W9-BAM-597

MacArthur's Eagles

MacArthur's Eagles

The U.S. Air War over New Guinea, 1943–1944

Lex McAulay

Naval Institute Press
Annapolis, Maryland

Naval Institute Press
291 Wood Road
Annapolis, MD 21402

Library of Congress Cataloging-in-Publication Data
McAulay, Lex, 1940–
    MacArthur's Eagles : the U.S. air war over New Guinea,
1943–1944 / Lex McAulay.
        p. cm.
    Includes bibliographical references and index.
    ISBN 1-59114-479-5 (alk. paper)
    1. World War, 1939–1945—Campaigns—New Guinea.
2. United States. Army Air Forces. Air Force, 5th. 3. World
War, 1939–1945—Aerial operations, American. 4. World
War, 1939–1935—Regimental histories—United States. I.
Title.

    D767.95.M42 2004
    940.54'265—dc22

                                    2004018242

Printed in the United States of America on acid-free paper ∞
12 11 10 09 08 07 06 05   9 8 7 6 5 4 3 2
First printing

Contents

Preface

The U.S. B-25 strafer crews could hardly believe their eyes. Ahead of them, lined up in the morning sun as if on parade in peacetime, were dozens of Japanese bombers and fighters. The sky was clear—no enemy fighters were overhead. The antiaircraft guns were unmanned. It was a strafer's dream target. A few minutes later, the Japanese airfields were scenes of destruction—and the balance of power in the air war over New Guinea was changed forever.

In New Guinea in August 1943 the U.S. Army 5th Air Force planned and executed a series of attacks on the Japanese army air force that effectively destroyed the Japanese offensive air capability in the theater. This was repeated in March 1944 and again in April. These campaigns provide dramatic illustrations of the understanding of airpower by the opponents in the South West Pacific war zone. They also illustrate the national characteristics of the combatants.

The U.S. squadrons operated a variety of aircraft that were prime examples of the innovative attitude of the U.S. aviation industry. The U.S. air command in the South West Pacific area conceived, planned, and executed daring, sustained, powerful, long-range operations that devastated their opponents.

The Japanese aviation industry basically refined existing aircraft designs, and in the South West Pacific war zone their commanders and forces were totally outclassed in the fields of operational concept, logistical support, planning, and execution. As long as their enemies were in disarray and poorly equipped, the Japanese command was able to exploit the situation. But when their opponents gained experience, were better equipped, were intellectually unrestrained, and, importantly, applied the principles of interservice and international cooperation, the conservatively minded Japanese command, in its chosen theater of war, was unable to achieve the standards necessary to prosecute modern warfare against such a capable enemy.

Gen. Douglas MacArthur's air squadrons, his Eagles, effectively destroyed the opposing Japanese air arm three times over—in August 1943 and in March and April 1944. The way to the Philippines was open.

The author has used unpublished information from captured Japanese documents and interrogations of prisoners, with decoded Japanese radio traffic, to give the Japanese side of the campaigns and to confirm the effectiveness of the U.S. Army 5th Air Force over Wewak and Hollandia 1943–44.

MacArthur's Eagles, with the author's earlier titles on the Bismarck Sea battle of March 1943 (*The Battle of the Bismarck Sea*), and the daylight bombing campaign against Rabaul in October–November 1943 (*Into the Dragon's Jaws*), is dedicated to all those U.S. Army Air Corps servicemen who served in the South West Pacific Area 1941–45.

Acknowledgments

The following people kindly contributed to, or assisted me with, gathering the material for this book. This opportunity is taken to thank them. John Brogan and Cy Stafford in particular provided details of the life in the U.S. Service Squadrons and Groups, from which the anecdotes are taken; my personal thanks to John and Cy. My thanks also to Larry Hickey, coordinator and publisher of *Eagles over the Pacific,* a series of excellent histories of the USAAC groups which served in the SWPA, who kindly made information on the U.S. units available to me for this book, and translations of histories of the JAAF fighter units, as well as the Garrett Middlebrook recollections of the Wewak missions.

Thanks also to Ian Affleck, Australian War Memorial; Jim Alexander, 90th Bomb Group; Bill Beck, 89th Attack Squadron, 3rd Attack Group; Jack Bleakley, WWII Australian Radio Intercept Unit; Edward J. Boone Jr., archivist, MacArthur Memorial; Joyce Bradley, formerly Australian War Memorial and a research consultant; John Brogan, 8th Service Group; John Bullen, formerly Australian War Memorial; Mike Claringbould, author, history of 312th Group; Ian Collier, Australian War Memorial; Dennis Glen Cooper, 475th Fighter Group; Steve Corvini, Australian War Memorial; Rick Dunn, aviation historian; Tom Fetter, 90th Bomb Group; Bill Fogarty, Australian War Memorial; Kevin Ginnane, photographic expert; Richard Grills, "Terry's Pirates," 90th Bomb Group; Bob Hallett, 90th Bomb Group; John Hampshire, RAAF B-24 pilot and squadron CO; Doris Heath, Japanese translations; Larry Hickey, International Research & Publishing; Andrew Jack, Australian War Memorial; Charlie King, 39th Fighter Squadron; Marion Kirby, 80th and 431st Fighter Squadrons; Robert McCandless, 8th Fighter Group; Kym Perry, computer expert/lifesaver #1; Robert K. Piper, historian; Geoff Purdue, computer expert/lifesaver #2; Raelene Purdue, computer whiz; Bill Martin, 90th Bomb Group; Bill Moran, 90th Bomb Group; Dalton Neville, photographic expert; Tony Rudnicki, Australian War Memorial; Bronwyn Self, Australian War Memorial; John Shemelynce, 3rd Attack Group; Cy Stafford, 482nd Service Group; John Stanaway, author and historian; John Stanifer, 80th Fighter Squadron; Osamu Tagaya, aviation historian and author; Larry Tanberg, CO, 38th Bomb Group; John Trouten, Australian War Memorial; Ralph Wandrey, 49th Fighter Group; William M. Webster, 8th Squadron, 3rd Attack Group; Andrew Weigel, 8th Squadron, 3rd Attack Group.

Special mention must be made of the staff of the Research Centre of the Australian War Memorial, for their tireless cheerful efforts bringing material from the highest and most distant stacks. Also outstanding for their speedy, efficient responses to letters and orders for materials are the staff of the MacArthur Memorial, Norfolk, Virginia. As a ready source of information on the SWPA, the memorial is outstanding and recommended to researchers.

Information on the notification of the deaths of 2nd Lts. John L. Stiles and Dale Ralph Lawyer, 400th Bomb Squadron, 90th Bomb Group, came from the U.S. Archives in College Park, Maryland, in the RG457 series, Entry 9012, Box 20, Folio 16850, and RG457 NSA Historical Collection, Box 637, Binder 1701aa.

MacArthur's Eagles

ONE

The Preliminaries

New Guinea 1942–43

From 1940 to 1942 the German Luftwaffe and Japanese army and navy air forces taught the Allies the practical uses of tactical airpower. The early successes enjoyed by the Germans and Japanese were achieved against unprepared and disorganized enemies in campaigns in which the German and Japanese air forces were subordinate to land and sea elements.

By mid-1943, however, the pupils had become the masters. On a much larger scale, Germany and Japan then were given powerful lessons in the use of both tactical and strategic airpower linked to strategic war aims. The Germans and Japanese had sown the wind in 1940–42, and in 1943–45 reaped the whirlwind.

Prime examples were the U.S. Army's 5th Air Force campaigns in New Guinea, against Wewak in August 1943 and March 1944, and against Hollandia in April 1944. The opposing Japanese army air force, the 4th Air Army, was effectively destroyed several times over in each of these campaigns. The 5th Air Force went on to operate over Japan itself, and a P-38 fighter of the 5th was the first Allied aircraft to land in Japan after the surrender.

The Wewak and Hollandia air offensives are clear indicators of the degree of understanding of the concept of airpower by the opponents, Japan and the United States, and also illustrate their understanding of what aviation industries can provide a nation in peace and war. The Japanese (and Germans) did not have in positions of authority high-ranking air officers who understood the use of airpower as an independent and essential third arm. The major Allies did have such officers.

The five major combatants in World War II were the aggressors, Nazi Germany and Imperial Japan, against the British Commonwealth, the United States, and the USSR. Aviation development in the USSR during the war 1941–45 is not in the context of this book.

Nazi Germany, a European continental landpower, lacked senior air officers and senior civilian government members with a true understanding of the airpower requirements of a nation that aims to dominate its neighboring regions. Germany developed short-range aircraft suitable for close internal continental employment, with only a few long-range commercial types such as the Focke-Wulf FW200 Condor for use between Germany and distant destinations.

Japan was controlled by a radical military clique, led and symbolized by Gen. Hideki Tojo. This group brought Japan into the war without clear objectives, or any idea of how to bring hostilities to a close. Japan was allied with the fascist regimes in Germany and Italy, and so desired some triumphs for status at any peace settlement with the British Commonwealth and the United States. Linked to this wish was the gamble that a quick series of victories against the United States and its Allies in the areas south of Japan would strengthen Japan and make for a better bargaining position against the United States at any peace negotiations.

As the Japanese militarist clique did not really know or understand either the British Commonwealth or the United States, the gamble failed to take into account the determination with which the British Commonwealth and United States would fight on to victory, and the gamble also failed to give importance to the enormous economic potential of the United States.

Japan, with the most militarized society of all, also lacked senior air officers who understood the use of airpower as it would be relevant to Japan, and despite being intent on the creation of an extensive empire in Asia and the Pacific, Japan also did not develop long-range load-carriers for military or civil aviation. The best that were produced to meet this need were the Emily and Mavis flying boats, but these were made in small numbers. Airliners were copies of Western designs, produced under license.

The British Commonwealth spanned the globe but contained so many dominions and colonies that there were relatively short distances between locations under British Commonwealth rule. The headline-making, record-breaking long-distance flights and air races by British aircraft and airmen of the 1920s and '30s did not lead to production of long-range military or civil aircraft capable of carrying a heavy payload, as the close proximity of British possessions and dominions did not require it. The class structure of British society was reflected in the airline arrangements, as only the wealthy could afford to fly, and the small numbers of passengers aboard were treated to personal cabin service during the daylight flying hours, after which the airliner landed and the passengers again received first-class service during the overnight stay in comfortable colonial surroundings. Then the next daylight flying leg began.

The Royal Air Force (RAF) was the first independent air service in the world, and its senior officers were proponents of airpower. A heavy bomber force capable of reaching targets in Europe had been part of the RAF concept of operations since the end of World War I. Although no major air wars were fought for twenty years, the RAF gained experience in the 1930s in airlifting troops and in the use of light strike aircraft against rebellious tribes in parts of the Empire, or Commonwealth.

The slogan "The bomber will always get through" frightened many civilians when the effects of aerial bombardment in the 1920s and '30s were publicized. But the British developed a modern, nationally coordinated system of radar, ground observers, radio and telephone network, and fast heavily armed fighters, with balloons and antiaircraft guns in support to defend Britain against air attacks from Europe. No such battle had ever been fought, and the commanders and their subordinates were forced to learn and adapt in the hardest school of all, but British victory in the Battle of Britain in 1940 was one of the decisive successes in the history of the Western world. The German Luftwaffe was unable to achieve air superiority over southeast England in summer, British defenses hardened over the weeks of battle, and German losses were unsustainable. All the while the Royal Navy remained a force against which no German invasion fleet could stand. Autumn and winter arrived. The Nazi leadership assumed that Britain was out of the war even if she did not make peace; Europe was conquered, and they turned their attention to the desirable spaces and riches of their eastern neighbors. All this had been achieved with short-range twin-engine bombers, dive-bombers, and short-range fighters.

Only the United States, isolated by the Atlantic and Pacific Oceans, was forced to consider the development of suitable aircraft to cross the oceans with a profitable payload of freight or passengers. It was this mental stimulus of needing to reach out to the rest of the world by air that marked U.S. aviation development from the early 1930s. No other nation grasped so eagerly all the latest advances in aviation technology and applied them to airframes, engines, and electronics.

The national characteristics of military aviation in Japan and the United States in the 1930s and '40s were clearly demonstrated in the Wewak-Hollandia air offensives.

The most obvious sign in aviation matters was the wide variety of excellent aircraft produced in large numbers by the United States for its own use and for its allies, which operated effectively in every war theater. One easily recognizable product was the Lockheed P-38 Lightning, with its twin booms and central cockpit nacelle with concentrated heavy firepower. The P-38 changed the nature of the fighter air war in the South West Pacific and brought many pilots in the SWPA to ace status.

The P-38 design used the latest all-metal technology and included a large number of "firsts" for a military airplane in squadron service: use of turbo-supercharged engines, power-boosted controls, tricycle undercarriage, and metal-skinned control surfaces. It was the first twin-engine fighter in U.S. service.

The P-47 was a triumph of engineering, with the huge Pratt & Whitney R-2800 radial engine harnessed to create a powerful fighter able to fight effectively at high altitude and fire a battery of eight .50-caliber guns.

U.S. bomber development was equally impressive and included the first modern aircraft, the B-24, and the Boeing B-29, which combined high-altitude performance with range, bomb load, and crew comfort in the greatest feat of aviation design and production of the war.

The operating range and capacity of the Boeing, Douglas, and Lockheed passenger designs in flying boat and land-based aircraft already in service across the Atlantic and Pacific oceans or soon to be available were unmatched by those of any other nation.

The speed with which these new aircraft, employing the latest advances and solutions to the problems of aviation development, were conceived, designed, built, and tested also was remarkable. The P-38 contract was awarded to Lockheed in June 1937, and the first prototype flew in December 1938; Republic had the XP-47 flying in eleven months; Martin had the advanced B-26 in production only twenty-three months after specifications were issued.

Another example of U.S. aviation enterprise was the Bell P-59 Airacomet, the first U.S. jet fighter. This aircraft was designed and flew in only one year, after a full set of drawings of the first successful jet engine was given to the United States by Britain. The British themselves were hampered by professional jealousy, professional blindness, commercial chicanery, bureaucratic indifference, and the worst aspects of the British class system—Frank Whittle, the inventor of the jet engine, came from a working-class background, and every possible bureaucratic obstacle was put in his way to deprive him of developmental control of this new means of propulsion. The British aviation industry squandered its advantage and failed to have jets in combat until the last few weeks of the war.

In contrast with the U.S. effort, the Japanese aviation designers and engineers were basically conservative, redesigning and improving proven developments in airframes, engines, armament, and metallurgy. The "standard" Japanese fighter was a maneuverable radial-engine monoplane with light armament, which evolved from the biplane era. Some technological advances were incorporated, but there were no radical departures from the usual concepts. The installation of 20 mm cannon on the Mitsubishi A6M Zero fighter was unusual, and the use of a liquid-cooled engine on the Kawasaki Ki-61 fighter was the sole example of such employment.

It was the U.S. aviation industry that was innovative; it designed, built, modified, tested, and produced a generation of bombers, fighters, and transport aircraft that have gone into legend.

After halting the 1942 Japanese advances, the Allies in the South West Pacific Area (SWPA) theater commenced a succession of offensives that began along the northern coasts of New Guinea in 1943 and ended thirty-two months later over the Japanese home islands. Behind the victorious Allies was the wreckage of Japanese military aviation. Not only were Japanese aircraft destroyed by the thousands, but flight crews and irreplaceable ground staff specialists and mechanics were lost in those distant campaigns as well. When Japan surrendered unconditionally in August 1945, some Japanese air units that had flown in the South West Pacific Area were reduced to a dozen or fewer survivors; some had no pilots alive.

U.S. Army 5th Air Force operations were planned and executed by personnel living and working in a hostile climate, with the added disadvantage of being low on Allied priority lists. With ideas and spirit harnessed only by equipment shortcomings, the 5th Air Force triumphed over an implacable enemy and hostile environment.

In January 1942, the experienced, numerically superior Imperial Japanese forces easily captured Rabaul on the island of New Britain and gained possession of strategically important Simpson Harbor. A force sent to Lae, New Guinea, captured it in March. Japanese naval aircraft from Rabaul and Lae ranged almost unopposed throughout the area. Bombing attacks on the administrative capital of Papua New Guinea, Port Moresby, began on 3 February. There was no fighter opposition because no fighters were available. The Japanese fighter escort performed aerobatics for the benefit of the Moresby garrison and indulged in surprise strafing attacks on the airfield and roads.

Wewak and Hollandia were small and little-known settlements on the north coast of New Guinea. In 1942 they were occupied by the victorious Japanese, but there was no urgency for defense works at either place.

On 12 January 1942, six Royal Australian Air Force (RAAF) PBY Catalinas made the first Allied attack on Japanese positions in the region, a mission to the big Japanese naval base at Truk, in the Marianas. From February 1942 small formations of U.S. 19th Bomb Group B-17s from Townsville, Australia, flew reconnaissance and bombing missions against targets in New Guinea and at Rabaul. RAAF Catalinas flew similar missions from Port Moresby.

The active Allied air defense of New Guinea began on 19 March 1942, when 75 Squadron RAAF arrived with Curtiss P-40 Kittyhawks. The urgency of the situation can be understood by the first three weeks in the life of the squadron: raised on 4 March, received its new P-40s in a few days, and two weeks later went into combat in New Guinea. Some P-40s still lacked the modern reflector gun sight, and some of the young Aussie pilots had less than twenty hours flying in P-40s on arrival at Port Moresby's 7-Mile airfield—so named from the distance to town. On the day they arrived, two Aussies shot down the daily Japanese reconnaissance plane, and two days later the squadron attacked the Japanese airfield at Lae. For forty-four days, this single Australian fighter squadron defended Port Moresby against the experienced and numerically superior Japanese and claimed eighteen Japanese destroyed, four probably destroyed, and twenty-nine damaged in air combats (18-4-29), with thirty-five more destroyed or damaged on the ground. Twenty-one P-40s and twelve Australian pilots were lost in combat, to ground fire, or from Japanese strafing and bombing. The RAAF squadron was reduced to one flyable P-40 when U.S. P-39s arrived to defend Port Moresby at the end of April.

Japanese losses recorded by them for April were thirty-four aircraft hit in air combat, with twelve lost, seventeen crew members killed, and eleven wounded; ten aircraft destroyed on the ground and fifty others damaged; thirty-one men killed and fifty-one wounded on the ground.

The U.S. 3rd Attack Group ("The Grim Reapers") departed San Francisco on 31 January 1942 and arrived at Brisbane, Australia, on 25 February. The 3rd Group comprised the 8th, 13th, 89th, and 90th Squadrons. The 8th Attack Squadron went by train to Charters Towers, 1,000 miles north of Brisbane, set up camp on 6 March, and trained with single-engine Douglas A-24 dive-bombers. The 75th Squadron RAAF was allowed two weeks from date of establishment to departure for New Guinea. The 8th Attack was allowed three weeks.

Thirteen A-24s from the 8th set off from Charters Towers for Port Moresby on 31 March 1942. The supply situation was such that Port Moresby radioed there were only two 500-pound bombs available; the A-24s had to bring their own. Three A-24s turned back due to excessive oil consumption, two were stuck in the mud after refueling at Cooktown, Australia, and when the remaining eight were making a dusk landing at 7-Mile Field, two collided. The squadron leader, Capt. Floyd W. "Buck" Rogers, became so ill that he had to be evacuated by air to Australia. Only five aircraft were available for the first U.S. tactical strike in New Guinea. The next day, 1 April 1942, the five A-24s, with six RAAF P-40s, attacked the Japanese airfield at Salamaua, New Guinea; all returned safely. Such were the beginnings of Allied airpower in the SWPA.

Meanwhile, Gen. Douglas MacArthur, commander of all U.S. and Philippine forces in the Philippines, had been ordered by Pres. Franklin D. Roosevelt to leave his command there and go to Australia, to assume command of all Allied forces in the SWPA. MacArthur had been extremely fortunate that the U.S. commanders at Pearl Harbor were made scapegoats for the disasters there when the Japanese naval air strike caught the U.S. Pacific Fleet unawares on Sunday 7 December 1941. The largest single force of B-17s in the world at that time was allocated to MacArthur for use against the Japanese. No investigative attention was focused on MacArthur, despite the fact that his powerful B-17 force was destroyed on the ground by Japanese air strikes nine hours after MacArthur was informed Pearl Harbor was under attack.

Destruction of those B-17s altered the strategic equation in the western Pacific. Much of the subsequent struggle in the South West Pacific, with all the pain and grief, the sacrifice, and the loss of life, health, and treasure, was caused by Douglas MacArthur's indecision and inability to perform on that morning. He later lied repeatedly and deliberately to those appointed to investigate the tragic events at Pearl Harbor about his foreknowledge of Japanese intentions, acquired through decoded radio messages.

MacArthur controlled the public relations machinery in the Philippines and carefully portrayed himself as the resourceful and courageous combat commander of numerically weak but heroic forces treacherously taken by surprise, valiantly fighting overwhelming numbers. In fact, the Japanese were outnumbered by MacArthur's forces in the Philippines but were qualitatively superior.

After his dramatic escape from the Philippines, MacArthur arrived in Darwin, Australia, itself already badly damaged by Japanese air raids, and was dismayed to find that there was no rail link to the south—he would have to continue by air. MacArthur disliked flying. A man of his immense ego and belief in his own importance was not happy about flying machines, so depressingly subject to mechanical failure and to forces of the implacable weather, machines which were known to crash with total loss of all aboard. The senior Australian air officer available was Squadron Leader (Maj.) Brian Walker RAAF, and he was called to confirm what the newly arrived U.S. general did not want to believe—there was no rail connection to the south and the best way to continue was in the same well-worn B-17 in which MacArthur had arrived.

Despite the urgency of the war situation, as soon as the B-17 reached a rail-head, MacArthur and his party finished their journey by train. On arrival in Melbourne, Australia, MacArthur was dismayed again to find that there was no great force assembled for him to lead back to liberate the Philippines. All he had available was a medley of units from convoys diverted to Australia after the Japanese attack on the Philippines. MacArthur apparently had not considered from where the expected large balanced force of air, land, and sea units, and the logistic support force necessary, had been conjured by the U.S. authorities or how it had been sent to Australia in time for his arrival.

Despite his self-proclaimed mission of returning to the Philippines, MacArthur responded to commands from the Joint Chiefs of Staff in Washington, D.C. For more than eighteen months after he arrived in Australia, Rabaul was his main objective, so ordered by the Joint Chiefs.

MacArthur received a Presidential Directive dated 30 March 1942, which ordered him to maintain U.S. installations in the Philippines, stem the Japanese advance to Australia, guard Allied lines of communication in and around SWPA, supervise shipping operations within SWPA, assist friendly force activities in the Indian Theater and Pacific Ocean area, maintain economic pressure on Japan by destroying facilities for transporting resources from newly conquered territories to Japan, hold areas of Australia most suited for establishment of bases to be used in future offensive actions, and be ready to mount an Allied offensive.

This order was far beyond the capabilities of the available forces in the SWPA. A further directive amended the previous directive on 2 July 1942 but still set aims beyond the capabilities of the Allied forces. The SWPA and adjoining South Pacific area commanders were to take and occupy Lae, Salamaua, the coast of Northeast New Guinea, and the remaining Solomon Islands; take and occupy Rabaul, plus an adjacent area in the vicinity of New Ireland or New Guinea; and seize and consolidate Tulagi and Santa Cruz Islands, with adjacent positions if necessary.

After the 1942 campaigns, on 28 March 1943, however, JCS 238/5/D directed General MacArthur to prepare to seize the Bismarck Archipelago; maintain the initiative to contain and inflict losses on the enemy by establishing airfields on Woodlark and Kiriwina Islands; take and consolidate the Solomons, including southern Bougainville; and take and consolidate Lae, Salamaua, Finschhafen, Madang, and western New Britain.

The Japanese suffered their first strategic reverse in May 1942 in the Battle of the Coral Sea, when their invasion force for Port Moresby was turned back by U.S. and Australian naval forces. If Port Moresby was secured by them, Japanese air and naval forces could dominate the northern and eastern coasts of Australia. The Japanese decided again to take Moresby but this time to come overland across New Guinea from the north and east.

From Rabaul, on 21 July 1942 the Japanese sent their South Seas Force to Buna on the north coast of New Guinea and began to move south through the uncharted Owen Stanley Range to Port Moresby. The Japanese force of two infantry regiments, with artillery, engineer logistics support, advanced south from the invasion beachhead and was first slowed by the outnumbered, partly trained Australian 39th Militia Battalion. The Japanese pushed on for Moresby, all the while looking for a nonexistent road through the unmapped mountains. The campaign was fought along the native path between villages journalists called the Kokoda Trail.

In these operations the Japanese made little use of their available airpower. The existing airfield at Kokoda was ignored and became overgrown. No tactical reconnaissance was flown in support of the advancing Japanese troops, and no close support missions were flown against the defending Australians. There was no cooperation between the army and air units. On the Allied side, every effort was made to use available aircraft to support the ground forces, every known technique and procedure were improved and adapted, and new ideas were tested.

Many RAAF and U.S. air attacks were made on enemy convoys but with little success. Bravery could not make up for technical malfunctions and bad weather conditions. The U.S. and Australian air commanders also sent out aircraft in small formations as soon as a few were ready. The Japanese defenses easily coped with the tiny forces that appeared at different times. Hundreds of bombs and thousands of flying hours were used against Japanese ships, but few were sunk. The Japanese cleverly used bad weather to cloak their convoys and often timed their arrival off their New Guinea beachhead for night hours to unload when air attack would be hampered by night and rain.

On 29 July 1942, the 8th Attack Squadron flew seven A-24s against a Japanese convoy off Buna. Despite becoming separated in cloud from the U.S. P-40 escort, Maj. Floyd "Buck" Rogers attacked through intercepting Japanese navy Zekes. From analysis of captured Japanese documents in the SWPA Allied Translator and

Interpreter Section collection, the author believes that Rogers scored a direct hit on one Japanese transport. The attack forced the ships to halt unloading and move out to sea at a time when every pound of supplies landed and every hour was vital to sustain their advance on Port Moresby. But only one A-24, flown by Lt. Ray Wilkins, returned to Moresby, and one other made it to Milne Bay. Rogers and other experienced crews had gone to their deaths in obsolete machines; there were too few of them, separated from their fighter escort, flying on to the assigned target, despite cannon-armed Japanese fighters attacking them. This blow removed the 8th Squadron from operations for many months.

It was to be another seven months before the policy of sending a few airplanes to attack as soon as they were ready was changed. "Concentration of Force" is one of the principles of war, but in the beginning it was not observed by the Allied air forces. It was not observed by the Japanese either; their grasp of the principles of war and understanding of airpower was far worse.

The advancing Japanese regiments were slowed further in August 1942 by three battalions of Australian Imperial Force (AIF) veterans from the Middle East campaign. The AIF found themselves making a desperate fighting retreat. The battle situation was made worse, because the quantity of air-dropped ammunition and food supplies the Australians had been promised as they departed Port Moresby failed to arrive in the combat area. This was due to the criminal negligence of U.S. airfield staff at 7-Mile, who lined up every available supply airplane in the open, despite a request to disperse them by the Australian army commander. The aircraft were destroyed in the 77th Japanese air raid on Moresby. There was no question of a surprise Japanese attack—they had been bombing the Port Moresby area for six months. The Japanese were halted by AIF and Australian militia infantry on the last mountain ridge before the coastal plain, thirty miles from Port Moresby. The Japanese could see, at night, the horizon glow of lights and Allied searchlights above Moresby.

The Aussies fighting in the mountains were supported by RAAF and U.S. air units that bombed and strafed, but the Japanese were barely troubled by these air attacks along the trail and rarely mention it in documents and diaries. Bombing their beachhead on the north coast was more effective.

While the fighting raged among the cruel ridges of the Owen Stanley Range, another Australian mixed force of untried militia troops and veterans of battle against the Axis in Africa achieved what had not been done before: they defeated a Japanese seaborne invasion. The Japanese landed on the eastern tip of New Guinea, at Milne Bay, to advance on Port Moresby from that direction. From 26 August to 6 September in merciless combat the Australians forced the Japanese to withdraw, leaving seven hundred dead. Finally, on 28 September 1942, the Australians began to advance north over the deadly mountainous Kokoda Trail.

No U.S. combat ground forces fought on the Kokoda Trail or at Milne Bay, but U.S. and RAAF air support, with air supply by free drops and parachute, was vital.

An important difference between the opponents in the theater and, again, one that showed which force better understood the application of airpower was the great amount of time and effort devoted by the Allied air forces to solving the new problems of how to resupply to units in jungle conditions by air, how to bring close effective air support to assist ground units in combat, and how to find and destroy enemy shipping of all sizes by day or night.

Another vital difference was the constant readiness of the Allied air forces to implement the benefits of airpower. Gen. George C. Kenney took command of the U.S. and Allied air forces in Australia on 4 August 1942. In September, at the height of the Japanese advance across New Guinea, Kenney convinced MacArthur to allow an airlift of the U.S. 128th Infantry Regiment from Australia to New Guinea to demonstrate that airlift was quicker than sea travel. By utilizing every bomber and transport airplane available, including borrowed Australian airliners and repaired airplanes returning to New Guinea, Kenney delivered the regiment in less than the time needed for sea movement.

In 1936 Junkers Ju52 three-engine transports performed the first military airlift when they flew 7,300 Spanish government troops from Morocco to Spain at the beginning of the Spanish Civil War. In May 1940 the Germans airlifted troops behind Allied lines in Holland and Belgium. In May 1941 the German airborne invasion of Crete faced defeat at the hands of the Australian and New Zealand defenders, but the Germans prevailed when fresh troops were airlifted directly into the battle area, despite heavy aircraft losses. The Japanese in New Guinea made a few small parachute supply drops but failed to match Allied determination to master the problems and combine air and land capabilities to achieve victory. The Australians fought north across New Guinea and were joined on the northern plain by the U.S. 32rd Division for the pitiless battles of Buna, Gona, and Sanananda.

The Japanese there, ordered to hold until the advance to Port Moresby could be resumed, obeyed and fought to the bitter end. The GIs of the National Guard 32rd Division, poorly trained and poorly led, failed at Buna, and Australians from Milne Bay had to be brought in to destroy the Japanese at great cost to the Aussies in dead and wounded.

By the end of 1942, the myth of Japanese invincibility had been destroyed. By the end of January 1943, the Japanese on the northern beaches had been eliminated. At the same time as this fighting in New Guinea, U.S. forces at Guadalcanal were locked in savage battles with the Japanese, which ended with Japanese defeat and withdrawal in February 1943.

Despite media reports controlled by him and carefully phrased statements, Gen. Douglas MacArthur never visited the battle areas. While it was strongly implied that MacArthur was personally conducting military operations at the front line in New Guinea, for most of the time he was in Brisbane, Australia. His headquarters had in key positions members of the "Bataan Gang," who escaped with MacArthur from the Philippines and whose role at this time was confined to sending orders and directives to the fighting units issued on a basis of ignorance of the battlefield conditions.

By February 1943 Australian and U.S. forces, at great cost, had secured space for airfields and harbors on the northern plains of New Guinea. The hostile Owen Stanley Range, with its dangerous weather and forbidding terrain, was behind the Allies instead of being a barrier to cross on each flight before reaching the Japanese. The advantage gained by the Allied air forces in achieving this cannot be overstated. MacArthur's forces really could begin the drive back against the Japanese.

The matter of airfields on the north coast of New Guinea also indicated the different qualities of the combatants. Australian and U.S. officers had visited the area to select airfield sites just before the Japanese invasion force arrived in July 1942. The Japanese made an airfield at Buna, but this location was swampy and had been ignored by the Allied officers in favor of better sites inland. The Japanese persisted with their bad choice, despite the field being described as of "the consistency of rice cakes." The Allies built a nearby complex of airfields that was superior, despite being only a few feet above sea level, in the Wanigela and Dobodura area.

The entire Australian and U.S. force north of the Owen Stanleys was reinforced and supplied by air from Port Moresby. Available Allied sealift simply could not be committed where the Japanese navy at Rabaul could reach out and destroy it. Whenever the weather intervened, the situation of the Allied forces at Buna, Gona, and Sanananda was endangered, but despite all the problems the air supply system improved, evolved, and made the campaign a success.

The Japanese not only failed to employ their own available airpower to their maximum benefit, but they failed to understand just how vital to their opponents was the air supply bridge over the Owen Stanleys. A few bombing raids were made on the new Allied airfields and a few fighter sweeps ventured into the area, but the interruption was minimal. Night bombardments by heavy naval guns from Japanese ships running down from Rabaul would have created havoc on the Allied airfields, but this seemed beyond Japanese understanding.

At the same time, the Casablanca Conference decided Allied policy for the remainder of the war. Germany was to be defeated first, so after "Defeat of the U-Boats," "Assistance to the USSR," "Operations in the Mediterranean," and the "Buildup in the United Kingdom," the Pacific and Far East were fifth on the priority list.

Of the five operations approved for the Pacific in 1943, only two concerned Gen. Douglas MacArthur's South West Pacific Area: the advance from Guadalcanal and New Guinea to take Rabaul and the advance along the New Guinea coast to Timor.

In the first week of February 1943, the defeated Japanese survivors on Guadalcanal were evacuated by destroyers deployed from their major base at Rabaul. This success was to be followed by a large ship-borne reinforcement of Japanese units to New Guinea, called "the Lae Convoy," comprised of eight transports and eight destroyers. The Japanese intended landing their 51st Division; farther north two other divisions waited to be shipped to New Guinea. Using their undisputed maritime superiority, the Japanese were about to reinforce at a far faster rate than the Allies and engage in harder jungle fighting. There was no Allied naval presence north of New Guinea, and the available Australian and U.S. army units were decimated and exhausted after bitter fighting at Buna, Gona, and Sanananda.

On 3 March 1943, land-based RAAF and U.S. aircraft changed the course of the campaign in New Guinea. Allied air units in the SWPA had been mostly unsuccessful in attacking ships but eventually had modified tactics and aircraft to cope. Group Capt. (Col.) Bill Garing DFC RAAF, an expert in air-sea operations, finally persuaded 5th Air Force commander Gen. George Kenney and Kenney's bomber commander, Gen. Ennis Whitehead, to wait until the maximum air strike force was available, and only then attack the Japanese convoy with all types of aircraft, flying at different heights, from different angles, all at once.

Australian and U.S. aircraft attacked the Lae convoy and sank four destroyers and all eight transport ships, most in a thirty-minute onslaught. This sudden devastation of a proud Imperial Japanese Navy force was almost totally achieved by mast-height attack by modified U.S. B-25s and A-20s, which flung bombs into the sides of the ships. (See the author's *The Battle of the Bismarck Sea,* St. Martin's Press, 1991.) It had been one year since Japanese air forces bombed and strafed with impunity the fleets of Allied ships fleeing the Philippines, Malaya, Singapore, and the Dutch East Indies. The destruction of the Lae convoy was a clear victory for Allied airpower. The Japanese were forced to use barges, landing craft, and submarines for supply runs from Rabaul to New Guinea. Barge-hunting became a major activity for Allied air force light and medium attack units.

General MacArthur's forces could continue the advance west to Timor and prepare for the encirclement of Rabaul. To assist intended Allied operations along the north coast of New Guinea, the Allied air forces were to provide air supremacy, air support, and air cargo operations.

By mid-1943 Gen. George C. Kenney, Allied air commander in the SWPA, had resources available that allowed his staff to plan the elimination of a large part of the Japanese army air force opposing him: the Wewak bases.

George C. Kenney

Gen. George Kenney arrived in the SWPA in July 1942 when the Japanese seemed unstoppable. Kenney, a lieutenant in the World War I U.S. Air Service, flew seventy-five missions, shot down two enemy aircraft, was shot down once, and ended the war with a Distinguished Service Cross and Silver Star. He remained in service and rose to lieutenant colonel in the next twenty years. During the interwar years, Kenney kept abreast of aeronautical developments and during exercises demonstrated the potential of airpower and air mobility. It was this open mind that was to distinguish George Kenney.

When Kenney arrived, theater supreme commander Gen. Douglas MacArthur had a poor opinion of the air forces, exacerbated by an opinion that Kenney's predecessor, Lt. Gen. George H. Brett, had been disloyal to MacArthur. Kenney had to assure MacArthur that he always had been loyal to his commander, and then convince MacArthur that he could bring the air units to a degree of acceptable efficiency.

MacArthur's dislike of Brett stemmed from the fact that while MacArthur was in the Philippines, Brett had been U.S. commander in Australia. The Australian and New Zealand governments had suggested to U.S. authorities in Washington, D.C., that Brett be appointed theater supreme commander. Brett was a contender for the office of theater commander and so had to be removed. Kenney was a fresh face from the United States. He was not, like Brett, an officer suggested by local government leaders as theater commander before MacArthur himself was nominated by Pres. Franklin Roosevelt.

Kenney was astute enough to realize that if he could gain MacArthur's support and trust, he could show what great benefits would accrue from intelligent use of available airpower. The advance back to the Philippines would be made across the large island of New Guinea and many smaller ones. Apart from the pressing requirements of Atlantic and Pacific naval operations, interservice rivalry meant an absolute minimum of ships would be allocated to the SWPA. The U.S. Navy chiefs had no love for MacArthur. The primitive nature of the islands meant that conventional military advances would be impossible. Airpower would be the dominant arm in the SWPA—if George Kenney could whip the air forces into shape and show MacArthur what could be achieved.

On 4 August 1942 Kenney took command of a collection of ill-equipped units, some worn down by combat experiences, and of a supply organization plagued with problems and spread across the eastern half of the continent of Australia. The Allied supply system was still hindered by the attitudes of some senior U.S. and RAAF staff officers, unable to change their behavior from peacetime, when every nut and bolt had monetary value and had to be accounted for to humorless auditors and inspectors. Now, despite a serious wartime situation, these cautious and conservative officers, molded in the days of miserly military funding, insisted on correctly completed and processed requisition forms, sent through recognized administration channels to supply depots far away from the operational airfields, while badly needed aircraft stood idle. So removed from reality were these bureaucrats in uniform that early in 1942, U.S. Army Air Corps units in Australia received an order that all officers were to grow a mustache and carry a swagger-stick.

On 9 August 1942, Kenney received permission from Washington to call his formation the 5th Air Force. On paper Kenney had a reasonable fighting force. His U.S. squadrons had 481 aircraft, but only 151 were operational. The RAAF in the region had 215 combat aircraft; 149 were operational. Many aircraft were grounded by time-consuming complicated administrative procedures for getting parts to the flight line. Airplanes were often worn out and obsolete, and many flight crews were tired after flying from remote and basic airfields on the Australian mainland and staging out of equally basic New Guinea bases to reach distant Japanese-held targets.

Kenney sacked many of the inefficient and tired U.S. officers and replaced them with men who would perform. The "book" on air operations in the SWPA had to be written and entirely new chapters composed, so Kenney sought out those men with new ideas and initiative. He promoted into command positions many young, aggressive, and intelligent officers. Incompetent Australians—and every bureaucracy breeds the type—were somewhat out of Kenney's command reach, but the Australian air force was not helped to perform at full potential by a merciless enmity between its two most senior officers, Air Vice Marshal William D. Bostock and Air Vice Marshal George Jones, who allowed their personal hatred to hinder the combat performance of the RAAF. The necessary political resolution to the situation between these two officers was beyond the will of the wartime Australian Labor government.

As well as confronting a determined foe and operating in primitive conditions, Kenney had to contend with lack of replacement aircraft and crews. Other theaters had higher priority, such as the Mediterranean and Europe, and the hostile and ungrateful communists in Russia. Kenney, adroitly publicizing the achievements of his meager forces and using personal powers of persuasion on visits to Washington D.C., was able to expand his force but never received an adequate supply of the types of aircraft he wanted or replacement flight crews.

Kenney had his faults. His early claims for the effect and flexibility of close air support over the effectiveness of artillery and tanks in the New Guinea campaigns were shown to be wrong, and he gave advice to MacArthur about the land battle situation from a position of ignorance: when the U.S. 32nd Division was failing in battle at Buna; when Robert Eichelberger, the U.S. army commander sent to Buna, was told to take the place or not come back alive; when Sutherland, MacArthur's chief of staff, was in danger of being sent back to the United States in disgrace; and when Japanese convoys were completing their voyages no matter how many ships Kenney claimed sunk. At these times Kenney, the newcomer, had to read MacArthur as astutely as any courtier of a medieval tyrant. But Kenney's enthusiasm and grasp of his chosen profession were evident, and he went on to achieve great things with the 5th Air Force.

The U.S. 5th Air Force

The 5th Air Force came from tiny beginnings. Seven merchant ships left Honolulu on 29 November 1941 bound for the Philippine Islands. Aboard were 2,600 U.S. Army Air Corps personnel, including forty-eight pilots; eighteen crated Curtiss P-40 fighters and fifty-five crated Douglas A-24 dive-bombers; 5,245 bombs and 9,000 drums of aviation oil and gasoline. There were also field artillery, ordnance, quartermaster, signals, and other units aboard, with cannon, motor vehicles, ammunition, and other equipment. Fortunately, the convoy was redirected south of the original route to skirt Japanese-held islands.

The convoy commander, Brig. Gen. Julian F. Barnes, later said that this alteration of course "no doubt saved the entire convoy from eventual capture and destruction." After the Japanese attack on Pearl Harbor, the convoy was ordered to Australia, and Brigadier General Barnes was designated commander U.S. troops in Australia. The ships arrived safely at Brisbane on 22 December 1941, the first of many in the next three years. From this small beginning grew the 5th Air Force, which four years later was based in Japan.

Ashore in Sydney: Scow-Class Travel

The 5th had its share of characters. M.Sgt. John Brogan, 8th Service Group, was determined to enjoy life and the war as much as possible. He went to Spain to see what was happening there in the Civil War, but rejected both Communists and Fascists and also decided against the French Foreign Legion, which offered marching in the sun and building roads. He ended up in Panama with the U.S. Army horse artillery, marching in the rain, so transferred to the Air Corps. With several thousand other Americans, he was aboard the liner *Queen Elizabeth* when it arrived in Sydney. The last thing the U.S. authorities wanted was thousands of Yanks running loose in Sydney when they intended sending them north to the war. No one was to go ashore until arrangements had been made for accommodations and travel.

Brogan, however, had worked out how to enjoy Sydney despite guards controlling access and exit from the ship, which was moored out in the harbor. With another sergeant he rolled his Class A uniform under his arm and went down into the ship to the hatch in the side through which garbage was thrown into a scow, pulled alongside by a tug. They jumped into the scow, and the friendly tug crew took them to a convenient harbor-side stair, where they washed off, dressed, went into the streets of Sydney, and enjoyed a great time. But how to get back aboard? Brogan had figured this out. When it was time, they went to the place where the crew of the liner gathered and went aboard with them.

In the first months of 1942, it was intended that the newly arrived U.S. aircraft be sent north from Australia to embattled U.S. forces in the Philippines, but problems of range, maintenance and logistic support, inexperienced pilots, weather, and relentless Japanese advance meant this came to nothing. Wrecked and damaged aircraft littered airfields, farms, distant places in the bush, and roadsides across northern Australia. Of 160 planes sent north only 38 reached eastern Java.

On 31 March 1942, operational U.S. aircraft in Australia totaled 261: 12 B-17s, 40 twin-engine bombers, 31 single-engine bombers, and 178 single-engine fighters. Of these, 120 were south of Brisbane, with some almost at the southern end of Australia, three thousand miles from New Guinea and the Japanese. Just over a year later, in April 1943, Allied air forces comprised sixty-eight squadrons: thirty-six USAAF, thirty-one RAAF, and one Dutch. Deliveries of aircraft in April 1943 were short by 224. Between October 1942 and April 1943, Kenney's overall combat strength decreased by sixty-eight, despite replacements. Only the total of transport planes increased, by 112. Five hundred thirty-eight airplanes were lost in accidents and 385 to the enemy, leaving him 772 first-line aircraft, plus 689 in RAAF units. His personnel strength was thirty-five thousand men.

Kenney was fortunate in that his first trip back to Washington in March 1943 was made just after the Bismarck Sea victory gained by his aircraft. Everyone else at the conference was keen to explain why he could not have more aircraft, but Kenney was able to acquire another heavy bomb group, two medium bomb groups, and three fighter groups, although he had to supply the men for one fighter unit. He also received another transport group, with which he determined to show the army and navy that resupply by air was feasible.

In May Kenney received the 345th Bomb Group, with B-25s. In June P-38s for the new 475th Fighter Group arrived; personnel were men already in the SWPA. Also due were Neel Kearby's 348th Fighter Group and their P-47s. In July 1943 the 5th had 565 aircraft, and in August, 598. However, 218 of these were the inferior P-39/P-400 or the P-40; half the airplanes were in depots. The average P-38 and P-40 had flown four hundred combat hours, equal to two thousand hours of peacetime operations. Only pilots in the China-Burma-India theater flew older and more worn-out planes.

There is one aspect of the aircraft supply line to the SWPA that should not be forgotten. Fighters and some twin-engine aircraft were delivered by ship, but other twins and four-engine bombers flew across the wide Pacific to Australia. Only a few years earlier, great pioneering flights had been made by Australian Charles Kingsford-Smith, opening air routes across the world's greatest ocean. "Smithy" was an experienced airman and was recognized as an international hero for these feats. Yet, in 1942, fresh young second lieutenants with a total of 250 to 300 hours flying time were setting off across that same ocean in brand-new B-17s and B-24s, machines barely out of the experimental stages, flying into and through weather they had rarely experienced as a mere first step into combat.

Not only were machines used to the last nut and bolt, but men also had the last drop of use squeezed out. Craven and Cate point out in their *History of the AAF* that 60 percent of the aircrew from other theaters who returned to the United States for medical reasons were able to return to flying status, but of those who returned from the SWPA it was only 5 percent, and the same ratio applied to army combat personnel.

Morale was affected by the quality of the enemy and his equipment, by the environment, and by the possibility of survival of a combat tour for rotation out of the combat area. In August 1943 the USAAF organized seven Air Sea Rescue squadrons for the various theaters of war, but in the SWPA a makeshift service operated already, using RAAF and USAAF PBYs and other light aircraft of various types.

The C-47, a Workhorse

Most accounts of aerial military operations concentrate on the more exciting aspects of the campaigns, missions flown by fighters and bombers, or daring rescues by flying boats under the noses of the enemy. The unsung heroes who flew in almost any weather, unarmed, into newly captured strips before they were ready for occupation by the fighters and bombers were the workhorse troop-carriers and cargo planes. The familiar shape of a C-47 droning over the jungles and coral reefs of the Pacific is as evocative of the times as the image of the P-38, B-17, B-24, or B-25. Perhaps deservedly, of all the aircraft of 1939–45, it is the venerable C-47 that still hauls passengers and cargo on almost every continent. Pilots rhapsodize about the P-38, P-51, A-20, B-17, . . . and the humble C-47.

In the Pacific and SWPA, the lack of roads and developed harbors meant ever-growing reliance and demand on cargo-carriers. Considering that they were operating in the same flying conditions as the bombers and fighters, statistics of the achievements of the C-47s of the 54th Troop Carrier Wing are impressive. Cargo delivered in 1943 increased from 4,120 tons in January to 32,184 tons in December. The total tonnage lifted in 1943 was 139,917, and ton mileage for the year was 16,831,457. In 1944 the Wing delivered 246,389 tons, for a ton mileage of 84,893,041. Without the C-47 and its crews, the fighters and bombers would have been severely restricted in their operations.

Australia: Base for the 5th Air Force

Australia was settled by the British after the North American colonies were closed as a repository for convicts. The separate Australian colonies gradually refused to accept convicts and instead supported immigration programs. By 1939 the Australian population was still only seven million. Like the other countries in the British Empire, Australia sent its raw materials to the United Kingdom and bought the manufactured items produced in factories there. Almost all Australian business enterprises and banks had head offices in London, and this was sufficient to stifle any attempt at industrial development in the Down Under dominion. Australian airmen had been world famous for their exploratory flights across the oceans and continents, but always in foreign aircraft. The local motor industry, shipbuilding, textiles, communications, and all the other components of a modern nation were allowed to develop only to the stage suitable to British head offices.

After World War II began in September 1939, Australia supported the British war effort in Europe and North Africa by training and dispatching formed units and trained individuals for the British Commonwealth forces. The Australian army, supported by the government, as in World War I, insisted on operating as Australian divisional formations and resisted attempts by British generals and politicians to split them into separate units and merge them with other British units. This infuriated the British. The RAAF and Royal Australian Navy were more amenable and were disposed overseas as British commanders required.

When Japan swiftly took the Philippines, Malaya, and the Netherlands East Indies (Indonesia), Australia had it brought home to the government and the people just how unprepared the nation was to fight a modern war in the region. The reassuring British promises that they would protect their southern dominions were found to be empty; Australia had only a small industrial base, no communications system able to support a nation at war, and many trained and experienced men and almost all combat-ready units were overseas fighting the Germans and Italians.

As in other nations, Australian aviators were volunteers and had to pass stringent selection procedures and training courses. In the Pacific area, however, they were sent to fight in some unsuitable and obsolete aircraft. At Rabaul, New Britain, in 1942, the RAAF Wirraways and Lockheed Hudsons at first had no armor-piercing or tracer ammunition and only one machine-gun belt loader. At one field the only tools were an ax and a cold chisel; galvanized iron was used to repair a Hudson. The Australian Wirraway was the North American AT-6 design built in Australia, much to the anger of the British, armed with three .303-inch (.30-caliber) machine guns, and used as a final training airplane, as a fighter, for army cooperation, and as reconnaissance airplanes. The Wirraways at Rabaul found they could not cope with the enemy. The Mitsubishi Zekes easily established air superiority. The local RAAF commander, Wing Commander John Lerew, asked for modern fighters but was told the plain cold truth: none were available. He then radioed in Latin the quotation from the Roman gladiators: "We who are about to die salute you."

Northern Australia was threatened by the Japanese advance, but it was the least developed part of the nation. Ports and airfields were few; roads were one- or two-lane dirt tracks between towns; and only one railway ran up the entire eastern coast, which for the last thousand miles was an unsuitable narrow gauge with reduced speed. Yet Australia was to become the SWPA base for the great counterattack against the Japanese. One factor in the Allies' favor was that the Japanese themselves were advancing into undeveloped areas, which affected their ability to maintain the momentum of their offensive.

Another factor favoring the Allies was a timely 1941 agreement between the United States and Australia for construction of a series of airfields in northeastern Australia for use by U.S. aircraft going to and from the Philippines. Australia provided the finance and effort for this project. By working three shifts, with local farmers loaning machinery, the chain of airfields was completed by the Queensland Main Roads Department in late 1941. This construction was for the bare runway and dispersal areas, and little or no accommodation, administration, or maintenance areas were able to be provided in the allotted time. Without this agreement and quick construction by the government roadbuilding organization, however, it would have been impossible for the timely northward deployment of aircraft that did reach Australia in 1942 to play their part in halting the Japanese advance.

Entire streets of private homes in northern Australian towns were commandeered for military use. Public buildings, schools, garages, and whatever was necessary were taken over by the military, despite protests from citizens. On 3 September 1942, Australia joined Allied Lend-Lease. During the war, Australia received 3.3 percent of total Lend-Lease, but provided the U.S. forces with 13 percent of total Reverse Lend-Lease, supplying U.S. formations in the region with 1.5 billion dollars of materials, equivalent to 70 percent of what Australia itself received.

"You shoulda been here when . . ."

The 5th Air Force existed to bring airpower to bear on the Japanese, and much responsibility for this devolved onto flight-line crews of the squadrons and groups as well as the maintenance squadrons and service groups. The generals and colonels could do only so much; after that it was up to the enlisted ranks. When it was not pouring rain, the burning tropical sun beat down, turning metal fuselages and engine bays into hot boxes. Yet, men had to work in the often confined and dark claustrophobic spaces on repair and maintenance tasks. Sometimes the master thermometer at the 8th Service Group reached 128 degrees Fahrenheit, but work had to go on. The factories and their experts were across the Pacific, weeks or months away. Problems arose that never had been considered in the United States, and field expedients solved many matters which, if the rules had been obeyed, would have seen precious aircraft sitting on the ground instead of flying missions.

As they advanced through the SWPA, the Allies had to contend with not only the human enemy but also the hostile undeveloped region through which they would fight. Everything had to be built while fighting continued, sometimes only a very short distance away. This aspect of the campaigns in the South West Pacific has rarely been given sufficient attention nor credit paid to all those who did the less glamorous but vital tasks in providing the very basics on which military advances were made and victories gained. While beyond the scope of this book, this should be kept in mind when reading of the Allied bases from which the air units operated.

By mid-1943, the Allied air forces had found, occupied, and developed sites for airfields in the mountains of New Guinea as well as on the north coast. General Kenney told MacArthur that he would be unable to deal with Japanese air formations at both Rabaul and Wewak, so he proposed to concentrate on Wewak. In early September fog often blankets New Britain and the Vitiaz Strait, so it was hoped the Japanese at Rabaul would be neutralized by this while the AAF flew in clear skies over New Guinea to the cluster of airfields around Wewak. By 10 August 1943, without detection by the Japanese, an airfield in the New Guinea mountains at Marilinan had been developed almost to completion, while in the past three months the Dobodura airfield complex on the northern coastal plain had been improved.

From Marilinan fighters could reach Wewak. As part of the overall Allied plan to recapture the major town and airfield at Lae, and so secure a base on the New Guinea side of the Vitiaz Strait, the Japanese air strength based around Wewak was to be destroyed. A Japanese reconnaissance aircraft had circled high over Marilinan on 14 August, and it was obvious that an attack would follow. General Kenney moved thirty-five P-39s into the new base just before dark.

The Allied Bases: Foundation for Success

By enormous efforts a complex of airfields had been built around the Port
Moresby area. Jackson Field had a bomber strip 7,500 feet long by 100 feet wide,
and a fighter strip 5,250 feet by 100 feet. Ward's Field had two 6,000-foot strips;
Durand and Schwimmer each had a 6,000-foot runway, and at Berry was
another, 4,500 feet by 150 feet. There were other airfields farther from the town.
On the northern coast near the former battlefields, at the Dobodura airfield complex were four strips, between 6,000 and 9,000 feet long. In addition to runways
at all these airfields, there were miles of taxiways and dozens of revetments. The
Japanese assigned nothing like this engineering effort to their own bases and paid
dearly for this lack.

The Bismarck Sea action had been decisively won in March, the Lockheed
P-38 was successful against Japanese bombers and fighters, and by July 1943 formations of up to twenty-five B-25s roamed the coasts of New Guinea on barge
hunts. On 11 July Japanese DDs *Ariake* and *Mikatsuki* were found off Cape
Gloucester, New Britain, by B-25s of the Grim Reapers 3rd Attack Group and
were battered to destruction. Kenney's squadrons were experienced, led by men
who had learned the lessons of operating in the theater, and all were buoyed by
recent successes. The Allies intended to take Lae in September 1943.

In mid-August 1943, photoreconnaissance showed the Japanese assembling
large numbers of aircraft on four airfields around Wewak, and, because of lack
of dispersal areas around the airfields, the airplanes were crowded together. This
confirmed information from a closely guarded source of intelligence available
only to senior Allied commanders and the few people who collected and worked
on the information.

Good intelligence on enemy strengths, locations, and intentions is equally
as important to a commander as his own combat and support units. The
Japanese believed in the inability of foreigners to learn the Japanese language and
assumed foreigners were similarly unable to defeat Japanese codes and ciphers.
This idea, combined with belief in the invincibility of the Japanese martial spirit
in every soldier, brought the Japanese to a series of disasters. The British had been
fortunate to benefit from a Polish breakthrough in mastering the German codes
and since 1940 had been able to decipher intercepted German radio traffic. The
British had given to the United States all their knowledge and samples of the

equipment necessary for this vital task. Japanese codes had been broken by brilliant U.S. cryptologists and an equally gifted Australian. Since the mid-1970s this revelation has inspired many books on the subject, and it is not necessary to go into more detail here. The radio intercepts, classified as "Ultra Secret," were processed as Daily Intelligence Summaries by a joint Allied organization, and a variation of these reports was supplied daily to MacArthur's GHQ SWPA as Special Intelligence Bulletins (SIBs) with a distribution list of four. Very few people were permitted access to this information. Rank mattered little; "need to know" was observed and enforced, and even the style of the reports was watched so that, if any fell into unauthorized hands, the source would not be immediately obvious.

From early July the arrival at Wewak of Japanese air units and formations had been reported in these bulletins. SIB 100, dated 10 August, reported a sharp increase in Japanese army flights between Rabaul, Wewak, and Hollandia. This flight activity decreased on the eleventh, but on the twelfth increased, with information of the move to Wewak by headquarters of the Japanese Army Air Force 6 Flying Division. Flight activity increased on 13, 15, and 17 August.

On 15 August radio intercept included in SIB 109 identified elements of the 13th, 59th, and 78th fighter units at Wewak. The 78th had not been identified in New Guinea before this date. More fighter and bomber units were identified by radio traffic in the Wewak area and indicated concentration of almost the entire 6 Flying Division.

Kenney's Strike Force

General Kenney intended to deal a tremendous blow to the Japanese Army Air Force (JAAF) in New Guinea, and the time was right. Some 5th Air Force squadrons and groups encouraged and used unit nicknames, some did not— "Flying Knights," "Wolfpack," "Headhunters," "Green Dragons," "Grim Reapers," "Jolly Rogers," and so on were well known.

Kenney was to launch the following units onto the Wewak area fields: four squadrons of Boeing B-17 Flying Fortresses of the 43rd Bomb Group, four squadrons of Consolidated B-24 Liberators of the 90th Bomb Group, five squadrons of North American B-25 Mitchells of the 3rd Attack and 38th Bomb Groups, and six squadrons of Lockheed P-38 Lightning fighters. There are many books that describe thoroughly these aircraft types, and it is not necessary to repeat that information here.

The U.S. military aircraft to be employed in this offensive represented some of the best efforts of the U.S. aviation industry. The B-17 entered service as the first bomber intended to operate in the stratosphere; the B-24 was the first truly modern multiengine aircraft; the P-38 represented a radical solution to the problem of high-altitude fighter interceptors; the P-47, to be employed in the second offensive, was another solution to that problem. No Japanese front-line aircraft in 1943 approached any of these production aircraft in concept, design, or engineering ability.

To enable his B-25s to reach out to the Japanese bases at Wewak, Kenney approved design, test, construction, and installation of a three-hundred-gallon fuel tank in the fuselage of the aircraft. The bottom turret was removed, vertical steel guides installed, spring-loaded doors added, and the tanks, fitted at top with bomb shackles, were made in local Australian workshops. These were used at the beginning of the flight, then jettisoned.

Lt. Gen. George Kenney had devoted his life to the advancement of airpower, had shown his theater commander the advantages of airlifting troops and supplies, saw his squadrons destroy the Lae convoy, and watched his P-38s achieve superiority over the vaunted Japanese Zeke. Now the opportunity to obliterate the opposing air force was at hand.

The Japanese in New Guinea

After their attack on the U.S. bases on Hawaii on 7 December 1941 and their successful annihilation of U.S. military presence in the Philippines, Japanese forces flooded across the Pacific. The Japanese won too many victories too cheaply and paid little attention to interservice cooperation or to solving the logistical problems posed by the sheer distances involved. After the setbacks of the second half of 1942, however, it was obvious to the Japanese that a reorganization in the southwest Pacific would be necessary. Early in 1943, it was decided the Japanese Navy Air Force (JNAF) would assume responsibility for New Britain and the Solomons, while the Japanese Army Air Force (JAAF) did the same for New Guinea. Accordingly, 4 Kokugun (air army), under Lt. Gen. Noriichi Teramoto, was formed on 28 July at Rabaul, to command

6 and 7 Hikoshidan (flying divisions). A major Japanese base was to be developed at Wewak.

An airfield had been built at Wewak by the Australian authorities in 1937 to serve the small town that was the administration center and chief port for the Sepik District. The Japanese concentrated on sites for airfields and controlled the region by patrolling. In general, they recognized the rights and privileges of the native people, with tribal chieftains allowed to remain and uphold laws and customs. However, areas had to provide a quota of manpower for labor, with men selected by the chiefs. As Japanese demands for food and labor became greater, and as local peoples realized the tide of war turned against Japan, supply quotas were not met and native disobedience was noticed by Japanese commanders.

Until it became obvious that the Japanese were being defeated, and the white men (Australians) could be expected to return to power, the local people almost always complied with Japanese demands. When the Japanese arrived at Buna in July 1942, the natives seized all the whites who had not escaped and handed them to the Japanese, who took the prisoners to the beach and beheaded them.

Four airfields were built by the Japanese in the Wewak area at Boram, But, Dagua, and Wewak itself. It was one thing to embark on a war of conquest but another to understand requirements to support modern combat units fighting at the end of long supply lines. Japanese leaders at the highest levels failed in this aspect of warfare. The Japanese never manufactured enough construction equipment to sustain a war effort in the SWPA or any other theater of the war, so infantry units labored to develop the Wewak airfields. Many unit reports and personal diaries recorded long weeks of hard manual work necessary before aircraft could use the fields. On 28 April 1943, 2nd Battalion 102 Regiment stated that But airfield was now complete, with one runway one hundred meters by two thousand meters, and a second eighty meters by fifteen hundred meters, plus forty revetments ready for bombers.

The airstrips, however, were so rough that the accident rate was high; there were never enough trained mechanics to repair damaged airplanes, and workshop facilities weren't provided in adequate supply. Propellers and tires were frequently damaged and supply requests for extra shipments of these were radioed to the rear areas and to Japan.

In mid-July 1943, 68 and 78 Fighter Sentai, with their new Kawasaki Ki-61 "Hien" (Allied code name: Tony) single-engine fighter aircraft, arrived at Boram, or "Wewak East," each occupying one side of the airfield. Their presence in the region had been detected in May and June, by radio intercept. "Ultra" SIB 22 of 23 May reported that the commanding officer of 68 Sentai was at Truk on 20 May and that about forty of the new fighters had flown from Truk to Rabaul on about 26 April.

Also on 9 and 10 July, 59 Fighter Sentai with Nakajima Ki-43 "Hayabusa" (Oscar) aircraft arrived at "But East," or Dagua. On 20 June 1943, army bombers had raided Darwin, Australia, escorted by Oscars of 59 Sentai. The 2 Chutai of the 59th was led by Capt. Shigeo Nango, well known and respected for his ability.

The 8th Naval Development Unit was formed by the Japanese to exploit the resources of British New Guinea. With headquarters in Wewak, about two thousand people eventually were employed by this unit. Military organizations the world over function with little regard to the personal wishes of their members, and like many of their Allied counterparts, a large number of Japanese found themselves in parts of the world they did not wish to see, nor had even known of in peace. A civilian member of 8 Development Unit had been encouraged to join by being told that although he would go to New Guinea, it was not a combat zone, and he could return to Japan whenever he liked. The reality was shocking. The constant bombing and strafing by Allied airplanes brought home to him the basic weakness of the Japanese occupation forces. High-level bombing allowed him time to get to cover, but his greatest fear was of strafing, as the planes were upon them so swiftly.

"Oda" was an unlucky civilian fisherman sent to help feed the forces. He had never heard of New Guinea or Australia before going to the region, and after capture, his interrogator commented that Oda thought himself so far away from his family, in this semimythical region, that he would never return to Japan or see again his wife and five children; he was amazed that seasons in the southern hemisphere were reversed and had trouble grasping this idea. Another disillusioned man was in 9 Shipping Engineer Regiment; he had believed such units were noncombatant. On arrival at Wewak in August 1943 he had a rude awakening. The whole unit was badly informed of events, all information coming from an officer who listened to a radio in the signals unit. This soldier soon greatly feared strafers after witnessing their devastating effect. Unhappy for different reasons was "Murata," whose military life had been miserable because of the way in which soldiers of the

Emperor were treated. Murata particularly disliked the physical beatings given by anyone senior in rank. In his opinion the public was not in favor of the war but had no choice. His only source of information was official victory claims, service newspapers, or news read out by an officer.

The victory claims presented by Tokyo to Japanese soldiers and civilians were so great and claimed such high enemy losses in personnel and material that if the claims came from Allied authorities, the average Allied soldier would have laughed in disbelief and scorned them as nonsense. But the Japanese had achieved fantastic successes. They had occupied vast areas of China; occupied French Indochina; destroyed the U.S., British, and Dutch Navies in the Pacific; overrun the Philippines and Netherlands East Indies; captured Bataan and the fortresses of Singapore and Corregidor; destroyed enemy air formations; captured tens of thousands of Allied troops; and ranged from Hawaii to Darwin, Australia, then to India and Ceylon. The year 1942 was the stuff of samurai legend. But later, when the cheap victories had ceased, the Japanese were told of events such as The Battle of Rennell Island on 4 February 1943: Allied losses were said to be 480 ships and 3,987 planes—such a huge defeat for the Allies that English radio did not mention it. There was no such battle. The truth of events in the combat zones was known only to the Japanese in the offices from which reports were sent. A chief petty officer in 2 Signals Unit sent to headquarters figures of Allied aircraft definitely shot down, instead of the inflated claims. In all August 1943, two B-25s were accurately known to have been destroyed, and until March 1944, only another five total were known to have been shot down.

In the Wewak area, Allied air attacks began as soon as the Japanese moved in, although at first little damage was caused. Japanese Anti-Aircraft (AA) defenses steadily increased, from four guns in January 1943 to twenty in March and forty in June. The coastline at Wewak favored defense as the airfields and installations were on the coast or only a short way inland, and the coastline formed a series of capes and headlands that allowed the gunners to place a series of cross-fires on attackers from seaward or flying along the coast. Warning of approaching Allied aircraft overland was given by radio and telephone from dispersed forward observation posts of 4 Air Intelligence Regiment.

The U.S. B-17s and B-24s that braved Japanese AA fire in the early days, although not causing great destruction, were an obvious symbol to the Japanese of 5th Air Force intentions and determination. Some Japanese who saw the bombers wondered why they were not shot down, and one soldier of the 80th Regiment paused from his labors at airfield construction, watched a B-17 sailing along apparently unconcerned among the antiaircraft bursts, and deduced U.S. flight crews were nonchalant because their aircraft were made of steel.

Allied action was only one problem, though. The area soon had a well-deserved reputation for malaria and other diseases, including "Wewak fever," for which there was no cure and patients either recovered or died. An NCO with 238 Regiment wrote of his arrival "in a coconut grove. There are many mosquitoes. Almost all the company has malaria. It rains every day, but we have no clothing to change into. We are building an airfield." A soldier in 26 Artillery Regiment wrote, "Our greatest enemy is the mosquito. Another is the Boeing."

Maj. Shigeki Nanba, a Nakajima Ki-43 Oscar pilot, who commanded 1 Chutai 59 Sentai at Dagua, described the adverse effects on the entire unit of the local food situation, climate, and prevalent diseases; dysentery weakened many pilots and ground crews. Attempts to cook and eat berries and vegetables that looked similar to those in Japan sometimes ended in poisoning and sickness.

The Japanese code of military justice was much harsher than those of the Allies, excepting the USSR. Typical examples of crime and punishment in the Japanese forces in New Guinea were: stealing sweets for sale to hospital patients, three months' imprisonment; going AWOL after a reprimand by the section leader, eight months' imprisonment; and self-wounding to evade duties, ten months' imprisonment. In general, the Japanese were as hard on their own people as they were on others. In the author's previous book describing the air raids on Rabaul, *Into the Dragon's Jaws,* more attention is given the Japanese state of mind, military code, and general attitude to prisoners.

Orders by Japanese commanders were captured by Allied forces and translated, opening a window into the Japanese system. Japanese treatment of prisoners contravened the Geneva conventions and resulted in war crimes trials for many Japanese military personnel. In the Wewak region, a 224 Infantry Regiment document stated that "the Division commander's policy is that PW will be put to death, but first will be sent to Regimental HQ, and dealt with at Division HQ." An engineer private was told that prisoners could be taken, but "there is nothing to prevent the shooting of pilots." A civilian in 8 Naval Development Unit at

Wewak was told that air prisoners were beheaded after a brief interrogation, with only senior ones sent to higher headquarters. He believed that about twenty were so murdered between December 1943 and April 1944.

The Japanese had gone to war with a mixture of feelings—worry, resignation, or joy at finally taking on the Western nations. Many did not believe Japan was responsible for the war in the Pacific. The Spartan life and rigid discipline imposed from the beginning of military service, and even before, ensured all ranks carried out their duties in adverse conditions. The harsh truth of the battlefront came as a blow to many on both sides. One Japanese diarist noted the many air attacks and his shock when told bodies in sunken ships would not be recovered for return of the ashes to Japan. In the privacy of their diaries or in conversation with close friends, alarm and discontent were voiced as it became obvious that the military situation had altered and was against Japan. But it was believed the only way out was to continue with one's duties. Surrender was not mentioned in diaries, and was not discussed. Whatever the conditions of capture, prisoners considered themselves dead, disgraced, and cut off from their families and homeland forever. Despite a progressively worsening situation for the Japanese, Allied propaganda had little effect unless the individual Japanese soldier was in a very desperate situation; the overall effect of Allied propaganda on Japanese groups and units was minimal.

Air attacks were one thing, but the general war situation another. In mid-1943, Wewak was not threatened by Allied ground forces, and conventional military thinking held that it would be months or years before the Allies could fight their way that far along the coast. There would be plenty of time for the Japanese to follow the plan of Imperial headquarters and hold the present perimeter of the Empire while the "Decisive Battle Force" was raised and trained near Japan before coming south to annihilate the Allied forces in mid-1944.

At the end of July 1943, General Teramoto's 4 Air Army was a strong organization. Under his command were 6 Flying Division, 7 Flying Division, and 14 Flying Brigade, with flying units and ground support units, and 12 Brigade, with support units, detailed in Appendix B.

The major Japanese aircraft available were:

Nakajima Ki-43 *Hayabusa* (Oscar)—highly maneuverable single-engine fighter, armed with a mixture of only two 12.7 mm or 7.7 mm machine guns

Kawasaki Ki-61 *Hien* (Tony)—the only inline-engine Japanese fighter, with two
12.7 mm or 7.7 mm machine guns, and, later, two 20 mm cannon

Kawasaki Ki-45 *Toryu* (Nick)—twin-engine fighter with 20 mm or 37 mm cannon and machine guns, intended to destroy B-17s and B-24s

Kawasaki Ki-48 (Lily)—twin-engine bomber with 800- to 1,600-pound
bombload, weakly defended by three 7.7 mm machine guns and vulnerable to
attack by the heavily armed Allied fighters

Mitsubishi Ki-21 (Sally)—twin-engined heavy bomber with 1,500- to 2,000-
pound bomb load, weakly defended by a mixture of three to six 7.7 mm or
12.7 mm machine guns

Nakajima Ki-49 (Helen)—basically the same as the Sally but with a 20 mm cannon at the rear

Other reconnaissance, communication, transport, and light ground-attack aircraft
were available in small or moderate numbers but are not relevant to this account.

Of all these types, only the Kawasaki Tony, with liquid-cooled engine and
(soon to be installed) 20 mm cannon armament, represented a departure from
the conformist Japanese design concepts. Almost all Japanese aircraft types represented the evolution of refining existing designs. The fighters and bombers provided by the Japanese aviation design offices and factories had little in the way
of radical thought applied to solve the problems of fighter interception and aerial bombardment.

The German Luftwaffe on the Channel Front contented itself with defense
from December 1940 and was eventually totally defeated by the Allied air forces,
which evolved into a modern offensive air arm. German aviation did provide the
outstanding Focke-Wulf FW190 and groundbreaking Messerschmitt Me262 fighters, and competed with Allied development work in every field of aviation, particularly development of jet engines, radar, and armaments. Japan's high command
and industry failed to counter Allied advances in aviation, however, and the unfortunate flight crews and ground units at the fronts were provided with only
improved versions of old designs, which in 1942 had been effective against the
ill-prepared Allied forces, but a year later were inferior in almost every requirement
of air combat.

A good example of the lack of understanding of airpower by Japanese senior
officers of the time is that of the bomb load of Japanese bombers. What the

Japanese classified as a "heavy bomber" was a twin-engine, with a crew of about six, and carried less than a ton of bombs. These might have been adequate for attacks on poorly defended cities in China but not for war against the Western democracies. Allied heavy bombers had four engines and carried several tons of bombs over comparatively long ranges. The outstanding Allied bombers—the Avro Lancaster, Boeing B-17 and B-29, and Consolidated B-24—showed the Germans and Japanese what was meant by the term *heavy bomber.* Allied medium bombers outperformed Japanese heavy bombers in almost every aspect of military operations. Eventually Allied fighters carried the same weight of bombs as a Japanese heavy bomber.

Of all the Japanese army aircraft available, by 1943 only the Tony was capable of meeting Allied fighters on anything like equal terms. The Oscar was nimble but underarmed. The Nick was rarely to fight B-17s or B-24s alone and was no match for Allied fighters. Japanese bombers simply could not exist in the presence of heavily armed Allied fighters, of which the lightest armament was six .50-inch machine guns. U.S. aviation technology in 1941 already had surpassed that of Japan, and even more advanced types of aircraft would be introduced. The Japanese, like the Nazis in Germany, made the fatal mistake of concluding that the aircraft inventory that served to win the early cheap victories would still suffice. This mistake was compounded by glowing reports of daily success by the existing aircraft in service.

Some Japanese fighter claims were ludicrous. Seven P-38s were claimed destroyed in the first combat with them on 27 December 1942 by pilots of 11 Sentai flying Oscars. In reality only one P-38 was seriously damaged, and it was repaired. On 6 January 1943, during a battle over a convoy to Lae, New Guinea, a Japanese pilot of 11 Sentai allegedly returned to base after a close-quarter battle with a B-24, with his Oscar sprayed with the blood that gushed from the pilot of the B-24. How the torrent of blood escaped the cockpit, how it remained concentrated in a torrent despite the effect of the slipstream, and how he flew through the four propeller arcs and missed the twin tails of the B-24 were not considered. This piece of nonsense has been repeated in postwar Japanese unit histories. Obviously any red stain on the Oscar came from hydraulic fluid leaking from the B-24, the pilot of which was unharmed. On 26 May 1943 over Madang, M.Sgt. Naoji Menya, an

Oscar pilot of 24 Sentai made a head-on pass at five B-24s and claimed to have shot down four, thanks to his "TA" explosive projectiles. Only the 90th Bomb Group operated B-24s in the SWPA at this time and has no record of such a combat or such losses. Menya received a citation and a special promotion to warrant officer.

In air battles over New Guinea in July and early August 1943, Japanese fighters claimed many victories, and the Japanese units and their headquarters command staff believed they inflicted significant losses. Unlike the Allied forces, the Japanese did not use many camera-guns for assessment of fighter claims but relied on the word of the pilot. On 15 August alone, the Allied base at Marilinan was reported destroyed, and eighteen U.S. fighters claimed shot down; actually four were lost, along with two C-47 transports. Heavy Japanese bomber losses in the combats were "regretted"—eleven were claimed by U.S. pilots—but it was thought that Allied installations had been badly damaged. Ground damage actually was slight, with four killed when a bomber crashed into a church and five others injured by bombs. Five first lieutenants were reported lost from 208 Sentai in the attack on 15 August, but junior and enlisted ranks were not included in this loss report. The newly arrived but experienced 59 Sentai claimed twenty victories in its first action in New Guinea on 15 August for an admitted loss of four Oscars: three from 2 Chutai and one from 3 Chutai. The two JAAF fighter units involved claimed thirty-nine victories, and U.S. pilots of the 40th and 41st Squadrons claimed three Oscars and eleven Sallys; four U.S. fighters were lost.

As a result of these large victory claims, an inspection party of senior Japanese officers from Rabaul arrived at Wewak on 16 August to deliver congratulations and present awards for this reported truimph as well as to inspect the assembled army air units. General Teramoto intended launching his force against another Allied field at Bena Bena right after the ceremonies. This staff officers' visit was to have a disastrous result.

After a year of confrontation, the Allied air forces recognized the weaknesses of the Japanese air forces. These were an inability to handle large masses of aircraft, a habit of making piecemeal attacks that were not followed up, confusion if the plan was upset, and no heavy bomber that could fight to and from the target.

The Japanese air forces in the Wewak area relied on the combination of local bad weather conditions and the five-hundred-mile distance from Allied air bases to keep them safe from air attack. After the battle experiences of the past twenty months, the Japanese should have had a higher opinion of the capabilities of their enemy. They did not, and they were about to have a bitter lesson administered by the U.S. Army 5th Air Force.

TWO

A Sea of Fire
Wewak, August 1943

17 August 1943

The U.S. 8th Photo Squadron had operated its Lockheed F-4 reconnaissance version of the P-38 and B-17s, often provided by the bomber squadrons, over wide areas of the SWPA, battling weather and enemy interception to bring back the vital photographs from which so much information could be derived by trained photo-interpreters. Wewak had been one of the many assigned targets. On 9 August, "impregnable weather" foiled the attempt, but on the eleventh and thirteenth successful missions were flown to the Wewak area.

The large concentrations of Japanese aircraft on the four strips at But, Boram, Dagua, and Wewak presented a target such as had been seen before only by the German Luftwaffe when they attacked Poland in 1939 and the Soviet Union in 1941, and again by the Japanese when they arrived over U.S. air bases at Pearl Harbor and the Philippines. But those occasions were at the beginning of hostilities, the most recent more than two years before. A combination of incompetent senior Japanese commanders and logistical and construction ineffectiveness, subordinated to operational requirements, resulted in too many aircraft crammed onto and close to four single strips of runway. Missions by the 8th Photo Squadron confirmed the information from signals intelligence—all four enemy fields were crowded. Gen. George Kenney concentrated his strike force at Port Moresby on the afternoon of 16 August.

In the late night of 16 August, thirty-seven B-17s and B-24s from all squadrons of the 43rd "Ken's Men" and 90th Jolly Rogers Bomb Groups took off for Hansa, Madang, Tadji, Wewak, But, Boram, and Dagua. Soon after midnight they droned back and forth showering fragmentation bombs across the airfields.

Bob Hallett of the Jolly Rogers 321st Squadron flew "8-Ball." In the United States, on the day the trainee crews were ready to receive new B-24s, only twenty airplanes were ready and these had been given to crews going to England. So the Hallett crew was forced to make the long journey from Kansas to New Guinea by Air Transport Command, train and troop carrier, before joining the 90th Group in June 1943. On this night raid to Wewak, Bob Hallett had a replacement navigator because his usual one, Lee Minor, was ill. Hallett's plane took its place in the queue for takeoff with aircraft leaving at three-minute intervals. The 43rd Bomb Group went first, followed by the 90th. To reduce the chances of midair collision, all aircraft were to fly the same course, which meant those destined for the most distant target had to overfly the others. Crossing the mountains at eighteen thousand feet, 8-Ball flew through good weather under a full moon. Just before the estimated time of arrival at the enemy coast, Hallett asked the replacement navigator how things were. The reply was that all was well, they were on course, a good checkpoint had just been identified, and they would soon cross the mouth of the Sepik River. Hallett descended across the coast when suddenly he noticed searchlights and flak to the right, and simultaneously they were held in six beams from below. Flak began to stream up at them.

Hallett broke violently and escaped the lights after about thirty seconds. The crew realized they were eighty miles off course and had just flown over the Japanese base at But, "fat, dumb, and happy" as Hallett recalled. They headed for their target and flew over the channel between Wewak and the islands of Muschu and Kairiru but again were lit by searchlights and shot at. By weaving down to bombing altitude of seven thousand feet, Hallett made it hard for the Japanese to fire accurately.

The first 90th Group B-24 over Boram was the 400th Squadron's Capt. Ellis Brown. Lt. Tom Fetter, the bombardier, dropped the full load of 4-pound incendiaries along the strip.

Bob Hallett lined up on Boram, and the sky ahead was "a literal hell of smoke and flame criss-crossed by searchlights." The B-24 roared on through the turbulence of the barrage, smoke from shell bursts flicked by, and shrapnel rattled on the fuselage. Hallett waited for what seemed an eternity until "bombs away" then whipped the B-24 into a dive to the left. He pulled out at four thousand feet, the air speed indicator showing nearly 300 mph, and left the target area. Behind them the raids went on.

Dusty Swanson, also of the 321st Squadron, flew the mission and noted in his diary:

When they said Wewak is a rough place, they were not kidding a bit. We left about midnight and were over the target about 3 A.M. They had a very active defense system. The ground to air fire and searchlights were all over the place. Needless to say we were glad to get rid of our bombs on target and get out of there. We were in the lights during the entire bomb run. I saw Joe Casale go down. He started his bomb run right in front of me and they received a direct hit. He went down in flames. It was not easy, going in for our run, after that. Joe was a heck of a nice guy, and it is really hard to realize it was him. His navigator lived in our tent, which really hit home.

Six B-17s of the Ken's Men 63rd Squadron attacked Dagua, and "The Mustang," flown by Lieutenant Glyer, was attacked by a twin-engine night fighter at the end of the bomb run, when the B-17 was held in searchlights; the fighter missed. The 63rd Squadron dropped fragmentation bombs [frags] across Dagua, resulting in three fires, and reported three passes by a twin-engine enemy fighter. The 65th Squadron attacked Dagua, But, and Madang, and also reported the twin-engine Japanese fighter. Of the 90th Jolly Rogers Group, one aircraft of the 319th Squadron had an engine shot out, a shell hit in the bomb bay, and other hits in the left wing, but the airplane returned to base. Crews from the 321st Squadron reported seeing aircraft in intense antiaircraft fire catch fire and crash off Cape Boram. The 403rd Squadron bombed the eastern end of the But revetments, and flight crews noticed four distinct small explosions and twelve to fifteen fires; crews from the other squadrons also reported the antiaircraft defenses, explosions, fires on the ground, and crashing bombers.

The twin-engine fighters reported by the bomber crews were Kawasaki Ki-45 Toryu "Nick" fighters of 3 Chutai 13 Sentai, commanded by Lieutenant Asahi. On 8 July, 2 and 3 Chutai arrived at Boram from Rabaul; this was their first real combat. The twin-engine Japanese bomber destroyer had been rushed into service, and many crews did not have great faith in its strength or reliability. On this night one bomber was claimed destroyed, and one probably was destroyed. Many Japanese on the ground watched the night raids, the falling bombers were clearly visible, and Sergeant Major Motohisa, 238 Regiment, noted in his diary that four aircraft were shot down. Two actually were lost.

These Jolly Rogers B-24s were Casale's "Yanks from Hell," 321st Squadron and Freas's "Twin Nifties" of the 400th. After the war, on 30 April 1946, local people led RAAF searchers to the wreckage of Freas's B-24 number 42-40348. Remains of three crew members were found in the wreck, and the searchers were told that one NCO crew member had parachuted but had been captured, taken to Wewak, and murdered there. Nothing was found of other crew members.

Of the losses, 13 Sentai claimed 1-1-0. Japanese 4 Air Army Intelligence Section records show claims for three destroyed and two probables, but records also show that the night raids resulted in thirteen Japanese aircraft destroyed, twenty badly damaged, and thirty-four slightly damaged. Some Japanese units were hard hit. Sentai records captured later and separate from the Air Army report total one hundred Japanese aircraft destroyed or damaged. Six Oscars were destroyed from 59 Sentai, an unstated number damaged, but only eight were available for operations. Only six Tonys were left flyable for 68 Sentai; pilots sent to Manila for replacement Tonys did not return until September. Only two Nicks from the twenty that 13 Sentai brought to Wewak were operational. So few aircraft were left to 13 Sentai that Major Nagano, the unit commander, decided to use the worn and battered Oscars left at Rabaul by 1 and 11 Sentai, when those units returned to Japan after service in the Solomons and New Guinea.

Capt. Akira Yamanaka, commander of the Japanese air intelligence units in New Guinea, was at Wewak waiting for dawn so an assessment of damage could be made. Captain Yamanaka wondered why the enemy made a heavy, prolonged raid on the airfields.

The B-24s were crossing back over the mountains and the tired crews were looking forward to landing. Bob Hallett, in 8-Ball, did not have an easy trip. After crossing the range at seventeen thousand feet, he found the coast under cloud down to sea level. He told the navigator he wanted a course to Moresby, but the navigator was not sure of their position so could not give a heading. Hallett decided to circle in a clear spot and radio Moresby for a bearing, but Murphy's Law was in effect and Moresby would not reply. It was 0545; gasoline was burning every minute. Finally, after a demand from Hallett, the navigator told him to climb on a bearing of 135 degrees. After about thirty minutes on instruments he broke into clear sky at twelve thousand feet. They passed over a break in the cloud but saw "nothing but cold gray ocean," said Hallett. "That was the last straw, so I took over the navigation myself."

He spiraled down through the break, swung out on a heading of 90 degrees, zig-zagged through the weather, and found the coast after twenty-five minutes. Coral reefs off the south coast of New Guinea existed only east of Port Moresby, and this natural feature was a basic navigation aid. There were no coral reefs below, so Hallett turned east along the coast, at two hundred feet height, twelve hundred yards visibility. It was dawn, there was fuel enough for two hours, and Hallett told the crew to prepare to ditch if he could not find a good stretch of beach. An hour passed, the weather improved, and a flight of B-25s passed overhead in the opposite direction. The navigator told Hallett they were going the wrong way, to make a 180-degree turn. Hallett told him to go to hell but tried the radio again. This time Moresby answered and gave a bearing almost the same as that they were on. They were only sixty miles out. "It sure felt wonderful to be on the ground" wrote Hallett in his diary. They had thirty minutes' fuel left. He determined to have Lee Minor back as navigator.

Before the planned daylight strike, two F-4s of the 8th Photo Squadron arrived to record the situation at the four airfields after the night bombing and to photograph the results of the coming B-25 strikes.

Meanwhile at Durand Airstrip, Port Moresby, at 0300, crews of the B-25 strafers of the 405th Squadron, the "Sunsetters" 38th Bomb Group, were called. Lt. Garrett Middlebrook realized that they were to have a long briefing because normally they were awoken an hour later. While they were dressing, Moffett, his navigator, said, "Rabaul, here we come." But Middlebrook had talked to the intelligence officer, knew of the congestion around the strips at Wewak, and suspected they would be flying northwest, not to Rabaul in the northeast. When they arrived for briefing, a glance at the map showed he was correct.

The day before, maintenance crews finished installing fittings for the jettisonable three-hundred-gallon gasoline tank inside the B-25. The tank had to be emptied first, and then dropped out, as fumes made it a veritable bomb, waiting for a single tracer round to explode it. The B-25s had to climb the Owen Stanley Range both on the way to Wewak and also on return, and part of the mission would be flown at maximum power, burning gasoline rapidly.

The B-25s of the Grim Reapers 3rd Attack Group flew from Dobodura on the north coast, southward over the Owen Stanley Range to the strip at Schwimmer, near Port Moresby, so the entire strike force would set off from the same general location. The intention was to make the approach across the island and not to fly along the north coast, where Japanese garrisons could easily see the formations and pass reports as the B-25s continued west.

For one pilot the Wewak missions began with a little excitement. Martin Radnik was a flight leader in the 8th Attack Squadron, and his copilot on the flight was a squadron character, "Cowboy" Brown. As they prepared for takeoff in the B-25, Radnik selected 15 degrees of flap, but Brown thought a few more should be added, and did so. He then accidentally moved the control handle past neutral—the flaps went back up. Neither pilot realized what had happened, so the B-25 went hurtling down the strip and used all available nine thousand feet, both men hauling back on the controls to clear trees at the end of the runway. When they landed at Schwimmer, the gunners asked why they took off with no flaps. Radnik looked at Brown asking an unspoken question.

The 90th Squadron of the 3rd Attack had a shortage of pilots, so Capt. Bob Reed came back from 5th Air Force headquarters to fly the mission. Bob Reed had flown missions with the 90th, including the decisive strike when the Japanese convoy to Lae was destroyed in one morning in the Battle of the Bismarck Sea. He had been working as an operations officer in Port Moresby for about a month but volunteered for this Wewak strike to be in on such an important mission, to drop parafrags, and to try the droppable fuel tank designed by Pappy Gunn. His work in operations at Moresby allowed Reed to become familiar with the bigger picture seen from headquarters level, and he knew the Wewak fields were packed with enemy aircraft. He also knew that the Japanese thought the Wewak area out of range of Allied strike aircraft.

Seven 90th B-25s were prepared for takeoff, led by Captain Hawkins. Pilots and crews had to contend with the weather, "mountain-filled clouds," and inhospitable jungle between the targets and base. However, fighter escort was to be provided: ninety-nine Lockheed P-38s were tasked on the mission. Fourteen returned for mechanical reasons, and eighty-five completed the escort. Missions to Wewak presented P-38 pilots with the potential for fuel problems. It would take about two hours to reach the target area, and it could be expected that combat would follow at full throttle, but always the flight back to Moresby or Dobodura had to be remembered. Any error in navigation on the way home meant more fuel consumption. It was a daunting prospect calling for a higher level of expertise. The P-38s flew to Port Moresby, landed and refueled, and waited for the B-25 strafers to assemble overhead.

For one P-38 pilot, the mission was to have enough excitement before it really began. The 9th Fighter Squadron, the Flying Knights, in fighter fashion was slipping in one or two at a time to land between the slower B-24s returning from the night raids on the Wewak airdromes. Ralph Wandrey was flying the last Lightning.

"As I was flaring," he recalled, "the B-24 ahead gave power, to go around again, and the prop-wash flipped me over on my back. . . . I was looking at the runway above me. If it hadn't been a twin-engine plane, I would have crashed."

Wandrey applied power to one engine, rolled right side up, landed, and taxied in; then he had to hold the shaking hand of his tent-mate who was trying to light a cigarette to calm himself after watching the near disaster. He gave Ralph an unprompted opinion: "You must be the greatest pilot in the world!"

The 9th was formed as part of the 49th Fighter Group in January 1941, and in January 1942 moved to the SWPA. Some of the pilots who joined the 49th in Australia took part in the debacle in the Netherlands East Indies. All three squadrons were active in the defense of Darwin, Australia, and later in New Guinea. While the 7th and 8th Squadrons continued to operate the P-40, the 9th was selected to convert to the P-38. The 9th, in their P-38s, narrowly missed shooting down Lt. Gen. Hatazo Adachi, commander of the Japanese 18th Army.

On 2 August 1943, Adachi flew in a Sonia reconnaissance plane from Alexishafen to go to the land battle area near Wau and Salamaua. He was escorted by Nakajima Ki-43 Oscars and Kawasaki Ki-61 Tonys with nine Oscars of 24 Sentai responsible for close escort. Near Finschhafen and Saidor, eleven B-25s of the 38th Bomb Group on a barge hunt found prey. Twelve P-38s of the 9th Fighter Squadron, the escort, joined the strafing. The P-38 pilots then noticed about fourteen Oscars and two fixed undercarriage airplanes assumed to be Nates, which approached from Madang at about fifteen thousand feet. The P-38s left the barges and engaged the Japanese, who were reported to be "experienced and willing."

Adachi's pilot saved the general by flying the slow and agile army reconnaissance plane at treetop height where the fast heavy P-38s were at a disadvantage. Two flights of P-38s chased the Japanese "wheels down and welded" airplane until they ran out of ammunition. Every P-38 made passes, but the Japanese pilot, at treetop height, cooly waited until the P-38s fired, then flung his plane into a steep turn out of the line of fire. Eventually the P-38s were out of ammunition and at the limit of fuel endurance. Then, according to one account, the Japanese pilot flew the Sonia to Cape Gloucester (New Britain) for a forced landing. Adachi's headquarters was thrown into gloom until word came of his survival. The ace Maj. Hachio Yokoyama, the commander of 24 Sentai, was reported lost along with one other officer pilot in what was described as "a desperate fight." Another version of the combat in Yasuho Izawa's history of Japanese army fighter units states that all the subunit commanders were lost with unit commander Yokoyama, and a junior officer assumed temporary command. The 9th claimed eleven enemy fighters destroyed, all seen to go into Dorfer Bay. The B-25s reported Tonys in the combat as well as Oscars and Nates, and confirmed destruction of three enemy fighters. One Nate reportedly flew alongside the B-25s and then turned for New Britain. This might have been Adachi's airplane or that of an accompanying staff officer.

On the morning of the Wewak strike at Port Moresby, as the 9th Squadron waited by their airplanes, a Red Cross girl drove up with Cokes and asked if the fighter pilots minded drinking dead men's drinks, because the bomber crews for whom the drink was intended had been shot down over Wewak. Wandrey was finishing his Coke when a B-24 flew overhead, the crew baled out, and some of the parachuting men almost were hit by B-25s taking off. Wandrey learned that the bomber had returned from Wewak and was so damaged it could not land. This was the 319th Squadron aircraft, damaged but able to make it back.

The Attacks Begin

The Sunsetters Group 405th and 71st Squadrons set off for their targets at Dagua and But. Flying with the 405th was the squadron's Australian army air liaison officer, Capt. John Massie, who had begun pilot training with the RAAF but was forced to give it up after severe air sickness problems. He transferred to the army, was attached to the U.S. squadrons, and flew many missions with the 405th, sometimes as a gunner.

The 405th took off, and the twelve B-25s slipped into formation as the squadron headed for the rendezvous point with the 71st Squadron, which was taking off behind them. Garrett Middlebrook was leading the 405th's second flight. He looked back and saw the 71st in takeoff position, but that was the last he saw of them that day. They aborted the mission. After circling at the rendezvous, the 405th set off alone. Middlebrook felt angry, as he believed the 71st could have pressed on through the cloud, into the clear, and joined the mission.

Middlebrook's frustration was only beginning. The 405th was to meet the Grim Reapers Attack Group and P-38 escort at a point near Marilinan, but no one was there. So the 405th flew on, sweeping well away from Lae so as not to alert the Japanese, and then slipped down into the Markham Valley to about one thousand feet.

Middlebrook began transferring the fuselage tank fuel into the wing tanks, but when they tried to drop the tank, it would not budge. There was no way Middlebrook was going to fly into combat with a fume-filled tank in the fuselage. Then he had an idea and told his engineer, Emminger, to put on his parachute harness, clip it to the fuselage spars above the tank, and jump up and down on the tank. This worked; the B-25 nose lurched down and then up, and Emminger reported the tank was out. "I hope you're still in!" joked Middlebrook, but Emminger was in no mood for humor and replied he wanted to test his guns.

Meanwhile on the Wewak airfields the Japanese were checking damage from the night attacks. About seventy men had been killed, and damaged or burned aircraft were being categorized. Captain Yamanaka, intelligence officer, went to the command post and sat chain-smoking, trying to deduce enemy intentions. Outside were the smoking remains of two Mitsubishi Sally twin-engine bombers, which had brought the staff officers from Rabaul the previous day. The south-ernmost Japanese observation post was at Koba, 250 miles southeast of Wewak. At 0600, the post reported two P-38s flying west at eighteen thousand feet. Then the radio station reported a break in the landline that prevented communica-tions with headquarters. Yamanaka could not do anything about this, so instead he sat, smoking. He was uneasy and suspected something was about to happen, but he had no information on which to base a decision. A trained and experi-enced intelligence officer, he tried to control his feelings and wait for definite information.

The staff officers from Rabaul arrived, looked at the scene, and then left for the headquarters in Wewak. Before they drove away, a military academy classmate of Yamanaka said he thought the night raids were what the Japanese classified as "restraining bombing"—a night attack on an airfield to damage communications and road systems so the aircraft would remain in place and be the target in a following attack. Yamanaka realized what was about to hap-pen—another heavier daylight attack on the four Wewak airfields was to take place soon. It was sometime after 0630 (Tokyo time; 0830 local time), and Yamanaka was the senior officer at Wewak airfield. He called an emergency meeting and ordered all efforts directed to re-establishing communications; he then tried to make contact with all higher and lower echelons. It was found the night bombing had severely disrupted line communications, and there were not enough men and materials available to lay new lines. It was 0700 (0900) before he could contact headquarters at Yotendai, where the Rabaul staff officers had gone.

Yamanaka realized the factors contributing to a catastrophe were falling into place: the airfields were packed with aircraft; one attack had been made and a second was to follow; communications were badly disrupted; enemy reconnais-sance P-38s had been sighted; and orders had been given for all aircraft to be brought out for inspection by the senior officers from Rabaul. Yamanaka did not have authority to stop this assembly.

When the formation of 405th Squadron B-25s crossed the Sepik River, Garrett Middlebrook saw, to his surprise and confusion, the squadron turning left 180 degrees, aborting the mission. He assumed it was because fuselage tanks could not be jettisoned and no one thought to do what he had Emminger do to force them to fall away. Then he saw ahead and a little below

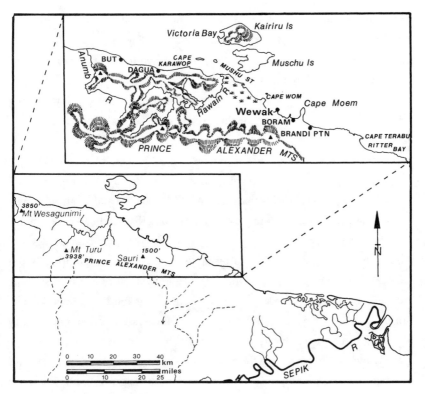

The Wewak area and airfields

one B-25 flying on to the target. He wondered who it could be. Middlebrook's crew called to say the fighters also were turning back. He recalled: "But here was this plane up in front, pulling away from me. At that moment I gave no particular thought to what I was going to do. I just wanted to see who this guy was who was going to the target, either alone or with whoever wanted to join him."

Middlebrook dived to catch the lone B-25, pulled alongside on the right, and noted another B-25 surging up on the left. "I came in close and found Mr. Determination to be Bill Gay, my friend from the first day I entered flying school." The third B-25 was flown by Berniece Lackness. Middlebrook thought about the situation: ahead was a heavily defended target; they had only three airplanes, which could not make a great difference to the war; he was responsible for his crew. He knew he had to make a decision: "When I looked over at Gay's ship again, a warm feeling of pride swelled up inside of me. I knew the decision had already been made for me. I had just been going through a mental exercise. We were following a courageous man, and neither I nor any of my crew were going to abandon him."

Middlebrook sat up a little straighter, and the crew realized he was going on to the target. He was not nonchalant about the attack, however; he knew there would be heavy ground fire and fighters and hoped the opposing pilots would be new guys "not the mangy old veterans of Rabaul, Madang, or Lae."

The tiny formation flew on with a low coastal ridge on their right and the foothills of higher mountains to the left. Middlebrook felt as if he already knew the area, as the briefing by John Massie was so good that landmarks were familiar. They knew they were passing Wewak on the far side of the coastal ridge and hoped the three B-25s could slip by undetected. There was complete radio silence, and they were flying along a peaceful green valley, with no signs of human inhabitation and peaceful white clouds sitting above on the peaks. The contrast, serene valley below and the hostile Japanese just over that little ridge to the right, made a deep impression on Middlebrook.

Meanwhile, after takeoff in the order 8th, 13th, and 90th Squadrons, the Grim Reapers 3rd Attack Group B-25s were en route to the target. Col. Don Hall, the group commander, was flying with the 8th Squadron. Bill Webster with Lieutenants Patton and Greene were the right flight of three, while Martin Radnik led the left flight. They rendezvoused with the P-38 fighter escort at nine thousand feet inland from Lae. Some crews, including Middlebrook of the 38th Group, admired the scenery. Bob Reed, with the 90th, noted that the weather was perfect. It was a Sunday; it had been a Sunday at Pearl Harbor. Radnik, Webster, and other pilots were impressed with the size of the attack force: 100 strafers and 100 fighters. After meeting the P-38s, the formation began a gradual descent under scattered clouds. Some fighters stayed high, but Radnik saw the P-38s of the 9th Fighter Squadron coming down with the B-25s.

At Wewak Captain Yamanaka believed a big attack was coming but knew he could do nothing more—he had no authority to countermand orders from senior officers for the inspection of all assembled airplanes. On the airfield itself, aircraft were in the open for testing engines and the inspection. At 0730 (0930 local time), Yamanaka's detachment at Hansa reported a large enemy formation flying west. He knew that, if Wewak was the target, in twenty minutes the enemy would arrive. Finally, the damaged communications were repaired and headquarters at Yotendai was informed of the sighting at Hansa and his deduction. Yamanaka tried to raise the alarm by shouting, waving his cap, and banging an oil drum with a wrench—all to no avail. The noisy engine tests drowned out his efforts. In a last desperate attempt, he sent his men running out to the airplanes lined along the runway edges. He began running down the airfield with his men.

Kenney's B-25s had achieved surprise.

Three Against Dagua

John Massie, the Australian liaison officer, had briefed the 405th Squadron to look for a distinctive two-hundred-foot drop in the ridge that looked like a snaggle-tooth because this was exactly perpendicular to the center of Dagua strip. As they roared along the inland slope of the coastal ridge, Middlebrook and Gay saw the spot, Gay rolled smoothly toward it, and the 5th Air Force began the daylight attack on Dagua—three B-25s.

Middlebrook realized that their attack path would be at a 45-degree angle, so the eastern end would not be touched. They sped up the ridge; suddenly Middlebrook had stomach cramps; he tried to swallow, but his mouth felt as though he had no water in weeks. He was taut, nerves tight, and mad at the Japanese. Alert, he was ready to react instantly; his adrenaline was flowing. As they leaped the crest, Gay crowded Middlebrook closer to the ridge. Middlebrook turned tightly to keep his right wingtip away from the trees, and suddenly they saw the target.

"My God, what a sight!" thought Middlebrook. Aircraft lined both sides of the strip, with gasoline trucks among them and activity all over the area. The three B-25s were not spaced widely enough to cover the entire target. Middlebrook swung left to bring his guns to bear, realized there was no ground fire, and concentrated on strafing the Japanese planes before him. He fired and eight .50-caliber machine guns and a 20 mm cannon began pumping out shells. Then his stream of bullets was joined by those from the other two aircraft: more than 14,000 rounds a minute flailed the Japanese aircraft.

To Middlebrook the hail of tracers flicking out and away from his B-25 looked like thousands of reddish-white lightning bolts, and the entire area ahead erupted in dust, fires, and explosions. His first burst hit a gasoline dump, which flared into red flames; then a plane exploded, and the blast lifted another plane into the air. A fighter was facing away from him, along his direction of flight, and the stream of .50-caliber bullets pushed it along the ground into another. A twin-engine plane exploded with a blindingly bright flash. Middlebrook's B-25 was flying over the massed targets, his machine-gun fire passing through plane after plane. Last of all, a gasoline truck was hit, but its reluctance to burst into flames somehow made Middlebrook angry.

Alongside him, his copilot had opened the bomb bay doors and was methodically releasing the parafrags about a half of a second apart to get a good coverage of the target. Careful to keep the bulletstream away from Gay's aircraft, Middlebrook kept on hosing the target until he saw rounds striking the water, beyond the airstrip edges. Then they were past, he felt the bomb bay doors close, and he knew it was time for the great metamorphosis to take place. Up to and during the attack, they had been aggressive and determined, but now, to survive, "we became outrageous, unabashed cowards! It was time to flee for our lives."

3rd Attack Group at Wewak

A few miles away, the Grim Reapers of the 3rd Attack were harvesting. Before reaching the Wewak area, Col. Don Hall took the Group down to the treetops, 8th Squadron leading and 13th Squadron one minute behind. On Hall's signal, the squadrons shook out into wider formation, with the elements almost abreast of the leader to avoid shrapnel from his bomb bursts, and spread out a little to allow the wing men to fishtail while strafing across the target area. Hall led the 8th and 13th Squadrons over Boram while the 90th hit Wewak itself. Eight B-25s had turned back, but twenty-seven arrived at the targets to find they achieved complete surprise, with Japanese aircraft massed, as the U.S. crews thought, ready for takeoff.

At Wewak, running and yelling futilely, Captain Yamanaka reached the middle of the airfield amid Japanese aircraft with engines turning and crews working on them. When he looked around he saw B-25s coming over the treetops and flung himself to the ground.

The Japanese airfields presented a strafer's dream: they were crowded with airplanes preparing to attack after the inspection; there were more aircraft present from the air base at Lae, and yet others there because Wewak was the end of the ferry route from Japan through the Philippines. Col. Koji Tanaka was one of the staff officers from Rabaul at Wewak as the attackers roared in. When interrogated post-war, he said many unserviceable planes had been collected at the Wewak airfields, and although the airfields were too small, with no room for dispersal, the Japanese believed they were out of Allied fighter range and that there would be no daylight attacks.

To add icing to this cake presented to the U.S. crews, there was no Japanese fighter-cover over the strips and the antiaircraft defenses were not ready. Hollywood could not have produced a better film scene for the time: fueled and bombed Japanese planes being lined up by blissfully unaware line crews for inspection by equally unaware senior officers, all crowded into the open as the Americans roared over the trees toward them, and the frantic lone officer unable to warn anyone of the looming disaster. But it was fact, not fiction.

Hall brought the 8th Squadron onto a westerly heading along the airstrip and they opened bomb bay doors. Bill Webster, on Hall's right, looked ahead after holding formation in the turn "and there was a whole line of Jap bombers parked wingtip to wingtip on the edge of the runway, with aircrew and ground crew nearby."

Hall thought it too much to expect that the enemy at Boram would be caught off guard after the night raids, but

that is exactly what happened. We held our gun switches down, raking plane after plane. The surprise was complete. Not an AA gun was fired. Not a plane got off the ground to intercept us. A fellow dreams of a situation like that, but never expects to see it. We let go our parachute bombs, in clusters of three, one after another. They drifted lazily down like a cloud of snowballs. As we turned left towards Wewak, it became apparent that the 90th had done a good job there.

Hall's flight went right up the runway, strafing and bombing the assembled aircraft while Martin Radnik's flight, on the left, hit the area south of the strip. As soon as they saw Hall's parafrags flicking out and back, they began toggling their own. Surprise had been achieved; all was going well. Suddenly Radnik heard a series of bangs, felt a rush of air in the cockpit. He thought shells were impacting on them; he looked over and saw Cowboy Brown had opened his window and was blazing away with his .45-caliber pistol. Radnik, his attention divided between the attack run and Brown, hit Brown with the back of his hand, and asked what he was doing. Brown's reply was that he had seen a Japanese down there!

Colonel Hall signaled a turn left to go home. This turn through 180 degrees meant Radnik's airplanes had to slow down and go as low as possible while the aircraft on the right had to speed up to complete the turn. When Radnik banked left, he lost sight of the rest of the formation. All he could see was the left wing man, and that man could not see any other aircraft making the turn. All went reasonably well; there was no fighter attack during the vulnerable turn, the P-38s stayed with them, and the flight home began. Tension eased, replaced by hunger, so cheese and hardtack were eaten and canteens were emptied. It was Martin Radnik's twenty-fifth mission, and he believed it the best he had flown.

Hall led five B-25s of the 8th Attack Squadron, and the crews claimed fifteen Japanese aircraft destroyed and "many" damaged, for damage to one strafer. Eight strafers from the 13th Squadron had roared over, and the crews estimated twenty to twenty-five Japanese aircraft destroyed, and the same number damaged. "Our radio chatter leaving the area was all happy-talk," wrote Bill Webster.

Five B-25s of the 90th Squadron, led by Captain Hawkins, shot their way along Wewak airfield, expending 6,000 .50-caliber rounds and 177 23-pound parafrags over the mass of Lily bombers, Oscars, and Tonys below them. Seven began burning at once, and the crews reported "the whole area seemed to be on fire."

For Bob Reed, "When we came over those low hills, it was a sight to behold! All gun emplacements were covered, there were Japs swimming in the sea, and their fighters were lined up along the runway. At treetop level we flew down the runway, strafing and dropping our parafrags, with no sign of opposition, much like a small scale Pearl Harbor!"

In Reed's B-25 was Bruce Greiner, who had been a sound recording engineer with the Republic film studio in Hollywood and was assigned to the combat film unit in the 5th Air Force. Greiner filmed the attack from Reed's B-25, and this film was later part of the documentary *Mission to Wewak* produced about the attack.

Ralph Wandrey, 9th Fighter Squadron, nearly killed when his P-38 flipped onto its back in the B-24 slipstream at Moresby, swung off to the side as the bombers began their run. Wandrey said, "There were no enemy planes in the air, and as we circled a short distance from the airstrips, we could see that they were lined with Jap planes parked so closely together that their wingtips seemed to touch. Some of their motors were running, and we could see the crews climbing around on the planes as the gas trucks drove from one to another." Wandrey watched the strafers pass "over the airstrips in waves of three, about 20 feet high with all guns blazing, and in their wake parafrags drifted leisurely toward the mass of Jap aircraft."

Wandrey had barely left the target when a voice began screaming, "Zeros over Wewak! Zeros over Wewak! Come back, P-38s!" There was no engine noise with the voice and the P-38 pilots could not see any aircraft over Wewak. When the voice refused to identify itself and began calling them foul names, the U.S. pilots knew it was a trick to lure them within range of Japanese guns.

Coming off the strip at Boram, Capt. John "Jock" Henebry of the 90th Attack Squadron saw a small freighter not far offshore and decided to hit it with his massed .50 calibers. He turned onto the ship and quickly realized he had "made a cardinal mistake. I made a turn bellying up to a shore battery that shot us up, blowing off our spring-loaded rear doors. I had my guns on that Japanese ack-ack that was firing on me and should have continued my run on that position. When you take your guns off him, you free him to shoot. He did. We made it home, relatively intact."

All around him at Wewak, Captain Yamanaka saw men hit and knocked over by the strafing. Then the field seemed to be covered in white parachutes as the parafrags showered from the bomb bays, and there was a rolling carpet of explosions. He got up to run back to the command post, but a second wave forced him to the ground again and then a third wave. Finally, he arrived at the command post and looked back at the field.

"It was a sea of flames. This was the first full-scale enemy counterattack I had experienced," he said.

In the immediate lull after the roaring B-25s, hammering massed .50-caliber machine guns and exploding bombs, there was a strange silence and what Yamanaka described as bewilderment and stupefaction. Then the screams of wounded were heard and rescue work began. Yamanaka stood in a daze, tears of self-reproach and remorse rolling down his cheeks, before he roused himself and sent an urgent signal to 4 Air Intelligence Regiment in Rabaul. The message was relayed to 4 Air Army where at first it was not believed because there were no other reports. Six hours later, 6 Flying Division sent a more formal report.

Outside the command post, Yamanaka heard voices calling that someone stank and found the person being abused was a driver who had been using the latrine when the attack began. Sizing up the situation in a flash, the man jumped down into the hole below him and survived. After the attack, feeling lonely, he went to join other men in the air raid trench. They were not thankful for his company.

The B-25 strafers flying away from the scene of destruction occasionally popped up a few hundred feet to look back at the roiling clouds of smoke rearing from the airfields behind them. The 90th Squadron reported smoke visible twenty minutes after leaving, and the 13th said it could be seen seventy miles away. A total of seventy-four tons of bombs and 37,500 rounds of ammunition had been expended, and it was claimed that about 120 Japanese planes had been destroyed.

The airfield at But was not attacked because the 71st Squadron turned back. Captain Yamanaka's warning was received at But, and larger airplanes were pushed back into protective pens while Oscar fighters took off looking for targets. They found them in the three 405th B-25s speeding from Dagua. Lieutenants Gay, Middlebrook, and Lackness were attacked by Oscars of 59 Sentai, and there were no P-38s to assist the B-25s. As the other two B-25s closed on Gay after the strafing run, an Oscar swung onto them, and the top turret gunners were presented with a close target: the entire upper surfaces of wings and fuselage. They hit the Oscar fatally; it went down to burn on the water not far from the beach.

More Japanese fighters dived from the left, firing, and their bullets kicked up foam from the water below and ahead of Gay, who adroitly lifted over the fire at the last second, climbed to five hundred feet, and stayed there. This was dangerous because it gave the Japanese space below from which to attack. Garrett Middlebrook was disturbed to see two Oscars coming in from ahead and below, but Gay did not seem to notice them. Middlebrook called on the radio, and Gay made a sharp diving turn into the oncoming fighters, passing so close the Japanese pilots could not bring their guns to bear. They flicked past "close enough to thumb noses," thought Middlebrook.

Gay leveled off close above the waves and began what Middlebrook considered to be a masterpiece of leading a formation under fighter attack, and he did it for forty-five minutes. The next few minutes seemed to be a nightmare as Oscars attacked from all directions. Two circled out wide, feinting in every now and again, while others zipped in, firing. Two were either damaged or out of ammunition because they left, but the others kept on. One in particular was adept at pressing right in, slipping past overhead only about twenty-five feet away, but he was not able to hit the B-25s and neither could the gunners get him. Not wanting to attract fighters from Wewak, Gay swung out to sea. Flashing along at minimum height did not allow the Oscars to attack from below, but glare reflected from the water made the flying difficult for the B-25 pilots, and they assumed that the Japanese had the same problem. The fighter attacks eased.

When he was past Wewak, Gay turned right, heading for the coast, but as they crossed it the fighters increased their attacks, and the B-25 gunners were coming to the end of their ammunition. Gay expertly used the contours of the land to assist his flight, using every hill, valley, and dip in the ground. The Oscars would pull alongside the bombers until almost ahead of them, then turn and come in firing, knowing B-25 turret guns could not shoot through the propeller disc. The B-25 pilots used a variety of quick climbing banks and dives in the opposite direction, never allowing the Japanese pilots a smoothly maneuvering target. All three pilots had to concentrate on the other two B-25s, on the agile enemy, and on implacable treetops not far below—at 250 mph one slip would mean cartwheeling to destruction in the jungle.

The gunners were calling for the bombers to be put into a good position for them to hit the fighters, but the main idea was to get away. Gradually the fighters turned back; there were six, then four, then two. They approached Lae; surely the Japanese would go back! But two remained with them, and way back, low on the trees, were two more, out of range but hanging there. Gay led the formation over the mouth of the Markham River, then along the rolling hills on the coast, zigging and zagging, following the shape of the land, never giving the pursuers a chance, making life difficult for them. Ahead were the peaks at Salamaua. Then Emminger called that the fighters had turned back. Still Gay led them on at almost full power, putting distance between them and the Japanese.

Finally Gay slowed and climbed to one hundred feet. They could relax a little, open the cowling gills to cool the straining engines, and check the planes. Middlebrook had about ten machine-gun holes in the rear of the fuselage. The clothes of all aboard the B-25s were wringing wet with sweat; mouths were parched. During the combat, concentrating on Gay and Lackness, on the Japanese fighters, on the glittering sea or the dangerous uneven green treetops, Middlebrook had noticed that his copilot three times had placed his hands loosely on the controls, in case it became necessary to haul the B-25 over some obstacle Middlebrook had not seen. It was not necessary, but he appreciated the precaution, and ultimate trust: the copilot had not actually grasped the controls. The only radio transmission had been from Middlebrook, telling Gay of the two fighters coming up below. He thought this a noticeable contrast to the fighter pilots, who tended to jam the channel with needless chatter, and the 3rd Attack Group, who also talked much more than the 38th.

They landed and were met with disbelief. No one believed they had actually gone on to the designated target instead of shooting up something closer around Madang or Lae. Cameras had been fitted in the aircraft tails to allow assessment of attacks and destruction behind the speeding strafers. Gay's camera had a malfunction, and Lackness's airplane did not have a camera fitted; only Middlebrook brought back proof of a mission to Dagua.

The three crews ate a poor lunch and then relaxed after the strain of the flight until news began to circulate of the devastation wrought by the 3rd Attack Group at Boram and Wewak. When he heard this, Middlebrook began to wonder if the three B-25s had made their return flight more difficult by avoiding Wewak, when, if they had gone close by it, they could have linked with the 3rd Attack and the desired P-38 cover.

Maj. Ralph Cheli, the 38th Group commander, called for them to meet him at Gay's tent. Middlebrook believed the conversation that followed might have led to tragedy the next day.

Ralph Cheli passed on the personal compliments of Gen. Ennis Whitehead to the three crews who had gone on to the target. Cheli had the respect and personal liking of the flight crews because he had proven himself and shown that he cared for his men. But, in Middlebrook's opinion, Ralph Cheli had one great fault: refusal to take the enemy seriously. He underestimated their ability, and he regarded combat missions as "fun," not dangerous operations of war.

Cheli said he wished he had been along to enjoy the fun, adding that he would lead the next strike on the same target the next day and the first strike on Rabaul, whenever that came to be flown. Gay replied that the mission was not "fun," that he never wanted another one as bad, and the flight was attacked by fighters for almost an hour. Cheli brushed this aside, pointing out that the attacks could not have been severe because of the lack of damage to the three B-25s. When reminded of the holes in Middlebrook's plane, Cheli laughed it off with a joke about Japanese gunnery skill. None of the three pilots were happy, and Gay asked why Cheli insisted on flying when he did not need to do so anymore. Cheli said that Wewak would be reduced in two or three missions, like Lae, but Middlebrook pointed out that Lae had needed more than two or three, and Wewak now was full of new planes and new pilots. He called them "the first team."

Then one of the three made the mistake of suggesting Cheli need not fly missions but should stay on the ground and run the group because his experience was needed and should be passed on to new pilots. Cheli flared up and said he did not need to be told when to fly and when not to do so. He added he would not ask men to do what he would not do, and he needed the respect of his men. Cheli ended the conversation on an angry note, although he tried to make a joke of it and smiled.

As Ralph Cheli drove off, Middlebrook said they had tried to give unrequested advice to the CO, and he personally would apologize as soon as possible. Gay replied that it was not the right time for Cheli to talk to them about milk runs and the fun of flying missions. Bill Gay made a statement Middlebrook would not forget: "Cheli has been very lucky on all his missions. I just hope his luck never runs out, because if it does the fun runs out too."

Officially, the three B-25s from the 405th Squadron were credited with seventeen planes destroyed at Dagua, but Middlebrook believed many more must have been hit, if not totally rendered useless. Throughout the 5th Air Force strike force, morale was high because, in Ralph Wandrey's words, "The first raid was a big morale booster as we caught so many Japanese on the ground, even though we fighters didn't shoot any down."

The 3rd Attack Group B-25 crews were debriefed at Schwimmer airstrip, near Port Moresby. After debriefing, when they were not told to return to Dobodura, the crews realized another strike on Wewak would be made the next day.

Jock Henebry was named to lead the 90th on the next strike. He later said that the first attack was frightening because it was a longer mission than any he had previously flown, but the success improved his confidence. He was sure of his own abilities and the capabilities of the weapons and of the entire squadron, and he had faith in Kenney's theories on attack aviation. Henebry had doubted the potential of the strafer version of the B-25 but soon was converted during the Battle of the Bismarck Sea.

Henebry had joined the Air Corps in 1940 and first asked to be assigned to the Philippines, but he changed his mind after an experienced officer told him that the aircraft there were old and not much flying was possible. He persuaded the clerk to put his name on the list assigned to units in the United States and ended up in Georgia, fortunate enough to be able to gain experience on the B-25 before he volunteered for overseas and arrived in Australia in June 1942.

Bob Reed, looking back at the mission, thought that in his opinion it was one of only three that contributed definitely to turning the tide in New Guinea. The other two missions were the attack on the Bismarck Sea convoy and the Rabaul mission of 12 October 1943.

The mission to Wewak marked a definite return to first-team status for the 8th Squadron. Since the disastrous A-24 strike against Buna on 29 July 1942, the 8th, for a variety of reasons, had been almost ineffective, sometimes acting as a repository for unwanted personnel, supplying men and aircraft to make up the mission numbers for the other 3rd Group squadrons. But after the Battle of the Bismarck Sea, the arrival of new B-25 strafers, and change in command, the 8th was reborn.

After the B-25 attacks, the 8th Photo F-4s tried to photograph the four Wewak airfields but ran out of film after passing above Wewak itself and had to return without the vital record of the destruction needed to confirm the accounts from the B-25 crews.

General MacArthur's general headquarters SWPA released Public Relations Communique 494. It described the massed Japanese aircraft, the surprise, and the damage claimed, with photographic evidence of 120 planes destroyed and "severe damage to at least another 50." The communique added that "it is estimated that 1,500 enemy air personnel were killed." The post-1945 official Japanese account of the war gives casualties to 4 Air Army personnel as nineteen killed and forty-nine wounded, with fifty aircraft destroyed or heavily damaged, another fifty lightly damaged, and three refueling vehicles heavily damaged. Captured documents taken in New Guinea later showed the aviation units had been hit harder than the postwar official Japanese history admitted. The 6th Flying Division was reduced to twenty-eight operational aircraft: 24 Sentai had only seven Oscars available; 59 Sentai, eight Oscars; 13 Sentai, two Nicks; 45 Sentai, four Lilys; 208 Sentai, one Lily; 14 Sentai, one Sally; 83 Recon Chutai, five Sonias. The 7th Flying Division had a total of only twelve aircraft operational: 68 Sentai had six Tonys; 78 Sentai, none; 7 Sentai, six Helens; 74 Recon Chutai, none of its Dinahs.

Captain Yamanaka, amid the wreckage at Wewak, was angry at what he saw as failure by senior staff of 4 Air Army to understand what the U.S. 5th Air Force was about to do. Senior officers had left junior officers such as himself to assess the situation, and then finally the senior officers took frenzied useless action. Yamanaka's anger was compounded when the Japanese Army Air Force again was heavily attacked at Hollandia in March–April 1944 and then suffered once more in the Philippines campaign of late 1944.

That day, 17 August, over the Darwin area, RAAF Spitfires shot down all four Mitsubishi Dinahs sent over on reconnaissance. In England hundreds of B-17s and B-24s were ready for the first raid on Schweinfurt, a great test of the concept that unescorted heavy bombers could fight their way over enemy territory to the target and fight their way back. Sixty four-engine U.S. bombers would be shot down and 168 damaged.

18 August: Ralph Cheli Shot Down at Dagua

One principle of air warfare is that targets must be hit repeatedly until they are totally destroyed; once is rarely enough. The Japanese failed to realize this and greatly overestimated the effect of their bombing attacks. Allied air staffs knew that every effort would be made by the Japanese to recover from the battering they had taken, so it was vital that pressure be maintained on Wewak. As always, New Guinea itself intervened. Clear weather of 17 August turned bad overnight and foiled the best efforts of the forty-six heavy bombers that set out the next morning to maintain pressure on the airfields. Twenty-nine did find their targets but results were not good.

The 90th Bomb Group was led by the CO, the highly respected Lt. Col. Art Rogers, in his B-24 named "Connell's Special" with the new Jolly Rogers emblem on the B-24 tail fins: a grinning skull and crossed bombs. Connell's Special was the first B-24 to have a nose turret to counter head-on fighter attacks. A B-24 tail turret had been successfully placed in the nose of the B-24 as a field modification, and later this was done in the factories in the United States. Six B-24s of the Group's 319th Squadron reached Wewak, bombed through poor visibility and rain, and claimed as destroyed one each of the dozen Oscars and Tonys that attacked. Only one 321st Squadron B-24 reached the target and salvoed six 500-pound demolition bombs from ten thousand feet with no result seen. Three aircraft from the 400th squadron dropped 500-pounders across the town, started four fires, and claimed damage to three intercepting fighters.

The antiaircraft fire was constant, and Japanese fighters flashed past through the clouds, attacking from all directions. T.Sgt. William W. Baker was on his first combat mission and claimed a fighter destroyed with his top turret guns, but he was so affected by the entire mission that he wrote home with instructions for his family to sell his car because he thought there was no hope of surviving a full combat tour of such bombing operations.

All nine aircraft of the Ken's Men Group's 64th Squadron turned back because of icing and weather. Lieutenants DeLoach and Sunderman of the 63rd Squadron turned back with engine trouble, but six others went on. One element made several runs and bombed the dispersal area between the mission and the airfield while the second element missed But airfield and their bombs went into the water. All of the problems were due to weather. Some of the 63rd Squadron's B-17s on this mission were veterans of many operations in the theater, including #357, "Tojo's Nightmare"; #381, "Panama Hattie"; #537, "Talisman"; and #554, the Mustang. By the end of 1943, the Mustang had flown 109 missions, had retired from operations, and was sent back to the United States.

The high-level heavy bomber missions, while distracting Japanese fighters and ground defenses, added little destruction around the airfields. Below the weather came the 3rd and 38th Groups.

Taking off at 0730, with P-38 escort, the strafers flew into thickening cloud. By the time the target was near, the fighter escort was having trouble keeping the B-25s in sight. In the Grim Reapers 8th Squadron formation, Martin Radnik thought it almost a miracle the strafers did not collide on the way to the target because the rain made visibility very poor. He led the left flight the day before and this day had the right. He was to go along the shore bombing piers, jetties, wharves, and boats while Bill Webster led the left formation and attacked storage areas.

The 8th was the second squadron in the group formation. As the leading squadron passed over a rocky outcrop a few miles east of Wewak, Radnik saw a black cloud rising and thought they'd bombed a fuel dump. As he flew toward the expanding black cloud, he realized that it was thousands of bats scared by the engine noise. Impulsively, he fired his nose-mounted .50s as they whipped through the mass of wheeling bats. None struck his B-25, but the left wingman, Robert H. Miller, had one hit an engine and crack a cylinder. The targets were just in front of them: Boram and Wewak. Fires were still burning from the attack the day before.

Boram, adjacent to Wewak itself, was attacked by ten 13th Squadron strafers who machine-gunned and bombed personnel and supply areas south of the runway; five more fires flared. The B-25 crews watched about twenty Japanese fighters swirling above with the P-38 escort and confirmed two Japanese crashed. Three of the 8th Squadron had turned back, but despite rain and intense accurate antiaircraft fire, the other nine, led by Maj. James Downs, roared in one long run over Boram and on to Wewak behind a hail of .50-caliber bullets leaving 100-pound demolition bombs in their wake.

As the formation turned for home, fighters attacked. This time, Martin Radnik's flight had the longest distance to cover as the squadron wheeled, and Lt. Richard Heinrich's B-25 simply could not keep up with the others. He became separated from the formation, and Japanese fighters shot him down two miles south of Wewak. There were no survivors; no Japanese prisoner taken later or any captured document referred to any of the crew.

Bill Webster bombed storage areas near the airstrip and recalled that "we got a bit scattered on the withdrawal." He remarked that this single loss—Heinrich—was the only drawback to an otherwise successful pair of missions, which marked the rebirth of the 8th Squadron. It was Webster's twenty-fifth mission, and he hoped that the next twenty-five were as satisfying and as destructive to the enemy as the last two. These had been six-hour missions, and he was "one tired cookie" when it was time to sleep that night.

Maj. Jock Henebry led six aircraft of the Grim Reapers 90th Squadron against shipping in Wewak harbor. They attacked five freighter transports with seventeen 500-pounders and left one sinking and one smoking. Launches and aircraft on the strip were strafed as the B-25s flashed overhead, and an Oscar that came in head-on was claimed as a probable. Two B-25s were damaged; two others turned back before reaching the target due to mechanical problems. Lieutenant Shull, who flew as copilot with Bob Reed the day before, also flew this mission with Jock Henebry.

Farther west at Dagua the Sunsetters Group's 405th Squadron hurdled the row of hills along the coast just before their target. Japanese fighters of 59 Sentai saw them and dived to attack. Despite damage inflicted by the strafing attack the previous day and through much work by the mechanics, the 59th had ten operational fighters. They had scrambled one and a half hours earlier after a report of large enemy formations approaching, but nothing happened. The Oscars were landing, then approaching B-25s were seen, and the Japanese pilots opened up their engines, climbing steeply to three thousand feet.

Ralph Cheli led ten 405th strafers. Garrett Middlebrook led the last flight of four B-25s. The flights had eased out to allow forty-five seconds between each, time for the bombs of the preceding wave to explode.

"As we approached the target from behind the same ridge from which we attacked yesterday," noticed Middlebrook, "the clouds were moisture-laden and heavy. They hung over the ridge, and out to sea beyond the target, they were even blacker."

On Cheli's left was Bill Pittman, with his copilot, Ed Maurer. Maurer remembered the mission vividly. The flights let down to treetop level a considerable distance from the target. The formation was close, at the most twenty-five feet from wingtip to wingtip. Maurer, in the right-hand seat and a little higher, was looking down into Cheli's cockpit. The terrain was not mountainous but hilly, and the B-25s were 100 to 150 feet above the trees. Speed was not the object; the strafers didn't start flying fast into targets until Maurer became squadron commander. He sat there observing, not flying.

As they approached Dagua, Maurer saw ten or fifteen Oscars wheel into them, making individual passes. One hit the B-25; the machine-gun rounds hammered the left engine nacelle, wing, and fuselage, but the B-25 went on. Then the Oscar turned onto Cheli's plane and put a telling burst into the right wing, engine, and side of the cockpit. Maurer, sitting next to Pittman, was looking at Cheli's aircraft, and

could see them getting hit. The plane caught fire. There was fire in the engines . . . there was fire in the cockpit, right in back, too. You could see the fire. The best I remember, both engines were on fire. They must have hit the fuel tanks. . . . I think Cheli must have had a window open; we often flew with the windows open because it was so hot. I don't know whether it (the fire) was from the base of the wings or whether they had their windows open and it was sucking as a draft, but there was fire in the cockpit. . . . It really bothers me, it appeared to me I could see the Australian (John Massie) who I really liked, and it looked like his shirt or back was on fire. The navigation compartment must have been pretty much on fire.

In the wing B-25, Sgt. John Wolf, top turret gunner, noticed Cheli's gunner, Sergeant Murphree, had not moved his guns after test-firing on the way to the target. The turret never did move, even when fighters attacked. What happened inside the B-25 will never be known.

Middlebrook, following, saw flak explode around Cheli's leading flight as soon as they appeared over the ridge, and he was shocked to see smoke and flames from Cheli's right engine as those B-25s reappeared through the first volleys of flak bursts. He remembered that Japanese fighters tended to attack the leaders on the way in to the target and the last flight on the way out, and also that they seemed to be much more determined when in sight of their base than when they were not. Middlebrook looked again at the clouds offshore as a haven from fighter attack.

In the combat area was the Satan's Angels 475th Fighter Group in its new P-38s. General Kenney had demanded men of good quality for all ranks of this new unit, formed from men already in the theater. This basis of local experience eased the short but intense training period after formation in May. The 431st Squadron of the 475th had the group's first combat only two days earlier, on the sixteenth, and claimed twelve Japanese over Marilinan. The 475th was keen to show what it could do with the powerful P-38.

Capt. Shigeki Nanba, with five Oscars of his 1 Chutai, made this attack on the B-25s but then saw P-38s approaching overhead and tried to signal his men to make only one pass, then break away and prepare to attack the P-38s. Two pilots did not see the P-38s or were slow in breaking, and the formation quickly was reduced to three, low down, under attack from enemy enjoying the advantages of height and speed.

P-38s of the 431st Squadron, 475th Fighter Group, engaged what were reported as "Zeros" (Oscars from this point in this account of the action). One Japanese dodged an attack by Lt. Tommy McGuire, pulled up, half-rolled, and split-s'ed down onto the tail of Francis Lent, McGuire's wingman.

Lent skidded down to the right, calling McGuire, who turned onto the Oscar and shot it down; Lent watched black smoke stream out of the Japanese fighter, then flames appeared. Looking down, Lent saw a B-25 with an engine on fire—probably Ralph Cheli. Another Oscar dived on McGuire's tail but passed in front of Lent, who fired a long burst that shot pieces off the nose, cockpit, and tail of the Oscar; McGuire saw it explode. It was the first of Lent's eleven victories. The two P-38s re-formed as an element.

Eleven fighter attacks were made on the first flight of the 405th Squadron, and Lieutenant Deptula claimed one fighter. It attacked from one o'clock below (ahead, slightly right and low), Deptula brought his nose battery of eight .50-calibers to bear and shot the Oscar down into the jungle.

In the leading flight, Ed Maurer was impressed with the precision flying of the Japanese pilots. He had the impression they were the cream of the crop; they knew what they were doing and did it quickly. As soon as they rolled out, the wings became very rigid and straight—then the guns could be seen firing.

Garrett Middlebrook, leading the last flight, dived to the right, as more Oscars popped out of the clouds from the south and west. Then John Donegan's plane, number four in the flight, was reported hit and out of formation, so Middlebrook radioed to the other two that they would attack as a three-ship flight. Almost at once he saw a fighter swing across from left to right directly in front of him and automatically fired the eight machine guns in the nose; he saw the Japanese plane slide with wing down toward the trees but then had to watch ahead and did not see him crash, although others in the flight did. Up ahead, crossing Dagua airstrip, Cheli, Pittman, Deptula, and Blain dropped their parafrags on aircraft, revetments, and gun positions.

Flames were streaming back from Cheli's B-25; conditions inside must have been indescribable. The luck and the fun had run out for Ralph Cheli, but in his last seconds of leadership of the U.S. 38th Bomb Group, he set an example that rarely has been equaled and not surpassed.

Fully aware he was on the attack run with other B-25s speeding along behind him, Cheli held course, bombed and machine-gunned the Japanese ahead, radioed Pittman, and then swung away for a landing on the water.

From Pittman's B-25, Ed Maurer watched Cheli's burning plane slide underneath, trailing a streamer of white smoke from burning gasoline; black smoke denotes burning oil. The B-25 streamed flames all the way down but was not out of control. Maurer watched as Cheli put the aircraft down gently across the surface of the waves, making a good landing. Another witness described it as "landing smoothly and under control in the surf." Unable to turn back, to slow down, or to circle and see what happened, the rest of the B-25s had to speed on, out of the antiaircraft defenses and with Oscars harassing them.

Dave Bryant, flying one B-25, realized they were in a serious situation. He reached into a suit pocket, took out a £5 Australian currency note (U.S. $20), passed it to Rodman Williams alongside him toggling out parafrags, and said, "Here's that five quid I owe you." Williams took the money while releasing bombs, muttering it was a fine time for that! Williams had seen red tracer from Oscar machine guns flowing under their right engine. Behind and above, their turret guns were hammering as Sgt. John H. Cooper shot at and hit the Oscar. Cooper

> could see his gun flashes as he tried to bring us down. I let go with a burst and he became a ball of fire, but his course did not alter, and I was afraid he would ram us. I raised myself on the turret footrest to get a better look at what he was doing, and when I was sure he was not going to hit us sat back down on my turret bicycle seat. Then came the shock of a lifetime. The seat was not there. In getting in, I failed to lift and latch the seat properly. In an instant I was hanging by my heels with one hand out that damn hole in the ship's bottom. Hanging out there, at about twenty feet over an enemy target, is terrifying to say the least. I could see Japs shooting at us with rifles and whatever they had. There was a burst of ack-ack near our ship, and I was hit but did not realize it. With one last great effort, I pulled myself up and out of the hole. I still wonder where the strength to do it came from. I went back into the turret, making sure the damn seat latched.

It had all happened so quickly that the radio-operator had only been able to stare in shock before Cooper hauled himself back inside. Cooper's back was pummeled with .50-caliber shell cases from the nose guns, which probably would have been enough to make him lose his grip, but his flight jacket, inflated by the rushing air, formed a cushion. Cooper looked out at what he called an unbelievable sight—hundreds of parafrags drifting over parked planes and, exploding among them, antiaircraft explosions and darting fighters.

In the last flight, Middlebrook was concentrating on the airfield ahead where the second flight was now crossing the target. Under attack by five Oscars, Middlebrook heard someone call that Cheli was going down, then Middlebrook swung left and went for the airfield. They were speeding across from west to east when he eased up a little, higher than he wanted, but it was necessary: ahead parafrags were still in the air. Flak was exploding behind, up near the crest of the ridge, as the Japanese presumably expected more strafers to come over it and down the slope to the airstrip.

Middlebrook took his flight down the length of the runway, then swung left and dived for the surface of the water. Still under fighter attack, he glimpsed one Japanese crash into the sea but could not look: all his concentration was on flying. His copilot slapped him on the shoulder, pointing out to the left, but Middlebrook did not look, thinking it was only another Oscar. It was Cheli's B-25 in the water.

Ralph Cheli put the burning B-25 down about two thousand yards from the shore, and many Japanese had seen it. Japanese civilian fishermen went out in their boat; others went to the shore to watch. The air battles moved away down the coast under the low clouds.

A cloud of 340 parafrags exploded among the Japanese planes, and 405th Squadron crews counted at least fifteen fires, claimed thirty aircraft destroyed on the ground, and claimed 3-3-1 from intercepting Oscars. Dagua had been hit hard again. Just out to sea, Middlebrook's flight slipped into the clouds at about two hundred feet, and he felt safer, relying on the bomber pilots' ability to fly on instruments and the knowledge that fighter pilots were not trained to the same standards. They flew through clouds for thirty miles and broke into the clear. All scanned the sky for fighters.

Shigeki Nanba and his two wingmen left the B-25s and tried to gain altitude but were fastened on by P-38s, who could outclimb them, especially with speed gained in a dive. The P-38s, probably the 432nd Squadron, closed to one hundred yards, and Shigeki could see at least ten in a column behind him. He regretted not having more wingmen and a little more height, briefly considered ramming, and then, like Middlebrook, decided to try to escape into nearby scattered cloud. He broke and dived, just as the leading P-38 fired and hit the starboard wing of his Oscar. There was no fire, but petrol poured into the cockpit and Shigeki blacked out from the violence of his maneuver, then recovered to find he was in a spiral dive, the airspeed indicator showing 800 kmph (480 mph). He looked back, saw no P-38s with him, and thought they believed him to be finished. Aware that previously he had not been confident of the fuselage strength of the Oscar, he pulled the throttle back and gently tried to pull out of the dive; the earth was leaping up at him. He leveled out just over Dagua strip. Nanba saw Lieutenant Hara making a landing southwest of the airfield, but the P-38s continued to attack while Hara was landing, after he was on the ground. Shigeki was infuriated and tried to attack the P-38s but found he was suffering from inhalation of gasoline fumes and noticed that the aircraft was handling strangely. Luckily for Shigeki, the P-38s did not see him and left. He flew the damaged Oscar from Dagua to But, landed east to west, and blacked out. Ground crews ran out and dragged him from the cockpit as B-25s approached. The 71st Squadron was about to attack.

The 431st Fighter Squadron had tangled with Oscars over Wewak. Tommy McGuire led the last flight in the squadron formation and shot down two near Dagua. The flight chased one Oscar down to one thousand feet over the water; Lowell Lutton shot it down, and Francis Lent saw it go into the water. Looking down, Lent saw large fires along the beach and runway, and three Japanese fighters falling, one on fire and the others streaming smoke; all crashed. McGuire, Lutton, and Lent had all destroyed enemy fighters. The P-38s pulled away through heavy flak, escorting three B-25s toward home.

Making up for their failure to get to But the day before, fourteen strafers from the Sunsetters Group's 71st Squadron thundered over, firing 23,000 rounds and leaving 490 parafrags drifting down behind them; crews counted eight bombers and six fighters on fire. An unidentified plane was seen crashing in flames offshore—it might have been Cheli at Dagua. Twenty Japanese fighters attacked, the B-25s claimed 10-2-1 and watched another crash-land on Muschu Island.

When Captain Shigeki revived at But, he went to inspect his battered Oscar. It was a total loss: there were bullet hits in the starboard wing, distortion of the fuselage and wing, and skin wrinkling in both wings and at the wing-fuselage joint. He realized the aircraft had been at the point of disintegration in the air when he landed. Then ground crews told him that another Oscar had been hit; the pilot baled out close to the northern side of the airfield, but too low, and had been killed.

Shigeki confirmed that the pilot was Master Sergeant Agemura, of his Chutai, which now was reduced to two flyable aircraft.

Crews of Cheli's 405th Squadron saw P-38s shoot down four enemy fighters over But. When thirty miles out they saw a Tony come in on a head-on pass and—possibly looking back at them and not above—the Tony pulled up into position for a perfectly placed flight of P-38s to shoot him down. The only Tony claimed that day was by Lt. Tommy McGuire ten minutes after he claimed the earlier two fighters. Francis Lent saw McGuire hit the Tony, and it was confirmed by the B-25 formation.

Garrett Middlebrook brought his rear flight up to the rest of the 405th, expecting to be chastised for taking them into the rain clouds immediately after leaving the target. The 405th flew on back to base, knowing Cheli had gone down in the target area. One passing crew glimpsed what they thought were four people standing on the sinking B-25, so it was presumed those in the front may have gotten out okay. No one knew what had happened to Donegan, last known to be under fighter attack and falling out of formation.

Sgt. John Cooper felt warmth around his feet, checked, and found his boots filled with blood. The other crew members pulled some antiaircraft shrapnel out of his back, poured sulfa powder over the wounds, and radioed for an ambulance to meet them at the revetment.

The lion's share of the fighter victories had gone to the 431st Squadron. Thirteen P-38s of the 431st had engaged an estimated forty Oscars in the combat area, with fighting swirling from sixteen thousand feet down to two thousand feet. The squadron claimed 13-2-0, but lost 2nd Lt. Ralph E. Schmidt. The individual claims by the 431st were three by McGuire; two each for Edward Czarnecki, Verl Jett, Lowell Lutton, and Maj. Albert Schinz; one each for Don Bellows, Robert Cline, and Francis Lent; and probables for William Sieber and William Haning. Ed Czarnecki was a future six-victory ace who began scoring over Wewak. His victory on this mission was witnessed by McGuire's flight.

The 432nd Squadron had seventeen P-38s dive into the melee and claimed one enemy destroyed by Capt. Bill Waldman, one probable by Vivian Cloud, and a damaged by Richard Ryrholm. Pilots reported seeing the Japanese red-brown and green camouflage and the red cowlings and fuselage stripes, red denoting 2 Chutai of the Japanese unit.

Capt. Hiroshi Onozaki, 59 Sentai, reported escaping a desperate combat at low level with what he thought was a force of twenty P-38s. The next day he would be evacuated to Rabaul with amoebic dysentery and later sent to Japan. He had made about fourteen victory claims for combats over Malaya, Java, Timor, Darwin, and New Guinea.

The entire Sentai, of 3 Chutai, had only eight operable fighters at the end of the day. Japanese pilots known to have been killed were Lieutenants Genbu and Hara and Sergeant Major Agemura of 59 Sentai. Sergeant Major Kobayashi of 78 Sentai, a Tony unit, was wounded and died on 22 August. He might have been McGuire's victory.

In Wewak itself a civilian with 8 Naval Development Unit estimated there were a hundred killed and thirty wounded, with the most serious damage done to antiaircraft positions that then were unable to answer later attacks. Sergeant Major Motohisa, who wrote happily about the falling bombers in the night attack on 17 August, reported this attack in his diary. He thought there were fifty enemy aircraft, and reported "there was AA and our fighters went up, but were on the defensive. Our damage is estimated to be great."

Three F-4s were tasked to photograph the results of the attacks but could not cope with the bad weather and returned without success.

Radio Tokyo told its listeners of the "Japanese eagle" who flew alone to enemy air bases, dropped messages of challenge to combat, waited, engaged all who flew up, downed them all, and then flew back to base, unharmed.

Back at Durand airstrip near Port Moresby when the 405th landed, "word spread like wildfire that Cheli was lost and the ground crews were dejected. It seemed that everything was in a state of confusion," recalled Middlebrook. "There was no friendly bantering back and forth between the aircrews and ground personnel."

When inspecting his B-25 after the flight, Middlebrook noticed the tears in the rudder fabric, which now seemed to happen every time, and a few machine-gun holes. What left him feeling decidedly weak was finding a large hole in the wing just outboard of the gas tank. But worse was the sight of Donegan's ground crew waiting by the empty revetment opposite and the hopeful questions they asked about the crew's chances of survival. He had to tell them not to hope for too much.

The crews waited for the intelligence staff to come around and debrief them. Middlebrook realized his copilot was giving a good account of the action, but he himself was too burdened by the loss of Cheli and Donegan to respond accurately. Pondering the losses of the day, he decided new improved techniques were needed and determined to do all possible to ensure his survival and that of his crew. By this time the squadron had lost two commanding officers, some original flight commanders, and many original pilots. Those remaining originals were feeling the loss of friends more and more, friends who were there at breakfast and gone after the next mission. A jeep sped up and word flew around that Donegan had crash-landed at 7-Mile Strip. Squadron members flocked to the operations office; it was true. The gloom was lifted by this good news.

Wounded by flak and aircraft machine-gun fire, Donegan apparently pulled up into the clouds, flying by reflex. The pain from his wounds was so excruciating that pain was the only memory he had of the next few minutes. Coming out of the clouds, he was jolted back to consciousness by the imminence of crashing into jungle-clad hills and he concentrated on flying the damaged B-25. Scammel, the navigator, and Charles Peebles, copilot, were unconscious from wounds, and both gunners were wounded: Don Bybee could not see because of blood running down from a head wound, and Joe Carroll had a leg wound. Donegan had no rudder control but had elevators and ailerons and could hold the plane in a slight climb. Joe Carroll crawled forward to assist, and they salvoed the bombs and then set about flying home. With no rudders, no hydraulics, no wheels, no flaps, various other damage, more than 250 holes in the B-25, all aboard wounded, and only one good arm, Donegan brought the aircraft onto the crash-strip at 7-Mile Strip at 170 miles an hour. No one suffered more injuries, but the B-25 was wrecked.

At lunch in the 405th Squadron, little was said; the mood was grim. Then, over coffee, talk began about Donegan's feat, with admiration for his courage and skill in bringing crew and ship home in the circumstances. Talk turned to Cheli. He had both respect and liking; often a commander has one or the other but not necessarily both or either. Pittman confirmed Cheli's engine was on fire long before crossing the target, but Cheli went on without wavering. Those who saw figures on the ditched plane recounted their sightings and speculation followed on who could have escaped. At first, despite reports of people seen on the sinking B-25, it was thought Cheli and his crew died in the crash. Later, Bill Gay, Lackness, and Middlebrook recalled the talk they had with Cheli after their running fight the day before; Cheli refused to accept there had been real hazards from Japanese reaction on that first Wewak mission, and he insisted on flying this day. Middlebrook told the others that Cheli once told him that it was not enough to be a good pilot to get through a tough mission—the pilot needed to be resourceful, a good thinker, and have a cool head. Middlebrook added he learned something else as he watched Cheli: never show yourself to the enemy until the last second, never give him a shot at you flying in a straight line, and never let him shoot upward at you. There was agreement.

On the beach at Dagua, many Japanese flocked to the shore to watch the return of a fishing boat that had picked up three men. The other three presumably died in the air, the ditching, or in the sinking B-25. One spectator was Captain Okada, 51 Airfield Battalion, who gave the following details to investigators when interviewed after capture in 1945. Cheli, wearing only pants, was able to walk unaided; the other two needed stretchers. They were examined by Dr. Yoshinori Hanada from 51 Airfield Battalion. Cheli was unhurt, Staff Sergeant Murphree had a bad stomach wound and another in the thigh, both from bullets, and Technical Sergeant Warren had two broken ribs and a damaged eye. Hanada thought Murphree was dying but Warren not seriously hurt. The prisoners were taken to HQ 59 Sentai and then to 9 Flying Brigade headquarters, and none of the local garrison at Dagua saw them again. Murphree was said to have died of his wounds. Later, Captain Okada was told by Major Fukuda of 59 Sentai that the prisoners were sent to 9 Flying Brigade, and nothing more was known of them. Fukuda was later shot down and killed.

Oscar pilot Capt. Shigeki Nanba arrived at Dagua by car from But, went to 59 Sentai headquarters to report, and met Cheli and Warren. He did not mention Murphree as being present at this meeting. Nanba thought both men were pilots, and—in the heat of the moment, having lost men in combat and survived his own dangerous fight—he struck one American in the face once or twice. He regretted his behavior and explained that he was still tense after combat.

On 3 March 1943, in the attack on the Japanese convoy in the Battle of the Bismarck Sea, Murphree had flown with Ralph Cheli as his top turret gunner. Lieutenant Ramey, Cheli's copilot to Dagua, and Sergeant Warren also flew that historic mission in the 405th Squadron.

Cheli was sent to Rabaul, where (it is now believed) he was murdered by the Japanese on 5 March 1944. The Japanese said Cheli was among a group of prisoners killed in an Allied bombing raid on that date, but the exact circumstances have not been verified. Surviving prisoners who went to the location after the Japanese surrender found intact shelters and no sign of bomb hits. Other surviving prisoners who had been on laboring tasks said that at least one batch of aviators had been killed in late November 1943. Of a total of sixty-nine Caucasian prisoners admitted by the Japanese as held prisoner at Rabaul sometime in the years 1942 to 1945, only eight were alive there at the end of the war. Twelve had been sent to Japan, and the rest had died of what the Japanese authorities described as "disease" or "accident," which meant bombing.

Almost certainly, in line with Japanese policy and once their ranks as enlisted men had been established, Sergeant Warren was murdered soon after capture, and Murphree probably died of wounds or was killed soon after coming ashore at Dagua. Other than those few pieces of information included previously, there is no reference found by the author in the entire collection of captured Japanese documents, personal diaries, or interrogations of Japanese to the presence elsewhere of Cheli's crew members, or their well-being, after the date of capture.

There were, however, several references to Cheli himself in captured Japanese documents, as a Major "Kelly" or "Cherry" who had been taken prisoner. Cheli was interrogated by his captors, who wanted to know everything a unit commander could tell them about the Allied airfield complex at Port Moresby, and had him draw maps of the areas. Their own reconnaissance aircraft had been over Moresby many times, and there was little Cheli could have told them that would have been of use.

No trace of Captain Massie, Lieutenant Ramey, or Flight Officer Yancey was found, and no Japanese prisoner or captured document referred to them. John Massie had flown with the 38th and other USAAF Groups since 30 November 1942 and was on his forty-second mission with more than 150 combat hours. He parachuted from Ed Adkins's plane on 13 July, when the crew baled out before Adkins landed the badly damaged B-25. Nine of the ten planes on that mission to McDonald's Junction had been shot up. Four with engines shot out opted to land at Dobodura rather than climb over the mountains. Massie noted in his diary that Middlebrook landed without brakes or flaps at 165 mph, and Legge's B-25 had fifty holes. Just thirteen days before the Dagua mission, Bob Herry had been shot down on a barge strafe to Madang. On all Herry's previous missions, Massie had flown with him, but that day Massie flew with Bill Gay. Herry liked Massie along to bring luck.

Sgt. John "Red" Cooper was treated by the squadron doctor and then slept for twenty-four hours. He was taken off flying status, sent back to Australia for medical treatment, and then sent on to the United States. He flew his first mission on 26 November 1942 and credited his survival through a number of tragic episodes to a St. Christopher medal, which he refused to let from his possession.

The official Japanese history of the war states that on 18 August, twenty-three fighters scrambled from the following units: 13 Sentai, two Nicks; 24 Sentai, seven Oscars; 59 Sentai, nine Oscars; and 68 Sentai, five Oscars—though it usually flew Tonys.

The Japanese claimed nineteen victories: seven P-38s, four B-24s, and eight B-25s as either destroyed or probables, for an admitted loss in this official history of two destroyed from 59 Sentai and one other damaged. Actual U.S. losses were only four: three B-25s—Cheli and Heinrich shot down, plus Donegan's wrecked on landing—and Schmidt's P-38. Real Japanese losses were certainly more than two, as there were multiple witnesses to some, including the lone Tony shot down by Tommy McGuire. Shigeki Nanba admits his Chutai was reduced to two aircraft. The commander of 1 Chutai 78 Sentai was Capt. Yoshichika Mutaguchi, and on this day he took a group of pilots back to Manila to collect replacement aircraft because the unit had no repairable fighters left.

Japanese 4 Air Army staff section intelligence reports were copied to 14 Field Air Repair Depot, and a collection of these totaling more than 625 pages for the period 17 August to 20 December 1943 was captured at Hollandia on 11 June 1944. This collection was included in the SWPA G2 intelligence translations as ATIS Enemy Publication (EP) 270. These records were compiled by the major Japanese air headquarters in New Guinea at the time and must be considered authentic, no matter what the postwar official Japanese history might state.

For 18 August, EP270 records that at Wewak-But, twenty-five aircraft were shot down or "uncertain if shot down," one was blown up, and thirteen were damaged, although the "damaged" category does not clarify if these were on the ground or in the air. U.S. fighter claims were for fifteen destroyed, three probably destroyed, and two damaged (15-3-2), and bomber claims were for 15-3-1, later reduced to ten destroyed. Taking into account the known inaccuracies in bomber crew claims, from information in Japanese records compiled at the time and location, U.S. claims for this day were accurate—twenty-five destroyed.

In addition, the EP270 documents include damages for Wewak-But for 19 August. No missions were flown to the area on that date, so it is probable that the losses listed in the Japanese records for that date refer to 18 August. These include fifteen destroyed and eight damaged, but the report does not clarify whether the aircraft were lost on the ground or in the air. One "large two-man fighter," a Nick, is listed as destroyed, as well as two Helens and three Dinahs.

Allied Air Forces Intelligence Summary 132 reported that nineteen B-24s, fifty-one B-25s, and ninety-five fighters had attacked and destroyed fifty-three Japanese planes on the ground and twenty-five in the air, started one large oil fire and fifteen others in the town, inflicted damage to the airfield and dump area, and left three ships on fire and some barges sunk. The Special Intelligence Bulletins of radio intercepts stated that on this day a Japanese plane inbound to Wewak called all four radio stations there but was able to speak to only one; it seemed the other three were out of action.

Public Relations Communique 495, from General MacArthur's GHQ, stated,

> We have completed the destruction of the remnants of the Japanese air force centered on Wewak. Of the 225 planes originally assembled, yesterday's surprise attack destroyed 120 on the ground, three in the air, and damaged fifty on the ground, leaving still existent fifty-two undamaged in addition to those fifty damaged. Our attacks in all categories were continued in incessant waves today. The enemy mounted thirty fighters to meet the onslaught. Twenty-eight were shot down. Only ten planes of the 225 escaped. The remaining 215 are now gone. We lost three planes, bringing the total to six. This closes the combat.

The communique reported the bombing attacks on shipping and supply dumps and the results. As ever, MacArthur projected optimism regardless of the real situation. The air war over Wewak continued until the end of March 1944.

From crew reports and photos it was clear that the Japanese had been heavily hit. It was also clear that they had little logistical support to improve their situation. The balance of power in the New Guinea air war was tilting in favor of the Allies.

On 19 August the damage at Wewak and Boram was recorded on film by two courageous U.S. F4 reconnaissance pilots who flew through accurate anti-aircraft and climbed away from intercepting Oscars. At least fifty-nine destroyed aircraft were counted in the photos, plus another fifty were damaged, but their condition could not be determined.

20 August

Bad weather on 19 August forced a halt to the pounding of Wewak targets, but on the twentieth the 5th Air Force returned. Japanese fighter opposition was fierce but relatively ineffectual. Oil fires and explosions in the target area were seen by the U.S. crews, but cloud and fighter attacks occupied their attention. The six-plane B-24 squadrons bombed with little observed result while fighter attacks came in at the formations.

One fighter hit a 319th B-24 with three bursts, but the squadron claimed 3-2-0. The lead plane in the 320th formation was attacked from behind by three fighters, but after three bursts from the tail gunner, one Japanese fighter exploded seventy yards from the bomber. The P-38 escort pounced, probably destroying a second airplane from the threesome, and three other Japanese were seen to go down to the Lightnings. Four B-24s landed at Dobodura, two making crash landings due to battle damage.

The 321st Squadron of the Jolly Rogers Group received twenty-three frontal passes from a mixture of Tonys, Oscars, and Nicks; one B-24 was damaged, and five crewmen were wounded. One Oscar was claimed as bursting into flame and then disintegrating with the fragments falling into the sea. The Group's 400th Squadron bombed the north side of Boram, but cloud and the aggressive fighter attacks, which closed to fifty feet, prevented observation of bombing results.

Technical Sergeant Baker, on his second mission, claimed a second fighter destroyed and now began to believe that he might make it through a tour of bombing missions.

In the nose turret of the leading 319th Squadron's "Yankee Doodle Dandy," Jim Alexander could only listen to the calls from others in his bomber. He could see nothing of the squadrons coming along behind and heard tail and waist gunners yelling on the interphone, "There goes a B-24 down in flames." Either intentionally or accidentally, a Tony flown by Capt. Takuo Ishiguro rammed Flight Officer John Stiles's

400th Squadron B-24, Miss Carriage. The bomber began to go down, burning; the wings folded and it exploded at about one thousand feet. Parachutes were seen, one on fire, and also Japanese fighters were also seen machine-gunning them.

Aircraft in following squadrons counted six open parachutes and a seventh burning as Stiles's crew bailed out while below a private of the Japanese 41 Mountain Artillery Regiment counted eight parachutes. He was told five men had been killed descending through the antiaircraft fire, but three were taken alive on the ground.

Seven months later, a Japanese radio broadcast named two of the crew as prisoners, but when Australian troops captured Wewak in 1945, no trace of them could be found and some of the crew were located buried in the local cemetery. On 10 February 1944, 4 Air Army officially notified its higher headquarters in Staff Message #2079 that 2nd Lt. John Lawrence Stiles, dob 23 November 1920, from Philadelphia, had died of malaria at Wewak on 30 January. Stiles had joined the unit on 30 July.

Captain Ishiguro, 24 Sentai, was posthumously awarded the Distinguished Service Award 1st Class for ramming the B-24. Joyfully, Sergeant Major Motohisa, who had described other aircraft losses, wrote, "Our invincible Type 34 [*sic*] fighters shot down four enemy bombers. Eight who bailed out were captured. Enemy losses were eight, ours was one."

Shigeki Nanba and the 59 Sentai pilots at Dagua had a different view of the action on 20 August. Because there were not enough aircraft to fly, they took cover in air raid trenches in the sand under large trees on the northern side of the strip. This was not prudent of the Japanese but again shows how they clustered everything, including precious trained pilots, close to target areas. The tree over Shigeki's trench received a direct hit, and the explosion caved in the trench, burying all in it up to their waists.

The 432nd Fighter Squadron of the Satan's Angels Group made no claims, as the Japanese dived away from the squadron. But the 80th Headhunters Squadron engaged many Japanese fighters and claimed ten: two to Maj. Ed "Porky" Cragg; three to Capt. George Welch; two to Lt. Jennings Myers; and one each to Lieutenants Daley, Gridley, and Mathers. Myers began scoring over Wewak on this day and eventually gained five victories.

The 80th Squadron split into two formations, each escorting part of the B-24 formations. Cragg had eight fighters with him twenty miles southeast of the target area when he noticed fifteen or more Japanese fighters. The Japanese flew an untidy formation, and Cragg brought his P-38s into a good position and dived to attack. He came in behind an Oscar and sent it down spinning in flames. After some dogfighting, Cragg went in behind a Tony and followed it in a pass through the B-24 formation, despite the hail of fire from the bombers, and hit the Tony, which spun into the sea. Out of ammunition, Cragg left the combat area.

Jennings Myers heard the warning that fighters were about, looked around, and saw an Oscar pop out of the clouds and shoot at his element leader. Myers fired, saw hits on the Oscar's wingtip, and walked his fire onto the fuselage; a cannon shell exploded in the cockpit and the Oscar began to roll and went into the ground. Now alone Myers saw an Oscar below. He dived and shot away its rudder and right elevator. The Oscar went out of control and crashed.

George Welch, who started his score during the attack on Pearl Harbor, went for a formation of Tonys and shot down three of them. He shook off a pursuer and arrived at base with minimum fuel remaining. A Tony had dived on Welch from above and with the speed of the dive was able to keep up with Welch, but he then set the P-38 into a climb at 250 mph, which the Tony was unable to hold and fell back.

The 80th Squadron had claimed more than fifty victories with the P-38 and was very pleased with the powerful Lockheed fighter. The 80th had a short eventful history up to this time. Raised in January 1942, it was in Australia by early March and by July was in action in New Guinea in the P-400 version of the P-39. In February 1943 the squadron returned to Australia to convert to the P-38 and had operated it in combat since March.

Tommy Lynch, 39th Fighter Squadron, destroyed two Nicks that were trying to get closer to the B-24s, for his twelfth and thirteenth victories. Lynch made an unsuccessful diving pass at an Oscar, joined the bombers, and then turned into a Nick making a pass. He circled onto the Nick's tail, and in two firing passes shot out both engines. The pilot baled out, and the Nick rolled to the right and down to the ground. Lynch rejoined the bombers. About sixty miles from the target, another twin-engine aircraft was seen closing on the bombers. Lynch made a head-on pass and saw the hits on the fuselage and right engine, which stopped. The aircraft "skidded back and forth," rolled onto its back, and went into the ground.

Lt. John Lane, a member of Lynch's flight, watched Stiles's B-24 blow up and took part in a chase after a single-engine fighter that escaped. Then the first Nick appeared, going in the opposite direction, but did not seem to notice the P-38s. Lane fired, and the flight swung after the Nick. Lynch fired and hits were seen on the Japanese, who turned toward Lane. Lane fired, hitting him. Lynch fired a long burst; Lane fired, but the Japanese already was smoking badly and in a vertical dive. Lane then saw him explode on the ground. Ten minutes later, another Nick appeared in front of the P-38s; Lynch fired a full deflection burst and the Nick went down vertically. Lane did not realize it was hit and started to follow, but the Japanese crashed and blew up. Lane witnessed the destruction of both and described the action in his combat report.

The only Ki-45 Nick unit, 13 Sentai, recorded the loss of one aircraft, flown by Second Lieutenant Fujino. However, both of Tommy Lynch's victories were confirmed by witnesses; the second aircraft might have been another type similar in appearance, such as the twin-engine Lily bomber, or perhaps an aircraft being delivered or ferried.

The 39th was another squadron very pleased with the P-38. Raised in February 1940, the 39th had more time than other squadrons to fully train maintenance crews and pilots in the Bell P-39 Airacobra. The squadron arrived in Australia in February 1942 but did not receive its P-39s until April when the 39th became part of the 35th Fighter Group. In May the squadron went into combat over New Guinea, and on 20 May Tommy Lynch claimed the first victories for the 39th. In July the 39th returned to Australia to be the first squadron in the SWPA to receive the P-38. This conversion took until November, but then the powerful Lockheed fighter began to make its mark, and by July the 39th claimed 104 victories in both types of aircraft, more than ninety of them in the P-38.

On the debit side for 20 August, some 432nd Squadron pilots stopped for fuel at Marilinan before going on over the mountains. One of the last to take off after refueling, 2nd Lt. Allan Camp apparently became disoriented and tried to land at Karema, about fifty miles from Moresby. He overshot, crashed into the river, and was killed, the first loss for the 432nd.

The 39th and 80th Squadrons, the only ones to engage the Japanese, claimed 13-1-3, and bomber crews claimed 5-2-0, for a total of 18-3-3. The 4 Air Army documents later captured at Hollandia recorded that Japanese losses were seventeen destroyed and twenty damaged, but again did not clarify the circumstances of the damage. Once again U.S. air combat claims were shown to be accurate.

The Japanese claimed 9-2-0. In the ramming, 24 Sentai lost Ishiguro;

Warrant Officer Chiyoji Saito, who had claimed twenty-four victories; and Corporal Sato. Another nine aircraft were reported lost by 59 Sentai. Saito was promoted posthumously to lieutenant.

Fortunately for the Allies in the Pacific, the Japanese operated mainly as individuals, rarely employing their available mass to best effect, and did not learn this lesson until later in the war. The defenses at Wewak seemed incapable of coordinating the available antiaircraft artillery and fighter force to deliver the greatest available force at the best moment.

Tokyo Radio said on this day that "further Allied penetration into the SWPA is not possible due to the long Allied lines of communication and they are now entering areas of Japanese air supremacy."

Again, the cloud cover hampered complete photo coverage of the four airfields, and the 8th Photo pilots were able to bring back only partial coverage, with Boram missed completely.

From MacArthur's headquarters, Intelligence Summary 515, written by the Military Intelligence Section, stated:

> The terrific toll taken from the first line Japanese air force probably will bring a change in offensive tactics. Conventional methods of attack employed by the enemy are proving too costly for him. No tactical procedure could be maintained in the face of regular combat losses of from 50 percent to 100 percent of the entire missions. Defensively, the enemy appears to be between the devil and the deep blue sea. Should he engage with only small forces, the effect would be limited, yet, if he employs large defensive forces, his losses are consistently heavy.

The summary went on to list probable methods of attack: suicide dives (*Author note*: The summary was written before the kamikaze attacks); approaches through weak spots in the Allied radar cover; low flying; better-coordinated attacks; night attacks; and small, quick attacks against a particular target.

Even allowing for optimistic Allied claims for Japanese losses, it was certain that the Japanese situation around Wewak was bad. Great damage had been done to 6 and 7 Flying Divisions. U.S. Army 5th Air Force formations were capable of returning to any target whenever this was desired, even in relatively bad weather. Also, the 5th Air Force had suffered minimal losses and was able to attack other targets while strikes were made on Wewak. Moreover, Allied squadrons operated from a wide network of developed bases, which the weakened Japanese air units could not hope to eliminate or even damage severely. The fatal shortcomings in the Japanese understanding of modern warfare were evident to their senior Allied opponents.

21 August

The U.S. strafers returned to the Japanese airfields to rake over the coals and maintain pressure. Garrett Middlebrook, on his third long mission in five days, led the 405th Squadron. Following his determination to use every advantage, no matter how small, to avoid giving the Japanese an easy shot at him or people under his command, he studied photos and maps of approaches to Wewak and found something of crucial importance. He kept it to himself until the last moment.

Larry Tanberg, the next senior pilot after Ralph Cheli, assumed command of the 38th Group and briefed the assembled crews of the 71st and 405th Squadrons. As they rose and began to file out of the room, Middlebrook called out for 405th people to remain because he had something to say to them. He waited for quiet to return and then outlined his own plan for the attack. The 405th would lag a little, and after passing Wewak would make a slight diversion into the valley of the Hawain River, go down to absolute minimum altitude, and follow the valley. They would keep the coastal ridge between the B-25s and the Japanese until the last moment, leap the ridge, and pour down the seaward side onto the target. In addition, to vary the direction of attack, they would attack from east to west, breaking right and out to sea when the attack was over, being careful to go behind trees along the shoreline to squeeze every bit of cover from ground fire. This took Middlebrook only a few minutes, including the time needed to reassure pilots who did not know that the Hawain River entered the sea at that point and to explain that there really was a gap through which they could fly into the valley and approach the target.

Cloud base was only at twenty-five hundred feet, 5/10 cumulus over the sky, but the P-38 escort was able to maintain contact with the bombers and engaged the Japanese fighters, who were up and waiting. It had been noticed by the Japanese that the Allied planes arrived at about the same times every day, and this made it a little easier for the defense.

Danny Roberts, already credited with four victories claimed with the 80th Fighter Squadron, led the 432nd Fighter Squadron in the Satan's Angels Group. As they approached the target, he took the squadron down to engage enemy aircraft attacking the B-25s while, as planned, the 80th Squadron went on to the target area. The 432nd found eleven enemy single-engine and twin-engine fighters at eight thousand feet. The yellow-cowled Oscars and Tonys stayed together and fought well. Some forty-five to fifty Japanese fighters were seen over the combat area, and the 432nd claimed 9-2-0. Roberts got hits on an Oscar, which was seen smoking, and took his wingman, Lt. James Michener, on to the target, where Japanese fighters were attacking the strafers. Roberts found an Oscar climbing away from Dagua and shot it into the sea off the airstrip; then he and Michener saw a P-38 being hammered by some six Oscars. Before they could assist, however, the P-38 went down vertically, in flames. Roberts went after the second Oscar, above and behind the burning P-38, hit it in the nose, and it half-rolled and dived, smoking, into the ground near But airstrip. The two P-38s were at only three thousand feet, so they left the combat area at full speed followed by about eight Oscars.

The other three flights of the 432nd engaged Oscars, Tonys, and Nicks. Paul Lucas hit an Oscar in a head-on pass, and the Japanese slipped past so close that Lucas could see the reflection of flames from the Oscar in the underside metal of his P-38.

The 431st Squadron reported a distinctively marked Nick, which had a checkerboard pattern on the engine cowlings and the fuselage near the hinomaru [Japanese circular red marking], and an attempt by an Oscar to ram. The squadron claimed 12-0-1.

Tommy McGuire, who claimed three victories on the 18 August mission, was leading Blue Flight of the 431st. He took them down to combat at lower level and fired a close-range 45-degree deflection shot at an Oscar, which burned and crashed, witnessed by Francis Lent. The flight became separated, but Lent stayed with McGuire; the two P-38s attacked another Oscar, shot down by Lent and witnessed by Ed Czarnecki. Lt. David Allen joined then, and they went down steeply to below one thousand feet after Japanese fighters attacking B-25s over Dagua; they shot down two, which were seen to crash on fire northeast of the strip. They turned back to the south and came across the twin-engine fighter with checkerboard designs, which Lent shot down into the trees. Another camouflaged twin-engine aircraft was attacked; McGuire saw hits and a small flame appear, but he lost sight of the aircraft when he had to climb to avoid a hill.

The 475th claimed twenty-three victories for the mission. Tommy McGuire was the first pilot to claim five victories while with the 475th. Other units that arrived in the SWPA went into action as soon as possible, and often the flight crews and ground crews had not properly completed their training. Some fighter pilots in the early days had not even fired their guns. But the 475th was composed of men already in the SWPA who began with a higher level of experience, especially in local conditions. McGuire already had flown one combat tour in Alaska and had the experience that came from flying in those difficult conditions. By the time he engaged the Japanese over Wewak, Tommy McGuire had some 550 hours as a pilot and was a flight leader.

Although hard on his assigned aircraft, McGuire was a good shot and frequently delivered killing blows from wide angles of deflection. He represented that collection of factors which makes fighter aces: courage and will to win, ability to fly, ability to shoot, a formidable aircraft, and contact with the enemy.

The Grim Reapers Group's 13th Squadron strafers had been attacked ten miles inland from Wewak by about ten Tonys and an Oscar. The Japanese made a series of diving attacks that were not pressed too closely. The B-25 crews reported revetments on the northern side of But strip were burned out, fires were still burning on Dagua, and the 13th crews watched the 405th set on fire two barges south of Wewak. Their own parafrags left six fires burning among the twenty or so planes below their attack path.

Garrett Middlebrook, leading the 405th to Dagua, was pleased to find that "it all worked so beautifully for a change." He slowed down a fraction after passing Wewak, and eased the squadron in perfect formation into the pass and into the Hawain valley, and then increased power until they were doing 280 mph. The other flights dropped back, spacing themselves for the attack as they slipped along the valley floor. Over on the right, they could see flak bursts above the ridge, a sign that the Japanese at every gun in range were giving their full attention to the 71st Squadron, who were running in on But aerodrome.

Middlebrook lifted his B-25 over the last covering hill, rose to two hundred feet, put his nose down, and opened fire along the south side of Dagua runway. There was no ground fire; every Japanese gun was pointing the other way, their attention on the 71st Squadron at But. There seemed to be little to destroy, however, and Middlebrook saw many wrecks and damage from the previous attacks. He saw two untouched twin-engine bombers sitting side by side, so strafed them, as did about six other members of the squadron, and then set them on fire.

The squadron report of the mission described in bare sentences the attack on the wooded area south of the strip and the dispersals and revetments, and it claimed two fires among parked Sallys with eight more of them damaged. A single-engine fighter caught taking off was shot down with .50-caliber nose guns, and the squadron also hosed down antiaircraft positions, huts, tents, vehicles, and barges as they roared across the treetops and beaches. They claimed two intercepting fighters and one taking off; crews reported destroyed aircraft on the ground throughout the airfield area. Photos showed seventeen destroyed planes, two burning, and "nine unhappy Nips" in a trench. One B-25 crash-landed at Jackson Strip, Port Moresby. As the 405th sped back along the coast, they came on two barges just east of Muschu Island. The unfortunates in them received the attention of massed .50-caliber machine guns of the two leading flights as the B-25s hurtled overhead, and the squadron turned out to sea to avoid Wewak.

Middlebrook was starting to relax under the P-38 fighter umbrella, so he rose to two hundred feet and began to swing back toward the coast when someone called that there were enemy aircraft ahead. He went back to sea level, pushed power up to 90 percent, and held course head-on for the Japanese, who were at about one thousand feet. There seemed to be about thirty enemy in no recognizable formation. The 405th pilots and crews realized that there were too many Japanese this time, and they would be able to inflict heavy losses on the B-25s— except for the P-38 escort.

The Lightnings dived and went head-on into the mass of Oscars, and there erupted a swirling combat just in front of the B-25s, whose pilots and top gunners watched entranced. Middlebrook thought at the scene, "Our P-38s are remarkable! They are dramatic, spectacular and somehow or other they make you proud to be an American—though patriotism is not something we discuss over here (in the SWPA)."

He swung the formation through a 45-degree turn to avoid the combat and then swung again to miss two Oscars and two P-38s; the B-25s then began flying away from the air battle. Some crews saw two Oscars crash into the trees, and many saw another Japanese pull into a vertical climb and zoom to about four thousand feet with a P-38 right behind; both leveled out and faced each other, fired, and made a series of head-on passes. No one saw how it ended.

Unable to resist the spectacle, Middlebrook eased the squadron back in a 180-degree turn so they could watch the fighting, but then he remembered that he was responsible for the formation and was supposed to be leading them back to base, not enjoying the show, so he banked right and continued. Later he thought he should apologize, but his attempts were rejected by the squadron, saying they liked the opportunity to see something of the action. His top turret gunner, Emminger, claimed a fighter with confirmation from other crews, but Middlebrook wondered how anyone could claim a particular plane in such circumstances with several gunners in action, and pondered why the Japanese seemed to persist in waiting to attack until after the bombers had attacked their bases, rather than before, when the attackers were laden with bombs and less maneuverable.

A head-on attack on four Japanese fighters by the 39th Fighter Squadron resulted in one claimed as destroyed. Tommy Lynch saw four Oscars offshore from Dagua, dropped his tanks, and went for them. He attacked one from below, scored hits on the front of the engine area, then swung around and went back after the Japanese, firing a long burst from behind. With Lynch two hundred yards behind, the burning, smoking Oscar went into cloud. Lynch made about five passes at other Oscars and saw hits on one before the P-38s broke contact. Other pilots saw a Ki-45 Nick go down after combat with P-38s—probably Lent's victim.

The Headhunters of the 80th Fighter Squadron attacked thirty to forty enemy south of Dagua at ten thousand feet and claimed ten: three each for Flight Officer Ed De Graffenreid and Cy Homer, plus one each for Ed Cragg, Jess Gidley, John Jones, and Paul Murphey. The 80th lost 2nd Lts. Robert E. Feehan, John Guttel, and Elwood G. Krisher.

Ed De Graffenreid was on the way home alone after this, his first combat, when a Japanese slipped in behind him and riddled the tail and right engine and blew pieces from the rear of the cockpit canopy before De Graffenreid could dodge into a cloud. De Graffenreid made it back to Moresby and ditched in the shallow water along the beach in the harbor. Cy Homer escorted Paul Murphey home after a Tony hit one of Murphey's engines.

To be successful, a fighter pilot needs one thing above all: contact with the enemy. Good eyesight, determination, the ability to get in close to the target, good shooting, a suitable aircraft, effective, destructive weapons—all have been enjoyed by many fighter pilots who simply had few or no combats. The Wewak missions provided the essential combat for fighter pilots of the 5th Air Force, and 21 August saw the first claims for enemy destroyed made by many pilots who later became aces. U.S. Army 5th Air Force fighter claims for the day were 35-5-7. In the 432nd Squadron, Elliott Summer destroyed the first of his eventual ten victories; Billy Gresham, the first of six; Fred Harris, the first two of eight; John Loisel, the first two of eleven; and Paul Lucas, the first of six. In the 80th, Ed De Graffenreid destroyed the first three of six, and Cy Homer the first three of fifteen. Several P-38 pilots became aces in this day's combats, including David Allen, Tommy McGuire, Frank Nichols. and Danny Roberts.

Three P-38s were lost; 13 Sentai claimed two for a loss of three, and 68 Sentai claimed 3-1-0 for two. Sergeant Kubo of 59 Sentai was killed, as were Lieutenants Ryoshei Harada and Nakamura and Sergeant Major Terada of 13 Sentai, and Lieutenant Hashimoto and Sergeant Nishikawa of 68 Sentai. Harada, commanding 2 Chutai 13 Sentai, led the only three fighters the unit could provide—two Oscars and a Nick. None returned. Shigeki Nanba had an unsuccessful combat at low level with two P-38s, possibly McGuire and Lent. Shigeki later saw an Oscar down in a marshy area about twelve miles east of the Wewak area; the pilot was standing on the wing, waving. Nanba flew back, landed, and reportedly went back to the crash site but was amazed to find no sign of aircraft or pilot; neither was seen again, and it was believed that the pilot must have been Kubo, 3 Chutai. Possibly the aircraft simply sank into a quagmire. In his diary, Sergeant Major Motohisa noted "over 100 aircraft in combat. Enemy loss was great, no damage to Wewak."

On page twenty-three of the original document created at 4 Air Army captured at Hollandia, and quoted above, Japanese losses were listed as:

Wewak-But	19–23 August:
shot down	38
uncertain if shot down	16
blown up	16
badly damaged	57
slightly damaged	47
Total	174

The "uncertain if shot down" category should be noted because the four airstrips in the target area were quite close together, and if a damaged fighter managed to land at any one of them, this would soon be known. Even if some went to distant locations such as Madang, Alexishafen, or Lae, they would have been reported. The sixteen airplanes in this category were lost, regardless of classification.

Therefore, at least 54 airplanes were recorded, in location and at the time of the missions by the Japanese themselves, as lost in air combat in the period. U.S. fighter claims for 20 and 21 August were for 48 destroyed: 13 on the twentieth and 35 on the twenty-first. Bombers claimed 5 destroyed on 20 August, to make the U.S. total for "destroyed" 53. Eight probables and ten damaged were claimed by the fighters and bombers, and these could be included in the 104 recorded by the Japanese as badly or lightly damaged. In addition, Japanese totals were not cumulative; aircraft once counted in a given category were not counted again unless specifically noted as such in the records. Therefore, later figures do not include aircraft destroyed or damaged that were counted and recorded previously. On the basis of these original Japanese reports, U.S. fighter claims and bomber gunner claims for this period of combats over Wewak were accurate. Furthermore, and despite what any official Japanese history might state, Japanese radio traffic intercepted and decoded at the time indicated that at least 165 replacement aircraft, both bombers and fighters, were sent to New Guinea in the month preceding 18 September.

Military Intelligence Summary 518 from MacArthur's GHQ reflected the view of the Allied staff that the number of Japanese fighters met in the air was "somewhat remarkable in view of the devastation to the enemy's strength at this New Guinea air stronghold." After describing sightings of Japanese aircraft in flight at what might have been points along the reinforcement route, the summary went on: "Accordingly, it is probable that the enemy planned to maintain a relatively strong fighter force of Army aircraft there, so long as he had access to immediate replacements. Such available resources, it would now appear, have been exhausted."

However, the Japanese would continue to funnel men and aircraft into the combat area, into the mincing machine operated by the experienced and confident P-38 squadrons. For 21 August, radio intercept operators reported in SIBs 114 and 118 that aircraft arrived at Wewak through Ambon and Hollandia;

radio conversations indicated that the crews were "very inexperienced." G-2 commented that this was probably a new unit moving in. Long-range flights for other destinations declined to only five airplanes.

The daily average of flights detected for preceding weeks had been between forty and fifty. On 23 August there was a sudden increase to eighty-five flights, with communications to sixteen air bases. The activity centered on Hollandia and Wewak but included bases as far north as Manila. One formation moving south was five Oscars. Wewak was reported short of aviation gasoline. All these were indicators that confirmed the impression of severe damage done to the Japanese by combat reports and photographs.

A planeload of pilots from 68 Sentai flew to Manila to collect new Tonys and returned in September with the new unit commander, Maj. Kiyoshi Kimura.

24–31 August

It was obvious that a major victory for Allied airpower had been achieved by the 5th Air Force in the Wewak strikes. The previous twelve months had seen the Australian army hold the Japanese during the fighting retreat over the Kokoda Trail, defeat the Japanese invasion at Milne Bay, and advance back over the Kokoda Trail to the north coast. Despite careful phrasing by some journalists and other writers, no U.S. ground combat troops were engaged in land actions in the Kokoda and Milne Bay campaigns. Then followed the Australian-U.S. capture of the Buna-Gona positions and the destruction of Japanese army formations in the eastern part of Papua New Guinea. A year after the Japanese began their attempt to capture Port Moresby, and a year after General Kenney assumed command of the 5th Air Force, decisive land and air victories had been won.

A matter of concern for the staff at MacArthur's GHQ was how the Japanese managed to put so many fighters into the air after the earlier successful bombing and strafing attacks. GHQ Intelligence Summary 518 referred to the matter:

> Last week it was noticeable that, despite the havoc caused by Allied attacks, the enemy was still able to maintain fairly large fighter groups in the air (approximately fifty in one engagement). This indicates that fresh replacements were brought in immediately. In part, it was also noticeable that the air groups engaged were composed of a mixed lot of unit markings. Aircraft movement from the Empire via Truk

to Rabaul is accelerating. As an expedient, until reinforcements can arrive from the Empire via the eastern route, the enemy can probably move more than 100-odd aircraft from Java, where there is not the immediate pressing need for them, into the New Guinea region.

For the next two days the Allied air forces turned their attention elsewhere but kept watch on the Wewak area. A reconnaissance on 23 August reported activity, so a B-24 strike was made next day. The town, airfield, and supply dumps were battered with 110 tons of bombs from thirty-six B-24s. Ten fighters scrambling to get away from below were caught by the P-38 escort. One Japanese was shot down by Lt. Harris Denton of the 39th Fighter Squadron for his second victory. The Japanese fighter made a pass at the B-24s and turned to attack again, but Denton caught it with a burst; it went down and was seen to crash. Sergeant Major Motohisa was glum and noted, "Wewak was heavily bombed. Our fighters were too late."

A single aircraft from the 8th Photo covered all four Wewak airfields with what the squadron record noted was "the usual efficiency" of the pilot, Rigsby.

Weather hampered accurate assessment of damage, but it was known to be greater than anything achieved since the campaign in New Guinea began. AAF Intelligence Summary 130 reported the attacks as "a gratifying catalogue of important Allied successes," adding that Advanced Echelon 5th Air Force estimated "in all 115–120 enemy airplanes have been destroyed or rendered permanently unserviceable in addition to the destruction of large quantities of supplies and heavy casualties to personnel." Summary 131 briefly related the attacks of 17, 18, and 20 August and described the scene: "the composite picture of these aerodromes is one of major devastation and damage. . . . It is impossible to assess with any confidence the remaining enemy strength throughout New Guinea until the situation clears. It is logical to expect some enemy strength was withdrawn to Hollandia to avoid the later attacks." The Intelligence Summary commented that it was thought bomber reinforcements would be held at Hollandia, but it was not known if aircraft were at Madang, Nubia, or Alexishafen; if Japanese aircraft from other areas might be brought into the Wewak area; or if the Japanese navy air force might find the burden unsupportable "unless the Empire could provide reinforcements." On 24 August, only fifty-two aircraft were visible on photos of all four airfields in the

Wewak area; the runways were serviceable, but buildings and wooded areas showed signs of much damage.

The top secret Special Intelligence Bulletins containing the "Ultra" radio intercept reports distributed to a very select few in the Allied hierarchy included references to flights of reinforcement aircraft from the north through Hollandia to Wewak. The SIBs included references to thirty-six Japanese army airplane crews flying into the Wewak area. By the radio messages intercepted, it was believed the arriving crews were inexperienced. In addition, Hollandia informed flights from the north that there was no aviation gasoline available. Air activity declined, but a week later Hollandia still was without aviation fuel.

Naturally, the Japanese were making their own claims, and Sergeant Major Motohisa wrote on 26 August that "enemy losses so far are 42 shot down at Wewak and 11 at But."

Weather again prevented photo reconnaissance of the Wewak area on 27 August, so the two 8th Photo pilots covered the Hansa Bay area instead and reported antiaircraft fire at thirty-one thousand feet. The squadron diarist joshed them with "Are you sure it wasn't just a little dark cumulus?"

On 28 August, thirty-five B-24s with P-38 escort attacked Wewak targets and were intercepted by an estimated sixty fighters. Only forty-four airplanes were visible on photos taken that day, and only thirty-eight on 30 August. AAF Intelligence Summary 134 admitted that "dispersal must be considered" when the low numbers of aircraft detected on the ground in the Wewak target areas were compared with recent fighter interceptions by several scores of Japanese aircraft.

Two 8th Photo pilots covered all four Wewak airfields, and one pilot photographed Hansa Bay as well. Japanese fighters were reported at twenty-six thousand feet but could not reach the higher-flying Lockheeds.

On 29 August B-24s returned to pound the wreckage at Wewak. Tommy McGuire led Blue Flight of the 431st Squadron over the bombers. Two Japanese fighters passed below the P-38s, heading for the B-24s, and McGuire dived after them. One Oscar pulled up in front of McGuire and received the full effect of the P-38 guns. Crews of the 320th Squadron confirmed the victory. McGuire then engaged a Tony and shot it down after head-on and tail attacks. It was his seventh victory in three combat missions. Climbing after this clash, McGuire noticed tracers flicking past and saw three Oscars and a Tony attacking. He dived, but his left engine was hit and started burning. McGuire stopped that engine, still in the dive with Japanese behind, and slipped down to nine thousand feet, which blew out the fire. He then dived into cloud at four thousand feet. The Japanese did not follow, probably well aware of the danger of being caught so low with P-38s in the area.

McGuire trimmed the P-38, set off away from the target area on one engine, and landed at Marilinan, 250 miles away. The P-38 had to be repaired there, so McGuire flew back to base the next day, hitching a lift in a B-25.

The 80th Headhunters P-38s took off to escort the bombers but broke away and returned because of the deteriorating weather. Two Headhunters went on to the target—Bob Adams and Albon Hailey. Over Wewak they became separated, but Adams shot down an Oscar and then a Nick. There were more Oscars above and below, and each P-38 pilot decided that it was not the best place to be alone, so they left. Hailey had fired but did not claim, and Adams was credited with two victories, making his total five.

John Lane, 39th Squadron, saw about ten enemy climbing to attack the bombers and dived on one as it moved to attack the lead B-24. Lane's fire hit the tail, and the fighter exploded. This was Lane's sixth victory.

Eight Japanese fighters dived on the 319th Squadron from ahead, and the top turret gunner in the Houston crew hit one with a long burst. The Japanese fighter went past burning and was seen to crash.

Capt. Shigeki Nanba, commander of 1 Chutai 59 Sentai, had seen Sergeant Kubo on the wing of his crashed Oscar on 21 August, and on 29 August saw another crash-landed Oscar. Shigeki identified the pilot as Umeoka, from 1 Chutai who walked north away from his plane, cheerfully waving to his circling friends. He entered the jungle and was never seen again. Nanba recalled that four Sentai aircraft did not return from combats on 29 August. Lt. Howard Round, 39th Fighter Squadron, claimed a "Hap" probably destroyed southeast of Wewak; this might have been Umeoka's aircraft.

Above all the action was a duo from the 8th Photo, who covered the target areas and reported five Japanese fighters about ten thousand feet below them. The next day they were tasked to arrive over the targets at 1220, an hour after the B-24s had bombed. On time, the 8th Photo aircraft arrived, and when their photos were developed there in the frames were the B-24s, just approaching the target. The 8th Photo diarist commented that the B-24s needed a couple of the reconnaissance pilots as navigators.

Total 5th Air Force fighter claims for the final week of August in the Wewak area were 8-4-4. Japanese claims for the week were 11-4-0 U.S. aircraft against their own admitted air losses of 4-0-16. However, five Japanese fighter pilots are known to have died in the last week of August: Lieutenant Yasuda of 13 Sentai, Sergeant Majors Shiroto and Aoki of 24 Sentai, and Lieutenant Umeoka and Sergeant Umetani of 59 Sentai. But a different report admits the loss of four fighters on 29 August alone; Shigeki Nanba stated that four from his unit failed to return on that date. The 14 Hikodan recorded fifty-seven killed and ninety-three wounded in the last week of August. The Japanese claimed thirty AAF airplanes destroyed for the month.

For Japanese on the ground, the surroundings were of widespread destruction. Corporal Nakamura of 208 Bomber Sentai had little work for the next two months because replacements for destroyed Lily aircraft did not arrive. He saw 1 and 2 Chutai 7 Sentai arrive just before the U.S. attacks and all twenty Helen bombers destroyed. A Sergeant in 51 Airfield Construction Unit counted at least one hundred wrecked aircraft and was told that one raid had killed 125 people and wounded 350, as well as destroyed supply and ammunition dumps. In all of the August attacks, he only saw three AAF planes shot down.

The frequency of flights over the Japanese areas was noted by the Allied radio intercept operators, and the low level of activity was another indicator that the entire Wewak complex of bases was hard hit. On 28 August only five aircraft were noted in communication with airfields; on 29 August, apart from the combats, only four flights were detected on radio in the area.

GHQ's Military Intelligence Section issued Summary 526 on 31 August, stating that the latest attacks on But and Dagua

culminated a series of assaults on enemy airpower in New Guinea, extending over a period of two weeks. Though initially able to sustain the pressure, via hurried reinforcements, it appears his power of recovery has dwindled. No enemy fighters were encountered in yesterday's raid, which took them well north of Wewak. The extension of our radius of effective striking action has virtually placed the Wewak chain of airdromes in the category of advanced landing fields. The net result will be the rapid development of rearward airfields, Tadji, Aitape, Hollandia, etc, for utilization as permanent bases.

The next day's summary referred to Japanese army aircraft identified in action in the Solomons and postulated that the Japanese headquarters at Rabaul was trying to cope with operations to east and west with the same pool of aircraft. This reinforced the idea of Rabaul being the key point in the region and suggested a possible new arrangement between Japanese army and navy air units. A final and conservative figure of 175 Japanese aircraft destroyed on the ground was accepted against a combat loss of two B-25s, three B-24s, and six P-38s. As August ended it was clear that Japanese aviation in New Guinea had been soundly beaten and was no longer the threat to Allied forces that it had been four weeks before.

At the end of August 1943, the 5th Air Force was mature. In eighteen months since the arrival in Australia of the small advance units, the 5th formed an organization that had demonstrated successfully the advantages of military airlift to land forces in the Kokoda and Buna-Gona campaigns from July 1942 to January 1943, had refined tactics and techniques before destroying the Lae convoy in the Battle of the Bismarck Sea in March 1943, and in this August 1943 series of attacks had annihilated the opposing air element on the ground and in air combat. After these three phases, the 5th Air Force was a fully functioning military machine for the employment of airpower.

THREE

Locked Horns

September 1943–March 1944

Having gained the initiative, Allied air forces reinforced their advantage, maintained pressure on the Japanese, and attacked any observed position or sign of activity. Because this book is concerned with the major attacks against Japanese airpower in New Guinea in August 1943 and March–April 1944, it is not intended to describe in detail the continuous strikes that followed the successful August missions to Wewak. To link the August 1943 missions with the next great concentrated series of Wewak strikes in March 1944, however, this chapter provides continuity.

In the ground war in August 1943, Australian and U.S. forces maintained pressure on Salamaua, defended by some five thousand Japanese. The real Allied intention was to capture Lae by amphibious assault while a simultaneous airborne assault captured Nadzab, inland from Lae, in the Markham Valley. After the Japanese had been pushed from that area, a major complex of air bases was to be constructed. The amphibious operation against Lae on 4 September was successful. Only three Japanese bombers attacked the ships and destroyed one landing barge, and an afternoon attack by an estimated one hundred Japanese aircraft was so disrupted by P-38 and P-47 interception that only two landing ships were damaged. The parachute drop at Nadzab was another success. A-20s of the 89th Attack Squadron laid a smoke screen to protect the eighty-two C-47 transports dropping paratroopers and equipment of the U.S. 503rd Parachute Regiment. Jumping for the first time were Australian artillerymen of 2/4th Field Regiment AIF, volunteers to take their guns into action by parachute without training jumps.

Work began at once on the airfields: two days later a strip for C-47s was operating, a week later two parallel strips were available, and ten days after the parachute drop the field could accommodate thirty-six C-47s. Lae itself was captured on 16 September by the Australian 7th Division. On 17 September Australian infantry in C-47s landed on the old airstrip at Kaiapit attacking nearby Japanese and eliminating them in three days, allowing the airstrip to be developed there. Similar operations resulted in the Ramu Valley being in Allied hands by the end of September with airfield sites at Gusap and Dumpu. Finschhafen was captured by Australians on 2 October, bringing the Allied line to the northern side of the Huon Peninsula. All this had been accompanied by intense air operations, including two attacks on shipping at Wewak, which cost three B-25s lost to flak.

The Special Intelligence Bulletin of 9 September reported Japanese aircraft reinforcement—in the previous six days, seventy aircraft arrived at Hollandia with twenty-five of them moving east to Wewak and Dagua. Sixteen Sally and Helen bombers with another seventeen aircraft arrived at Hollandia on 5 September alone, and twenty more arrived on 9 September. On 10 September, 6 Flying Division had the following aircraft operational: 13 Sentai, nine aircraft; 14 Sentai, thirteen; 24 Sentai, sixteen; 45 Sentai, five; 59 Sentai, fourteen; 81 Chutai, two; 83 Chutai, four. This was a total of sixty-three aircraft, including forty-four fighters.

At the same time, 7 Flying Division could call on about half that many: 7 Sentai, four planes; 68 Sentai, ten; 78 Sentai , six; 61 Sentai, eleven; 74 Chutai, three. This was a total of thirty-four aircraft, including sixteen fighters.

Eleven more Oscars were identified in transit on 12 September. On 16 September at least thirty-two aircraft flew in to Hollandia, including Lilys, Dinahs, and unidentified types with an escort for navigation. Thirty-three more were noted on 18 September. On 22 September, about fifty flights between the bases at Rabaul, Wewak, and Hollandia were noted.

Wewak was pounded constantly for the rest of 1943 by heavy bombers and strafers, and fighter sweeps continued to grind down fighters and bombers in the air. Allied superiority was established. Before the AAF attacks in August 1943, Japanese staff estimated that their forces were outnumbered in the air by about three to one. They realized they were hindered by poor preparation of their air bases and by an air repair organization that was too small, not properly equipped, and not properly supported from Japan. The Japanese staff realized that by mid-1943 the Allies had excellent facilities for establishing bases; comparatively enormous replacements and supplies; good ability getting these replacements and supplies into action; superior equipment in aircraft, including bullet-proofing; increased range for bombers; and excellent radio and radar facilities and aids. The situation after August was simply compounded—nothing improved for the Japanese. Their highest command levels did nothing of use to restore the balance of power to Japanese forces. More aircraft of the types that had been destroyed in such large numbers were produced and sent forward, but the Japanese aviation industry could not conceive or design anything likely to match U.S. aircraft such as the P-38, P-47, and B-24. The B-29, in concept, design, and engineering capability, was far beyond Japanese capabilities.

Allied units fought on through the darkest days of 1942 against the superior Japanese aircraft types waiting for the promised better aircraft to arrive. Arrive they did, along with fresh aviation units. The Japanese in New Guinea were merely fed propaganda claims, and a few units arrived from other battlefronts equipped with marginally improved airplanes of the old types.

Many Japanese aircraft that reached New Guinea became unserviceable because of a lack of trained maintenance crews. Finally, Japanese commanders in the Home Islands understood this, but it was too late to begin to train the flight crews and essential maintenance personnel in the large numbers needed.

September 1943

By the end of September 1943, 59 Sentai was reduced to fifteen aircraft and only two officer pilots. The unit handed over its Oscars to 68 and 78 Sentai, went to Manila to re-equip, and returned to Wewak in November, but 59 Sentai was again ground down. On 15 December, Captain Nango wrote, "We are at the mercy of the P-38s. The time of our Type 1 fighter is past."

After the death of Nango on 23 January 1944, unit effectiveness slumped. By 1 February 1944 only ten pilots remained; 1 Chutai consisted of a single sergeant pilot. The pilots and half of the ground crews left for Japan, and 59 Sentai did not fly again in New Guinea. Capt. Shigeki Nanba, commander 1 Chutai 59 Sentai, weakened by dysentery, had been ordered to Akeno Flying School, Japan. At the end of the war, only he and Master Sergeant Shimizu remained alive of the 59 Sentai pilots who flew from Java to Wewak in July 1943.

On 19 September, for the second time in a month, 78 Sentai sent pilots to Manila for new aircraft. They returned late in October with new Tonys. The arrival of twenty Tonys was noted in the Special Intelligence Bulletin 172 for 24 October. The 24 Sentai already had been reinforced with new pilots and aircraft but lost them in three weeks and left for the Halmaheras early in October.

Japanese records for September 1943, translated in EP 270, show some of the losses reported to 4 Air Army:

13 September, at But: 45 Sentai lost three bombers destroyed and six damaged (3-0-6).

15 September, at Wewak: 7-0-20. The 90th Bomb Group fought a savage action this day, when an estimated seventy-five Japanese fighters kept on attacking. The Group claimed forty-four destroyed: six to the 319th Squadron, eleven to the 400th, and twenty-seven to the 321st. U.S. fighters claimed an additional 9-2-1 in the day's combats.

17 September, Wewak area: six destroyed and eleven damaged on the ground; three lost in the air.

26 September, Wewak area: 13-0-12.

For September 1943, in the Wewak area, U.S. fighters claimed forty-four destroyed, fourteen probably destroyed, and six damaged (44-14-6) for a total of sixty-four, but Japanese records admit 23-0-38, a total of sixty-one. The combination of four airfields in close proximity allowed badly damaged aircraft to land or to be recovered if nearby. How many of the thirty-eight listed as "damaged" were made flyable again is unknown. Appendix E shows the constant flow of replacement aircraft to Wewak, despite which Japanese air strength fell from ninety-seven aircraft on 10 September to seventy-five on 1 October.

The Japanese bomber effort in September was negligible by comparison. Raids on Nadzab caused little or no reportable damage, and in the Finschhafen area bombing results were the same.

The fate awaiting downed Allied flight crews was often recorded in Japanese diaries, letters, and official instructions. A diary captured in April 1944 included a note that the diarist guarded Allied air prisoners on Wednesday 8 September. Then on 9 September he wrote that "prisoners were killed at this time. We watched the execution take place. After thinking it over, I felt sorry for them, but it was something that had to be done. Five persons."

Jeep Parts for Lockheed

On 28 September, Cy Stafford of the 482nd Service Squadron was at Marilinan and saw a P-38 preparing to land with what looked like smoke coming from an engine. Cy flagged the plane into a revetment. It was Tommy McGuire, and the P-38 had been hit in the coolant line. Again McGuire had made a 250-mile flight on one engine to Marilinan. The simple repair consisted of sawing out the damaged section of pipe and replacing it with a section of radiator hose from a jeep secured with clamps. While this was done McGuire was treated to a can of pineapple from the secret hoard of the 482nd, who had to unload C-47s bringing in supplies. After forty-five minutes, McGuire was on his way.

October 1943

The 5th Air Force maintained pressure on targets across the region, as well as over Rabaul, New Britain. Again the Japanese bombing effort was small by comparison with the Allied intensity of operations, and Japanese raids often were a waste of time and aircraft. Any single Allied bomber squadron achieved a higher sortie rate and inflicted more damage than the entire Japanese bombing force managed to achieve in response.

On 2 October the thirteen remaining Oscars of 24 Sentai were handed over to other units and the surviving pilots flew to Manila, made a delivery flight of fighters back to Wewak, and then left the theater for Japan. The unit claimed eighty victories but admitted the loss of twenty pilots in a little more than four months of operations.

Some Japanese losses at Wewak in October 1943 are available to historians in translations of captured documents in the Allied Translator and Interpreter Section collection. These confirm some U.S. fighter claims. An entry in the Japanese document states:

11 October

Lt. Col. Tamiji Teranishi, CO 14 Hikodan, and Capt. Shigeru Koyama, CO 68 Sentai, listed as "missing."

This was the day Neel Kearby, commander of the 348th Fighter Group, claimed at least six Japanese aircraft destroyed, and his wingmen accounted for another three. Kearby's victories were assessed and confirmed by camera gun film, and more would have been claimed but the film in Kearby's camera ran out.

Kearby was determined to prove that the P-47 could be effective in combat in the SWPA and was angry at the slurs from the P-38 believers. Wewak was the place to find enemy aircraft, and it was there that Kearby would prove the value of the big fighter from Republic Aviation.

An attempt to fly a sweep over Wewak on 10 October was foiled by weather. On 11 October, Kearby tasked a flight to see what could be found over the Japanese bases: Kearby, with Capt. John Moore as wingman; Maj. Ray Gallagher, commander of the 342nd Fighter Squadron, and Capt. Bill Dunham as Gallagher's wingman. Kearby had three victories, gained in September; Moore had one victory, Gallagher had no victories, and neither did Dunham.

John Stanaway's history of Kearby's unit gives considerable detail of this combat. The Japanese were aware of the approach of the P-47s and apparently had scrambled a large formation of at least twenty-five Tonys and Oscars under command of Lt. Col. Tamiya Teranishi, commander of 14 Hikodan. Colonel Teranishi flew in defiance of policy from 4 Air Army but was determined to provide leadership to his pilots.

From twenty-eight thousand feet the four P-47s were able to watch the airbases below, assess the Japanese reaction, and select the time and place of their own attack.

Kearby saw a lone Oscar—misidentified as a Zero—at twenty thousand feet and dived on it at 1115. The Oscar took no evasive action and was destroyed by a burst at three hundred yards' range from Kearby's eight .50-caliber machine guns. It is speculation that this Oscar possibly was flown by Teranishi, attention focused downward and looking for the climbing fighters under his command, or it could have been someone on a test flight, intrigued by the sudden activity below and not alert to his surroundings. In their book *Japanese Army Fighter Units and Aces,* Ikuhito Hata and Yasuho Izawa state that Teranishi was killed by "surprise attack" while flying alone over Wewak.

Kearby led the P-47s around to the rear of a formation of Tonys and Oscars, dived, and shot down two more Oscars. A Tony turned on Kearby, but Bill Dunham shot it down. This might have been the Tony leader, Capt. Shigeru Koyama, commander of the 1 Chutai 68 Sentai.

The P-47s shot down several more Japanese, and at one time Dunham looked down and counted seven patches of fire on the sea where aircraft had crashed. Others were shot down over land. Moore and Gallagher also saw varying numbers of enemy crash and fires on the sea. Kearby was credited with six victories, Moore with two, and Dunham with one for a total of five Tonys and four Oscars.

The U.S. Army 5th Air Force fighter claims a total of ten on 11 and 12 October including one Dinah on 12 October for Lt. Col. Bob Rowland, 348th Fighter Group. There were no other fighter claims against JAAF aircraft.

The Japanese misidentified the P-47s as P-40s and so reported them in various documents. Captured 4 Air Army records list only the two officers, Teranishi and Koyama, as "missing" and two more aircraft "damaged" for this day. The total aircraft reported available for operations to 4 Air Army on 11 October was seventy-two and increased to seventy-five on 12 October, but this number dropped to sixty-seven on 14 October.

For the period 11–14 October, the JAAF fighter units reported variations of only one or two aircraft on strength. The only unit that reported a significant drop in number of aircraft available was 45 Sentai, which operated the Lily twin-engine bomber, with numbers decreasing from thirteen to six.

Just which Japanese fighter units launched the forty or so fighters airborne, as reported by Kearby's formation? (This was later estimated as about twenty-five by historian John Stanaway.)

Fifteen Oscars were reported available for 11, 12, and 13 October by 13 Sentai; 24 Sentai was involved in ferrying Oscars from Manila at this time and did fly in thirteen aircraft on 2 October and another twenty-one late in the month. Pilots from 59 Sentai were sent to Manila on 2 October to bring back twenty-three more Oscars, which arrived at the end of the month. Ten Oscars and four or five Tonys were reported available by 68 Sentai for 11, 12, and 13 October. No Tonys or Oscars were reported as operational for 78 Sentai between 1 and 15 October.

Some units had been removed from combat missions and were ferrying aircraft from Manila, others apparently had none available according to their reports, and those with operational fighters of the types reported in the combat did not report any losses, even though two senior officers were killed in this combat.

Kearby's camera gun film and the reports of his wingmen indicate a day of outstanding results over Wewak, but no decoded Japanese radio transmission or captured document relevant to this day's combat detailing greater JAAF losses than two destroyed and two damaged has been located. One must wonder if Teranishi and Koyama had not been killed, would this combat have been reflected at all in 4 Air Army's documents?

Another entry in the Japanese documents states:

16 October

Over Wewak, four Tonys of 78 Sentai were destroyed in combat, and thirteen various types damaged. 78 Sentai lost four killed in action and one wounded, while 68 Sentai lost one killed in action.

Both Tonys and Oscars were flown by 68 and 778 Sentai at this time, and in the morning over Boram, the 80th Headhunters Squadron claimed four Tonys (to Taylor, Freeman, Myers, Smith) and an Oscar (to Myers) destroyed, and later Neel Kearby claimed a "Zeke," the pilot seen to bale out—a total of six. The U.S. claims over Wewak and Japanese records match.

Near Madang on the 16th, Sergeant Major Fujii, 68 Sentai, claimed three P-47s before being shot down and wounded by P-38s and is probably the Zeke claimed by 2nd Lt. George Haniotis, 9th Fighter Squadron, over Madang. No P-47s were lost.

Flying Oscars, 13 Sentai lost its commander, Major Nagano, Second Lieutenant Nishide, 3 Chutai commander Captain Asahi, and Sergeant Major Ikeda, a total of four killed. However, a separate Japanese report on aircraft lost includes 13 Sentai losses at Alexishafen as 3-0-4. Kearby's 348th Group P-47s claimed 13-3-0 over Alexishafen and Madang but lost no aircraft. The author has not located any Japanese record for the Alexishafen combats, but the U.S. fighter claims for Wewak and Madang are confirmed in captured Japanese documents.

For 19 to 22 October over Wewak 4 Air Army records admit losses as 5-0-3.

U.S. fighter claims by the 342nd Fighter Squadron were for three Japanese army aircraft destroyed on 22 October. On 19 October Neel Kearby and other members of his flight claimed six Mitsubishi F1M1 Pete floatplanes caught taking off, but because the Pete was operated by the navy, they would not be included in reports from 4 Air Army. In November Japanese losses over Wewak were reported as 15-0-19, and U.S. fighter claims for November over Wewak for army aircraft were fifteen.

However, combat also took place over other parts of New Guinea in November 1943. Some captured documents indicate high Japanese losses, which is confirmed in that, by the end of October, 68 Sentai had lost its Tonys and Oscars, and Capt. Shogo Takeuchi took the pilots to Manila for a month and returned in November with twenty-six new Tonys. In only two weeks, 78 Sentai, which returned from Manila in mid-October with new Tonys, was forced again to fly Oscars from the departed 24 and 59 Sentais. The 78th lost a steady stream of pilots and leaders, including the Sentai commander, Maj. Akira Takatsuki, over Wewak on 22 December. Captain Takeuchi, leader of 2 Chutai 68 Sentai, was wounded and hospitalized for fifteen days in October. Takeuchi discharged himself from hospital and returned to his unit still heavily bandaged. He insisted on flying missions, and his example was a great morale booster for the pilots and ground crews. But on 21 December after an escort mission to Arawe, New Britain, Takeuchi was killed when trying to land his damaged Tony at Hansa. By late December the 68th had only three pilots left.

For October, November, and December 1943, U.S. fighter pilots claimed 71-6-3 over Wewak; a captured 4 Air Army document (EP 270) admits loss of 26-0-35 in the area to the end of November.

The admitted Japanese losses in air combat in some Japanese records often do not agree with U.S. fighter claims, but to be considered also in this matter were the frequent departures from New Guinea by parties of Japanese pilots to collect new fighters in Manila and return with them to Wewak. A few weeks later, the sequence was repeated. Either the replacement fighters were being shot down in considerable numbers, or damage inflicted in combat was so severe that even if the airplane did manage to crash-land somewhere, it was written off as beyond repair, or pilots were wrecking large numbers of valuable aircraft. There are also the frequent documentary references to units reduced to a handful of pilots or fewer.

The re-equipment rotations to Manila and back to Wewak by the Japanese fighter units in New Guinea indicate steady destruction in combat or loss of their aircraft by various causes:

19 September: 78 Sentai went to Manila for the second time in a month. They collected new Tonys and returned in mid-October but in two weeks were flying old Oscars.

End of September: 59 Sentai sent pilots to Manila, picked up twenty-three fighters in late October, and on the delivery flight lost Major Fukuda to non-operational causes at Geelvink Bay. On 31 October, flew on to Wewak, but by February the unit again was reduced to ten pilots and departed for Japan.

The Japanese documents report:

Early October
24 Sentai, having already used up a batch of reinforcements in three weeks in September, moved to the Halmaheras.
End of October
68 Sentai flew to Manila, re-equipped, and returned, by December was reduced to three pilots. 24 Sentai delivered twenty-one Oscars to Wewak, then the pilots flew to Japan.

On 17 October "Ultra" intercepts identified a large movement of at least sixty-five aircraft to army bases in New Guinea, including two Sallys escorting forty-one others. A special intelligence bulletin revealed that all forty-three airplanes were Sallys. On 22 October Wewak reported that thirty-two bombers and twenty-four fighters were available, and another twenty fighters were en route. On 30 October Ultra again detected a total of forty-eight flights bringing aircraft into the army bases.

Obviously, the truth about U.S. fighter victories in the New Guinea campaigns is somewhere between the admitted Japanese losses and those claimed by the U.S.

pilots. The frequent requirement to replace entire unit batches of aircraft is a strong indication that U.S. fighter victories in these Wewak combats were considerable.

The Ultra intercepts gave an idea of the scale and frequency of Japanese air replacements and the routes they followed to the SWPA. Frequently a formation was escorted by a bomber for navigational guidance and for radio communication with the air base network. The normal radio traffic from these flights allowed Allied staffs to assess the flow of aircraft and their dispersal to airfields, and to confirm this by photographic reconnaissance.

The Allied air offensive pressure on Wewak was so strong that the air navigation aid control radio station closed and moved west to Wakde Island.

The 5th Air Force mounted a series of heavy attacks on Rabaul between 12 October and 11 November, contributed to the destruction of Japanese aircraft and shipping, and distracted the Japanese while U.S. Navy and U.S. Marine Corps units made a successful landing on nearby Bougainville. These 5th Air Force attacks on Rabaul did not have the success they deserved. The weather often intervened and limited operations over Rabaul to one or two days between blocks of successive days when the Japanese were able to recover, repair damage, and improve defenses. The Allied air forces flew another intense series of missions in December in support of the landings at Cape Gloucester and Arawe, both on New Britain, as part of the strategy of isolating Rabaul rather than attacking it directly. In fact, although cut off from useful outside assistance, the Rabaul garrison continued to improve its positions and train for the expected Allied assault—which never came. At the end of the war, the Rabaul garrison considered itself undefeated and cast a medal for its members before they returned to Japan.

Meanwhile fact and fantasy seemed to be closely associated at headquarters in Japan. On 3 November 1943 citations were awarded to flying units for their alleged victories over New Guinea and New Britain, such as the action on 15 October when the bomber element of 582 Kokkutai (Naval Air Group) and fighters of 204 Kokkutai attacked Oro Bay in New Guinea, allegedly shot down eight U.S. fighters, sank four transports, and set one of the transports on fire. Again, citations were awarded for supposed successes on 15–16 December when 201 Kokkutai, commanded by Lieutenant Oba, attacked the Allied force at Cape Merkus, New Britain, and claimed to have shot down five planes, set one cruiser on fire, and sunk three transport ships and fifty landing barges. The 201, 204, and 253 Kokkutai at Rabaul were commended for supposedly shooting down

653 Allied aircraft in thirty-eight days ending on 29 January 1944. This is a minimum of seventeen victories a day, every day, for thirty-eight days. Other units received commendations for similar feats.

In Japan itself, public morale in early 1943 was high due to propaganda and other tales of exaggerated successes fed to the population by the military authorities and because in mid-1943 2,320 airplanes were financed by public donations. There was disagreement about the need for quality or quantity in aircraft production. In November 1943 Giro Takeda of Mitsubishi, said in a speech: "Victory or defeat depends on aircraft. We must realize that the aircraft we have produced are inadequate. Have we not relied on the prowess of our men to make up for any deficiency in strength? This is a big mistake in the fierce air war of today."

Professor Itakama agreed and pointed out that inferior aircraft cannot defeat superior ones, and Japan was no match for the United States in production of aircraft. But in an example of how the acceptance of optimistic statements instead of hardheaded investigation and establishment of facts can result in wrong attitudes, Professor Tsuji said that Japan did not need the mass production methods of the United States, as war results showed they were 12- to 13-to-1 in Japan's favor.

The Japanese estimated the numbers of Allied troops and aircraft opposing them, but their estimates of enemy strength often were far beyond reality, and far beyond what common sense should have told them. Early in October the Ultra network intercepted messages, reported in SIB 154 of 6 October, that revealed the Japanese version of the forces gathering around the southwestern Pacific: 90,000 U.S. paratroops, 12 infantry divisions, and 1 mechanized division were believed to be in northern Australia, and another 85,000 paratroops and 3 mechanized divisions were in eastern India; 10 infantry divisions were in New Guinea, and 5 in New Zealand. The enormous airlift logistics system to accommodate 170,000 paratroops was beyond the dreams of the Allied commands but apparently not beyond acceptance at the higher levels of the Japanese military.

November 1943

In the southern combat zones, the cold hard truth was apparent to Japanese officers and enlisted men. Inadequate technological support was typified by the experience of 248 Sentai, a fighter unit equipped with Oscars. The unit formed in Japan in August 1942 and after almost a year's training was ordered to New Guinea in October 1943 to replace 24 Sentai. On 31 October, the Sentai arrived at Wewak with thirty Oscars and thirty-four pilots under the command of Maj. Shin-ichi Muraoka. But the fatal weakness in Japanese combat deployments is again shown clearly when the unit's supply, maintenance, and engineering component is known. The unit had three starter trucks and three fuel tankers, thirty-three mechanics, nine armorers, five electricians, six radio technicians, three drivers, and four "general workers." These sixty men were to service, maintain, and repair all the Oscars of a fighter unit of a headquarters and three flying subunits operating in combat from a rough airstrip. Two hundred other ground crew were lost when their ship was torpedoed on 2 November, so ground crew from destroyed units leaving New Guinea were transferred.

Between 7 and 16 November 1943, the Sentai took off fifteen times from Wewak airfields to engage the enemy. Despite having radar control, the formation failed to be directed to the enemy on thirteen flights, one time they intercepted friendly aircraft, and only once did combat occur.

The Sentai also flew other missions in November. On the sixth, it flew to Alexishafen for the attack next day on Nadzab, but in what seems to have been a series of landing mishaps, it lost the commander of 3 Chutai who was killed at Alexishafen, another pilot was injured and went into hospital there, and a detachment of seventeen men had to go to Alexishafen to work on damaged Oscars. On the seventh, during the Japanese air attack on the Allied air base complex at Nadzab, the unit lost two pilots killed, two were wounded, and four made forced landings at Alexishafen. On the ninth, eighteen Oscars took off to attack Nadzab. One pilot was killed at the mouth of the Markham and one killed at Alexishafen; two others were missing, and two more made forced landings at Hansa and Alexishafen. On the fourteenth, nineteen Oscars flew to attack Finschhafen; Lieutenant Murakami was forced down twenty kilometers north of Finschhafen but made his way to safety in Sio. The next day the other eighteen airplanes attacked Marawasa, and six were lost. On the sixteenth, twelve Oscars from the unit took off to engage P-38s over Wewak, and one was lost; this was Corporal Aihara, who parachuted off Wom Point, was rescued, and then taken to the hospital. Aihara probably was one of the two victories claimed by Maj. Meryl Smith, 475th Fighter Group, who saw the Oscar pilot in his parachute. There was no combat for a week, but on the twenty-sixth, fourteen Oscars took off to support an attack on Heldsbach; two were reported missing and one made a forced landing at Hansa.

Thus, thirteen pilots were officially reported lost from this one fighter unit in its first month of operations in New Guinea. At the end of November only seven 248 Sentai Oscars remained operational, but fifteen replacement pilots arrived in December.

The poor state of support and resultant lack of combat readiness was known to many in the Japanese air units, but the situation did not improve. Instead of training the new pilots, those with the most experience received the most opportunities to fly to maintain their skills. The 248 Sentai records for November show the flying hours of 3 Chutai: the ace Nishihara logged 90.25 hours, but flying time among the others gradually diminished to 17 hours for Corporal Nakayama and only 11 for Lieutenant Ota.

Reinforcements and replacements continued to arrive at the Japanese bases. Air reconnaissance photos taken on 19 November showed eighty-two twin-engine bombers at Hollandia. More bomber arrivals were detected by radio on 28 November.

In Japan information had been received from "a spy in Washington" that led them to believe the Japanese forces had been successful in actions fought off Bougainville in November. U.S. losses were alleged to have been two battleships (one of the 45,000-ton *Wisconsin* class) and nine cruisers (four of which were new large ones launched in 1942, including the *Wichita, Savannah,* and *Juneau*), with heavy damage to another battleship. Of these ships only about half the crews had been rescued.

The report went on:

Fearing this defeat might cause agitation and unrest among the general public, the military authorities are trying to decide whether they should deny the Japanese claims or announce the facts to the U.S. people.

At present, the result of this defeat is to discourage landing operations on New Britain and New Ireland scheduled for 6 February 1944, for the 40,000 troops waiting in Australia and New Zealand. As things are now, the attack is thought impossible.

However, the Japanese army insisted on moving forces to defend those areas and the navy was forced to assist.

December 1943

In December 248 Sentai claimed eleven victories in five combats: two B-24s, five P-38s, two B-25s, and two P-47s. The B-24s were claimed on 1 December, against the recorded loss that day alone of sixteen Japanese aircraft destroyed on the ground. Operating Dinah reconnaissance aircraft, 10 Sentai lost every one and 81 Independent Chutai was "considerably reduced." In 248's records, on that day Captain Tozuka led seven other pilots up, and "Lieutenants Fueki, Ejiri, and five NCOs failed to return." Tozuka was the only one to get back. U.S. fighters claimed five victories over the Wewak area. The U.S. 90th Bomb Group lost three B-24s to flak and fighters on this mission. One Tony made a head-on pass at the 321st Squadron and fired a single burst that hit accurately and shot down Lt. Oliver Sheehan's aircraft.

On 16 December 248 Sentai sent nine Oscars as part of the escort for Japanese bombers attacking Arawe; 248 lost three. On 22 December in a convoy escort two of the four unit Oscars that flew the mission were lost and the pilots were killed. The 248 had only six fighters available for this task and noted that 68 Sentai could not participate in the escort because of "loss of men"; 248 had to fly the escort alone.

These few documents alone show that in two months 248 Sentai lost nineteen pilots killed (or "failed to return") and three wounded. Seven fighters were so damaged in combats that they made forced landings. Twenty-five airplanes were recorded as lost in combat, but the recovery or loss of those making forced landings was not clarified in the documents. This information is for only one participating Japanese air unit in New Guinea at this time.

The experience of Sgt. Iwao Tabata, 68 Sentai, on 22 December confirms the poor state of the radio and radar support provided the flying personnel. The 3 Chutai launched two elements of two Tonys, led by Lt. Akinori Motoyama with Corporal Furuhashi as Motoyama's wingman and Tabata leading the second element with Corporal Oakada on his wing. The Tonys scrambled to intercept the oncoming U.S. formation and headed east. There was no radio contact with the ground, so the Tonys basically searched on their own. Tabata looked back at Wewak and saw smoke billowing up, obviously the result of a bombing attack. He flew up alongside Motoyama and indicated to him that the enemy were behind them at Wewak. Motoyama turned back, led the four Tonys into the action, and engaged a formation of P-38s.

Tabata maintained position behind Motoyama to protect the leader's tail. Then Motoyama's wingman dived away. Tabata slid up on Motoyama's left to show that he was now the wingman; Motoyama looked across and nodded. In that instant both Tonys were hit by P-38s and burst into flame. Tabata managed to bale out into the jungle and was found three days later by men of 78 Sentai who were searching for Major Takatsuki, the unit commander, also missing since 22 December. Motoyama was taken to a naval hospital but died on 25 December.

Postwar research by California historian Henry Sakaida indicates that Tabata was shot down in a head-on pass by Paul Murphey, 80FS. It has not been established who shot down Motoyama. Major Takatsuki was not found, and in John Stanaway's history of the U.S. 8th Fighter Group, *Attack & Conquer,* he speculates that Takatsuki could have been the unfortunate pilot whose parachute was accidentally rammed and torn to pieces by Maj. Ed Cragg, CO 80th Fighter Squadron. Hit by another P-38, a Tony pilot bailed out and opened his parachute right in front of Cragg, who did not have time to avoid the parachute.

The 248 was tasked to provide part of the escort for Japanese bombers attacking the U.S. invasion fleet off Cape Gloucester, New Britain, on 26 December. While seventeen fighters from 248 did meet the bombers, the unit after-action report stated that another seventeen promised from 59 and 68 Sentai "did not arrive," and 78 Sentai was on other tasks elsewhere. The 248 then found itself "surrounded by P-47s," which made a series of attacks. No aircraft from 248 were lost "due to excellent handling by our pilots," but the bombers were unprotected. The writer of the report, Major Muraoka, the commander of 248 Sentai, then went on to complain that "Joint command in combat is not good. Someone should be appointed overall air commander. It is impossible in the present organization for the Flying Brigade commander to command in the air. It is not good from the standpoint of control for an elderly air brigade commander to appoint someone else to give commands in the air."

This is a classic example of the shortcomings of the Japanese command: some two years after the beginning of the war in the Pacific, and after their previous combat experience in China, the Japanese fighter and bomber units flew missions without an overall flying force commander appointed. The most serious fault was that the Japanese operated to detailed orders given by older nonflying commanders who dictated tactical decisions before the mission began. The situation must have been serious for a Japanese junior officer such as Muraoka to criticize his superiors.

On 25 December 4 Air Army reported to Tokyo that officers in subordinate units had confirmed that the Tony was superior to the Oscar. Linked to this admission, by the end of December 1943, it was necessary for Capt. Yutaka Kozuki and other experienced pilots of 248 Sentai to compile a paper listing combat lessons learned in an attempt to assist the inexperienced pilots. Basically, the paper was a list of "dos and don'ts" on how to avoid being shot down but little on how to destroy the enemy. It was defensive in nature and content, not offensive. But Allied fighter leaders of the time produced papers emphasizing how best to destroy Japanese aircraft using height, speed, teamwork, and gunnery.

Pilots from the fighter units were not the only pilots who were not fully trained. On 5 December, 4 Air Army endorsed a recommendation from the reconnaissance units that a list of twenty-one pilots be sent back to Japan for retraining as gunners or radio operators "because of their lack of competence."

In late 1943 the Allied air forces under General Kenney truly demonstrated the flexibility available from efficient air forces. Their achievements were limited only by the capability of the aircraft. By year's end the 5th Air Force contained seventy-eight squadrons, and its power was brought to bear on every aspect of the Japanese presence. Ships and barges of all sizes were hunted; sixty fishing trawlers from Wewak were sunk in November alone. Any sign of military activity or occupation was bombed and machine-gunned. Airfields, roads, vehicles, bridges, barracks, buildings, radio masts, gun positions, villages, trenches, ports, wharves, and anything afloat were lashed with bombs, 20 mm cannon, and .50-caliber machine-gun fire.

The diary of one Japanese soldier gives some idea of the intensity of the air raids of the time. Private Mihara was a member of the Labor Unit, 78 Infantry Regiment, who arrived at Wewak on 20 November, from Korea via Palau.

27 Nov—Before our embarkation we were bombed and strafed by a formation of 30 enemy airplanes; embarkation cancelled.

28 Nov—Attacked by 150 enemy bombers at 1005 hrs.

01 Dec—Today we came to Wewak No. 2 embarkation point but at 1030 were attacked by a formation of 26 North Americans. Our unit sea truck received a direct hit and sank in 30 minutes.

Mihara kept his diary through his journey to Kankiryo, writing on 27 December that "enemy artillery and air attacks are terrible." His last entry was the next day, and the diary was captured on 1 February 1944.

The Japanese had examined their opponents, and a 2 Area Army report of 15 December described U.S. flight crews as "men with about 200 hours experience. When they encounter difficulties their morale drops and there is a marked decrease in fighting power. They believe their aircraft are better and that they will always win, and are always in high spirits. They do not persist in using the same tactics, and avoid our strong points while attacking the weak ones."

In addition to the purely military aspects of their presence in New Guinea, the Japanese were simultaneously trying to develop its natural resources and ease the burden of support from the Home Islands by local production. Units on the perimeter of the Empire would feed themselves and export to Japan. Whole development units were raised and sent to fertile lands in newly occupied areas. Ryoji Oshi was in one such unit, which had only three hundred men in it instead of the intended five hundred. They arrived at Wewak on 23 September 1943, but constant bombing and strafing made vegetable gardening impossible, and only small quantities were harvested.

The requirement to feed themselves meant units had to divert manpower from military duties to agriculture and fishing. By October 1943 the Army's 41 Division at But had thirty-eight acres under cultivation. Each unit was allocated an area and a quota of produce, while laborers had to clear more land. Each man allocated to gardening had to maintain his cleared eighty square yards while clearing another forty. A first season crop was calculated to be forty square yards of vegetables and eighty of potatoes for each worker. Farther west at Hollandia, 8 Naval Construction Unit was responsible for setting prices paid for food from local villages and arranged for the surrounding area to produce food for sale to the Japanese, who would collect it by boat or truck or even carry it to the stores themselves.

But all this was done in a hostile environment, and sickness and disease were prevalent. The Medical Officer of 41 Airfield Battalion at Wewak was a twenty-eight-year-old who arrived in September 1943 but was himself continuously ill with malaria from December on. There were nine hundred patients in the hospital, many with the mysterious "Wewak fever," for which there was no cure and which had a 20 percent fatality rate. All the while they were "in fear of the four-engine bombers," and eventually the patients were told to go into the jungle. The medical staff of 2 Special Base Unit calculated that their patients were 60 percent dysentery, 50 percent malaria, and 10 percent gonorrhea.

In Japan by December 1943, all commodities were scarce, rationing had been applied—as in all other combatant nations—and taxes increased at places of entertainment. The greatest shortage was of petrol; all civilian transport was powered by charcoal gas. But morale was high, and generally higher still in country areas because of the availability of food.

For the Japanese, 1943 ended with the knowledge that their enemy was growing stronger each day while they were struggling to maintain the levels of a year ago. Gen. Hideki Tojo had taken Japan to war in the expectation that the Western democracies would ask for peace talks after a series of Japanese successes, but instead the war had continued and Japan and her allies were confronted with the demand for unconditional surrender. Defeat for Japan was unthinkable, but Imperial headquarters staff had assessed the situation and decided to hold the present extent of the Empire while preparing for a decisive naval battle in mid-1944.

For the benefit of those fighting in the southern areas, a great new offensive force was said to be in preparation. Lack of airplanes in one location was explained by saying the planes had been deployed elsewhere. Many Japanese did believe in the imminent arrival of the "Decisive Battle Force" with thousands of new superior Japanese planes; others realized it was only talk. In their diaries many Japanese recalled the events of the past year and wondered what the coming year would bring. One optimist hoped to be dining in Sydney, Australia. Others, realistically, wondered if they would see Japan again.

Two years after the attack on Pearl Harbor, it was obvious to some Japanese that Japan simply was not able to fight a modern, drawn-out war. This warfare had developed when the Western democracies fought on rather than surrender after their first defeats. The industrial base of the Japanese Home Islands was inadequate. In 1942 the Japanese had sown the wind; in 1944 they started to reap the whirlwind.

January to March 1944

As 1944 opened, attention of both opponents in New Guinea turned to Hollandia. The Japanese emphasized the importance of its harbors and airfield complex. General Adachi, commanding 18th Army, declared that it must be defended to the last man. However, on orders from 2 Area Army in the Philippines he heavily reinforced the Wewak-Madang area to oppose expected Allied landings in that location. Once again the Japanese staff underestimated their opponents.

There were changes in the Japanese air forces. The 4 Air Army's area of operations expanded to include the Celebes to the west, and 7 Flying Division went there to replace naval air force units that moved to Rabaul. The Commander of 4 Air Army was Lieutenant General Teramoto, and his remaining formation in New Guinea was 6 Flying Division, commanded by Lt. Gen. Giichi Habana.

The 6 Flying Division comprised eleven Sentai and two Chutai. In practical terms, the Division had about 240 aircraft to attack the expected Allied landings. But due to lack of parts and heavy equipment, and a high accident rate, only about 25 percent would be operational. The Division comprised:

14 Hikodan, commanded by Colonel Tokunaga, with the fighter Sentai: 33, 63, 68, 77, 78, and 248

8 Hikodan, Major General Morimoto, with 45 and 60 Bomber Sentai

Training Hikodan, Colonel Moritama, with 34, 75, and 208 Bomber Sentai.

Also in New Guinea but under direct command of 4 Air Army was 9 Hikodan, with 61 Bomber Sentai, 10 Reconnaissance Sentai, and 7 Transport Unit. The allotment of aircraft to 4 Air Army for January 1944 was 117 fighters, 92 bombers, and 8 transport aircraft.

The Japanese reorganized their supply system for air units in New Guinea. At first the flow of men and equipment went from Japan to headquarters in the Philippines, which then allocated assets to the front-line senior headquarters. From the beginning of 1944 a direct supply system from Japan to the front-line commands was introduced.

On 2 January 1944 troops of the U.S. 32nd Division landed at Saidor, catching the Japanese in a trap between the U.S. and Australian army units advancing from the south. Maj. Kiyoshi Kimura, commander 68 Sentai, was killed in action over the landing area. However, it was not until 16 January that the Japanese reported by radio the loss of the commander of 68 Sentai among a total of nine; the information was passed on for Allied commanders in SIB 285. Possibly his death was reported only after wreckage was found or hope of his return was given up. Major Muraoka, commander 248 Sentai, was also killed in action over Cape Gunbi, but the unit reported that "morale was higher than ever" as a result. The land fighting was nearly over by 10 February, and the Huon Peninsula was in Allied hands. Some fourteen thousand Japanese were killed or died in the campaign.

The Allies benefited immensely from a great intelligence find. Japanese troops of the 20th Division retreating from Sio were charged with safekeeping of the army codes in a large metal box but decided to take the easy way out and simply buried the codebooks, in the box, in a mud-filled crater. They removed the codebook covers as "proof" the books had been destroyed. In the process of checking the area for mines and booby traps, an Australian engineer found the box with his mine detector. The intelligence officer called to the site realized what a prize was before him. The priceless books were flown to Australia, and then the pages were dried and photographed for other offices in the Pacific and United States. At last Allied codebreakers could read mainline Japanese army code.

The Allied forces secured more airfields near Saidor and developed those at Gusap, four hundred miles east of Hollandia. The main Allied air base was the complex of seven airfields at Nadzab. But before Hollandia could be attacked, the Japanese presence at Wewak had to be beaten down again. Allied pressure continued, and over Wewak in January the Japanese counted 358 Allied sorties and claimed 30-14-0 U.S. planes for an admitted loss of eight in combat. U.S. fighters claimed 38-6-6 Japanese planes in the Wewak area for that month.

When the new commander 248 Sentai, Maj. Takebumi Kuroda, arrived at Wewak on 21 January, only ten operational fighters were left, and by the end of January, no officer pilots remained. In February the unit was reduced to making single aircraft night sorties into the Ramu Valley area. On 1 February, 1 Chutai 59 Sentai had only one pilot, Sergeant Kumatani.

From photographic sorties of their fast high-flying Dinahs of 10 Reconnaissance Sentai, the Japanese estimated on 31 January that the Allies had 750 aircraft available for operations against central and western New Guinea. By 15 February they counted 850 Allied planes on airfields and 739 Allied sorties over the Wewak sector. They claimed 29 Allied aircraft destroyed, for their own losses of 36-0-40. Teramoto's staff believed "the conspicuous decrease in P-38s is due to their use in other areas." However, 5th Air Force was accumulating new P-38s and improving older ones for use in force.

After U.S. forces went ashore at Aitape in April 1944, a file of Japanese intelligence reports was found and passed through the Allied system. Like the other reports that were found at Hollandia that gave detail of the Japanese side of the campaign from August to December 1943 (quoted previously), this file contained reports from HQ 4 Air Army for the period December 1943 to March 1944 and included details of operations by Japanese aircraft in that period. The "Aitape" file of spot intelligence reports (immediate reports) was translated and issued by the Allied Translator and Interpreter Section as ATIS Bulletin 1560. These reports, as with all other captured documents, provide a valuable window into the campaign as experienced by the Japanese. Although details of their own losses are not complete in these spot intelligence reports found at Aitape, they are an indicator of damage suffered by the Japanese.

The Japanese view of losses inflicted by them on the U.S. forces included in these reports is interesting, both because of the high numbers of U.S. aircraft claimed shot down and also because these figures were included in official intelligence reports at a senior HQ level. If these claims were accurate, the sea should have been littered with U.S. survivors in life rafts, the shorelines crowded with other survivors trying to escape, and many more prisoners should have been expected to be in Japanese captivity. Any reasonably intelligent person, and any trained staff officer, should have queried these claims, but they were reported to a HQ and reissued to other units in the theater, apparently without confirmation.

The culmination of this poor staff work came in 1945 when the Japanese relied on verbal reports from survivors of the escorts for the kamikaze attacks. They came to the conclusion that enormous losses were being inflicted on the U.S. forces to the degree that the appearance of the Allied invasion fleets off Japan itself was welcomed as the opportunity to inflict an even more gigantic defeat on the Allies. This information, available through Ultra radio intelligence intercepts to the highest levels of the U.S. command, linked with other complementary information that surrender was not considered, led inexorably to the decision to use the atomic bomb rather than endure the tremendous human slaughter that would follow an invasion.

The Japanese in early 1944 made air attacks on Allied airfields and the Saidor beachhead. None were much more than annoyances and in no way compared to Allied blows against Japanese bases. Formations of up to fifty Japanese fighters intercepted Allied raids, the fighter Sentai launching between six and fifteen planes each. The pilots put in excessive victory claims.

According to the documents captured at Aitape, thirty-three Japanese fighters attacked Nadzab on 15 January and claimed between sixty and eighty Allied aircraft destroyed on the ground, including thirteen definite and four probable P-38s. Warrant Officer Takashi Noguchi of 68 Sentai was credited with a C-47 "shot down for certain." Actually the U.S. 312th Bomb Group lost four P-40s shot down or crashed on landing, one C-47 was damaged in the air but landed, and eleven U.S. aircraft were damaged on the ground. The attack force was made up of twenty-two fighters from 68, 78, and 248 to attack Nadzab and Gusap, and eleven Oscars from 59 Sentai to attack Gusap and Dumpu. The 59 Sentai shot down the 312th P-40s. Admitted Japanese damage was to only four aircraft, two each from 78 and 248 Sentai. Noguchi was shot down the next day and taken prisoner.

On 18 January, fifty-six Japanese fighters intercepted ninety P-38s and P-47s over Wewak at 0900 (Tokyo time). The defenders claimed 13-4-0 from the P-38s and admitted the loss of three, including Captain Kojima. U.S. P-38 and P-47 pilots claimed 13-3-1.

On 23 January, fifty-one Japanese fighters engaged fifty-five B-24s, P-40s, and P-38s, which attacked Wewak and claimed 13-5-0 for a loss of six. Actual U.S. losses were one P-40 and four P-38s; no B-24s were lost but some suffered damage. U.S. Army 5th Air Force fighter claims were for 19-2-4, and the B-24s claimed 12-8-0. Capt. Shigeo Nango, who claimed fifteen victories with 59 Sentai, was killed in this combat. His brother was a JNAF ace killed in China. Also killed was Capt. Nobuyoshi Tozuka, commander 2 Chutai 248 Sentai. The 248 launched eight airplanes and lost two.

Captain Nango was greatly admired for his personal qualities of bravery, leadership, lack of selfishness, and a down-to-earth nature with superiors and subordinates. He was promoted two ranks posthumously.

At the end of January, at least one Japanese HQ was annoyed enough to radio that "the enemy has been using B-24 and B-25 bombers without even a fighter escort to bomb our positions."

The developing situation was clearly seen by those in command at the Manila Air Depot, which was responsible for ferrying new and repaired aircraft to the combat areas. On 27 January, the unit reported "a rapid supply of fighters is going to be needed in the New Guinea area. At present, the entire strength of our unit is used to transport Type 1 fighters, but then 16 to 18 Type 3 arrive for delivery."

Other problems in operating from the rough New Guinea fields resulted in urgent orders for tires of all sizes for the different types of aircraft. In early February 7 Flying Division asked "suitable instructors" be sent from Japan to assist with the "relatively large amount of motor and propeller trouble." The Ki-61 Tony had many accidents attributed to the rough conditions, but little effort was assigned to improving the airfields.

The constant submarine and air attacks on shipping were successful and gathered force as the war went on. Twenty ships from Palau and Truk set off for Rabaul during January, but seven were sunk en route. More were sunk around Rabaul and on the return, and only six ships made the round-trip. This loss rate could not be sustained.

On 3 February U.S. aircraft attacked Wewak and But. The Japanese claimed 14-6-0 Allied aircraft, all B-25s except one P-40, for an admitted loss of fifty-seven aircraft destroyed, burned, or damaged on the ground. Fighter losses reported in the Aitape file were severe, totaling fifteen Oscars and nine Tonys "burnt" or damaged. Four Lily bombers were listed as destroyed and another five as damaged. The 431st Fighter Squadron claimed six Lilys destroyed over or near But airfield. Total AAF fighter claims were for 15-0-0, but no Japanese aircraft were recorded specifically as lost in the air in the reports found at Aitape.

After moving its forces around, 4 Air Army on 7 February reported that 33 and 77 Sentai were at But, 45 was at Aitape, 75 was at Hollandia, and 60 at Wakde. "To avoid former waste," the units were to be moved again so that 33 and 77 would be at Hollandia, 45 at Wakde, and 60 at Galela.

On 10 February a report to 4 Air Army showed the total number of Japanese aircraft available for operations that day in New Guinea was ten reconnaissance, twenty-nine fighters, and twenty-six bombers. Two days later 7 Flying Division submitted a request for supply in March of twelve Dinahs, five Sonias, and thirty Nicks.

On 15 February eleven Oscars and two Tonys intercepted fifty-four twin-engine bombers and thirty P-40s and claimed 8-0-0 for a loss of two destroyed and one damaged. Three U.S. twin-engine bombers were claimed destroyed with one air-to-air bomb. No U.S. aircraft were admitted lost, but 5th Air Force fighter claims were for 10-1-2.

Warrant Officer Shimizu of 59 Sentai claimed five B-26s and P-47s over But on 15 and 16 February. Despite claims for ninety victories in six months of operations in New Guinea, 59 Sentai was reduced to about ten surviving pilots by 19 February. They boarded a bomber as passengers and flew to Japan. Some of the ground crew were returned to Japan by ship, but the others remained in New Guinea and died in the land battles.

On 8 March seven B-24s and one P-40 were claimed, for a loss of one Japanese. The seven B-24s were claimed destroyed by air-to-air bombing, for a loss of one Type 1 fighter (Oscar). In reality, one B-24 was lost and four were damaged. U.S. fighter claims were for one Japanese fighter destroyed. Capt. Arland Stanton, 7th Fighter Squadron, claimed an Oscar twenty miles southwest of Wewak, his sixth victory.

Between August 1943 and February 1944, Japanese aircraft losses in New Guinea were recorded in their documents compiled at the time to total 710. Two hundred twenty-five were lost in combat, 373 were destroyed on the ground, and 112 were wrecked in accidents and to other causes. Only one-third of the Japanese aircraft delivered to New Guinea in these six months were lost or destroyed in combat. The other two-thirds were lost in accidents or destroyed on the ground, a fatal situation for an air army. U.S. fighter claims for the period 1 September 1943 to 10 March 1944 in the Wewak area were reasonably accurate, at 193-32-21.

Col. Rinsuka Kaneko served on the army headquarters staff at Rabaul, and then spent thirteen months from August 1943 as a supply officer at the headquarters of 4 Air Army. He was interrogated postwar and estimated that losses were 30 percent in air combat, 50 percent on the ground, and 20 percent in operational losses. He added, "I can remember occasions when entire flights failed to come back."

Colonel Kaneko attributed the high number of aircraft lost on the ground to the lack of machinery and manpower available to construct dispersals, resulting in aircraft held in a relatively small area, and to the lack of ground crews, resulting in aircraft that could not be made flyable to move them away from an area about to be attacked. He stated, "In my opinion we failed not only because we received insufficient planes but because we did not have sufficient personnel and heavy machinery to build proper airfields and properly maintain what we had."

After Japan surrendered in August 1945, their records showed that Japanese aircraft production of bombers, fighters, and reconnaissance aircraft for the last quarter of 1943 and January 1944 totaled 3,120. Approximately one-quarter of their production was lost in New Guinea, and this loss rate would continue. The Japanese air armies were also fighting in the Pacific, China, Burma, and India.

Allied losses in air attacks on Japanese bases were reported with official claims for Japanese successes that should have been suspect by any thinking person. For example, at Wewak on 15 February 1944, the defenses claimed twenty-two U.S. aircraft shot down; at Kavieng on 14 and 15 February 1944, the defenses claimed twenty-six U.S. aircraft shot down; and in the five days 10–14 February 1944, Japanese defenses at Rabaul claimed 207-31-0 Allied planes allegedly destroyed or damaged for a loss of twenty-nine. In New Guinea, for the month of February 1944 alone, Japanese antiaircraft fire was credited with destruction of 129 Allied aircraft in the zone west of Hansa Bay. These fanciful figures were reported to higher headquarters and intercepted by the Ultra organization.

The Japanese often were enraged at the destruction inflicted by Allied bombing and strafing, but much of that anger could have been directed at their own higher echelons or staff. Repeatedly, even when it was known AAF formations were in the area, planes were caught on the ground and destroyed. One such incident was the strike on But airfield on 3 February 1944, which made a deep impression on the lieutenant commanding 20 Airfield Battalion. Despite warning from headquarters at Wewak, all three Chutai of 248 Sentai were on the ground when waves of B-25s roared over. Caught in a maelstrom of blaring engines, .50-caliber machine guns, and parafrags, the lieutenant dived under an Oscar, which caught fire, forcing him away. Thirty fighters were destroyed, and at least one pilot was killed.

Headquarters 14 Flying Brigade reported that action and described how 59, 63, 78, and 248 Sentai launched fighters to attack approaching B-24s but fought P-47s while the bombers hit Boram and Wewak fields. Then the Japanese flew to But, were given the signal to land, and did so. The report goes on: "However at this time sixty B-25s attacked the strip, causing the following damage: (total) 43 destroyed or damaged."

A separate Japanese report gave destruction at But as fifty-one aircraft, and a third quoted twenty-six aircraft destroyed on the ground. The Japanese air repair depot reported that seventy-six aircraft were destroyed in the first fifteen days of February.

However, while documents such as those mentioned indicate the loss of between twenty-five and fifty airplanes, reported strengths from Sentai to superiors show small losses over the period 3 to 6 February. On 3 February 248 Sentai reported strength as seven and as five three days later. This is another example of conflicting figures, which make it difficult to establish Japanese losses.

Disasters like this were happening before the eyes of Japanese soldiers, who came to wonder at the truth of communiques from Imperial headquarters. A private in 4 Air Intelligence Unit at Wewak wrote of an attack in February 1944, when B-24s, B-25s, and P-38s bombed, strafed, and completely destroyed the barracks alongside the airfield, and attacked thirty antiaircraft positions; twenty-eight men were killed by a direct hit.

As well as the pressure applied to airfields, Japanese ground positions were attacked constantly and the fleet of small ships that shuttled cargo and men along the coast was hunted almost daily by aircraft and nightly by PT boats. The Japanese lost 59 barges and equivalent ships to bombing and strafing in January and 85 barges in February. They radioed for 170 to replace them; 100 remained in use. Crew training was "urgently necessary," and the radio message stated that the continued existence of their forces in New Guinea depended on this force of small ships and barges. A network of sixty large-caliber guns was strung along the coast to provide sheltering fire for the barge traffic against aircraft and PT boats. This situation also was reported by radio and intercepted by the Allies.

The effect of shipping losses along the coast was such that the transport situation was recognized by the Japanese to be "most acute," and it was realized that there was only a small hope that replacements would arrive in useful quantities. From mid-February, only barges were permitted to go east from Hansa. Sea trucks and other coastal vessels were to be used between Hollandia, Wewak, and Hansa but not forward of there. On 13 February Wewak radioed that the situation there was critical due to losses. It was decided to establish a shipping center at Hollandia to coordinate all coastal supply activities.

Headquarters for 4 Air Army reissued a report on Allied air raids that originally came from Imperial headquarters. The report stated that heavy bombs were not used in large numbers, and about half the parafrags were duds, but bombing accuracy had improved. It was noted that Allied air raids took place between 0900 and 1100, but this report admitted the Allies suffered "comparatively small losses." Counters to Allied successes were obvious: concentrate the defending fighter strength, use camouflage, disperse aircraft, and move antiaircraft guns. Meanwhile, Japanese antiaircraft units received copies of a January 1944 analysis of AAF attacks by 2 Area Army headquarters. B-25 strafers were mentioned particularly; their low-level approach was hard to detect, and establishment of "remote observation posts" was recommended. Daily training in antiaircraft engagements of "surprise targets" was emphasized. The report admitted that successful engagement of aircraft flying higher than 12,000 feet was difficult, and units were reminded to concentrate antiaircraft fire in front of formations of bombers in order to upset the bombardiers.

The fast Dinah reconnaissance aircraft were able to arrive over Allied coastal areas and report the assembly of Allied shipping, obvious indicators of future Allied intentions. But the Dinahs could not maintain a constant presence and report the directions in which the ships sailed.

Realizing the Allies were going to strike but not knowing where, 6 Flying Division prepared its available fighter force for the coming actions. On 9 March 1944, the six fighter Sentai were organized into three attack units. The 68 and 78 Sentai combined under Captain Tateyama as Attack Unit 1; 63 and 248 under Major Hara as Attack Unit 2; and 33 and 77 Sentai were Attack Unit 3 under Major Matsumoto.

The quality of both men and machines was privately acknowledged to be below the standard necessary to cope with the coming battles. In October 248 Sentai had arrived in New Guinea. Originally, pilots had at least six hundred hours of experience, but by early 1944 many had fewer than four hundred hours and were put into combat as soon as they arrived. The leading ace was Warrant Officer Nishihara, with ten victories. The experienced pilots produced an honest appraisal of the situation for the younger men, acknowledged the inferiority of Oscars in combat, and emphasized their only advantage: turning ability. Major Kurata was the CO, but unit orders show Warrant Officer Matsumoto often led the unit in combat. Well aware of dangers to health in the region, 248 Sentai had an efficient antimalarial precaution program and had only five malaria cases, one of the lowest rates among units in the Wewak sector.

The 33 Sentai arrived from Indochina and Burma; they were detected on radio and reported present in New Guinea. This unit, formed in 1938 in China, was battle-hardened after operations in Manchuria, China, Burma, and India. In its early combats in New Guinea, it lost fifteen pilots killed and others wounded. Formed in February 1943 in Japan, 63 Sentai began operational flying in New Guinea and sent its 2 and 3 Chutai to Wewak in mid-January. By the time 1 Chutai arrived in mid-February, with twelve Oscars, the other two Chutai had been reduced to a total of eight aircraft. Experienced leaders had gone, and Lt. Hiroshi Endo led the flying, claiming about ten victories in the period.

An example of the wastage rate in Japanese fighter units is provided by 63 Sentai. In January 1944, the unit lost twelve Oscars in accidents: one was hit from the rear during its landing run, one overshot on landing, two swerved into the jungle on takeoff, two crashed due to selection of an empty tank on landing approach, four hit trees when landing or taking off, and two collided. The official cause for six losses was "incompetence."

In February 1944, 77 Sentai arrived at Hollandia. This unit formed in July 1938 in China and had war experience in China, Thailand, Burma, and the East Indies before arrival in the SWPA. The entire unit had thirty-six Oscars, forty pilots, and 120 ground crew, but 75 percent of the pilots had fewer than two hundred hours and were being trained by the experienced cadre, men with up to one thousand hours. Once the unit went into combat, it became impossible for the "old hands" to cope with numerous aggressive enemy while leading inexperienced wingmen. Lieutenant Nagata had been away from Japan since July 1941 and arrived in New Guinea with 77 Sentai. He believed they could have coped with the P-38 in one-on-one combat but were unable to deal with the diving line-astern attacks employed by the Lightning flights.

Many Japanese fighter pilots thought it useless to attack Allied bombers, while Japanese bomber crews feared most the P-47—its eight .50-caliber machine guns tore their planes apart. Pilots regarded the Allied fighters in order of superiority as P-47, P-38, and a bad last, the P-40. The unfortunate ground crews had great respect for the strafers but most feared "those devils" the B-24s.

Japanese bombers once again gathered on the New Guinea forward airfields in early 1944. Yasuo Imamura, 38 Airfield Battalion, had been away from Japan since 23 December 1941. He arrived at But on 4 September 1943 and endured constant attacks. He recorded in his diary the arrival of the bombers and the animated atmosphere as 33, 34, 60, 61, and 208 Sentais landed. To the west Hollandia was a scene of great activity. On 5 March 1944 Sohei Ogawa, Signals Office of 90 Garrison Unit, counted more than 300 aircraft on Sentani airfield with more arriving daily.

Depending on the headquarters estimate of the situation, the fighter and bomber Sentai would be deployed for training, attack, or interception. Individual airfields were allocated for these operations. To cope with weather and terrain, 4 Air Army ordered training in attacks on landing craft in a beach assault. Flying conditions in the area were as hostile to the Japanese as to the Allies.

Another 130 aircraft of all types were allocated to the New Guinea theater for March 1944, and 4 Air Army was informed that in February it had received a total of 42 Oscars, 15 Tonys, and 56 bombers. However, the Japanese did not have adequate logistic and maintenance backing for the airplane force they accumulated. Captain Naniwa took his Mobile Repair Section to Hollandia and found to his disappointment that although it was the major rear base for the region, only light work could be done. No milling machines were available, and the nearest complete workshop was on Palau. Naniwa was aware of health problems and insisted on correct antimalarial precautions. Other Japanese noted that although the Hollandia airstrips themselves were acceptable, the resident airfield battalion had no maintenance capability, there were few refueling and starter trucks and few facilities for air-to-ground communication, and only a small amount of training was done. The only well-equipped unit was the intelligence signals network. At But, where many bombers concentrated, the airfield repair unit was equipped with 1,545 laborers, 41 trucks, 7 rollers, 1 tractor, and 1,514 shovels. In March 1944 this was in no way adequate to cope with offensive operations or with damage from a modern air offensive.

Material damage and destruction inflicted by Allied air attack was often great, although generally personnel casualties were low; letters and documents referred to the small numbers killed and wounded. By early 1944 there were few who regarded air attacks as a spectator sport, and personnel were under cover when the Allied air forces came over. Capt. Takaki, Medical Officer of

8 Hikodan, Wewak, wrote on 11 February: "Enemy air attacks are always between 0800 and 1100, about 200 aircraft take part, with targets the houses, fuel dumps, et cetera. The attacks are always made in the morning but strafing casualties are very low. There have been a few mental cases, a few with loss of voice or temporary paralysis due to concussion. We have tied cases of explosives to the trees and brought the aircraft down."

In addition to battle casualties, ever-present health problems continuously drained unit strengths. In December 1943 and January 1944, 49 Anchorage Unit evacuated 5,300 patients to Truk. A survey showed 30 percent were wounded; the rest were ill of various diseases, including the incurable "Wewak disease." On 29 February 1944, 66 AA Battalion had 479 men on strength, but 99 were ill with fever, 21 had stomach problems, 22 suffered with lung problems; only 3 were wounded. A shipping medical unit recorded for the first week of April 1944 a total of 224 patients: 70 malaria, 12 beriberi, 31 stomach disorders, and 16 wounded; the remainder suffered from a collection of various other sicknesses. A malaria prevention unit formed under Maj. Rikuro Tomura, who reported that due to better antimalarial precautions and drugs, cases fell sharply to 9.7 percent in February 1944.

On 29 February 1944, MacArthur's forces invaded Los Negros Island in the Admiralties group, northeast of New Guinea. Ultra intercepts revealed that the Japanese command thought that further landings would be made on New Britain, New Ireland, and Hanover Island, and they moved units to defend selected probable landing areas. Other Ultra information revealed that the Japanese thought the next Allied landing on New Guinea would be at Hansa or Wewak, and forces were moved to those areas. With the Admiralties securely in Allied hands, Rabaul was effectively surrounded and neutralized, "left to wither on the vine," and MacArthur could turn his attention back to the move along the north coast of New Guinea and on to the Philippines.

There was disagreement within the Japanese staff levels. In his postwar interrogation, the senior staff officer of 25th Air Flotilla, Capt. Takashi Miyazaki, said that the opinion of the officers at Rabaul was that the Admiralties were more important than Green Island, but this was overruled by higher headquarters because Green Island was closer to Rabaul.

In discussions with air forces commander Gen. George Kenney, and with that vital knowledge from Ultra intercepts, it was decided to bypass Hansa Bay and Wewak and leap to Hollandia on about 15 April 1944. General MacArthur and Admiral Halsey agreed to use some of Halsey's carriers to support the Hollandia invasion. The Joint Chiefs of Staff in Washington approved and also directed that Hollandia be captured for use as a base for Admiral Halsey's invasion of Palau on 15 September and the projected invasion of Mindanao in the Philippines in mid-November.

The Japanese tried several times to gather a strike force to send against the invasion shipping off the Admiralties, but each time bad weather caused the attack to be postponed. These moves were detected by the Ultra system. An important indicator that some Japanese officers at higher command level at Wewak doubted the effectiveness of the available aircraft types was shown in a message to Tokyo, reported to Allied commanders in a decoded version, in which Wewak asked if Tokyo believed that the capacity and bomb load of Army aircraft were adequate to attack warships.

Tension obviously was high in some parts of the Japanese command, as one message in reference to the Admiralty landing contained a statement that said there was "no excuse for not having been able to smash them yet."

The increasing Japanese aircraft strength at Hollandia was reported frequently to MacArthur and Kenney. An intercepted message informed them that in February another five Sentai were to be sent to New Guinea to be used against the expected Allied landing at Madang, and later messages related the progress of this reinforcement with unit identities. On 24 January, 22 fighters and 82 bombers were counted at Hollandia; on 31 January, 34 fighters and 106 bombers; and on 13 February, 200 aircraft including 150 bombers. This concentration of bombers, not quickly used against Allied targets, was noted by Allied intelligence offices not provided with Ultra information but working from photoreconnaissance material. The weight of Japanese airpower had moved west, from the Bismarck Archipelago to a complex of five bases at Hollandia, Aitape, and Wakde. Wewak was slipping to secondary status, and Rabaul was defended less vigorously. Why the Japanese had gathered so many bombers but not used them was pondered by the intelligence staff, who thought that some of them could have been used as transports, or the bomber force was a mobile reserve, or the crews had not finished training. The "conclusion" of Intelligence Summary 692, 12–13 February, was "the probability is at least projected that air support operations within New Guinea proper are imminent."

Ultra intercepts confirmed the aerial photography results. Messages between Tokyo, Manila, Hollandia, and Wewak gave details of aircraft flights and destinations of the fighters and bombers throughout January and February 1944, and it was reported that Hollandia was to receive another 130 aircraft in March. The 4 Air Army had asked for an additional 50 fighters, 15 two-seat fighters (Nicks), and 15 heavy bombers.

Meanwhile, combat crews on both sides flew and fought. New pilots came and lived or died, hardly noticed until they established themselves as veterans. They fell to the enemy, were swallowed by weather, or dragged down by an immutable law of aeronautics. Outstanding men on both sides died over the seas and jungles of the theater. On 2 November 1943, B-25s and P-38s made the famous low-level attack on shipping in Rabaul harbor, and Maj. Ray Wilkins, CO 8th Attack Squadron, died on his eighty-second attack mission; on 9 November the respected Danny Roberts, CO 433rd Fighter Squadron, 475th Group, died in a collision with his wingman over Madang; and on 26 December Ed "Porky" Cragg, CO 80th Fighter Squadron, bailed out over New Britain and was never heard from again. On the Japanese side, in addition to the leaders already mentioned, on 21 December, Capt. Shogo Takeuchi of 68 Sentai, who claimed sixteen victories over New Guinea, died trying to land his shot-up Tony at Hansa; in February Lieutenant Takimiya, who claimed seventeen victories with 78 Sentai, died in a night landing accident at Wewak when his aircraft hit a fuel tanker. That month 5th Air Force claims for destruction of all types of Japanese aircraft, in the air and on the ground, were 199, including 102 fighters. In the Wewak area, claims were for 35-1-2.

The 5th Air Force was about to concentrate its power even more forcefully on Wewak again.

Tommy Lynch's Victory, Neel Kearby's Loss

On 5 March Captain Kuwabara, experienced leader of 77 Sentai, was over But with Lieutenant Miyamoto and Warrant Officer Mitoma. Two P-38s pounced and Kuwabara broke, but all three were hit, and Miyamoto went into the sea north of the airfield. Below, a Japanese writing in his diary about hunger saw the destruction of the Oscar, which did nothing to improve his morale. The P-38s were flown by leading American aces Tommy Lynch and Dick Bong, nineteen and twenty-four victories respectively.

Lynch fired at the rear-most Oscar (Miyamoto), and his first burst resulted in flames streaming back from the target, which fell on fire. The agile Oscars survived the next passes from the P-38s, and as the combat had lost height and another formation of Oscars was seen in the distance, Lynch called Bong to break off and they climbed to the cloud base at six thousand feet. They started to leave the area but turned back to make another pass. Lynch hit an Oscar in a head-on pass, and a piece of debris from the Nakajima hit Lynch's left engine cowling. After a few more passes, the P-38s broke off the action and flew back along the coast.

Lynch claimed one destroyed and one damaged, and Bong claimed one probable and one damaged. Miyamoto was Lynch's victory, and the other two Oscars were hit, as claimed by Bong, confirmed by Japanese records. Kuwabara claimed a P-38; none were lost.

On 6 March 78 Sentai recorded the loss of Lt. Mitsusada Asai, who had claimed seven victories, but because there were no claims by U.S. pilots that day, it could be that Lynch killed Asai in that head-on pass, in addition to Miyamoto.

This combat, well inside the Japanese-occupied area, demonstrated the effectiveness of the P-38 flown by two superior, experienced pilots against a greater number of enemy, right over an enemy base.

Neel Kearby, original commander of the 348th Fighter Group and leading P-47 ace in the theater, had almost tied with ranking theater ace Bong. News came in early afternoon of the latest claims by Lynch and Bong over the Wewak area. This spurred Kearby into taking his headquarters flight of Capt. Sam Blair and Capt. Bill Dunham to sweep Wewak. Kearby had twenty-one victories, Blair six, and Dunham seven. This was an expert flight of P-47 pilots with six months' experience in the theater.

At 1700, the P-47 flight saw four Lily bombers of 208 Sentai approaching Dagua from the sea. The P-47s dived from twenty-two thousand feet and caught the bombers as they were flying parallel to the strip at only five hundred feet. The P-47s engaged: Kearby, Dunham, and Blair attacked, and three bombers were shot down. But Kearby broke all his own rules; he pulled his P-47 around for a second pass, and one of five Oscars from 33 Sentai, an escort for the bombers, slid in behind him, scoring hits with 12.7 mm machine guns in the cockpit area of Kearby's fighter. It was fatal.

Dunham completed his own turn and saw the Oscar shooting at Kearby; he fired head-on and hit the Oscar in the engine and cockpit, and as they flashed past Dunham saw the cockpit canopy flick back from the Oscar before it crashed in the same area as the burning bombers. Dunham joined another P-47, and as they left the area he saw yet another aircraft burning at the opposite end of the strip to that where the bombers went down.

Japanese records show that four Lilys of 208 Sentai escorted by five Oscars were airborne and report the loss of three bombers. The 33 Sentai claimed two P-47s in the combat. No Japanese fighters were listed as lost or damaged, though Capt. Bill Dunham claimed the Oscar that hit Kearby after he saw the Japanese fighter explode and Blair saw a radial-engine aircraft crash at Dagua. This victory could be over Lieutenant Asai, rather than by Tommy Lynch.

On this date 33 Sentai requested five replacement Oscars, and a document captured at Hollandia lists these five aircraft, their factory numbers, engine numbers, and propeller numbers, as supplied to the Serita and Hirata formations of 33 Sentai. There is no record that any of these five were to replace losses in this combat.

It was thought that Kearby crashed below the combat, but postwar investigations showed he managed to fly 140 miles, trying for air bases at Gusap, Nadzab, or Marilinan. Natives of Pibu village told RAAF personnel in 1946 that they saw an aircraft falling on fire and the pilot bail out at low level. When they reached the spot, the pilot was dead of injuries inflicted when he hit the trees. After removing personal items, the natives buried him, but a Japanese patrol later took away these items. The RAAF search team found P-47 #222668 with fuselage number #72. Neel Kearby had been located.

Bill Dunham, later a fifteen-victory ace and commanding officer of the 460th Fighter Squadron, 348th Fighter Group, wrote about his experiences in the SWPA, as did other experienced fighter leaders. He said that the height advantage must be attained before an attack, speed must be kept above 250 mph, and the minimum altitude in combat should be five thousand feet to allow the P-47's diving speed to be used. Dunham emphasized, "It is imperative that no turn greater than 90 degrees be attempted before breaking off the attack."

Bill Banks, when deputy commander of the 348th, with nine victories, also contributed to the collection of experiences. Banks included the same points as Dunham: maintain high speed, keep a minimum altitude of six thousand feet, never turn more than 180 degrees with a Japanese fighter, and never fail to retain at least a two-plane element in combat.

Bob Rowland had been deputy commander of the 348th and assumed command when Kearby went to 5th Air Force headquarters on 12 November 1943. Rowland had claimed eight victories up to 27 February and later submitted his combat principles with the other commanders in the 5th. Rowland also emphasized the use of speed and height and specifically warned against fighting the Japanese when the agility of the enemy fighters could be used against the P-47: "Any attempt to turn and fight him close in is throwing away the best qualities of your ship and allowing him to use the superior qualities of his." Rowland then put in capital letters, "Almost all of our combat losses have been due to pilots becoming overeager and forgetting this most important point."

Neel Kearby joined the long list of fighter aces who broke the rules by which they had flown successfully, with fatal results. Others include Baron von Richthofen in April 1918, who broke his own rules for combat, chased an enemy at low level over the front lines, and was shot down by Australian ground fire (though the British and the RAF refuse to accept the well-established facts and claim the Baron as an aerial victory); Tommy McGuire in January 1945, who, with two almost-full underwing tanks, tried to turn with a Japanese fighter at low level, stalled, and went into the trees; and George Davis, who—with seven victories in the SWPA and after a string of fourteen more in Korea—was shot down by a third Chinese MiG pilot after Davis downed two others.

Sometimes, when the situation was in their favor, the Japanese enjoyed some success. On 8 March 1944, 33 Sentai engaged fourteen unescorted B-24s. The allocated U.S. fighter escort had been prevented from taking off when the runway was blocked by the takeoff crash of the lead B-24 of the 90th Group. The fighters were held back for some forty minutes. The B-24s' primary target was Dagua, but the weather precluded an attack and the secondary target at Hansa was selected. Captain Doi combined with Lieutenants Shigemura and Koraki to shoot one B-24 down, and Lieutenant Ueki, 63 Sentai, claimed two with air-to-air bombing. Five other B-24s were claimed with air-to-air bombing. The fighter passes continued for some thirty minutes, well into the return flight.

Some of these B-24s were from the U.S. 380th Bomb Group, which usually operated out of bases around Darwin, Australia, against shipping and targets in the Netherlands East Indies (Indonesia). They had moved to New Guinea to boost the sortie rate of the 43rd and 90th Groups. On this day the 380th and Jolly Roger 90th formations were heavily engaged among thick clouds, and bomber crews reported the Japanese pilots as aggressive and eager but poor shots, although all U.S. squadrons suffered damage. The 380th's 529th Squadron flight of Jennings, Dow, and Blake became separated from the main formation, and for the Jennings crew time ran out on their twenty-fifth mission. With two engines on fire, the B-24 went down, and crew members who parachuted were machine-gunned by the exuberant Japanese. None of the B-24 crew survived. The next day, having lost two other crews in flying accidents, the 380th returned to their usual stomping grounds in the west.

The Japanese were quite impressed with the seeming effectiveness of the new air-to-air bomb, and in a radio message from Wewak to higher headquarters, reported that thirty-eight fighters intercepted the bombers and claimed a total of eight enemy, for the loss of one. The Japanese reported that the B-24s "were thrown into extreme confusion, their formation was broken, they dropped their bombs into the jungle, and they withdrew."

The single Japanese loss, confirmed in their reports, was claimed by Capt. Arland Stanton, 7th Fighter Squadron: an Oscar, twenty miles south-southwest of Wewak. The B-24 gunners claimed about twenty-five more, but in the prevailing conditions none were confirmed. Only one Japanese fighter is mentioned as lost in both captured documents and radio intercepts.

This interception on 8 March was the first combat mission over New Guinea for Sgt. Maj. Harumi Takemori, 2 Chutai 33 Sentai. On arrival at But that morning, he saw three aircraft that had been destroyed in night raids. At 1100 he took off to engage the B-24s with air-to-air bombing. In his excitement he forgot to arm the bombs, which fell harmlessly past the Liberators. He returned to But and landed. Later he was disturbed to find there were only five maintenance men for the entire Chutai.

Tommy Lynch Lost

On 9 March 1944, the great Tommy Lynch died. He and Dick Bong had been successful in the Tadji area, so they set off to sweep the location again. The 78 Sentai sent two Tonys to intercept but did not make contact. The P-38s strafed three luggers offshore and sank *Yashima Maru*, with the captain and one other man killed and three wounded. The P-38s turned for another pass at twenty feet height.

Unknown to Bong and Lynch, a forty-five-man detachment of the Japanese navy's 90 Garrison Unit, commanded by Warrant Officer Hideo Ezawa, was onshore, equipped with two light 7.7 mm and three heavy 13 mm machine guns, with 7,000 rounds of ammunition. Some of the unit personnel had only just arrived in New Guinea from Formosa, arrived at Palau on 20 February, and went on to Tadji. They fired at Lynch and Bong, and Bong later reported that on Lynch's P-38, "the entire nose section [was] blown off and starboard engine on fire." Lynch pulled up to twenty-five hundred feet to bail out, but did not get out until the P-38 was down to one hundred feet; the fighter exploded, and simultaneously Lynch's parachute streamed but did not have time to open. Leading Seaman Amano was credited with the victory, but the Japanese merely claimed a P-38, never knowing they had shot down one of the greatest fighter leaders in the SWPA. Tommy Lynch joined the long list of superior pilots brought down by ground fire.

The Japanese navy gunners shot well and almost downed two leading aces, because Bong had to feather one engine to return to base, and his crew chief at Nadzab found eighty-seven bullet holes in the P-38. The loss of Lynch was the only time the ground crew saw Dick Bong show any signs of nervousness. Bong did say that Lynch's death was the hardest blow he suffered in the war.

The Allied air forces could absorb the loss of such experienced leaders as Roberts, Cragg, Kearby, and Lynch, but the Japanese could not replace their own fighter and bomber leaders. The second great hammering of Japanese air forces at Wewak was about to begin. The U.S. Army 5th Air Force was to demonstrate its superiority once more.

Theater commander: Gen. Douglas MacArthur. *Beryl Stevenson*

Air commander Gen. George C. Kenney, commander Allied Air Forces SWPA. *Beryl Stevenson*

U.S. B-24 crew. The Hallett crew, 321st Squadron, 90th Bomb Group. Back row, l. to r.: Bob Hallett, pilot; Al Cerone, co-pilot; Lee Minor, navigator; Sandy Ophner, bombardier; Lem Gibson, engineer; front row, l. to r., gunners and radio: Howard Ostler, nose; Jesse Miller, radio; Junior Oakley, right waist; John Bitner, left waist; C. E. James, tail. *Bob Hallett*

B-25 strafer "Star Dust," 405th Squadron, 38th Bomb Group, en route to Wewak, August 1943. *USAAF*

Targets: Dagua under B-25 attack. Oscars and a Helen are lined up and the wreckage of three Lilys is to the left. *USAAF*

Air commander Gen. George C. Kenney, left, returns a salute from Maj. Ralph Cheli. At Dagua, Cheli won the Congressional Medal of Honor, 18 August 1943. *USAAF*

Australian liaison officer Capt. John Massie, who flew more than 40 combat missions with the 38th Bomb Group, accompanied Ralph Cheli on the 18 August mission to Dagua. *Massie family*

The unglamorous, sturdy workhorse C-47, "Boozy Lou," of 374th Troop Carrier Group.
USAAF

"Jock" Henebry, right, receiving his rank emblems from Gen. George C. Kenney.
Henebry was, perhaps, the outstanding attack pilot of the theater, with 219 combat missions. He rose from squadron pilot to commander of 3rd Attack Group and later was
commander of the Combat Crew Replacement Training Center. *Beryl Stevenson*

A rising star. The P-38 of Tommy McGuire, with seven victories marked, receiving attention from men of the 482nd Service Squadron, left to right, Corporal Norilla, Sgt. Cy Stafford, Vince Coffman, and Albert Lee. All seven of McGuire's victories pictured here were claimed during the August 1943 missions to Wewak. *Stafford*

P-38 ace. Capt. C. M. "Corky" Smith, 11-victory ace with the 80th Fighter Squadron "Headhunters." Two of his victories were claimed over Hollandia. *C. M. Smith*

P-47 leader. Ralph Wandrey flew the Wewak and Hollandia missions in both the P-38 and the P-47, and on 19 March 1944 single-handedly attacked a Japanese fighter unit, but his gun-camera failed and he had no record of his success. He later commanded the 9th Fighter Squadron. *Wandrey*

Combat photographer John Shemylence, with the 3rd Attack Group, flew 46 low-level missions. *Shemylence*

Longer legs for P-38s. Extra fuel tanks were installed in the P-38s in a major modification performed in the field, to allow the fighters to escort bombers to Hollandia. Here members of the 482nd Service Squadron work on an airplane of the 433rd Squadron. *via Bruce Hoy*

Australian B-24 crew. The first RAAF crews to operate the B-24 flew some missions with the 43rd Bomb Group to gain combat experience on the airplane before forming Australian squadrons. The first such crew is, back row, l. to r., gunners and engineer: L. G. Bradley, Monty Oakes, Arch Wallis, Noel E. Cochrane, Ken P. Gilicat; front row, l. to r., co-pilot, gunner, pilot, navigator, and bombardier: Keith Chapman, A. H. Smith, John B. Hampshire, Lloyd A. Morris, Robert A. Gilder. Hampshire was on his third combat tour. *Hampshire*

"Pistol Pete" at Hansa Bay. This Japanese Type 88 75 mm antiaircraft gun and crew were well known to Allied airmen operating in the area. Victory markings can be seen on the barrel. An Australian soldier, Corp. R. Currell, examines it after capture. *RAAF*

But under the B-24s. Twin-engined Lily bombers shown would fit into the craters of the bombs dropped by the B-24s. *USAAF*

"Listen Here, Tojo," a well-known B-17 of the 43rd Bomb Group. *USAAF*

Massacre at Hollandia. 1135 3 April 1944. The 90th Attack Squadron starts more fires among the parked Japanese aircraft. A burned-out Dinah of 10 Sentai is below. *USAAF*

Hollandia, 1135. A fireball erupts behind the 3rd Attack as the A-20s speed over. The "Tony" in the foreground had crash-landed off the edge of the runway, earlier, left its propellor behind as it slid along, and burned. Several U.S. fighter combat reports described similar incidents and this could be one U.S. air victory. *USAAF*

Victim of Hollandia. B-24 #42-40077 "Yankee Doodle Dandy," 319th Squadron, 90th Bomb Group, on its 102nd combat mission, was shot down on 12 April 1944. The crew of Lt. Bernard Donohue was killed. *Jim Alexander*

Hollandia aftermath. Battered Oscars of 63 Sentai pushed aside into the palms. *RAAF*

The distinctive shark's mouth marking on the 39th Fighter Squadron P-38. *USAAF*

Wewak, 15 March 1944. A B-24 of the 64th Squadron, 43rd Bomb Group, passes over the target. *USAAF*

Boram under the 500th Squadron, 345th Bomb Group. A fuel dump burns at center. *USAAF*

Wewak. The collection of wrecks at Wewak, with the runway at top right. Visible are examples of almost every type airplane used by the JAAF in New Guinea. *USAAF*

A preview of the ultimate doomsday at Dagua is this 5th Air Force minimum-altitude attack on a Japanese airstrip eight miles west of Wewak on 3 February 1944. The leading B-25, left, unloads parafrags on three Tonys, while other parafrags pepper the strip. At right, a B-25 cuts through dense smoke from a burning Helen. *National Archives*

Bombing of Humboldt Bay. *National Archives*

Bombing of Humboldt Bay. *National Archives*

Bombing of Hollandia. *National Archives*

An A-20 skip-bombing a freighter. Four splashes can be seen, two of the bombs having been dropped from the airplane in front, which is taking the picture, and the other two by the plane just clearing the ship. *National Archives*

FOUR

The Mincing Machine
Wewak—March 1944

Ultra information was the basis for the next and greatest leap forward by General MacArthur's forces. Inability to read many intercepted Japanese army messages had held back estimates of enemy strength and locations up to the end of January 1944, but the opportune breakthrough into Japanese army codes provided full detail of the Japanese military situation and their intentions. The plans of General Imamura at Rabaul and General Adachi in New Guinea were revealed.

The Japanese were going to hold Hansa, Madang, and Wewak in the belief that the next Allied landings would be at those places. Hollandia and the Admiralties were weakly held and poorly defended.

The accuracy and timeliness of Ultra information was proven when the Admiralties were taken quickly, and enemy strength was shown to be as reported in the signals intercepts.

MacArthur advanced his timetable, dropped the intention of landing at Hansa, and decided to go all the way to Hollandia. This was risky and would be the biggest operation of his command since the beginning of the war: eighty thousand men would move one thousand miles into enemy territory. With Ultra providing immediate information on the enemy, though, this was a chance to be seized and exploited.

The G-2 (Intelligence) branch of MacArthur's headquarters played a significant role in planning for these operations along the north coast of New Guinea and presented a plan for deception that was adopted. G-2 reports for February 1944, in addition to the Ultra material, showed that the Japanese were strengthening their bases at Hansa and Wewak, and as March began this was confirmed. On 1 March 1944, the G-3 (Operations) office produced an estimate of the situation, which concluded that because of recent Allied successes, the Allied forces available, and indications that the Japanese were strengthening west New Guinea, an opportunity for exploitation by the Allies was presented. It was therefore suggested that Allied planning should be guided by the principles of a speedy advance along the north coast of New Guinea, using aircraft carriers to support leaps of more than two hundred miles to the west; if no aircraft carriers were available, the frequency of the leaps should be increased.

On 7 March G-2 submitted a plan for deception to G-3, which intended strengthening the Japanese belief that the next Allied landing would be in the Madang-Hansa area. The G-2 deception plan involved frequent aerial reconnaissance over the Madang-Hansa area and a strong Allied feint into the area. It was intended that this would bring Japanese air units forward from their distant bases. If the feint was coordinated with the actual landing at Hollandia, and if the Japanese detected the convoy, then they would assume it was for the feint operation. The deception plan was adopted, and 5th Air Force intensified attacks on Madang and Wewak and made increased and conspicuous air reconnaissance. As part of the plan, navy operations were mounted against the area, PT boats were concentrated against parts of the coast near Hansa Bay, empty rubber boats used by scouting and intelligence teams were left for the Japanese to find, and parties of Allied Intelligence Bureau were moved openly toward the coast, making sure the natives saw them.

After the Allies captured Nadzab in September 1943, another enormous construction effort provided a complex of airstrips there with four runways, two of

5,000 feet and two of 6,000 feet. In addition, there were taxiways, hardstands, camps, and squadron areas provided. However, the 450 miles from Allied fighter bases at Gusap and Nadzab to Hollandia presented problems for fighter escort, and General Kenney had only one fighter aircraft type that could fly that far and return: the twin-engine Lockheed P-38. Its range was 350 miles, but new models with extra tanks in the leading edge of the wings and droppable external tanks could stride out to 650 miles. Thirty-seven of the new P-38s had arrived, the Townsville Air Depot modified fifty-six more, and a special program by Maj. J. J. Summers's 482nd Service Squadron modified another thirty-seven P-38s at Nadzab.

M.Sgt. Cy Stafford, of the 482nd, was a very experienced NCO. He arrived in Australia at the height of the Allied retreat in the SWPA and went to New Guinea in July 1942 when trained enlisted men of the maintenance units were worth their weight in gold to the Allies, and in fact had a higher priority on the evacuation schedule—if the Japanese reached Port Moresby—than the lieutenants. Cy recalled of the P-38 modification effort:

We had planes all over the place waiting to be repaired, but we got hit with an order that about bowled us over. They were going to put fuel cells in the leading edge of the wings of 125 P-38s to make them a plane for longer flights. The maintenance officer told them that we were going to need some help, plus the outfits the planes belonged to would have to bring them in, plus be responsible for getting the planes back to their squadrons. One of our officers was in charge in case there was any friction with men from the other squadrons who were to come and help. Work was to be in two shifts—1600 to midnight and midnight to 0700, so the planes could be brought in and taken out in daylight. There were 147 screws in the leading edge of each wing, and some would have to be removed by hand screwdrivers. We were still going to do other repair work in our area during the day.

Generators and air compressors were brought in, along with a forklift. The leading edge of the wing was marked, removed, placed out of the way where a crew put in the rubber tank, and the other leading edge removed. We ran into a problem trying to hold it while refitting it to the wing. It was nearly impossible to hold it by manpower exactly in place to get the screws begun reseating. So, boards were placed on the forklift and nailed together to make a platform, then sandbags placed on it so as not to damage the leading edge while the forklift jammed it into place and held it while the screws were installed. Our men supervised each phase of the job. Then the plane was moved to the next place where the fuel lines were connected, tanks filled and checked for leaks, and if everything was found to be okay, it was cowled-up and returned to its unit. It took about three weeks to get that modification done, and we were glad when it was finished.

RHIP: Rank Has Its Privileges

One problem that annoyed the line crews was that flight crews would not assist with work on the aircraft but stood about and watched. A B-17 going back to Australia needed fuel tanks installed in the bomb bay at Port Moresby. Because all available men were busy, Sergeant Norilla of the 482nd Service Squadron was sent to the B-17 to tell the flight crew that work would begin on it as soon as possible, but at the moment everyone was busy. Asked on return to the squadron headquarters if the B-17 crew made a fuss, Norilla smiled and replied that there was no problem because they installed the tanks under his supervision. People wondered about the secret of getting flight crews to actually work. A few nights later, Norilla did it again. But the next night, Major Elliott drove up and told Sgt. Cy Stafford that he had heard that an enlisted man was impersonating an officer and asked if Norilla knew anything about it. Norilla put on an innocent look and said he had not heard about it; who would be that stupid? He agreed to inform Elliott if he did hear anything, and the major drove off. Norilla looked at Cy, grinned, pulled a set of captain's bars out of his pocket, and threw them away, saying, "I have got about all I can out of them anyway. I just threw a little rank around and got some of the crews busy who would never help one iota with anything to be done to the airplane!"

The air strike force assembled for the campaign against Hollandia was a balanced grouping of heavy, medium, and fighter aircraft: 113 B-24s, 300 B-25s and A-20s, and 106 P-38s.

Some B-24 crewmen were Australians. The Royal Australian Air Force (RAAF) operated four-engine heavy-bomber squadrons in England and the Mediterranean theater since 1942, many RAAF airmen flew as individuals with British squadrons against Germany, and many Australians flew Liberators in the antisubmarine campaign in the Atlantic. For some time the RAAF had wanted four-engine bombers in its Pacific squadrons to allow them to take part in the heavy-bomber campaign there. General Kenney arranged for B-24s to be made available.

In comparison with modern high-technology air forces and currently accepted "lead times," it might be of interest to recall the way things were done at the height of a war. The RAAF needed B-24 crews before the aircraft arrived. The first experienced Aussie pilot nominated to train on the B-24 in Australia was Wing Commander (Lt. Col.) John Hampshire. He had flown extensively in the SWPA, had been at Rabaul when the Japanese attacked, and had continued against them for two combat tours. In mid-November 1943 he was attending a unit commander's course in Victoria when he was pulled out and told he was to be captain of one of the first five Australian B-24 crews at Townsville. Then began an odyssey up the east coast of Australia. Everyone knew about these B-24s, but no one had any definite information; it might be at the next place north. The RAAF commander in Port Moresby suggested going to Gen. "Big Jim" Davies, commanding V Bomber Command, and added it might be a good idea to bring any scotch Hampshire had brought up from Australia. So, with two bottles, they went to see Davies. He had heard of RAAF B-24s but knew nothing more. Hampshire told him the crews would assemble at Townsville, and Davies replied that U.S. B-24 training in-theater was done at Charters Towers, one hundred miles west of there. The scotch flowed. Davies said he would tell the U.S. commander at Charters Towers to put the RAAF crews through the B-24 training course, and paperwork could sort itself out later. Hampshire went to Charters Towers, and the Aussie crews commenced training. There was no official deal for this below government level, and the arrangement was made at a cost of two bottles of scotch.

Hampshire had twenty minutes dual instruction before his first takeoff as an aircraft captain. The Aussies at Charters Towers were trained like any other member of a crew. Training lasted from 29 December 1943 to 27 January 1944, and then the five crews went to the 65th Squadron, 43rd Bomb Group. Later RAAF B-24 crews trained in New Guinea, and then RAAF B-24 crew training was by the 380th Bomb Group, in the Darwin area, until RAAF schools were established in southern Australia. Hampshire's first combat mission was 14 February, to Kavieng, New Ireland. He flew eleven missions with the 65th and then went to command the first Australian B-24th squadron, 24th Squadron. Hampshire recalled that the Aussies were "entirely integrated with the 65th. They [the 65th] were wonderful people, and I have the highest regard for them. There were no RAAF crews as such." The Australians liked the B-24, and it compared well with other bombers they flew in the SWPA.

Americans also were converting to the B-24. The "Red Raiders" 22nd Bomb Group had flown B-26s and B-25s from April 1942, but as more heavy bombers became available, General Kenney phased out the B-26, so the 22nd became his fourth B-24 group. Those who had flown the B-26 through the hard times had deep feelings for it, and many regretted its end. Roy Parker "can clearly see the line of mighty machines on the tarmac at Amberley (west of Brisbane). We had flown them down from New Guinea to the RAAF base, where they were to be cut up for much-needed aluminum." Parker went to Charters Towers and after ten hours of flying was a B-24 captain. He flew back to Nadzab in an arrangement that later seemed to make sense: he did not know the aircraft but did know combat, while the copilot had gone through operational training in the United States and knew the B-24 but had no combat time. By March 1944 Roy Parker felt "a bit more familiar with the aircraft, but nothing could really take the place of formal training." His confidence was increased by the quality of the B-24, added to the high standard of maintenance and engineering support from ground personnel. Parker believed quality equipment was a major contributor to the defeat of Japan.

The Red Raiders made their return to combat in the B-24 on 10 March with a two-squadron strike against Lorengau in the Admiralties. Bad weather between Nadzab and the target broke up the formations, but those that got through did bomb the assigned areas.

The Allied air forces began a masterfully orchestrated series of operations that perfectly complemented overall Allied activities in the South West Pacific. In the past the Japanese had shown that they were slow to react to setbacks, and the invasion of the Admiralties on 29 February 1944 again demonstrated that weakness. It was forty-eight hours after the landing before Japanese aircraft appeared, and Allied air cover was superior anyway. Distance and weather made it difficult for Japanese aircraft to operate effectively over the Admiralties, except from New Guinea fields such as Nubia and Alexishafen. Allied fighters were eager to engage them, and if more Japanese aircraft moved forward from Hollandia, so much the better.

Special intelligence bulletins included information on Japanese aircraft serviceability numbers. On average for the week to 7 March, the JAAF had available

73 serviceable bombers and 55 fighters in New Guinea for a total of 128, and another 75 at Manila. As Japanese ground forces deployed forward to repel an Allied landing at Hansa, Madang, or Wewak, so too had 4 Air Army moved flying units; they crammed the airfields and provided the targets General Kenney wanted. The signals intercepts showed that as of 5 March, Manila held a total of 81 aircraft.

Unknown to almost all in the Japanese high command and discovered by U.S. investigators after the war, Rear Adm. Soichi Takagi of the Japanese Imperial Navy general staff in September had commenced a study of the battle lessons of the war. He completed the study in February and presented his report in March. Rear Admiral Takagi presented his findings verbally to Admiral Yonai, an Imperial councillor, and Rear Admiral Inouye, commander 4th Fleet. Takagi had arrived at the conclusion that Japan would lose the war unless some moves toward peace were made soon. But any such move, or even any such statement, had to be made with the very real prospect of assassination by the army and navy fanatics who had brought Japan into the war.

11 March

Starting on 11 March, Kenney unleashed a concentrated series of attacks on the But-Boram-Dagua-Wewak areas, increasing the pressure that had been on these same targets since August 1943. To begin the offensive, Boram was to be hit by eighteen B-24s, nineteen B-25s, and forty-eight A-20s. The B-24s and strafers went for the old targets while the escort fighters searched for Japanese defenders. The antiaircraft defenses were well practiced by now, and the Jolly Rogers 400th Squadron reported the flak as "terrific, unbearable, solid black." Two bombers were damaged as they dropped their 1,000-pound bombs on the searchlight and antiaircraft positions on Cape Boram. A Japanese report stated that eighty-nine men were killed or wounded in the antiaircraft artillery position.

The Red Raiders 22nd Group followed the Jolly Rogers, but only the 33rd Squadron hit Boram, and the 19th bombed Alexishafen and Hansa. As the 33rd approached their bomb run, Japanese fighters made head-on attacks, and the top turret gunner in the lead B-24 claimed hits on one, seen smoking and spinning. Crews reported a total of about eighty passes from the fighters, and two victories were credited to gunners. The bombs went down on antiaircraft positions on Cape Moem, but with intense antiaircraft fire exploding around them, and fighter attacks speeding past, bombing accuracy was not reported.

As in the big August attacks, these missions gave fighter pilots opportunities to score. The 41st Fighter Squadron escorted the 400th and 321st Bomb Squadrons, engaged twelve Tonys and Oscars, and claimed 6-2-0. The Japanese were in no apparent formation; some were line abreast, and six were in elements of two. Then, when one attacked, they all turned in. Japanese tactics were steep turns to left or right, half rolls, dives, split-s'es, fast chandelles, and slow rolls. Below, on the airfields, more were seen taking off, and it was assumed these were decoys to bring the American escorts down so that higher Japanese could gain a height advantage. Given the lack of communication and coordination among the Japanese, however, the later takeoffs possibly were pilots who wanted to get into the fight or others who were removing aircraft from the target area.

The U.S. pilots reported that, with two exceptions, the Japanese were "experienced and very aggressive, the best encountered in combat so far. They pushed their attacks closely and exploited brilliantly executed maneuvers." However, the Japanese failed to score, primarily because they were too dispersed.

The 348th Fighter Group's 340th Squadron launched its P-47s for what was to be a major day in the life of the unit. The Thunderbolts fought a fifteen-minute combat with the agile Japanese, and at the end of the day claimed fourteen victories; only three P-47s were damaged. Maj. Harvey Carpenter led the squadron and shot down two Japanese but was hit in the fighting and made a wheels-up landing at Saidor.

Capt. William Chase led Yellow Flight and took the P-47s in a diving attack on a formation of Oscars. Chase picked one Japanese and gave him a long burst, saw smoke come from the Nakajima fighter, and then "pulled up to 7,000 feet and saw the Oscar smoking badly in a shallow dive onto a small island off But strip, where he crashed and burst into flames."

Blue Flight was led by Lt. Richard Fleisher, who shot down two Oscars. One pilot bailed out but no parachute opened, and the second Oscar went into the water west of Kairiru Island.

Climbing to engage the first waves of U.S. bombers, Sergeant Major Takemori's oxygen failed, and he swung back and down to land at But along with Fukusu and Sugiura. They refueled and went to Hollandia. Lt. Myron

Hnatio, 340th Squadron, engaged a six-plane formation and became an ace with his fifth kill:

> When first observed they were coming from the west, circling to the north. They were brown, with greenish-gray bellies. They had what appeared to be red feathers painted on the top of the wings. We dropped our tanks and the Zekes (*author:* They were actually Oscars) made a frontal attack from 30 degrees, then a tight diving turn to the right. I came on one from 30 degrees astern and observed my tracers falling low. I pulled into a tighter turn and saw my tracers hitting his engine. I came in dead astern, firing all the way. He started smoking, rolled over, and crashed into the sea two miles off But airdrome.

The end of this Oscar was confirmed by Lt. William Carter. Hnatio also described markings visible on some of the enemy, which identified 77 Sentai. Lloyd Zaage broke off the combat due to low fuel and settled into a return flight at four thousand feet. He did not check behind. Bullets began to strike the P-47; Zaage dived left, but his engine was running very rough. He trimmed the Thunderbolt at sea level and then saw what he recalled as a "black" Tony slide up onto his wing. The Japanese slid in behind Zaage and fired the rest of his ammunition. Zaage could only sit there and feel the hits on the P-47. Ammunition gone, the Japanese turned away. Zaage landed at Saidor almost out of fuel.

At 1300, three minutes after the first wave, B-24s of the Jolly Rogers 320th Squadron aimed thirty-two 1,000-pounders at six antiaircraft positions at Boram. Some aircraft could not get a clear run because of clouds, so they bombed Hansa on the return flight. But here, unfortunately, accurate Japanese antiaircraft fire hit "Heaven Can Wait," and the B-24 went down on fire into the sea. Three crew jumped, but no parachutes were observed; Tennyson's crew was gone. At 1330, nineteen B-25s of the Sunsetters 38th Bomb Group, covered by their old friends in the 9th Fighter Squadron, came across the target, put fifty 500-pounders and nine 500-pound aerial burst bombs into Boram, and left 75 percent of the area covered with explosions and fires. Karl Foster, in B-25 #220, noted in his diary that the fighter escort of two squadrons of P-47s was not met at Annenberg, as expected, and the B-25 squadron approached the target at ten thousand feet, over scattered cloud. The 405th Squadron, leading the formation, overshot and came out over Wewak Point into considerable antiaircraft fire. The B-25s made a 360-degree turn to the right, came back into the antiaircraft fire, bombed, and made "a very fast diving turn to the left out over the mountains." The second flight of the 71st Squadron did not follow into the bomb run but dropped their bombs into the sea. Two Japanese fighters attacked, putting a one-foot hole in the flight leader's starboard wing.

Ten minutes later, forty A-20s of the Grim Reapers 3rd Attack Group and the 386th Bomb Squadron, 312th Group, followed and dropped 184 500-pounders into the chaos. Three A-20s were damaged by accurate antiaircraft fire. By the fortunes of war, some bombs from one of these attacks fell on and near compounds holding civilian and military prisoners, apparently killing them all. The Japanese 41 Mountain Artillery Regiment were witnesses and later were told no one survived. A soldier in 13 Airfield Survey Construction Unit who saw the attack estimated that 350 planes took part and thought he saw two B-25s destroyed by bomb explosions from the previous wave.

The 40th Fighter Squadron saw Japanese fighters in the traffic pattern over But and dived on them. One P-47 got out of control in the high-speed descent and flew into the water three miles off the strip; three others were damaged by antiaircraft fire.

Returning from Hollandia after earlier oxygen failure, Sergeant Major Takemori joined three fighters of 77 Sentai, and they claimed a P-47. He noted in his diary that two men of 77 Sentai were wounded. Another captured Japanese document states 33 Sentai claimed five P-47s destroyed and one probable for two Oscars damaged. Maj. Yoshio Kuwabara, 77 Sentai, who narrowly escaped Tommy Lynch and Dick Bong on 5 March, claimed a P-47 destroyed. His unit claimed four enemy destroyed for ten of its own aircraft damaged, six on the first mission and four on the second. The 63 Sentai lost Lt. Takeshi Hamasuna and Sgt. Hajime Watabe. Other Japanese documents give conflicting figures of claimed victories and admitted losses, but one report listed damage by unit:

33 Sentai		2 damaged
3 Sentai	1 destroyed,	4 damaged
68 Sentai	1 destroyed	
77 Sentai		3 damaged
78 Sentai	2 destroyed,	4 damaged
Total	4 destroyed,	13 damaged

This document also details losses by aircraft type: three Tonys and an Oscar destroyed, as well as eight Tonys and five Oscars damaged. In another report

77 Sentai recorded ten damaged in two interceptions, and independently, one unidentified Japanese diarist watched four fighters shot down by P-38s; only one parachute appeared.

A separate Japanese intelligence report stated that five Tonys were lost and one damaged, and an Oscar was destroyed plus one more damaged. Yet another report states seven Tonys and two Oscars were lost with four pilots escaping by parachute. Japanese radio broadcasts reported that the 130 raiders were "hotly engaged" by Japanese army fliers who shot down twenty-six.

The 4 Air Army reported the events: "Between 1050 and 1140 a combined force of 130 fighters and bombers attacked the Wewak and But areas. Brought down in air combat: two B-24s and 16 P-47s. Brought down by AA: two B-24s (unconfirmed), two B-25s, four A-20s. Losses: Type 3 fighters—six badly damaged or burned, one not yet returned, pilots of four escaped by parachute; Type 1 fighters—one badly damaged, one not yet returned." Separately, however, 4 Air Army reported that 63 and 248 Sentai were reduced to a total of eleven Oscars, and 68 and 78 Sentai had only seventeen Tonys available on this date.

Allied air forces headquarters compiled Intelligence Summary 190:

The aerodrome area was bombed (120 tons) successfully in adverse weather. The target was left covered with a heavy blanket of smoke. Enemy fighters came up in force and intercepted our planes vigorously and almost continuously for almost two hours after engaging P-47s on the latter's sweep preparatory to the raid. In all, twenty-six enemy fighters were destroyed and six probably destroyed. One B-24 was lost and several were damaged by antiaircraft.

Total USAAF fighter claims were for 23-0-1, with combat reported over the entire area. The 40th Fighter Squadron claimed three destroyed and one damaged, the 41st claimed six destroyed, and the 340th claimed fourteen destroyed. It was the most intense day of action for more than a month. Robert Yeager of the 40th and Richard Fleischer of the 340th also became aces, and Edward Hoyt of the 41st scored the first of five victories.

12 March 1944

The heavies and strafers returned to deny the Japanese time to repair and recover. Japanese at Alexishafen reported the B-24s passing toward Wewak, and 63, 68, and 78 Sentai took off. When more B-24s were reported, 33 and 77 Sentai launched.

At 1030 fifteen B-24s of the Jolly Rogers Group 320th, 321st, and 400th Squadrons attacked antiaircraft positions at Boram. Flak was reported as intense and accurate, building to a barrage. Bombing results were described as "excellent, the target covered with explosions and smoke to 2,000 feet." Eighty thousand pounds of 1,000-pound demolition and 2,000-pound aerial burst bombs battered the Japanese. The 320th's 2,000-pounders caused a large explosion with orange flames shooting high into the air over the target. Because of equipment malfunctions, the 400th Squadron's bombing was disrupted and bombs fell "near the target." The 22nd Bomb Group, the Red Raiders, flew their third mission with the B-24. The 22nd squadrons reported their attack as accurate, covered the target with sixty-four 1,000-pounders, and claimed the antiaircraft positions destroyed. Thirty minutes later more heavies from the same two groups attacked as the second wave. In the antiaircraft positions, forty-two men were reported killed and two antiaircraft guns destroyed.

Seven fighters of 77 Sentai engaged the first formations of B-24s twelve miles east of But. Japanese documents show that in the following combat, five of the seven were destroyed: Hashimoto returned with engine trouble; Fukushima, on fire, landed at Wewak; Capt. Yoshihide Matsuo and Lieutenant Fujii bailed out; and three pilots were killed—Mitoma, Taguchi, and Obayakawa. Mitoma had escaped Bong and Lynch a week earlier. Matsuo, 2 Chutai leader, was wounded and died with many other pilots in May on the overland trek to Sarmi. At dusk six operational aircraft remained for the Sentai, but claims were made for two P-47s and a P-40 destroyed, plus seven B-24s and two P-40s as probables.

Five Oscars of 2 Chutai 33 Sentai took off to engage the second formation of B-24s, but Sergeant Major Takemori, who flew to Hollandia with oxygen failure and claimed a share in a P-47 the day before, lost formation and did not engage. He returned to find the bombing left "a gruesome spectacle." Five men of 77 Sentai had been killed, and M.Sgt. Tatsuo Tomatsu of 1 Chutai 33 Sentai had been killed in combat. The Sentai claimed one B-26 and a P-47 for the loss of Tomatsu. Takemori also had a diary entry about the death of Tomatsu the day before.

A quarter of an hour later, fast twin-engine strafers came over the trees, pounding the same antiaircraft positions. Squadrons of the Grim Reapers 3rd Attack and 312th Bomb Groups placed their 500-pounders among the guns, stores dumps, and personnel areas at Boram and in Brandi Plantation. The antiaircraft gunners fought back: 2 Company 61 AA Battalion claimed 3-2-0 strafers for the loss of two men killed in action. Watching the action, Yoshio Yusuki, 54 Lines of Communication Unit, counted 150 enemy planes and thought he saw four shot down.

Twelve A-20s of the Grim Reapers 90th Squadron, led by Captain Rosebush, went for the south dispersal area of Boram strip. Twenty-eight of their thirty-two 500-pounders fell into the target area and fires were started, but damage could not be assessed. Leading the second flight of the 38th Group's 71st Squadron was Karl Foster, who dropped five 500-pounders with instantaneous fuses on Boram. He noted that the mission was identical to that of the previous day but with no fighter interceptions and no friendly losses despite flying through intense inaccurate antiaircraft fire.

The 4 Air Army reported by radio: "Because about 60 P-47s engaged in combat before the concentration of the main strength of the defenses had been completed, fighting was difficult and only a few planes attacked the enemy. As we had no "TA" shells, results were insufficient. A-20s were used at extremely low altitude and the strength of our AAMG against them was great. The enemy objectives are gradually changing to AA positions, and they carried out destructive attacks at frequent intervals."

The U.S. fighter escort of P-47s and P-40s engaged numerous Japanese fighters. Eighteen victories were awarded, five to the 7th Squadron, nine to the 8th, and four to the 41st. The U.S. pilots reported enemy crashed in many locations: three in the water off Boram, and one on land south of Boram strip. In addition, three Japanese parachuted, one fighter with a black engine cowl and fuselage stripe went down into a hillside at Ritter Bay, one more crashed four miles northeast of Brandi, and another fell one mile north of Cape Terebu.

Capt. Arland Stanton, 7th Squadron, claimed his seventh Japanese, an Oscar, ten miles southeast of Brandi Plantation. Stanton led the 7th in a pass onto a bunch of Oscars that were attacking the A-20s. In that single pass, Stanton and four other pilots—Ferris, O'Neill, Pollack, and Suggs—each claimed an Oscar destroyed. Three were seen to fall in flames into the trees and two into the bay.

The 7th pilots reported combats with the agile defending fighters in the following paragraphs:

I climbed towards two Oscars above Brandi Plantation. A P-40 dived on them and they dived. I pulled up on one, on the way down, and got a long burst into him before he turned inside me. I was so close to his tail that I observed the texture of the catwalks on the wings. Soon after one of the other P-40s shot the Oscar down in flames.

Approximately over Brandi Plantation we sighted enemy fighters ahead and below and dropped our belly tanks. One Oscar pulled up into our flight going in the opposite direction. I made a sharp right turn as he turned on my tail, fired in a diving turn but was unable to turn sharp enough, spun out, and headed for a cloud as he ended up on my tail.

We turned to the left and there were two Oscars. We followed them down into clouds, my element lost the first one but caught the second one. He had dived to the water and another P-40 was making a pass at him, both in a tight climbing turn to the left. The P-40 was obviously missing him, because I could see bullets hitting way behind the Oscar in the water. As he came climbing up off the water, I made a head-on pass. He kept on turning to the left; I continued turning and got in behind him as he leveled out, firing another good burst at him. He made a sharp turn to the left; I could not follow so pulled up and watched. He did a high-speed stall, dished out of the stall, and mushed into the water.

I jumped on the Nip's tail, firing a short burst, he did a tight turn to the right and I could not follow him, so pulled up. Two other P-40s made a pass, again he went into a sharp bank, which left me right on his tail. I started to fire again. We were right on top of the water and he started a turn to the left. I stayed with him and fired until his wingtip hit the water when he practically disintegrated.

The 8th Squadron met what they took to be a unit of inexperienced Oscar pilots who merely circled to avoid the U.S. attacks. The 8th came along above and behind the 7th Squadron and was well placed to hit the Oscars that survived the attack by the 7th. Eight more claims for destroyed Oscars were made by the 8th, including three by 1st Lt. Don Meuten, making him an ace.

Lt. Averette Lee, 8th Fighter Squadron, met a Japanese who might have been trying to maneuver him into the treetops: "I made a turn to slow down and turned onto the tail of an unknown type enemy fighter. I fired as I closed on him until we reached Cape Moem; he was on the water and pulled up sharply trying to run me into the trees. I was well back and it was easy to hold him in my sights. I kept firing until I reached the coast, and from fear of ack-ack I pulled up. Then I saw where he had hit in the middle of the peninsula."

Again, the agility of the Japanese fighters was noted by many P-40 pilots: "A P-40 attempting to attack an Oscar 500 feet below found the enemy turning with him every time he attempted to pull away for a pass. . . . Each attempt I made to turn so I could drop on his tail, he turned with me."

Headquarters Allied Air Forces SWPA Intsum 191 gave the attacks a brief paragraph: "Seventy-nine tons of bombs were dropped over Boram aerodrome and A/A positions. The target was blanketed and smoke covered the area. Eighteen enemy planes were shot down in air combat. Our losses were two."

In the target area, Japanese staff officers compiled Intelligence Report 127 to 4 Air Army headquarters, with claims that 47 fighters engaged 188 enemy, with 1 B-25 and 6 P-47s shot down by fighters, and 19 A-20s destroyed by antiaircraft. Losses admitted in this report were 6 Tonys destroyed and 2 damaged. Another Japanese report listed fighter losses as 1 destroyed from 33 Sentai, and 3 destroyed and 3 damaged from 77 Sentai— but neither operated Tonys. Yet another document included 6 Oscars destroyed. A decoded message listed 6 Oscars lost and 2 more returned with "heavy damage." Therefore, from several captured records with differing detail, at least 6 Tonys and 6 Oscars were destroyed in the air. Again, this is an example of the problems met when consulting Japanese records compiled in New Guinea at the time.

The Grim Reapers 90th Squadron lost four aircraft to the hostile flying conditions in the theater. Captain Rosebush and Lieutenant Ladd, who was on one engine, had to land at Gusap. Lieutenant Rutters continued on with Garlick, Short, and Trzaskowski, and it seemed that Garlick was in some sort of trouble. When the other three came out of cloud, Garlick had disappeared. With Garlick was Staff Sergeant Adams and a photographer from 3rd Attack headquarters, Sergeant Newcomb. Because the remaining three could not see the Markham valley, they became lost and flew clear across New Guinea. Short and Trzaskowski crash-landed in the water off the southern shore, and Rutters also was forced to crash-land in the Port Moresby area.

To the west, at Hollandia, the Japanese "Ikeda" arrived on this day and noted in his diary that "only half the aircraft are operational."

Tokyo radio, broadcasting for the home islands, reported the attacks of the past two days:

This is what happened on the 11th and 12th of this month. Enemy bombers and fighters, numbering 130 planes, at 11 o'clock on the 11th, appeared over Wewak area, but were hotly engaged by our Army Air Force units and ground fire. Twenty-six planes were instantly brought down. At 9 o'clock on the 12th, 190 enemy planes reappeared. This time, our AA units intercepted, and with support from our air units shot down twenty-six of them. On the two days, we lost six planes. Throughout the New Guinea area, from the 1st to the 12th of this month, about 850 enemy planes attacked. Of these enemy raiders, seventy-one were brought down and two others damaged, while in the whole period our losses were only six planes. While our losses are small, we nevertheless must strive further to increase our plane output in order to repay our frontline officers and men for their difficult fighting.

13 March 1944

Again the bombers returned to Wewak, but results were mixed. A force of forty-three B-24s, seventy-five B-25s and A-20s, and fifty P-47s and P-40s attacked targets around the Wewak area. Aerial burst bombs exploded across Wewak point: 34 2,000-pounders, 116 1,000-pounders, and 24 1,000-pound However, three of the Jolly Rogers 400th Squadron turned back with engine problems, and all the bombs of the other three aircraft that reached Wewak landed in the water. The leader of the first flight of the group's 320th Squadron had a bomb hang-up at the release point, so the flight's bombs dropped late and impacted five to ten miles inland; the bombs of the second flight hit the western side of the peninsula and in the water, causing no damage. Other B-24s attacked antiaircraft positions and Brandi Plantation. Fighters dodged the P-47 escort and attacked, but the claims were three destroyed by the B-24 gunners and several damaged.

Behind the heavies, much lower, B-25s and A-20s attacked Brandi with 137 500-pound bombs and machine guns, leaving smoke and fires in their wake. The 61 AA Battalion suffered many direct bomb hits in all unit gun positions, and twelve guns were put out of action. Five hundred rounds of antiaircraft ammunition were destroyed and four hundred drums of gasoline burned. The 4 Air Army reported, "Use of the airfields has almost stopped." Later, radio messages to higher headquarters reported that the headquarters of the Japanese navy's 9th Fleet and 2nd Special Base Force had been destroyed by bombing, and all documents were lost.

Because of the low flight level, high speed, smoke, and debris below and around them, observation during attacks was often very difficult, and crews could give only vague or general accounts of the target and results. The mission was described in AAF Intsum 191: "Brandi Plantation, A/A positions, and Wewak area were hit with 210 tons of bombs. The target area was covered with smoke from numerous fires and explosions. A/A was of all calibers and intensity, from accurate to inaccurate. Escorting fighters shot down eight enemy fighters of the heavy intercepting forces; one squadron engaging about thirty-five enemy fighters." The total available defending fighter force was forty-six aircraft, and forty-four took off, led by the commander 14 Flying Brigade (Hikodan), Col. Kenji Tokunaga. Combats erupted over the area.

Ralph Wandrey, 9th Squadron ace, had just managed to get his P-47 formation back together after an inconclusive mix with a number of Oscars when he heard a call on the radio, "There's a Zero on my tail—somebody get him off!" Wandrey looked around and saw five P-47s with enemy on their tails, and all the Japanese shooting at the Americans. He broke into the closest, forced the Japanese to leave the P-47, and heard the same American voice saying he was going straight down and was going to crash. In a calm voice, someone said, "Roger." Later Ralph found the pilot who rogered the distress call, asked why he said it, and got the reply: "The poor guy seemed to expect somebody to answer him, and that was all I could think of!"

Ralph had Lt. John Crowder on his wing; it was Crowder's first combat mission. In the engagement, Wandrey pulled up and there in front were two Oscars making a right-hand turn. He pulled in behind the leader and fired. Crowder was watching Wandrey, looked out ahead of his P-47, and, to his amazement, there was another Japanese plane directly in front! Crowder fired and hit it. The plane Wandrey hit dropped, fluttered—so he knew the pilot was hit—and went down into the sea.

The 9th Squadron attacked nine single-engine Japanese fighters, claiming 1-1-2. It was noticed that some Japanese did not release their wing tanks in combat, and this was reported. No one knew it was unlucky Sergeant Major Takemori of 33 Sentai, futilely heaving on the tank release lever while watching the Thunderbolts diving and climbing around him. His oxygen failed on 11 March, he lost formation on the twelfth, and on the thirteenth, he could not drop his tanks.

The 2 Chutai 33 Sentai had five Oscars airborne, Captain Senda leading Nakamura, Kumagai, Inagaki, and Sergeant Major Takemori. Due to "faulty communications" they took off late, so the Americans were higher; then Takemori's sight light failed and Murphy's Law came into force—he could not release his wing tanks. He left the area in company with another Oscar in the same predicament. All he could do to stay alive was turn as tightly as possible when diving passes were made by his enemies. M.Sgt. Joshu Kumagai was killed in the combat—Ralph Wandrey's victory—but Senda claimed 2-1-0 P-47s for the loss of Kumagai. It is believed that Kumagai shot down Neel Kearby.

At eight thousand feet southwest of Wewak, P-40s of the U.S. 7th Squadron hit five Oscars, assessed as "inexperienced." The P-40s saw the enemy first, then climbed while turning to reach a position to attack from above and behind. They dived, and the Oscars did not break until tracers were flicking past. Two escaped, but the other three were shot down. The combat report was reprinted in AAF Intsum 193:

> Of the three, one made a steep turn to the left, smoking heavily, and the pilot bailed out. Another pulled straight up with a P-40 on his tail firing steadily until he reached stalling point where the Oscar burst into flames and the pilot bailed. The third chandelled to the right, smoking, and the pilot bailed out.

It was thought the Japanese were returning from a previous combat and waiting to land, seeming to be "oblivious to all proceedings, taking no evasive action and seemingly intent only on getting back on the ground. The position and attack of the P-40s was well timed, placed, and executed. The position, timing, and action by the enemy was strictly cold turkey."

The Oscars were a formation of 63 Sentai preparing to land. Capt. Koji Takemura, the leader, was hit in the ankle by a .50-caliber round. His Oscar burst into flames; he parachuted and landed near a field hospital. His wingman, Corp. Takaaki Yamamoto, parachuted into the jungle and was not seen again. The unit record did not identify the third parachutist.

The 77 Sentai launched six fighters and claimed 1-1-0 B-24s for the loss of Sgt. Soichi Hashimoto. Hashimoto had returned to base with engine trouble the day before. The Japanese reported six fighters lost and four pilots parachuted.

The 4 Air Army was told 44 fighters intercepted 170 Allied aircraft and claimed 10-2-0 B-24s and fighters, while antiaircraft defenses claimed 1-2-0 bombers for a loss of 2 Oscars destroyed and 1 damaged. Another document put losses at one each "missing" from 33 and 63 Sentai and two "heavily damaged" from 63, but there was no reference to 77 Sentai.

Victories awarded to U.S. pilots were 5-1-2, almost a mirror image of the Japanese reports. Lt. Frederick Helterline of the 9th Squadron claimed a Tony "probable," which could well be one of those admitted destroyed. The confirmed victories for the day were one to Ralph Wandrey, two to 49th Group headquarters pilots who flew with the 7th Squadron (Lt. Col. David A. Campbell, fourth victory, and Capt. Robert A. McDaris, second victory); one to Francis Dubisher, 41st Squadron, who became an ace; and one to Joel Paris, 7th Squadron, who shot down the first of his nine victories.

Back at the Allied fighter bases, there was a certain amount of acrimony caused by overenthusiastic P-47 pilots shooting at other P-47s and P-40s. Ralph Wandrey's Group CO, Col. David Campbell, had flown a P-40 and had almost been shot down by a P-47. When the angry colonel came barging into the room and asked if Wandrey had shot at him, Ralph told him seriously, "When I shoot at you, you won't be around to bitch about it later!"

The results of the air attacks were reported in a letter from Sergeant Haikawa of 14 Field Air Repair Depot to Sergeant Major Fujiyama in Hollandia.

Because of the daily raids, no work can be done in the morning. Because of the bombers at night, we cannot sleep. All the fighters are destroyed. Of three fighter Sentai, only eight planes are available to fly. The enemy comes in hundreds, in perfect formation, and drops numerous bombs. This happens every day. To make it worse, our AA guns have received direct hits, the HQ and living areas and workshops have been destroyed. Only the airplane motor workshop is still standing, and we work by improvization. The coconut palms are now craters.

Though the bombing is daily, no one is wounded.

The headquarters of 6 Flying Division was at Wewak, and Lieutenant Horie noted the events in his diary while posted there. On this day, he saw 150 enemy aircraft overhead and was told four B-24s, six P-47s, and a P-40 were shot down.

The valuable information from intercepted Japanese radio messages reported that the 21st Wewak Convoy was due into Hollandia on 16 March and Wewak on the eighteenth. The 5th Air Force had three to five days to prepare to deal with these ships. At South West Pacific Area GHQ, military intelligence staff covering the previous two days' actions stated in Intelligence Summary 721: "Enemy is not capable of defending strongly his entire salient or sustaining his effort over any important point within it. From the air standpoint, it is clear that the enemy is incapable of serious interference with Allied air operations."

Ultra intercepts revealed that on 5 March the Manila air depots held 81 airplanes for 4 Air Army with another 14 en route from Japan, and 23 already were on the way to Hollandia, for a total of 118 aircraft assigned to the New Guinea theater. However, on 13 March, only 18 aircraft of those remained held at Manila—in eight days, 100 had been sent to the forward areas in New Guinea.

14 March 1944

Despite their hammering by high-level bombing and strafers in earlier attacks, the Japanese antiaircraft defenses at Wewak still fired, so it was decided to target them again, but this time the B-24s were to deliver larger bombs against the gun positions. Twenty-one B-24s, fifteen B-25s, and forty-seven A-20s attacked targets in the Boram-Brandi area, while another seventeen B-24s went to Tadji. In addition to bombs, propaganda leaflets intended for the local native people were dropped. B-24s of the Red Raiders Group 19th Squadron and Jolly Rogers Group 319th, 320th, and 321st Squadrons in flights of three sailed over the now-familiar landscape and dropped 1,000- and 2,000-pound bombs. The 319th observed a line of seven 2,000-pounders at fifty-foot intervals across eight antiaircraft guns near the airfield dispersal. A 75 mm antiaircraft shell made a direct hit on the right wing of Capt. John Bird's "Glo-Hop," passed through it, and then passed through the fuselage above the right waist window and detonated about twenty feet farther in its flight. It was presumed the shell's fuse was on time-delay, not impact.

An estimated fifty Japanese fighters pounced as the 320th Squadron was on its bomb run, and closed to one hundred feet, but the bombers claimed 1-1-0. The Oscar destroyed came from the ten o'clock direction. The waist gunner of Capt. John W. Kline's crew hit him with a long burst, and although no visible damage was seen, other crews watched the fighter dive vertically into the water. Another coming in from one o'clock was hit; it began smoking heavily and went into a dive, seemingly out of control, but was not seen to crash. The 320th crews reported the enemy fighters as dull gray, silver, or greenish, and some light gray or cream colored with green bands across the wings. The Japanese attacks were made mostly from ahead and above but were not coordinated, although some turned to attack in close succession at the same angle. Crews of the Red Raiders 33rd Squadron saw a P-47 shoot one Oscar into the sea. The P-47s followed the Japanese fighters through the bomber formations and claimed 5-0-0 for loss of two and one damaged.

Capt. Yoshio Kuwabara led seven Oscars of 77 Sentai. Kuwabara was acknowledged as their best pilot, with more than fifteen hundred hours and twelve victories claimed in Burma, plus two P-47s claimed in the SWPA. From the times stated in the reports of the combatants, it was 77 Sentai that engaged the B-24s and the escorting 41st Fighter Squadron. One B-24 was claimed but Kuwabara, Corp. Shuhei Nagasaka, and Watanabe were killed* and Aoyanagi was wounded; all four fighters were destroyed; and Corporal Tamaguchi survived a forced landing at sea, making a loss total of five Oscars for the Sentai. Kuwabara was reportedly last seen in combat with P-38s, but no P-38s were claimed here this day. The 41st claimed five Oscars destroyed in the target area, matching the Japanese report, with two victories to Edward Hoyt and one each by Robert Johnson, Denby Noble, and Philip Walcott. The 41st lost two P-47s.

From But, Captain Senda again led the 33 Sentai Oscars, with Nakamura, Sugiura, Yamaguchi, Inagaki, Matsumoto, Oya, and Sergeant Major Takemori. They engaged P-47s and claimed three for the loss of Sergeant Matsumoto and Corporal Oya. Once again Takemori had oxygen and wing-tank problems and found that his Oscar could not climb. He looked up, and above was a formation of U.S. fighters. Carefully watching them for any sign that he had been seen, Takemori flew away toward Hollandia. He wondered if anything would go right. The U.S. fighters were very cautious about diving onto a single enemy fighter in the middle of the combat area, seeing the situation as a trap.

The U.S. 9th Fighter Squadron with sixteen P-47s engaged Oscars over Boram at the same time reported by 33 Sentai. The 9th reported their adversaries

---

* The author's source for this date as the death of Kuwabara is a decoded message in the signals intelligence collection.

as inexperienced but willing and reported two Japanese down in flames and two others smoking in steep dives. Capt. Wallace Jordan and 2nd Lt. Ed Howes were credited with one victory each, almost certainly Matsumoto and Oya, and Lt. Richard Kirkland received credit for a probable.

A separate Japanese report listed losses for the battle as six destroyed and five damaged, but only two in that list were from 77 Sentai, which, in its own documents, recorded five fighters lost. One has to wonder why there are such discrepancies between unit reports to higher headquarters and reports from that headquarters to its own superior formation. The 5th Air Force claims were 8-2-0 and eight Japanese fighters, as confirmed by their records, were destroyed in air combats this day: seven by P-47s of the 9th and 41st Squadrons and one by Kline's 320th Squadron B-24.

From the Ultra system, intercepted Japanese messages first reported a loss of six aircraft and then a loss of eight aircraft and six fliers, including "a formation leader," obviously Kuwabara. Ultra also reported that fourteen replacement aircraft arrived at Hollandia on this day and more were on the way, and Wewak reported that 114 aircraft were "ready" for operations in that area. MacArthur's G-2 staff commented that this figure was average, and that replacements equaled losses. The SIBs reported Japanese messages about a concentration of aircraft at Hollandia, which Allied staffs interpreted to be the establishment of a pool of aircraft from which reinforcements would go east.

But the B-24 attacks were only part of 5th Air Force operations against Wewak on 14 March. Twenty minutes after the B-24s struck, at 1120, the 38th Sunsetters and 345th Air Apaches Group had thirty-five B-25s drop 166 500-pound bombs into Brandi Plantation followed in twenty minutes by a similar bomb load from thirty-seven A-20s from the four squadrons of the Grim Reapers 3rd Attack Group.

Allied Air Forces Intelligence Summary 191 reported:

Boram and Brandi Plantation were bombed with 174 tons, including 27 x 2,000-pound demos. Fuel dumps were set afire and other damage caused in the well-covered target areas, which were also strafed. Thirty enemy fighters were intercepted, of which eight were shot down. All our planes returned. . . .

Sixty-eight tons of 1,000-pound demos were dropped on the aerodrome with excellent coverage. Fires were started. The runway was rendered unserviceable, and one airplane on the ground was damaged or destroyed.

The 4 Air Army issued order A-244 that directed units to "take safety measures against an enemy landing one moonless night west of Madang." The 10 Sentai was to do reconnaissance, and others were to train to attack the enemy while they were still at sea.

Japanese of all ranks could now expect air attacks each day, not only in the immediate area of Wewak, but also along the coast, on roads and trails, and wherever a sign of their presence was visible. The defending Japanese pilots were faced with the prospect of combat whenever the Allied pilots could fly. No matter how many U.S. aircraft they shot down, or claimed to shoot down, more returned and were just as aggressive. No matter how many replacement aircraft arrived from Japan and Manila, these were soon destroyed or rendered useless.

15 March 1944

Pressure on Wewak was maintained with a strike force of 129 bombers escorted by seventy-nine fighters. The number actually arriving over the targets was somewhat less due to returns to base caused by equipment problems. As the B-24s approached, the U.S. fighter escort engaged Japanese defenders. P-38s of the 433rd Squadron 475th Satan's Angels Group claimed three yellow-nosed Tonys. Yellow denoted the third Chutai in a Sentai. At 1020 three enemy at low altitude were seen by the 433rd, and the P-38s dived on them. The first flights hit one Tony in the wing and the pilot bailed out, while another went down in a tight spiral into the sea, and the leader of the third flight shot the tail off the last one. Victories were credited to Capt. Richard Kimball, Lt. Paul Peters, and 2nd Lt. William Grady.

The 36th Fighter Squadron P-38s also engaged; they claimed one Oscar destroyed and one other single-engine fighter as a probable, for the loss of two Lightnings. William Giroux destroyed the first of his ten victories. P-47s of the 41st Squadron used "dive-attack-climb" tactics against Oscars and Tonys that split-s'ed and dived left to avoid the U.S. fighters who claimed 4-2-0 Japanese. The 9th Squadron attacked sixteen Oscars and three Tonys, with Lieutenant Huisman claiming a Tony that dived into Dagua. This was the final 9th Squadron victory with the P-47.

The Red Raiders Group's 19th and 33rd Squadrons attacked antiaircraft positions with seventy-four 1,000-pound bombs while the Jolly Rogers Group hit airfield defenses. Bombing was reported as good, though equipment malfunction resulted in a fortuitous success: Lt. Hoot Bassett's bombs hung up, so Lieutenant Presly salvoed them, and they hit what appeared to be an oil storage area. It exploded into a large fire. Elsewhere, A-20s of the Grim Reapers and 312th Groups went for targets on Kairiru Island with a total of 209 250-pound bombs. B-25s of the Sunsetters Group hit the Mission area on Kairiru.

The 312th Group had a lengthy period of training in the United States; they also had several changes of title and type of aircraft assigned, as well as destination, but by this time had worked up to operational standards. After attacking other targets with less-intense defenses, they were assigned to strike the Wewak area. The 386th and 387th Squadrons of the 312th were tasked to attack the seaplane base on Kairiru Island. The group's A-20s took off in turn: six aircraft from the 386th and six from the 387th Squadrons. Colonel Strauss, Group CO, was flying and Major Carroll led the 386th. The second flight of the 387th was led by 1st Lt. Edward Pool with Lieutenants Nicholas on the left and Bistika on the right. Before takeoff Bistika had begun to put on a lifevest that he thought would not be needed that day, but Nicholas owned it and asked for it back. Bistika handed it over, and they drove out to the flight-line together.

The squadrons attacked in flights of three abreast, coming off the target heading out to sea. As they banked away from the target, Lieutenant Bistika saw the A-20 on his left burst into flames and glimpsed the gunner bailing out despite the low altitude and speed. "His chute failed to open just before the aircraft hit the water and disintegrated. The abrupt realization that it was piloted by Nicholas numbed me. It had happened so quickly."

Pool, the flight leader, noticed Nicholas lag slightly, then seem to be catching up to his place in formation. But Pool saw smoke coming from Nicholas's right engine, and it became obvious the A-20 was losing height. As the fuselage caught fire at the wing root, Nicholas jettisoned his bombs, but the burning engine fell off, the fuselage exploded, and the A-20 dived into the sea. From the gunner's position in the leading aircraft, Sgt. Leo Mandabach watched the episode and noticed Nicholas's cockpit hatch flip along the surface of the sea, ahead of the rest of the A-20's wreckage. Colonel Strauss, in the cockpit, asked Mandabach if he had seen "that plane," and Mandabach affirmed, but Strauss was talking about a Japanese fighter to their left.

Japanese fighters attacked the 312th formation. One passed in front of Jessie Sowell's A-20. Sowell pressed the nose-gun trigger, but the safety pin was still in place, and the fighter flicked on by. However, Sgt. Norman Rye, gunner for Lt. John Roby, shot one Japanese down, the first fighter destroyed by the 386th, confirmed by Major Carroll.

The 312th Group report described the action:

There were dogfights all over the sky and only two Jap fighters were able to attack our formation. Our airplanes were at 200 feet doing about 250 mph. An Oscar made a head-on attack, but no hits were scored. One Tony attacked the last airplane in the formation from below at 5 o'clock. The turret gunner held his fire until the Tony was within 300 yards and then opened fire. Tracers were observed going into the Tony, which began trailing smoke. The Tony dove below the A-20 and pulled up again into the same position, giving the gunner another good shot. Again hits were scored and the Tony was seen to hit the water.

The 7th Fighter Squadron P-40s met about ten silver or slate-gray Japanese fighters in no particular formation but with pilots who seemed experienced and eager to fight. From eleven thousand feet the 7th dived on the fighters, which were attacking A-20s near Brandi Plantation. One Oscar, with a hinomaru on the left wing only and camouflaged a dirty brown and green, was hit, rolled onto its back, righted, hit the water with a flare of spray, bounced, and fell back into the sea. Bob DeHaven was credited with his ninth victory. In addition to Japanese attacking the A-20s, others were mixing it with the fighter escort with losses on both sides.

The Sunsetters 71st Squadron B-25s, at seventy-eight hundred feet, attacked Muschu Island with 500-pounders fitted with instantaneous fuses. Karl Foster, in the first flight, noted that they began a gradual climb after meeting the fighter escort, and that, as they approached the coast near the mouth of the Sepik River, the formation turned out to sea to avoid Cape Moem and then swung back to attack from east to west. There was no antiaircraft fire, and crews saw a Japanese fighter, shot down by two P-38s, fall into the sea near Cape Moem. They returned to base over the clouds so that enemy fighters could not stalk the B-25s from above using cloud as cover.

Flying as squadron leader for the first time, Lieutenant Prince of the Grim Reapers 90th Squadron took eight A-20s to the floatplane base on Kairiru Island. They hit it with fifty-three 250-pounders and 10,700 rounds of machine-gun fire, leaving an oil fire, destroyed houses, and the floatplane ramp damaged. The 90th lost two crews: 1st Lt. James L. Scarlott, 2nd Lt. Vernal J. Bird, S.Sgt. George D. Henderson, S.Sgt. Daniel G. O'Connell, and S.Sgt. Roy F. Davis. The two A-20s lagged behind the formation when it reached the target.

U.S. bomber crews saw some results of fighter combats. As the strafers passed through the target area, the Sunsetters Group's 822nd Squadron saw two single-engine fighters fall into the water between Wewak and Muschu Island at the same time the 405th Squadron saw two Oscars shot down by four P-38s. The 822nd also saw a P-38 in the water off Kairiru and called the Air Sea Rescue PBY but got no answer. This was one of two P-38s lost from the 36th Squadron, 8th Fighter Group, flown by Captains Warren Danson and James McLaughlin.

After rescue McLaughlin described his adventures. The squadron was to be high cover in the fighter escort, and, after several aircraft returned to base, he moved to Danson's wing. At twenty-five thousand feet over Kairiru Island, they saw about a dozen Oscars some two thousand feet below, dropped their tanks, and dove on the highest flight of Japanese. McLaughlin discovered that he could not get full power from his Allison engines. As the combat continued and Danson dived, McLaughlin became separated from him. Then, at about ten thousand feet, his cockpit began to cloud up as moisture formed on the inside of the Plexiglas. Unable to see clearly with little height and with no friendly planes near, McLaughlin decided to go home. He said, "At about seven thousand feet I felt bullets striking my airplane. I turned right and the Oscar pulled up and made another pass at me. This time bullets began invading the cockpit, causing splinters of Plexiglas to sprinkle all over me. I could not see out of the canopy so decided to bail out. The airplane was not on fire."

He released the canopy, turned on his IFF, and had a moment to note that the P-38 was clocking 250 mph in a two-thousand-feet-per-minute dive. He released his seat belt and was sucked out of the cockpit; he grabbed the canopy rim and held on until his feet were out on the wing, then let go and slipped close under the tail and elevator. The parachute opened at about two thousand feet, and he slipped air from it to get down as fast as possible in case the Japanese performed their usual trick of machine-gunning parachutes. It seemed the two Oscars above did not see him as they swung away to the mainland.

McLaughlin splashed into the water and, after some difficulty, climbed into his dinghy and released the shroud lines from his legs, entangled after the parachute canopy settled into the water. After tying all his equipment to the raft with lines cut from the parachute, he noticed that he was only about a mile and a half from Muschu Island and two miles from Kairiru. He tried to attract the attention of the A-20s by waving part of his parachute at them as they swept past on their attacks on Kairiru. He watched the A-20s bombing and strafing and realized both islands would be populated with unhappy Japanese, so he paddled north and alternated paddling for an hour and resting for the same time. He estimated he covered five miles in six hours but dared not put up a sail in case Japanese saw it.

Meanwhile, a U.S. Navy PBY was airborne searching for a missing P-47. The PBY pilot, Lt. H. L. Dennison, was about to return to base because radio static made it impossible to receive directions. Then a message was received about a P-38 down off Wewak. Dennison acknowledged that he would be able to go to the location, but all aboard the PBY knew Wewak was a very dangerous location for a PBY, even with fighter escort. The position for the downed pilot was given— a few miles off Kairiru, almost under the gun muzzles of the Japanese defenses. Dennison set course for the area. Around 1530 McLaughlin reported that he "heard a plane approaching from the southeast. The plane was low and about a mile and a half away, headed straight for me. I could not recognize it from that distance as friendly, so quickly covered up my chute and laid low. The plane got within half a mile and turned to sea, and I recognized it as a PBY. I tried to start my smoke bomb but it was wet and would not function. I then billowed out my chute and was at once spotted and picked up."

The mission report recorded McLaughlin's coolness, praised his use of issued equipment to assist in survival, and also mentioned his useless smoke bomb and that his .45-caliber pistol became rusty so quickly that it was unable to be used after a few hours in the dinghy.

The 33 Sentai had twelve fighters airborne, and they joined three from 77 Sentai on patrol at twenty-three thousand feet. Sergeant Major Takemori had Inagaki on his wing, and they dived on a P-47, which saw them and "easily put its nose down," diving out of reach. The formation did claim one P-47, but Takemori gave no details of this.

Sergeant Tsugio Shimada was an experienced pilot with 77 Sentai. He had been with the unit in Burma, flown to New Guinea with it, and arrived at

Wewak on 29 February. He took part in the combats of the first two weeks in March but could see the way things were developing. He wrote on the fifteenth: "We are gradually losing our aircraft." The 77 Sentai recorded no losses this day but claimed one P-47 destroyed and one probably destroyed.

A captured Japanese document recorded six fighters destroyed in combats on 15 March: three Oscars from 63 Sentai, one Tony from each of 68 and 78 Sentai, and one Tony from an unidentified unit. Another report also gives a total of six but identifies three as Tonys of 78 Sentai. However, a message from 4 Air Army listed ten pilots killed or failed to return on 15 March. The 78 Sentai listed three pilots: 2nd Lt. Shogo Saito and Sergeant Majors Shoichi Tajimi and Naotoshi Tanaka; 68 Sentai lost Lt. Michihiro Kato and Sgt. Mjr. Kiyo Nagae (name not deciphered fully); and 63 Sentai lost Corp. Hajime Watanabe. Also listed were four aircraft from 79 Independent Chutai: three sergeant majors and one other rank, whose names were not deciphered.

Nine U.S. fighter victories were confirmed for the day, a total of four Tonys, three Oscars, and two Zekes: to Dehaven of the 7th Fighter Squadron and Huisman of the 9th, Tuuri and Giroux of the 36th, Bomar and Rowell of the 41st, and Kimball, Peters, and Grady of the 433rd. The fighter claimed by the 312th makes ten. Once again, these claims are confirmed by Japanese documents, although these documents differ in detail.

One thing is certain from captured documents: many replacement fighters were supplied to all the Wewak units in March. One unidentified fighter unit recorded a total loss of fourteen airplanes in the six weeks to the end of March 1944. It was also reported that in combat 11–15 March, Japanese losses were twenty-three aircraft destroyed and twenty-one damaged in the air, and eight destroyed on the ground. However, simple arithmetic applied to the admitted Japanese losses derived from captured documents included previously for each day in that period result in a total of at least thirty destroyed.

On the Japanese side, the loss of experienced pilots such as Kuwabara on the day before could not be made good. The general quality of Allied pilots was superior, as were their aircraft and the use made of them. By now no Allied pilots engaged the agile Japanese fighters in dogfights but instead employed superior speed and height to make diving attacks and then sped back up above the fuming Japanese. The Japanese pilots claimed excessively, but there were few camera guns to use as an impartial witness, and the toughly built Allied planes absorbed a great deal of punishment and then returned to base while an exultant Japanese claimed a victory.

The mission of 15 March was reported in a large paragraph in AAF Intsum 192:

From minimum altitudes to 11,000 feet, installations and personnel areas were attacked with 225 tons of bombs. Bombing was effective with hits observed on machine-gun positions, docks, and warehouses—the floatplane ramp was damaged and a lugger probably destroyed. A definite oil fire was started in a stores area, demolishing several buildings. Direct hits were observed on antiaircraft and search-light positions in Wewak township, and fires started that were visible from seventy-five miles distance. Eleven airplanes were damaged by antiaircraft, and two crew members were slightly wounded. Of an undetermined number of Tonys and Oscars encountered by the fighter escort, eleven were destroyed and one probably destroyed. One Tony was shot down by an A-20. Two P-38s are missing.

The unceasing aerial offensive was being felt brutally by the antiaircraft gunners. Pvt. Hiromi Machiyama, 61 Antiaircraft Battalion, had been in the actions since May 1943. He had watched the gradual decline of the defenses and on this day wrote, "I don't know where our airplanes are, but there is no sign of them." One Japanese report estimated that one hundred 1,000-pounders blanketed the antiaircraft positions with many direct hits but stated that no casualties were suffered. It was reported elsewhere, however, that fifty men had been killed in one shelter, five guns were hit in one battalion, and the bivouac area and 6 Flying Division headquarters had been badly damaged with much destruction.

At higher levels of the chain of command, 4 Air Army was aware of the destruction caused by the daily attacks, and in order A-246 designated "rear operational airfields" for the flying units. Fighters and reconnaissance planes were to use Manokwari, light bombers were to use Kamiri, and heavy bombers and transport planes were to go to Moemi South. Not only were the Japanese forced to think defensively, but they also began arranging to move their air units west, out of the mincer of the relentless daily attacks from the east.

At night B-24s of the 63d Squadron attacked a convoy to Wewak from Hollandia and claimed as sunk two 1,000-ton ships; another was forced to beach. These sorties were planned with information from Ultra radio intercepts.

The Japanese recorded the attacks from 0100 on the 21st Wewak Convoy but only slight damage was reported to *Tenshio Maru,* and *Yakumo Maru* and *Taiei Maru* were not hit.

16 March to 31 March 1944

Weather for the March attacks on Wewak was mostly good, so flying was possible, and on only two days were attacks halted. The period was the changeover phase between wet and dry monsoons and was used to advantage by the Allied air forces. During the October–November 1943 daylight air offensive against Rabaul, weather reduced the program to missions flown on single days or over a short period of two or three consecutive days of good weather separated by three, four, or more days of bad weather. This allowed the Japanese to make repairs, improve defenses, and recover from the bombing attacks. In these attacks on Wewak, however, the weather pattern was to the advantage of the 5th Air Force. During April 1944 the New Guinea weather would play another tricky hand with the 5th Air Force.

When the daily air attacks on Wewak targets showed no signs of slacking, the Japanese command thought of removing the remaining fighters and bombers from the danger zone. On 16 March, the fighter Sentai flew to Hollandia to cover the 21st Wewak Convoy because the Japanese could not defend Wewak itself and also cover the ships. It was one year after the important Battle of the Bismarck Sea, and that action was to be replayed. Because the fighters went to cover the ships, on 16 March there was no fighter defense over Wewak visible to Japanese on the ground. Lieutenant Horie, 6 Flying Division headquarters, wrote that he "felt very keenly the lack of air cover." During the March combats to this date, 63 Sentai claimed twelve victories, but then withdrew to Hollandia, out of range of the U.S. fighter sweeps. The 68 Sentai sent its pilots and fifty maintenance men to Hollandia, where they took part in further actions. The rest of the unit remained in Wewak and fought as ground troops against the Australian army in the hills until the Japanese surrender in August 1945.

Continuing the daily onslaught, on 16 March four squadrons of B-24s attacked Wewak peninsula and antiaircraft positions. As the B-24s approached, crews could see winking muzzle flashes as antiaircraft guns fired at them. After all the destruction heaped upon them, the Japanese gunners continued to man their weapons, and three B-24s were hit by antiaircraft fire. The B-24 flown by Captain Homen, leading the Red Raiders 19th Squadron, had a three-inch shell enter the belly, bend the pilot's left rudder pedal, and explode against the left inboard engine. The engine was badly damaged, and Homen was wounded in the arms and legs.

The oil bled away and the propeller could not be feathered; then the engine began to vibrate and pound as it started to seize. Homen had gone to get his wounds tied, and the B-24 went into a dive with the left wing flexing violently. At about five thousand feet, the aircraft was pulled out of the dive after Homen climbed back into his seat and assisted the copilot. The outer engine was shut down to lessen vibration in the wing, and gradually control was regained. The three remaining engines had to be at full power to overcome the drag from the propeller blades on the dead engine. Meanwhile the engineer, S.Sgt. H. K. Goldey, had to collect urine from the rest of the crew for emergency use in the hydraulic system.

The B-24 was flown as far as the fighter strip at Gusap and landed safely. The B-24 was repaired and rejoined the squadron, but Captain Homen had to go to Townsville for medical treatment.

At treetop level B-25s and A-20s attacked Brandi. In a Sunsetters Group B-25, Karl Foster, 71st Squadron, flew with the usual load of 500-pound bombs, and as they approached the target, he noticed the 405th Squadron ahead swinging onto a secondary target. The 71st strafed and bombed along the length of the plantation, broke off before reaching Cape Moem, and left the area "low and fast." Near Madang, a Japanese fighter was seen circling a formation of B-24s, breaking in for attacks on them, and near Gusap another enemy fighter made an unsuccessful pass at the B-25s and then departed. This was the only Japanese fighter presence noted. Foster recorded that there were "nil losses, nil ack-ack."

The attacks were included in AAF Intsum 192: "A/A positions in Wewak township and Brandi Plantation were attacked with noticeably lessened ground opposition. Buildings were demolished and fires started. Black smoke rose to two thousand feet from a blaze in an airplane salvage dump. Fires and an explosion were seen near an A/A Battery. One hundred and fifty-five tons of bombs were dropped."

The feelings of the Japanese—under ceaseless attacks at Wewak, all along the coast and inland, and on distant islands such as Bougainville and New Britain—are well represented in captured diaries and letters. One such diary belonged to Lieutenant Uchimura, 41 Division: "In air superiority, to put it briefly, we are about a century behind Germany and America. If you have not experienced continuous bombardment by formations of Lockheeds and North Americans of fifty or sixty bombers, a true appreciation of air superiority is well-nigh impossible. Those in the war in New Guinea, even the Privates, voice the same opinion: 'if only we had airplanes!' Ah! If we only had air superiority—air superiority! I'm greatly irritated by their arrogance."

It had been two years since the first Allied fighter defense of New Guinea consisted of the single P-40 squadron of 75 Squadron RAAF, some without gunsights and some pilots having only twenty hours' flying in the new Kittyhawks before being sent into combat two weeks from activation of the squadron. The only daylight attack force available then was the Douglas A-24s of the U.S. 8th Attack Squadron, which was sent into combat three weeks after its airplanes were delivered. Bombs were in such short supply that A-24s from Australia had to fly to Moresby with bombs slung.

The 5th Air Force on 17 March 1944 sent thirty-six B-24s and sixty-five B-25s and A-20s to repeat the strikes on Wewak targets; an enormous explosion resulted from the Red Raiders B-24 attack with smoke clouds up to ten thousand feet still visible to the departing bombers as far away as the Sepik River. On the 18th they were back again and had one B-24 badly damaged by flak. Attacks by the Allied air forces continued, not only on Wewak areas but also on Hansa Bay, Nubia, Bogadjim Road, Madang, Alexishafen, Tanimbar Island, Aitape, the Admiralty Islands, New Britain. Night missions also continued to Hollandia, as well as long-range searches for shipping well out across the seas. Weather and aircraft permitting, the crews maintained a high level of attacks against the Japanese.

By this time the incessant daily raids had made the Wewak airfields useless, their surrounds pocked with huge craters up to thirty feet deep and seventy-five feet across. The Japanese were incapable of coping with such sustained damage and destruction. Aircraft caught on the ground were hit again and again, reduced to ripped and torn wreckage. The trees had been stripped of foliage and branches by explosions and .50-caliber bullets. The 248 Sentai had no operational aircraft; other units were reduced to six and eight. Japanese repair capability was simply swamped in a rain of bombs. The attacks are described in brief by paragraphs in Allied air force Intsums:

18 March: Seventeen tons of bombs landed on Brandi Plantation, black smoke rising to 300 feet.

19 March: The Cape Moem and Cape Boram target areas were excellently covered with 118 tons of bombs and thorough strafing. A six-gun heavy A/A position was covered with 500-pound bombs. P-47s jumped four Oscars at 3,000 feet, destroying one. Twelve other enemy fighters were seen departing the area. Three bombers were damaged, and one was brought down by the reportedly weak and scattered A/A.

B-25 Miss Ellen of the 499th Squadron Air Apaches Group flew into blast from bombs of the preceding plane, was blown onto its back, and went into the trees out of control.

Lt. Robert Sutcliffe, in a 342nd Squadron P-47, claimed an Oscar over Wewak on 19 March, and 248 Sentai recorded the only Japanese loss that day. This was the fourth of Sutcliffe's five victories.

Also on 19 March, the hapless 21st Wewak Convoy was massacred. The convoy consisted of two merchant ships, a sea truck, and three sub-chasers. Information about the convoy had been included in special intelligence bulletins four to five days earlier. The 5th Air Force was notified, and bombers were routed to locate the ships. The ships had been bombed by radar-equipped B-24s of the 63rd Squadron but made the dash to Wewak, arrived on the afternoon of 18 March, and unloaded during the night. Now they were trying to leave the area. While the 5th Air Force bombers were returning from the strike, the convoy was located, and forty B-24s were diverted from a planned mission and sent after the ships.

This mission was the twenty-sixth for Morgan Terry and his "pirates" in the Jolly Rogers 320th Squadron. The group saw two "Fox-Able" class freighters and two gunboats twenty miles off Boram and attacked. Watching from his tail turret, Dick Grills saw the 90th Group bombs miss the ships, but he watched the following 43rd Group fly through accurate ack-ack and "blow them both out of the water. Very pretty bombing and the ships were blown out of the water; really did it right." The Ken's Men Group's 64th Squadron claimed fifteen direct 1,000-pounder hits.

The Japanese fighter units could keep few aircraft operational, and only two had more than ten; 78 Sentai reported ten, and 33 reported thirteen able to fly. Seven Japanese fighters attacked the Red Raiders 19th Squadron, pressing in to fifty feet; one was claimed by gunners. Roy Parker, former B-26 pilot, was flying the mission and recalled:

> It seemed to me that they were all out after me. This was the first time I had been jumped on Liberators, and I don't mind saying that my mouth was very dry. I remember wharves, shipping, and the little specks of Japanese anger darting about the place. Being in such a situation results in a great involuntary concentration, there is nothing else in the world at the time. With adrenaline pumping, one's performance is at its peak, but all the time you wish you were somewhere else—which in fact you were very quickly.

Dick Ellis from Group headquarters led the Grim Reapers as a horde of strafers converged on the convoy. Formation discipline evaporated. B-25s and A-20s simply swarmed over the ships, attacked regardless of risk of collision, and obliterated the defenses and then the vessels themselves. One A-20 from the 89th Squadron went too low, hit the ship's mast, and speared into the water. Luckily, the pilot, Lieutenant Soloc, was seen and picked up seventeen hours later. S.Sgt. Donald L. Bradley went down with the A-20. Six other strafers were damaged. The Grim Reapers 90th Squadron more or less ganged up on a transport ship and hit it with nine of their ten 500-pound bombs. The Grim Reapers's A-20 flown by 2nd Lt. Norman L. Craig with S.Sgt. Howard Ball and S.Sgt. Ottis Cunnagin as his crew was seen to have its left engine flaming and go into the sea. It was believed shot down by the hail of .50-caliber bullets from a strafing B-25. A second A-20 landed at Dumpu with holes in the gunner's compartment, also from B-25 guns.

The 312th Group sent six A-20s led by the CO, Colonel Strauss. It was the group's first shipping strike. The formation, last to arrive, entered the target area when only one small ship was left, the sky full of eager attackers, the ocean littered with survivors and debris from the destroyed convoy. Strauss saw that there were more aircraft than necessary and "felt that the 312th's contribution was the damnedest waste of bombs I ever did see."

Photos show debris and Japanese in the swirling waters as the last convoy to Wewak disappeared in a rain of bombs and machine-gun fire. The next unloaded in Hollandia. Among the personnel lost in this convoy were 111 members of 6 Flying Division units, including those for a new radar installation.

Japanese records state that twenty-eight fighters were tasked to cover the convoy, but their efforts were futile. As these fighter units returned to the Dagua area, they began joining formation over land. Ralph Wandrey, flying a 9th Fighter Squadron P-47, found himself up-sun of the Japanese, watching and wondering how he could engage and get away. He noticed that as each Japanese approached the formation, he would slide in from the rear, do a barrel roll (which seemed to be a signal of friendliness), and tack onto the top of the echelon-down line of Oscars.

Ralph was confident he could do this, so he dived, flew up behind the line, "did the best barrel roll of my life," and surged up to the top of the stack. He kicked on rudder and, as his sight came onto the Oscars, fired his eight .50-caliber machine guns and hosed down the row of Japanese fighters below him. Wandrey saw that the sixth Oscar down the row was new, so bright and clean that the paint and canopy glittered. He was so close that his .50-caliber bullet streams passed the nearest Japanese, converged beyond him, and hacked off the wing of the second. Ralph hung in position until the last instant, firing along the line of Oscars, watching them break, catch fire, and lose a wing and other pieces. But others swung onto him, looping back onto the lone P-47. He shoved the nose of the seven-ton fighter down, firewalled the throttle, and roared away from the formation for Dagua beach. Behind Wandrey the Japanese scattered, except for those after his scalp and other body parts.

As Wandrey came lower, he noticed a bunch of Japanese in the surf and one other, wearing a white coat, sitting on a bicycle-type apparatus that traversed an 88 mm antiaircraft gun. This fellow was "pedaling like a fool, and I could see that muzzle swinging around onto me, and as I went past, about 100 feet up, it fired. I saw the muzzle-blast, and in the center the tiny black dot of the shell, and hunched down waiting to get hit, glanced at my airspeed indicator, and I was going 400 miles an hour. The shell missed behind!"

The Oscars had no hope of catching him, and Ralph flew on back to base, to disappointment—torrential rain the night before had ruined his camera film; there was no record of the attack on the formation, no way to confirm any claims; and his wingman had been separated from him earlier. This disappointment at the lack of confirmation of victories was one reason why Ralph Wandrey insisted on wingmen sticking to their leader; he got the nickname "Ironass" by threatening to court martial anyone who failed to do so. No captured Japanese records or survivors' accounts located by the time of publication of this book refer to the combat, but Ralph believes he might have destroyed as many as five or six Japanese in that point-blank hail of .50-caliber machine-gun fire along the row of Oscars.

After the convoy melee, it was perhaps provident that there was no mission the next day due to weather. Kenney's headquarters reported that forty B-24s, sixty-two A-20s and B-25s, and twenty-eight P-38s flew against the ships. The report continued:

> Attacks continuing throughout the day resulted in the sinking of two Japanese transports of 6,000 and 4,000 tons, and three escorting corvettes, with heavy destruction of enemy personnel. One lugger and one barge were also claimed sunk in the general shipping strike. Seven to eleven Japanese fighters reported in the area were attacked and one HAMP was destroyed, and three enemy fighters were claimed damaged. A P-38 and an A-20 were shot down by antiaircraft fire. Two B-24s were damaged. An A-20 crew member was seriously wounded.

Wewak reported that though losses were "severe," the bomber force had not suffered greatly.

On 21 March the strafers attacked Kairiru Island, unopposed except for antiaircraft from the beach north of Dagua. By this time antiaircraft over Wewak was so slight that B-24s began to fly individual bomb runs of up to four minutes, and the Ken's Men Group's 403rd Squadron reported only twelve "pitifully inaccurate" antiaircraft bursts. The runs were made at 10,000 to 13,000 feet, with 1,000- and 2,000-pounders. The strafers bombed from medium altitude, 500-pounders from 7,600 feet at 220 mph. Karl Foster was leading the Sunsetters Group's 71st Squadron, and they banked out to sea to avoid antiaircraft fire from Cape Moem and Dagua. The B-25s turned left onto the bomb run, made difficult by smoke over the target, held course for photos, and then dived to low altitude and home with "nil losses, nil sightings, results unobserved."

Commenting on the situation, the military intelligence staff stated that despite the buildup of Japanese aircraft farther west, at Hollandia, the enemy "neither can afford nor intends to counter our raiding with large fighter elements of, say, 100 fighters. The Wewak interceptions, the largest in weeks, involved maximums of 40 fighters. The enemy cannot, accordingly, protect his bases with adequate forces, nor engage offensively in effective strength, except initially against a prime target."

The Japanese had long realized the times within which the bombers came, and life on the ground began to be organized around this. Food was cooked and distributed early; those who could leave target areas went into the jungle during the danger period to return in the afternoon or night. Much effort was put into repairing the dirt runways each night, but the cumulative effects of the bombing were becoming more and more obvious. Yet there were some who were confident, or perhaps putting on a brave face, or were simply unable to recognize reality. Major Tanaka, commanding 208 Sentai, equipped with Lily bombers, wrote "enemy airplanes are excellent, but cannot be compared with ours."

Morgan Terry, "Terry and the Pirates" of the Jolly Rogers Group, was a flight leader on the mission to Wewak Point on 22 March. Looking out from his tail turret, Dick Grills was surprised to see the clear sky: no fighters, no ack-ack. The seventy-one heavies returned to base, and Terry had to circle for an hour and forty-five minutes while the formation slid down to land and his turn came. But it was all combat time mounting up.

It really seemed that a turning point had been reached in the air war. Wewak and its fighter force had been ground to small pieces, and the bomber force was incapable of even assembling anything like a formation capable of inflicting worthwhile damage to any Allied target that might be selected. On 22 March, in a pitiful effort compared with the ceaseless pounding the Japanese bases had received, 75 Sentai managed to launch four Lilys in a night attack on Gunbi airfield and claimed "damage to billets."

The Japanese 18th Army headquarters released a summary of claims of damage inflicted on the Allies. From September 1943 to March 1944, 6,000 Australian and U.S. troops had been claimed killed, with 4,000 wounded; 434 aircraft were "confirmed" shot down and another 160 "probably" shot down, with a loss of 1,730 flying crews; 25 PT boats had been sunk and another 6 damaged. Japanese losses totaled 6,500 killed, wounded, and missing.

On 21 March, however, Imperial headquarters was forced to declare that due to heavy shipping losses, use of large vessels between Palau and Wewak would be discontinued. Shipping already had been discontinued to Rabaul, which was left to fend for itself. These messages were intercepted and reported in the Ultra intelligence system to senior Allied commanders.

Of 114 aircraft reported available by 4 Air Army, only forty-eight were fighters. Tokyo advised that only six Oscars were available.

However, all through the New Guinea campaigns the fast Ki-46 Dinahs had managed to provide some photographic evidence of Allied airfields and harbors as well as sight concentrations of ships. Before the invasion of the Admiralties, the Dinah crews had reported the ships but had not been able to keep them under surveillance as they moved to the island group. Now, off Finschhafen, the Dinahs again reported the invasion fleet massing, but again the Japanese command fit this information into their appreciation of Allied intentions: landings near Madang.

On 24 March, due to bad weather, there were no missions to the Wewak area. On that day, Special Intelligence Bulletin 322 included the text of an order from the Japanese 2 Area Army dated 21 March, which gave new missions and boundaries to 4 Air Army. One mission assigned was "immediate strengthening of Hollandia." General Itabana believed the ceaseless battering at Wewak was to prepare for an Allied landing, probably at Madang.

On 25 March, with cloud cover 90 percent, the three U.S. heavy-bomb groups flew against Wewak town, the airfield, and Cape Wom, which also were hit by A-20 and B-25 strafers of the four twin-engine groups, all escorted by P-38s and P-47s. With no damage to Allied aircraft, 207 tons of bombs were delivered. However, the airfields were repaired by the busy Japanese and reported as usable soon after noon.

General Teramoto moved his 4 Air Army headquarters from Wewak to Hollandia, out of the constant pounding. His ground echelons were told to walk, and hundreds of trained and valuable men died on the trek. The Japanese army air force in New Guinea was on the brink of disaster.

General Itabana told his air force troops of "the glorious victories" being won in Burma and reminded them of the most important duties of an aviation formation. The first four were to break up landings, smash enemy air power, make successful interceptions, and conduct successful reconnaissance. These duties show the state of mind of the Japanese command: they were defensive, not offensive, and they accepted that the initiative lay with the

Allies. Because of the incompetence of Japan's high command and its failure to provide adequate logistic support and trained technical staffs and flight crews, by late March 1944 none of the four assigned duties were within the capabilities of the Japanese air units.

At Hollandia twenty-one Oscars were issued to two unidentified fighter units; one received sixteen and the other five. Wewak advised Tokyo that 4 Air Army had 113 aircraft available for operations, 47 of which were fighters. On 23 March the Manila air depot had only 8 airplanes available for units in New Guinea, with another 15 listed as "damaged" and 27 "under repair," with 20 more classified as "other," but presumably not fit for issue to units.

But more importantly on 25 March, Allied radio intercept intercepted and decoded an Appreciation of the Situation by Gen. Korechika Anami, commander 2 Area Army. This was priceless for MacArthur. The appreciation accepted that the Allies would land at Hansa and Madang and would probably operate in the western Caroline Islands, but it did not consider seriously any offensive or landing against Hollandia. At the time proposed for MacArthur's Hollandia operation, the bulk of the Japanese 18th Army would be around Wewak.

The 2 Area Army from Davao politely exhorted 4 Air Army to continue the struggle. On 25 March, Davao radioed that the forces

> had made progress beyond all expectations, and morale of officers and men has been high. However, there is an urgent need for a brief recovery in both fighting strength and position. In the present situation we cannot put to good use our air bases in Hansa and Madang. The enemy will land in Hansa in the dark of the moon, but will avoid fighting a decisive battle. Wewak must be secured and the air force become extremely active. Bases in the Admiralties will exercise a very great influence and will also be bases for the development of enemy designs.

Japanese records for 26 March list by unit the aircraft available to 4 Air Army: 7 Sentai, two airplanes; 10 Sentai, three; 20 Chutai, four; 33 Sentai, sixteen; 34 Sentai, ten; 45 Sentai, twelve; 60 Sentai, twelve; 61 Sentai, four; 63 Sentai, eight; 68 Sentai, eleven; 75 Sentai, sixteen; 77 Sentai, four; 78 Sentai, eleven; 83 Chutai, three; 208 Sentai, six; 248 Sentai, four. Total: 126 aircraft.

Fifty-four of these were fighters and sixty-two were bombers capable only of carrying small bomb-loads. As a fighting force it was incapable of inflicting any serious damage on its opponents. Technologically and quantitatively, the Japanese air armies were being left far behind, and the Allies were still increasing their strength.

On 26 March 5th Air Force units returned to pound But and Dagua. Two hundred twenty-four 1,000-pounders were dropped by squadron formations, and another twenty-four by individual aircraft that made deliberate bomb runs on antiaircraft positions. The Dagua guns were still firing. One A-20, one B-24, and two P-38s were damaged; no defending fighters were seen. While keeping up pressure on the surrounding area, the 90th Squadron, Grim Reapers Group, sent nine A-20s led by Lieutenant Prince along the coast to Aitape. They attacked three barges, and again the dangers inherent in low-level attacks were emphasized. Lieutenant Richardson, leading the third flight, flew into the waterspout from an earlier bomb explosion; the A-20 nosed up and then went into the sea. One person was seen to get out of the plane. With Richardson, who had been with the 90th since November 1943, were two old-timers, Staff Sergeants Casillas and Divers.

After a series of attacks lasting sixteen days, the Wewak area had been battered to wreckage, and the Japanese air units that operated from the four airfields there had been forced back to the west. To accomplish this the 5th Air Force lost eighteen fighters and sixteen bombers to enemy action and accident. It was a remarkable demonstration of air power, despite limitations set by climate and terrain. It was the second time the 5th Air Force had inflicted such destruction on its opponent in New Guinea. Nothing like it had been achieved in any other theater. The Luftwaffe destroyed a considerable number of Polish and Soviet planes on the ground but in surprise attacks at the commencement of hostilities. The 5th Air Force records for the missions from 11 to 27 March show 1,543 bomber sorties, which dropped 3,036 tons of bombs, plus 911 fighter escort sorties. The seven fighter pilots lost represented 0.7 percent per mission, and the fourteen bomber crewmen represented 0.16 percent per mission. The 5th Air Force claims for Japanese aircraft destroyed in combat were 59-13-0 by U.S. fighter, and 7-2-8 by bombers.

The 4 Air Army claims for the fighting between 11 and 24 March were for seventy-six U.S. aircraft destroyed for a loss of nineteen and destruction of twenty antiaircraft guns. Other Japanese documents—mentioned previously— give a higher total of aircraft destroyed, at least thirty. Craven and Cate, in the U.S. official air forces history, refer to Japanese documents admitting a loss of 37-0-24 in the air and 6-0-18 on the ground. But a document captured at

Hollandia listed, by serial number and receiving unit, sixty-five Oscars supplied to fighter units in February and March. The 77 Sentai received twenty-seven replacement Oscars, and 33 Sentai received twenty.

For the month of March, in New Guinea, the Japanese counted 4,066 Allied sorties, more than the total for February of 3,600. For March the Japanese claimed 103 Allied aircraft shot down, including 16 probables or unconfirmed over New Guinea, the Bismarck Archipelago, and the Solomon Islands.

The achievement of the air offensive was reflected in Allied military intelligence summaries for 26 and 28 March, which noted that of 291 planes counted on photographs of Japanese airfields, 260 were at Hollandia, but none were at Hansa, But, or Tadji, and added, "The air abandonment of the Bismarcks, and of Hansa Bay and the Wewak area in New Guinea, is paralleled by diminishing ground fire against Allied planes, except at Rabaul."

The plight of the Japanese is recorded in their diaries and documents. Colonel Okada arrived at Wewak to take command of 49 Anchorage Unit. He wrote:

15 March—Office shot full of holes. The situation is dangerous.
22 March—Entire anchorage is burnt and in Wewak there is no habitable
    building.
24 March—To Hollandia.
25 March—General Teramoto, commanding 4 Air Army, arrived Hollandia.

Four hundred men of 9 Fleet headquarters set off to walk to Hollandia. A petty officer among them who survived recalled that one hundred died of sickness, air attack, and lack of food. Lieutenant "Moto," 20 Airfield Battalion, decided that Imperial headquarters concluded that New Guinea was a failure, so he sent no reinforcements and left the men and units there to fight to the end. Two hundred men of his battalion set off for Hollandia, and as far as he knew, only four reached there. The traditional army-navy rivalry came to the minds of some, and the army felt they had been let down by the navy, who failed to halt the Allied landings.

At Hollandia, on 26 March, Sergeant Major Takemori of 33 Sentai was less than happy with the situation, despite being in a relatively safe area. He wrote, "Only thirty to forty planes available against hundreds. It is damned annoying!" Takemori complained in the privacy of his diary of the lack of better aircraft and of the small number of those models they did have.

On the same day, however, Radio Tokyo declared to its audience, "Out of 20 enemy B-24s, ten or more are shot down, sometimes with their wings disintegrating after one burst of fire. The quality of enemy aircraft is suffering."

The truth was known to the Japanese in New Guinea if not to those in authority in the Home Islands.

Some Japanese units were tasked beyond their ability to perform adequately. The 14 Field Air Repair Depot was to support the aircraft supply route to New Guinea through Truk and Rabaul and also through Manila and Palau. The unit had personnel at Truk, Lakunai, Vunakanau, Kokopo, and Rabaul to assist the pilots of 68 and 78 Sentai flying Tonys to New Guinea along that route, as well as personnel at Manila, Palau, and Wewak. During March at Wewak the 48 Airfield Battalion worked on 474 aircraft of all types, trying to repair damage from bombing, strafing, and aerial combat. The battalion kept its own count of AAF aircraft passing overhead: 489 B-24 sorties, 518 twin-engine bombers, and 254 fighters. More Japanese airplanes were fed into the pipeline for issue to the front-line units. In March staging through from Manila, at least 40 Oscars and Tonys were issued to fighter units at the Hollandia branch of this unit alone.

Australian army forces fought and defeated the Japanese at Wewak in 1945 and occupied the airfields. Allied air force technical intelligence personnel checked all wrecked and abandoned aircraft in the area of the airfields and counted 490 wrecks of Japanese combat aircraft in their search for items of intelligence value. There were 33 at But, 133 at Dagua, 116 at Wewak, and 177 at Boram. The searchers found that in only a little more than one year, the prolific growth of New Guinea flora was such that aircraft easily seen on aerial photos had to be searched for on the ground. Saplings up to fifteen feet high had sprung up, and grass growth was so tall that sometimes only the tip of a propeller blade could be used to locate an airplane. Yet more aircraft remained hidden, unable to be located, uncounted, and unexamined. The same situation applied to other Japanese airfields in New Guinea.

Reconnaissance photos of the Hollandia fields showed 264 operable planes, plus 62 that were either wrecks or unserviceable. Radio intercepts indicated another 21 were due in the next four days. Small numbers of B-24s went to Hollandia at night to harass the Japanese and reinforce their belief that Allied aircraft did not have the range for large daylight attacks. In August 1943, believing they were out of range, the Japanese crammed the Wewak fields with aircraft; in March 1944 they did the same at Hollandia.

As they had done since mid-1942, the Japanese commanders miscalculated both Allied intentions and capabilities. Given the nature of war, there may have been some excuse for the former error, but there can be little for the latter. From late 1942 the Allied air forces had been a potent part of the force opposing the Japanese. From March 1943 the Japanese command witnessed Allied air power destroy the Bismarck Sea convoy, the development of the Dobodura airstrips, and the construction and development of Marilinan. Then came the August slaughter at Wewak; in September, the pounding and airborne landing at Lae and Nadzab; in October–November the Rabaul raids and hammering of Cape Gloucester; and the seizure and development of the Markham Valley complex of airfields. In February were the isolation of the Admiralties and the invasion and the isolation of Rabaul. In March 1944 they saw the grinding down for the second time of the air units and ground installations in the Wewak area. The 5th Air Force had demonstrated repeatedly an ability to deliver smashing blows to important targets. For Japanese commanders to plan based on the belief that Hollandia was "out of range" was an example of an abysmal lack of understanding of enemy capabilities.

In March, of the twelve antiaircraft artillery guns at Hollandia, ten were under repair but were expected to be ready "soon." Four thousand seven hundred thirty-three rounds of ammunition were available. One branch of the Japanese military had learned some lessons, and all signal equipment and personnel were placed in caves at Hollandia as early as February 1944.

Nothing seemed to go right for the Allies in the early days of 1942, but in two years the wheel had turned and now it was the Japanese who saw everything crumble in their hands. In 1942 the Allies were unprepared for war in the Pacific but had been forced to fight a trained, experienced enemy. Now, despite two years of battle, it seemed as if the Japanese were the unprepared amateurs, outsmarted, outmaneuvered, outflown, and outfought in every campaign. Soon, in desperation, they would resort to Special Attack Units, the kamikaze.

Not all the Japanese commanders were unaware of Allied capabilities. Some realized that even if Hollandia was not the objective of the next invasion, it must certainly receive attention from bombers, if only at night. They tried to prepare for these attacks and make plans for some eventualities. An unidentified officer who commanded the Ordnance Depot at Hollandia made a lengthy speech and detailed those aspects of ordnance work that he believed were not satisfactory. He said that better service would be possible because of the strengthening of the office, but then he berated those who did not understand the fact of limited home production and the long supply line, and he pointed out that aircraft losses from noncombat causes and destruction on the ground were higher than losses in air combat. Four hundred eighty-five aircraft had been destroyed on the ground since August, most not by direct hits but because the revetments were weak or too low. He called for "a protective feeling toward Ordnance material" and emphasized the importance of Hollandia, reminding the audience that the large collection of material there was useless if it was not dispersed, camouflaged, and protected, "especially as we expect Hollandia to be bombed."

He then made admissions: management of the antiaircraft defense was haphazard, some damage had already been done to aircraft and supplies, and, after the long delivery flight from Japan and "a long time in the rain in Manila," some airplanes were not ready for combat operations. He called on the repair depot to bring these machines up to combat standard as soon as possible and directed that all aircraft be dispersed and camouflaged, that shelters for personnel be prepared and improved, that units cooperate more, and if an aircraft was sent for repair, that it be accompanied by a statement of what was the problem.

The officer reminded his listeners that ammunition and fuel needed protection. He pointed out that Hollandia had been reconnoitered by the enemy, and if it had not yet been bombed, that must be expected. Fuel and ammunition were to be dispersed in amounts of not more than fifty drums or one hundred boxes, always at least one hundred meters apart. If bombing did begin, then—as at the time of his speech—the antiaircraft gun crews would suffer heavy casualties, so shelters had to be prepared for them as well, and second positions must be "perfected without delay." When the bombing started, he said, servicing units were to collect all usable parts from a wrecked airplane, not just take the one they wanted and leave the rest. Only absolute wrecks were to be left, and even they should be rearranged to appear as whole airplanes. All useful parts were to be delivered to the repair depot. The Japanese commander also told his officers to get away from their desks and actually work with the men among the planes to see what was required; he reminded them that it was useless to give an order and not check that it had been carried out.

Unfortunately for this officer, time was not on his side. He gave the speech on 27 March. On the 30th, 5th Air Force bombers struck Hollandia in daylight.

On 27 March at Wewak the final attack in the series was made by the 5th Air Force. Sixty bomber sorties were flown, escorted by eighty-four fighters. Clouds hampered the bombing, but there was no antiaircraft or fighter defense. Morale among the Japanese in the Wewak area varied from high to low. Air and ground crews of 208 Sentai were happy, because they thought they would all be going back to Japan to re-equip. But the antiaircraft gunners, under daily hammering with no word of relief, were more despondent. The 40 AA Company arrived in February, and by late March one officer wrote, "It can be said the AA guns hardly fired a shot. It seems there is no ammunition left. It is really depressing." He watched aerial combats, saw Japanese aircraft fall into the jungle and sea, and knew there was little hope of change.

The relentless submarine warfare took a continuing heavy toll of Japanese ships from Japanese waters down to the combat zones across the Pacific and Southeast Asia. The air attacks in the Wewak area and the constant pressure maintained on barge traffic along the coast meant a great reduction in the passage of supplies to eastern parts of New Guinea. In March 20,939 cubic meters of supplies were unloaded at Hollandia; most of it stayed there. Although 2,341 tons of fuel were unloaded, only 32 tons were sent out. In its report for March, 31 Anchorage Unit recorded that ship losses on voyage and in harbor reached 65 percent, "a distressing situation for the future," and called for "rigorous and complete protection against persistent and superior enemy aircraft counterattacks." The report also referred to careless packing, which resulted in loss of up to half of many items including aviation fuel, and finally made reference to the growing problem of lack of quality among ships' crews.

The Japanese, very conscious of security at home and overseas, prudently had gathered eighty-two missionaries and fifty "aliens" in detention at Hollandia by 23 March. When their losses began to mount and ships were sunk in the harbor or after leaving port, when aircraft were destroyed on the ground time and again, it seemed reasonable to deduce that someone was spying. Because it would not be a Japanese, suspicion fell on foreign people such as those in the religious groups. That these foreigners had no means of communication only added to the mystery.

The number of Japanese at Hollandia has been the subject of some disagreement, but figures were quoted by 27 Field Freight Depot for the number of personnel it supplied. On 19 February 1944, it supplied 12,779 people, including 888 flight crew; and on 19 March, 16,297 people, including 2,250 flight crew; on 10 April numbers supplied were almost the same, at 16,339, but flight crews had fallen to 1,917. Combat and logistic troops had been sent east to areas along the coast that were expected to be invaded, and flight crews and airplanes had been gathered at the complex of airfields. Japanese deployment to the eastern locations was described in detail in their messages, and then repeated for the top Allied officers in Ultra bulletins. Air units had been congregated at Hollandia with little dispersal and few defense works to protect them. This was just what General Kenney wanted. The second part of the 1944 lesson in the use of airpower was about to be delivered.

FIVE

In the South West Pacific

Service in war was vastly different from the life experienced in peace. The following anecdotes illustrate some experiences of 5th Air Force members in the SWPA.

"If It Ain't Broke . . ."

One day in 1942, a B-17 was taxied to the 482nd Service Squadron with a report that the right landing strut was leaking fluid. The 482nd had no facilities to remove and repack a B-17 landing strut, but the pilot was told they could fix it well enough for him to fly to home base where the work could be done. Instead of hydraulic fluid, the strut was filled with ordinary 10-weight motor oil and air, and when the strut was wiped clean, it showed no sign of leaking. For the information of the regular maintenance crew, the defect was entered in the B-17's Form 1A by Sgt.

Cy Stafford as a temporary repair. Two days later the same B-17 returned, and Cy asked if the strut had been fixed. The crew chief replied that because it was working okay, it had been left as it was.

"That's the Crew Chief's Job!"

Apart from well-known fighter aces, the legendary Paul "Pappy" Gunn seemed to wage his own war in the theater and was at the center of the adaptation of the North American B-25 with eight .50-caliber machine guns in the nose. Larry Tanberg, CO of the Sunsetters 38th Bomb Group, realized Gunn played the various groups against one another. He would go to Tanberg and say, "Larry, you ought to see what the 3rd Group is doing. God, they're doing this and that and you guys aren't doing anything at all." Then he'd go to the 3rd and reverse the statement. Tanberg always remembered the first time he flew with Gunn, in a B-25 at 14-Mile Field outside Port Moresby. Tanberg was in the righthand seat, buckling up as Gunn quickly swung out onto the runway, opened the throttles, and took off. Tanberg leaned over and asked if Gunn ever did a magneto check. "Hell, no," replied Gunn. "That's not my job, that's the crew chief's job."

To Hell with the Paperwork

M.Sgt. John Brogan arrived in Port Moresby, New Guinea, with the first U.S. units in July 1942. He was wounded in a Japanese air raid on Port Moresby and evacuated to Townsville, Australia. When Brogan decided he was fit enough, he went AWOL from the hospital and hitched a ride on a 19th Bomb Group B-17 flying to Moresby to rejoin his unit. The paperwork was fixed somehow.

John Brogan's outfit, the 8th Service Group, had to cover the entire New Guinea area, sending men to distant force-landed airplanes to strip them of excess weight to allow flight out and also sending men to wrecks to salvage anything of value. Field expedients and ingenuity were used to solve problems for which there was no normal solution.

As master sergeant, Brogan was involved in several notable examples of "field solutions." One of the simplest involved the B-24. Parked out in torrential rain, many B-24s were unusable because electrical systems were shorting out. The solution was to drill holes in the bottom of the junction boxes so water did not accumulate. Sand was packed into the tires of a damaged B-17 so it could be flown from Moresby to Townsville. Another time coolant was used instead of hydraulic fluid. A C-47 was hit by a Japanese bomb and cut almost in two, but the edges of the tear were trimmed, the fuselage splinted with 4 x 2 timbers, and it was flown to Townsville. A DC-2 had one outer wing replaced with a DC-3 wing, the three-foot difference balanced by removing the DC-3 wingtip. "Pappy" Gunn reportedly flew that plane out of Marilinan.

Forty-one Cups of Tea

In the early, disorganized days of the United States's move into the SWPA, almost everything that the Americans saw or did was new and adventurous. The rear echelons struggled to establish themselves, become organized, and cope with the long distances from southern Australian ports and cities to Darwin, and thence to Java and the Philippines. Airplanes straggled back from the fighting, and it was decided that some sort of organization in the north of Australia was needed to provide servicing for these and future air units. The first detachment was forty men from the 482nd Service Squadron to be sent from Sydney to Brisbane. Then–Sgt. John Brogan was assigned to take them there by rail. He got his detachment aboard the steam-driven train, and away it puffed on the 600-mile overnight northern journey. There was no dining car, and Brogan went to see the conductor, who said the detachment would have to pay for meals at railway diners along the way. Brogan explained that the U.S. government should have arranged rations or meals. Finally the conductor supplied a cup of tea and a bully-beef sandwich for each of Brogan's forty-one men. In payment Brogan signed a promissory note, addressed to Gen. George C. Marshall, explaining the matter and requesting payment. As a precaution Brogan signed as "Sergeant Shoes" (Brogan = Shoes). They arrived in Brisbane and got on with the war.

Twenty-five years later, in Vietnam, Brogan got to know a USAF colonel who told him that when he was a captain, he was assigned the duty of sorting through and paying all the claims on the U.S. government made during the war. One of the strangest was a bill for forty-one cups of tea and forty-one sandwiches from a sergeant in Australia in 1942. "Sergeant Brogan, did you ever use the name 'Sergeant Shoes'?" asked the colonel. Brogan admitted he had and was pleased to find that the U.S. government did not want him to pay for the tea and sand-wiches consumed so long ago.

A Great Place to Visit, but . . .

In the very early days of the buildup of U.S. forces in Australia, Brogan had been in Java, seeing what would be needed in the way of aircraft servicing assistance from Australia. On one flight from the north to Sydney, in a KLM (Dutch airline) DC-3, engine trouble caused them to land at Cloncurry, Queensland. The engine was removed and sent to Brisbane with a request for another to be sent up. Days passed, weeks passed while the crew and John Brogan waited in Cloncurry enjoying local hospitality and hotel life. After a month an engine arrived—the same one that had been sent to California for repairs and then returned. Such were maintenance and logistics arrangements in early 1942.

Yankee Know-how #1

The shortage of aircraft resulted in extraordinary efforts to keep them usable. Although the Bell P-39 was not highly regarded in air-to-air combat against the light, agile Japanese fighters, it was used extensively for ground attack. The 482nd Service Squadron came up with an ingenious method of getting a damaged P-39 from Marilinan back to Port Moresby. The P-39 was parked at Marilinan, and a member of the 482nd was under the wing, reading, when Japanese bombers appeared. One bomb went smack through the right wing, into the ground, and failed to explode. When the reclining reader "saw the hole in the wing and in the ground," said Sgt. Cy Stafford, "he took off for the jungle like a cougar and was gone for two days." The P-39 had only sixty hours' flight time, but a spare wing could not be fitted into a C-47. The damage to the P-39 included the right undercarriage, which could not be retracted, and the tanks in the wing had been holed and made useless.

The problem was solved this way: Guns and ammunition were removed from the left wing but retained in the right; a sheet metal patch was placed over the holes in the wing; the undercarriage was locked in the "down" position; a drop tank was filled under the fuselage and the left wing tanks filled; and a pilot was found to fly the plane over the mountains, first using the fuel in the left wing and firing the ammunition in the right wing to balance the loss of weight, and then continue the flight on the fuel in the drop tank.

Yankee Know-how #2

The official supply system did not contain some tools and equipment that would have speeded repair jobs. The 482nd Service Squadron was blessed with men who had a "can do" attitude, who designed and produced the following items for the squadron. The wood shop made a band saw by cutting round wheels and using old saw bands. The plastic shop made an oven by joining two field stoves. They used this to heat sheets of plastic to replace broken windows in aircraft. A pattern maker, using plaster of paris from the medical staff, made a mold to the shape of the window. Four men with pliers lifted the heated plastic from the oven, pulled it down over the mold, and held it in place while another man cooled it with compressed air until it set in shape after about five minutes.

Low on the Totem Pole

For almost all of its time, the 5th Air Force was low on the priority list for all items and classes of supplies. Capt. James B. Peterson joined the Group's 90th Squadron at Charters Towers, Queensland, on 1 October 1942. He found the squadron vehicles to be three half-ton pickups made from Australian 1941 Chevrolet coupes, one Australian one-and-a-half-ton Ford truck, one 1940 Ford, and one 1940 Dodge staff car, two old weapons carriers, two panel-body light trucks, two one-and-a-half-ton trucks, and three two-and-a-half-ton trucks. These were simply incapable of meeting the requirements of a twin-engine bomber squadron at a remote base. None were four-wheel drive, and all had to be disposed of for the move to Dobodura in May 1943.

"We Also Served"

An aspect not normally considered success in the battlefield of the heavily armed strafers was that of the Armaments sections. When the B-25 was equipped originally with .30- and .50-caliber machine guns for its role as a medium bomber, the number of armorers assigned was sufficient for that quantity of weapons. When the extra eight .50s were fitted and ammunition expenditure rose considerably, there was no immediate increase in the table of organization for extra personnel; more work had to be done.

Darn Fool Pilots!

Brig. Gen. Paul Wurtsmith had a personal P-40, which had the front fuel tank removed and a seat installed. It needed an engine change and went to the 482nd Service Squadron. Cy Stafford takes up the story.

> The engine was changed, test-hopped, and given to a P-40 squadron to fly back to the general. They decided to do a little playing around with it, and in so doing, they ground-looped it, bending the prop. Back it came, the engine was changed, and it was given back to the squadron to deliver to the general. Out they went again playing around, and while buzzing a village they hit a treetop, damaging the lower surface of the right wing, which took a sheet-metal shop four days to repair. It was sent back with a stern warning—no more horseplay!
>
> Kiss my grits if they did not fool around and ground-loop it again, bending the prop. We were getting hot under the collar with such foolishness. We were running out of parts for P-40s. The engine and prop were changed, but we could not get an oil cooler anywhere. After four or five days waiting for a cooler, and some nasty phone calls about why was it taking so long to get the plane back, one morning an Australian sergeant drove up with all the papers for supply of a generator for one of their P-40s.
>
> I asked him if they had a serviceable oil cooler; he said they did, so I arranged a swap. I got a crew to install the cooler at once and a pilot to test-fly the plane. At 1500 that evening, the maintenance officer had a pilot fly it back to the general. He told the pilot what a time we had with that plane, that he was going to watch him take off, and all he wanted to see was the tail of that plane going home!

Other lighter moments concerned the P-47 on which exhaust gases passed so close to the tail wheel that carbon would form on the wheel-locking pin, and it sometimes stuck. A major had this happen on his first flight in the big fighter, and a mechanic of the 8th Service Group jumped into a jeep, drove out to the

P-47, climbed out, and gave the pin a kick to free it. The major saw all of this. Later, people scratched their heads as they watched this pilot land a P-47, leap out of the cockpit, kick the tail-wheel, and taxi away.

Field Expedient

A B-25 was to be flown from New Guinea to Townsville, with John Brogan of the 8th Service Group aboard. But John really wanted to go to Cairns to visit a girlfriend. Before takeoff from Moresby, John rigged a wire from the magneto of one engine so he could cut power. Out over the sea, he did this several times, and finally convinced the pilot that they might not reach Townsville, so, as Brogan intended, he diverted to Cairns. The pilot went on to other duties in Townsville, while Brogan enjoyed a twelve-day stopover with his girlfriend.

Revenge Forgone, Justice Later

Working around aircraft can be dangerous, and more so at night in a war zone with enemy aircraft on the way to bomb. One night on a Port Moresby strip, a B-17 ran a wheel into a small bomb crater. Japanese planes were expected, and returning Allied bombers needed to use the strip and taxiways. By this time the service squadron crews knew shortcuts and faster ways of doing things, but they also knew the limitations of their equipment. The only available cletrack nearby would not be powerful enough to haul the B-17 out of the hole, and John Brogan, in charge of the night crew, went to bring a bigger tractor, which was some distance away in the darkness. While he was away, a major from a day fighter unit arrived and began to give orders. He demanded the B-17 be moved at once and ignored the explanations of the service crew. The "know-it-all" officer ordered the engines of the B-17 revved to full power while the cletrack was linked to the plane and pulled as hard as it could. All the ground crew knew this was extremely dangerous and tried to tell the officer that the B-17 would surge out of the hole and run up onto the cletrack, and that a bigger tractor would soon arrive to do the job. The abrasive and arrogant major repeated his orders and insisted they be obeyed at once.

Exactly what the enlisted men tried to caution against did happen. The B-17 roared up out of the crater and came forward suddenly, and the man on the cletrack was literally cut to pieces by the propeller blades. Brogan arrived back and demanded to know what the hell was going on. The crew told him and stated their intention of killing the officer when the next wave of Japanese flew over. Already their engines could be heard in the distance in the night sky. The major heard this and realized he was alone in the night with a group of people whose advice he ignored, and who had lost a friend and family man as a direct result of his interference. He disappeared into the darkness and soon after left New Guinea but returned with a new P-38 group. He was later killed in a flying accident in the United States. The officer was not one of the theater aces.

The Fearsome Jungle

There are many memories held by the servicemen who went to New Guinea. Some are humorous, but many reflect the arduous living conditions. The island was little known to the new arrivals, and their ideas had been formed from the prewar Tarzan movies. As everyone who saw these epics knew, the jungle was inhabited by headhunting warlike cannibals, lions, tigers, leopards, elephants, giant snakes, and crocodiles—a very dangerous place.

The Morgan F. Terry crew, 320th Squadron, Jolly Rogers 90th Group, flew from Charters Towers, Australia, to Port Moresby, arrived late in the day, and then were taken in the dusk "into the jungle." The truck drove for what seemed miles through this new and scary environment, and finally the crew was dropped at a collection of tents. Around them they could see nothing but dark, menacing jungle. Then, in the distance, started what they recalled as "weird music and chanting, repeated over and over," and it was getting louder and louder, closer and closer, very quickly. Were they about to be attacked by charging savages?

Several truckloads of singing natives coming back from some laboring project went past on the nearby road, and hearts slowed down in the Terry crew. But it was not until after the war, at a reunion, that people admitted to being frightened that first night in the New Guinea wilderness.

Terry and his crew, known as Terry and the Pirates, flew sixty-two missions and 405 combat hours before returning to the United States. The radioman, Butts, was an expert scrounger and often returned from his private missions with all sorts of good things. Once he somehow acquired a whole case of eggs from the high-living U.S. Navy, and more than one crew had to eat eggs, eggs, and more eggs to get rid of them before they went bad.

My Dog Can Lick Your Dog!

Marion Kirby, Headhunters 80th Fighter Squadron, recalls the clash between two of the senior members brought on by their pets. Ed "Porky" Cragg, the CO, was nicknamed because of his resemblance to the cartoon character and his love of food, and lots of it. The operations officer was George Welch, one of the few pilots to get airborne at Pearl Harbor, with four claims for Japanese shot down. Following several brushes with military discipline, Welch ended up with the 80th at Port Moresby. Kirby recalled:

Welch and Cragg were as different in character as chalk and cheese, and a rivalry grew between them in an unusual way. Welch was the owner of a dachshund, and about the same time, Cragg returned from leave with a parrot. The parrot was kept in a cage in Cragg's office. Welch's dog would lay just outside the door, following the bird's every move. One day the inevitable happened; the dog ate the parrot.

Furious, Cragg scheduled himself for leave and scoured Sydney with a fine-tooth comb until he found the biggest and ugliest bull terrier available. He came back, proud as a peacock, with just one thought in mind—complete and utter devastation of the dachshund.

The bull terrier was turned loose and, to Cragg's evident pride, soon became top dog. But one day, an enlisted man digging a latrine accidentally clipped the dog's tail with his shovel, instantly turning the dog from the "greatest fighter in camp into the biggest coward in the world." Then one day the dachshund beat the terrier, and Cragg was completely deflated.

Welch went on leave, leaving his dog in care of a bunch of new pilots. One night they gave the dog a drink in the officers' club. Then another, and another, and soon everyone was roaring with laughter at the antics of a drunken dachshund. But Welch was due back, and the "dog sitters" decided they would have to walk the dog out of drunkenness, a job that kept them up all night without sleep so the operations officer would be met by a sober dog.

"But Back in the States They Said . . ."

Charles P. Martin was assigned to the 89th Squadron, 3rd Attack Group, as assistant intelligence officer on 11 February 1943. He later became group intelligence officer and group executive officer and stayed with the 3rd until 26 August 1945. On arrival in 1943, he immediately found that almost everything he had been told in the United States about the modern equipment and accessories that would be available for use in the field was just not true. No projectors, slides, and other items were available, and none arrived until mid-1944. Crew briefings would have been much better if projected photos of target areas could have been shown; maps were inadequate, inaccurate, and insufficient in quantity; and forward-aiming cameras for the strafers were sought by squadron and group in an attempt to improve strafing attacks but were not made available. Martin made the point that U.S. ground forces provided almost no information about the positions of their units, and if it had not been for Australian liaison officers, the squadrons would not have known the locations of friendly forward troops.

"When the Jungle Goes Quiet . . ."

Japanese air raids are the source of many memories, and they affected people in different ways. One day in April 1943, Clint Solomon, 3rd Attack Group, noticed some activity around a 90 mm antiaircraft gun position, so he walked over and asked what was happening. He was told that 120 bombers escorted by 120 fighters were approaching. Solomon noticed the absolute quiet during the wait for the raid. Everything, even the animals and jungle, was silent.

Marion Kirby had a tent mate, a buddy from aviation training who decided to fly as many missions as quickly as he could, so Marion let him fly in his place on an escort to Marilinan. When the aircraft had gone, the air raid warning sounded, and Marion looked up to see "thirty-five or forty of the biggest, blackest Jap bombers headed for our airstrip. Our camp was right off the end of it. We jumped in the foxholes, the earth shook, the noise was deafening. . . . It was quite an experience. I never was willing to trade places on a mission again!"

Another group of interested watchers were observing their first Japanese daylight raid, and one person remarked casually that the wind was really howling through the power lines. The wind noise got louder. Someone said there were no power lines, and the group scattered as realization struck that the wind noise was made by Japanese bombs on the way down.

"It was often said," recalled Robert McCandless, "that the best air raid warning we had was three bombs on the airstrip."

Smoking Can Be Hazardous to Your Health

In 1942 as the Japanese advanced ever closer over the northern mountain ranges, nerves grew tighter, and a variety of official and unofficial plans were made for evacuation and escape to Australia. At this time the aircraft flew up from Australia to Moresby, were assigned targets, flew their bombing missions, and returned to Australia. Personnel were issued weapons and ammunition in case the Japanese got through to the airfields. Then one night word went around that enemy paratroopers had landed. Close to the 80th Fighter Squadron, in the pitch black of a tropical night, a few glowing embers on a burning log were thought to be men smoking. When calls to put out the cigarettes were ignored, it was assumed the little red lights were made by the Japanese paratroopers, "so the shooting started," said Marion Kirby. "The men by the log thought they were being fired on by Japanese and themselves fired back. We had a real good little war going on right in the camp for about half an hour."

"But We Are Officers! . . ."

In the 482nd Service Squadron, Cy Stafford and his friends began

serious planning when explosives were placed under the machine shop and in all mobile trailers to blow them up. Also, a list was made for the order in which to evacuate the men. Some of the Ninety-Day Wonder officers began to gripe not receiving priority. They were told, "You can be replaced in ninety days, but a mechanic takes twenty-two weeks schooling, plus what experience they have gained. That is too much to throw away."

The Usual Spy Rumor

One story going round at Moresby was that of the nurse at the 17-Mile hospital who was a spy for the Japanese and passed much information to them, but finally was caught by giving details of tail number and crew particulars in a B-17 crash, all of which was broadcast by Radio Tokyo within hours.

"And the Food We Had to Eat . . ."

Food has always been a subject of discussion and comparison among military personnel. All agree that the standard in the early days in New Guinea was low. Bread arrived with weevils and flies cooked into it. The dehydrated foods tasted bad because that aspect of science was in its infancy. There was little in the way of fresh fruit and vegetables, and milk was almost unknown. On rotation to Australia, crews amazed themselves by their hunger for fresh salads, vegetables, and milk. Many gorged themselves, putting back the weight they had lost "up north," but some did not manage to do so until they returned to the United States. Weight losses of thirty or forty pounds were common. A few put this weight loss down to the constant running up and down hills to the air raid shelters when the Japanese bombers came over.

To improve the food situation, many bomber units used aircraft not suitable for operational flying to collect fresh fruit and vegetables from places such as Cairns, Queensland, or even farther south around Brisbane or Sydney. These aircraft were called "Fat Cats" and sometimes did not exist officially, having been built from parts and wrecks. On one memorable occasion, a B-25 Fat Cat made a heavy landing, the bomb doors popped open, and the fruit and vegetables fell onto the runway, creating a large, instant but messy salad.

The Cavalry from Nadzab

While serving with the 5th Air Force as a special service officer, Robert McCandless was called on to make a mounted mission. A sergeant in a remote lookout post way up in the Nadzab valley had sent a letter to say that if the lieutenant in command of the thirty-three-man unit was not removed, the sergeant would kill him. McCandless was a former cavalryman, and because the only way to the unit was by horse, he was sent to investigate. The horses turned out to be "Chinese-size." In company with a member of the Australian New Guinea Administration Unit (ANGAU) and a guide, off he went. The trail wound along the tops of the ridges and was definitely not the quickest, most direct route, so McCandless decided to go cross-country.

Despite the ANGAU's protests, I started down the side of the mountain into the valley. The kunai grass was so tall I could only keep my orientation by guiding on the distant point on the other side. After a short while of descent the pony stopped. All the urging, kicks in the side, laying on of reins would not budge him an inch. I dismounted, took a wrap of the reins around my wrist, and took a step forward, using my weight to pull him. . . . To my utter surprise, I found myself dangling in space, suspended only by the reins and the pony holding back. The kunai hid the sheer drop.

Thanking his lucky stars for the good leather in bridle and reins, McCandless pulled himself back up to the grinning guides on the trail. After crossing flooded creeks and passing a tribal war, the travelers finally reached the unit with the pretext of delivering mail and taking inventory. They stayed three days to assess the situation and started back, intending to meet a C-47 at a grassy field in the bush and fly back. But at the noon stop a Japanese patrol was seen running toward them.

We mounted and took off at the fastest gallop the little horses could muster. We discovered the running Japanese were moving ahead of us. We knew we had to beat them to our rendezvous, and the C-47 better be on time! When we came to one of the streams that had been flooded, we found that it was down to about six inches of clear cool mountain water. My horse stopped, put his head down, and gulped twice before I could raise his head. I pulled him up and urged him on. He bounded through the stream and down the trail when he died as if he had been shot, head going down and hindquarters coming up and over. I kicked out the stirrups and landed with a forward roll, then came up on my feet. The horse did not move. As hot as he was from running, the cold water had killed him quickly. The ANGAU circled back, stuck out his arm, and I caught it, doing a flying mount.

As we approached the field the C-47 was on its down-leg approach. The co-pilot had seen the running Japanese. The three of us galloped up, swung off the ponies, and hit the ground running. As soon as the first was aboard, the plane began moving, we scrambled in, and as we shut the door and locked it, shots were fired at us. We climbed, banking sharply right to avoid the peak closing on us. The ponies were left to be spoils of war.

McCandless's other duties were not as hazardous.

There was a short time at Moresby when we had a thirty-foot pleasure yacht, which we would use to take pilots and nurses to a close-by secluded beach for swimming and relaxing. We also constructed a gathering unit for fresh water by stretching a large piece of canvas between two tall poles, funneling it downward to empty oil barrels. This gathered rainwater, and we carried it in buckets to a built-up platform that held several barrels, the water running into homemade shower heads. Nurses used to visit [so they could] use it to wash their hair.

The group also had ice for the beach which they "made by flying tubs of water in an airplane at high altitude." They created tents that were decorated inside with silk parachutes. "There were several colors, and in one the occupants had taken apart different colored parachutes to make varicolored sections. Inside the tent was a row of six helmets, each fitted on a frame supported by poles, for morning shaving."

Some units managed to live with more comfort than others. The type of unit often had a direct bearing on how much comfort could be managed. Charles King, 39th Fighter Squadron, noticed:

The bomber and headquarters people generally had things nicer than the fighter jocks, because they had planes that could ferry goodies up from Australia. It did not take the good outfits long to be resourceful, and trade was one of the ways to do it.

We were able to put up tent frames and good wooden floors because one of our enlisted men used a broken-down jeep to make a sawmill. Other outfits brought us wood; we sawed it and kept half as payment. After a time, the 39th got Donald Dake, who had been a hotel manager in the United States; he was a good administrator and a chef of such talent that he could show the cooks how to do it. He would visit ships in the harbor and arrange delivery of excess food from ships that were returning to the United States and did not need it. The 39th mess became so well liked that visiting pilots would stop there rather than where they were supposed to be fed.

"Remember Nadzab?"

Many 5th Air Force veterans believe that the Nadzab area was the best of their many camp locations from Australia to Okinawa. It seemed that the mosquitoes and bugs in general were fewer, there was less illness, the food was better, and the supply system somehow seemed to function more smoothly. The Port Moresby area was thought of as a place they were happy to leave behind. Also, the Owen Stanley Range, and the abominable weather, did not have to be crossed on every mission. In the Nadzab area, however, it became obvious that some Japanese were still loose, creeping down from the hills to steal food and perhaps carry on the war. One morning a 320th Bomb Squadron crewman was found strangled to death with a wire, killed in his sleep, and it was believed infiltrating Japanese had done this.

Definitely Not the Hollywood Version

All these things were really minor efforts at achieving some standard of civilized living in what was basically a wilderness. John Shemelynce was a photographer with the 3rd Attack Group, which moved from Townsville to Port Moresby by landing craft.

> The moment we landed, life took a big change. Dusty or muddy roads, depending: before rain, dust; right after, mud. Food: no bread, hard-tack, the famous Australian bully-beef, dehydrated eggs, milk, et cetera. Mosquitoes, bombing, and no social life. The outdoor movie was the most important entertainment we had. No Post Exchange; our supply issued toilet articles, cigarettes, and other basic items. No beer.
>
> So every night the outdoor movie was it. You tried to get there early so you could get a good seat, and generally brought your own, in addition to a raincoat. If it didn't rain you could always use it to keep mosquitoes from biting through your clothes.

Being only nineteen years old, brought up on a dairy farm, and used to a rough life, young Shemelynce found little difficulty adapting to the conditions.

The ones who suffered most were the married men. They may have had a child born just as they left the United States, by now it is two years old and they have not seen it. I have personally seen tears in their eyes when they read letters from home telling them of their child. Most of these men knew also that they would not see the child until the war was over, or, possibly, never.

"All kinds of bugs and creatures and snakes" used to pester Bill Martin, B-24 pilot in the 90th Group.

Mosquitoes, holy smoke, they just ate you up and you had to learn to sleep with your arms by your sides inside the mosquito netting. You could tell a new crew. When they went to the mess hall, their arms, from the elbow halfway up to the shoulder, would be a solid mass of red from the mosquitoes that had feasted on them during the night. It wasn't uncommon to just sit there in the officers' club and kill mosquitoes while writing letters. I remember killing twenty-one mosquitoes when I wrote a letter, just piling them up on the desk by the letter. Of course, we had screens, but they did a lousy job.

Apart from the movies, some of the 321st Squadron, 90th Group, had fun for a while out on the waters of the harbor. Bill Martin was one of the players who would "use those tough steaks. We'd trail them behind a boat on the harbor, and when a shark attacked we'd bring him up with grenades and then chop him up with Thompson submachine guns . . . and you've heard about those shark-feeding frenzies!" Only later did realization sink in that if anything had happened to the boat, the happy Thompson gunners would have been in the water with the sharks. "That's the kind of amusement we had, because there were no women. A simple thing like a chocolate bar or a Coke was just beyond reach."

Some people were able to plan a little before going to New Guinea, as did Dennis Glen Cooper, squadron and later group intelligence officer for the 475th Fighter Group.

I was careful to select things that might be useful to me when I got there, for I knew that once I was in New Guinea it would be impossible to purchase anything. One day, when I had time off, I journeyed into the village [of Ipswich, Australia] to look about and to purchase a couple of items: pajamas, two bed sheets, two pillowcases, and a comfortable pillow. Those were some of the wisest purchases I ever made, for I am six foot three inches tall and an army cot will not hold me. I was also able to get an air mattress, and I tell you, I slept in luxury, with air mattress, clean sheets, comfortable pillow and case, and pajamas. Of course, we never used a blanket.

"And the Rain There . . ."

Morgan Terry's B-24 gunners had a good position on a grassy slope in the Nadzab camp area, and all enjoyed it until the first heavy rain fell. Then a sheet of water swept down the slope and kept on flowing around, under, and over everything in its path. A disgruntled crew decided to do something about it. Lumber was "acquired" and a beautiful level floor erected, about two feet high at the back and nice and flush with the ground at the front. Everyone was really happy with it until the next rainstorm. The sheet of water swept down the slope and kept on flowing around, under, and over everything sitting on the level floor, cascading off the back in a little Niagara. A lot of effort was expended in digging drains to divert the floods.

Check and Check Again

Under the pressure of preparing the big B-24s for operations, sometimes little things were not checked, with frightening results for other people. Bill Moran recalls a take-off from Nadzab when the crew became all too aware that the cap on a fuel tank in the wing had not been replaced properly. As they were roaring down the strip under full power, petrol began streaming back, and the fumes were so intense that the gunners went onto oxygen. The pilot radioed their predicament and was told to go away for half an hour so the rest of the group could take off, and then come back for a landing. Bill has vivid memories of "sweating out a landing when we were terrified that one spark could send us into a fireball."

On another occasion, the day after his twenty-second birthday, he was photographer of a crew tasked to do a reconnaissance up into the Halmaheras. Two 1,000-pound bombs were carried, but the B-24 was loaded down with wing tanks and two extra bomb bay tanks. Finding a convoy, they went down to attack, shot down a Jake floatplane, and then straddled the largest ship with the bombs, which blew in the hull plates and the ship began to sink. The aggressive crew in the B-24 made a series of passes at six hundred feet, machine-gunning the hapless Japanese on the ship for twenty minutes. Then Murphy's Law came into force, and engine trouble intervened to remind them all just where they were, how far they were from base, and that their recent targets were probably in no good mood.

They set course for distant New Guinea and, owing to an unsympathetic U.S. Navy, had to bypass Hollandia (now in Allied hands) and go on back east along the coast to Nadzab, anxiously watching the fuel gauges drop. Dean, the pilot, tried unsuccessfully to land at the Gusap fighter strip but had to go all the way to Nadzab. He radioed for landing priority, but as he approached the runway threshold, he was horrified to see a B-25 landing from the opposite direction!

The B-24 was committed and had to go on and land, and red flares alerted the B-25, which applied power and leaped over the B-24 as its wheels touched the runway and all four engines stopped. The tanks were empty.

Well, not quite. As the helpless bomber was towed away and postflight checking began, it was discovered the extra wing tanks had not been emptied into the normal tanks, and there were still one hundred gallons available. The flight engineer had to make himself scarce for an urgent debriefing, but some of the crew wanted to have a serious talk with him.

Escort with a Difference

Richard "Dick" Grills, rear gunner in B-24 Terry's Pirates, had noticed how the fighter escort would discreetly slide away from the bombers as they entered the flak zone over the target and then swing back when it was all over. But one day he watched an RAAF P-40 maintain station on the B-24 as the others swung out, and then it crept in closer and closer to sit just off the right tailfin and stay there through all the flak and to the end of the bomb run. The pilot was looking across at Dick, grinning and waving all the while. Dick never did find out who the pilot was, or why he did it, but it increased his regard for RAAF P-40 pilots.

SIX

Hammer Blow

Hollandia, March 1944

The Ultra signals intercept service had been able to acquire good details of the flights into western New Guinea by Japanese formations. The lead airplane often radioed information about the number in the formation, the unit it was to join, and the airfield destination. The passage of many such formations from Manila south through the island chain was tracked, and general headquarters intelligence and operations staffs knew the status of the enemy air arm. Many of the strikes that destroyed so many Japanese aircraft on the ground were planned around this information. The Hollandia area radio traffic was constantly monitored by the RAAF 3 Wireless Unit at Darwin, and this Australian unit later was praised for its part in the Allied air force successes against the Japanese air forces.

Despite the flow of information from air photos and the signals intercepts, it was decided to send a party of army personnel to the Hollandia area to check the situation on the ground and to report Japanese strengths, locations, and dispersal efforts. Such parties had been successful since the start of hostilities in the Papua New Guinea and Solomon Island campaigns. Some of the men became legends for their bravery and determination in remaining deep in Japanese-held territory and radioing warnings of air and ship movements. The Japanese showed no mercy, and of those who were captured only one of the men survived the war. Natives also often betrayed them and led Japanese troops to the Coast Watcher camps.

The Coast Watcher team of eleven men selected for the Hollandia operation was experienced and had operated in New Guinea and on New Britain and the Admiralties. The plan was that the submarine USS *Dace* would land them in Tanahmerah Bay. The first boatload went ashore and found the selected landing place was not suitable, so they signaled by torch that the landing was not to go ahead. The codeword for go ahead was *groggo,* and cancellation was *washout.* Aboard the submarine whoever was responsible for reading the light signals was incompetent, negligent, or worse, because the remainder of the party was sent off for shore in their rubber boats.

Then it became clear that natives nearby had quickly betrayed them to the Japanese, and a battle followed. Six of the team were killed and the others survived and endured great hardships until the invasion force arrived. The mission was a failure, with loss of Allied lives, mainly because the submarine captain or his officers were incompetent or afraid to be close to shore.

At a much higher level of the Allied command, there may have been other influences at work. When the Ultra system reported accurate details of the Japanese from regional commanders down to tactical level, and photoreconnaissance confirmed this information, the author wonders if Coast Watcher and similar operations really were sent to Japanese-occupied territory as decoys to distract the Japanese and provide a ready explanation for the successful Allied air operations.

Hollandia had been harassed at night by a small number of B-24s as part of General Kenney's plan to make the Japanese believe it was out of Allied fighter-escort range and safe from daylight attacks. The weather, as always, was an important factor, and for the Morgan Terry crew in B-24 Terry's Pirates, it provided a rough flight on 28 March. This mission is one of Dick Grills' most vivid memories of his time with the 320th Squadron, 90th Group. They flew to Finschhafen to load bombs and make final preparations for the flight. While there they were twice interrupted by Japanese air raids. Finally they took off for Hollandia. The first hour was smooth flying, but then a series of storms was met. Grills recalls:

We tried to go under it, over it, and around it, but couldn't find any end to it. Finally we drove through at high altitude—19,600 feet. That's where the trouble began. There were winds going every direction. First we were going up, then down, then sideways. Sometimes we dropped 3,000 to 4,000 feet at a crack, but immediately after would be going up just as fast and usually sideways at the same time. Several times we'd be going 190 miles an hour, dropping 1,000 feet a minute, but next minute be going up 1,000 feet a minute at 150 miles an hour. All the time it was raining.

About halfway through, two things happened to make it worse. It started snowing and icing up, and my electrically heated flying suit stopped working. Inside the tail turret became all white with snow and ice, just like refrigerator walls, and, of course, it was all wet with the earlier rain, so this froze on me. . . . My hands and feet were nearly stiff, but I managed to keep my hands moving. Static electricity was hopping all over the guns and turret. All the time we were buffeted by the storm.

When we finally got through and went down a little, it was like heaven, but it didn't last long. In thirty minutes we ran into another storm. Terry, the pilot, was determined to make it to the target, so we plunged on into the second storm. Exactly the same thing happened again, but we were thrown around worse than before, and after twenty minutes our oxygen began to run low. We sweated it out for thirty minutes; a nightmare. Then we ran into another storm, our oxygen was low, and we had to turn back. We only hit one storm, thank God, and that was the end of it.

We spent seven hours on this run and next day were a mass of aches and pains, sore throats, hands, and feet. My knees fitted very tightly under the brackets that held the ammo, and the pressure from the up and down motions of the flight actually forced blood through the skin, despite the layers of olive-drab pants and heated flight suit. Never, as long as I live, will I forget that night.

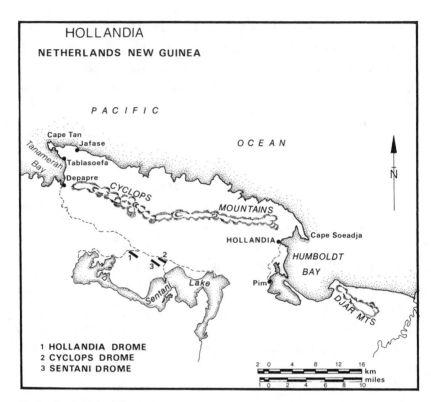

Hollandia airfields and towns

Hollandia, 30 March 1944

Before dawn, seven B-24s harassed Hollandia and the airfields. Farther east ground crews put finishing touches to preparations for the first daylight strike with P-38 escort. Flight crews were woken and prepared. In the early morning light, the big B-24s began rolling down the long runways. Leading the bomber force was the Jolly Rogers Group. Waiting to go were the P-38s, some new, some older with recently installed tanks in the leading edge of the wing. Because of a shortage of P-38s in theater, only four squadrons were available to escort the bombers on this mission. Hundreds of P-38s sat in depots in the United States.

Gradually the formations closed up and set course west. Japanese below them reported the bombers heading for Hollandia, but little notice of these alerts seemed to be taken at Japanese higher command. After all, Hollandia was out of range of daylight raids and escorts. However, Allied radio intercepts detected a number of Japanese transport aircraft flying west before the bombers arrived over Hollandia.

With very little warning to those in the target areas on the Hollandia airstrips, at 1035 seventy-five B-24s showered 5,900 20-pound and 120-pound fragmentation bomb clusters from 10,000 to 12,500 feet and laid a deadly pattern across the exposed dispersal areas and unprotected aircraft. A steadily advancing explosive carpet unrolled over airfields where 350 aircraft were parked without protection. Again Japanese commanders had been criminally negligent with their force, built and dispatched at substantial cost from the Home Islands.

Surprise on the ground was widespread. "Sagawa," medical officer of 113 Lines of Communication (L of C) Hospital, was caught unprepared with others, and in great haste they began to dig under the officers' quarters as the thunder of B-24 engines drowned out the shouting and yelling of orders.

Sergeant Major Takemori, 33 Sentai, who had flown in defense of the Wewak area despite being plagued with defective oxygen, gunsight, and wing tanks, was caught on the ground. With others he fled the obvious target zone and went to the bivouac area in the mountains. In many areas there was no warning, and a diarist wrote that because of this lack, "we lost eighteen killed by bombs."

The size and irresistible force of the USAAF formation impressed a forty-year-old lieutenant in charge of telephone communications. He watched the squadrons pass overhead and witnessed the bombing, but he felt remote from the entire event; it all seemed abstract, without any feeling of personal danger. The demonstration of enemy power reinforced his disbelief in the reports about the massive Japanese relief force said to be assembling to come to the aid of units in the South Seas.

After the bombing, at the hospital, Sagawa was told the Hollandia antiaircraft defenses and 100 airplanes were destroyed. One reason for the weak antiaircraft fire was that some guns were in still-wet concrete, and only 6 were able to fire. The bomb carpets had been impartial, and pilots and flight crews died with ground troops. Sergeant Shimada, 77 Sentai, noted that bombing killed Lieutenant Nanango and Matsumura, and another diarist was told that at least 5 pilots were killed. A private was told that up to 30 March, night bombers destroyed a total of about 70 planes and killed about 60 men, but in this attack,

200 U.S. bombers destroyed 80 bombers and 70 fighters, killed 124, and wounded 60.

A member of 208 Sentai had counted about 300 aircraft at Hollandia and estimated that 200 Lilys, Helens, Dinahs, and Oscars were destroyed. An armorer from 208 saw all 15 Lilys of 3 Chutai destroyed and 10 men killed. As he gazed around in the aftermath of the raid, at burning aircraft, the huge columns of smoke that blotted out the sun, and the dust haze settling after the bombing, it seemed that every aircraft in his sight, regardless of unit, was wrecked or damaged beyond repair. One Japanese in an antiaircraft artillery unit counted the wrecks visible from his action station. He saw 109 destroyed aircraft, and the attack brought home to him just how hopeless was Japan's position, particularly in New Guinea. Because the gunners stayed at their posts, that unit suffered heavy losses, and 95 percent of their casualties were deaths from bomb fragments.

In his postwar interrogation, Colonel Kaneko stated that the most effective U.S. aircraft for inflicting losses on the ground were the B-24s and B-25s, "particularly the formation of thirty or more B-24s. Also, the use of many small bombs was effective in this sort of operation."

Jay Robbins led twenty-three P-38s of the 80th Fighter Squadron. They arrived over the target area, and he saw Tonys and Oscars to the right. Robbins warned the 475th Group squadrons. Only the 65th Squadron, the 43rd Ken's Men Bomb Group, was attacked by Japanese fighters and claimed two of the estimated twenty-five enemy engaged for no losses. The 80th Squadron P-38s saw seven Oscars just as the Japanese began to split-s onto the B-24s, and some Japanese slipped through to the bombers. The U.S. pilots reported that the Japanese tactics "seemed to be almost totally lacking in any organized manner. Except in very few cases they seemed to be unwilling to mix with our fighters. Their favorite maneuver was the half-roll or split-s. The majority of enemy contacted were in disorganized bunches, or in pairs, and occasionally alone. Most of the enemy sighted were slightly below bomber level and to northwest of the target area where they seemed to mill around with no apparent purpose."

Extracts from some of the combat reports in AAF Intsum 199 give an idea of the day's actions.

I then made another pass at an airplane which was in a sharp turn. I couldn't turn tight enough to get enough lead and my shot fell behind him.

They came at us in a line abreast for a head-on pass. I opened fire at 500 yards and saw pieces fly from the Oscar. He passed under me and the last I saw of him, he was still going, apparently not too badly damaged.

I found myself in the middle of about six to eight Oscars; I fired snapshots at two of them but without enough lead. Next pass was made at an Oscar that was in almost a completely stalled position. I observed strikes from the tail to the cowling, but he peeled off into a vertical dive, apparently under control.

Jay Robbins reported: "One dived and turned right and I had a 30-degree deflection from rear. I got numerous hits and he burst into flames and crashed (*Author:* another aircraft being attacked). I made a very fast diving turn to the left and got on his tail again and immediately he started a turn and half-rolled again. The Oscar was too low and crashed as he attempted to pull out of the dive."

Cy Homer, 80th Headhunters Squadron ace, destroyed one Tony and damaged two in the combat. Seeing an Oscar behind a P-38, he dived and forced the Japanese away, and then swung behind a Tony, which went into a 60-degree dive while making vertical reverses as he went down. Homer hit him in the left wing, but the Tony hauled around in a turn beneath the diving P-38, and Homer lost him. He made a head-on pass at a distant Tony, with no result. Then he slowly

pulled up behind and underneath a Tony flying over the target. He had a bomb, probably aerial, slung underneath his wing. I closed to 100 yards and fired, my shells going ten feet beneath him as my sight was off. I pulled up and saw cannon shells explode beneath the fuselage, causing parts of the fuselage to scatter in the air. He rolled over onto his back and stayed in that position ten seconds, then fell off, rolling downward. His prop was windmilling, and I think I got his engine.

I searched for five minutes and pulled up behind another Tony. It dived at about a 45-degree angle and I followed, closing very slowly. I came in range at about 6,000 feet and fired, and pulled out as I was indicating 480 [mph]. I saw cannon shells hit his fuselage before I broke away, pulled up, looked, and saw him hit the water about a mile offshore fifteen miles northwest of the target.

This was the ninth of Cy Homer's fifteen victories. He started his score on 21 August at Wewak. Jay Robbins claimed the fourteenth and fifteenth of his twenty-two victories. The Headhunters claimed a total of seven: two for Captain

Robbins and one each for Lieutenants Homer; Vernon Jenner, Jenner's first victory; Paul Murphey, his fourth; and Louis Schriber and Charles Ray, the second of five victories for both Schriber and Ray. Schriber saw Robbins's second victim hit the ground when he could not pull out of the split-s in time. Other 80th pilots claimed two probables and five damaged. Only one 80th airplane had been hit, and that by one large bullet.

The 431st Squadron, 475th Satan's Angels Group, claimed a damaged Tony, shared by the Group CO, Col. Charles MacDonald, and Lt. Alvin Kidd. The 432nd did not claim any damaged. Four P-38s fitted with the new fuel system had to return due to faults with the new kit, but eighteen others reached the target area.

The 33 Sentai was airborne and claimed a P-38 destroyed, but it lost five fighters damaged on the ground, with six men killed and two wounded. Captain Tagashira led six Oscars of 77 Sentai, claimed one B-24 and one P-38 destroyed and three B-24s and a P-38 damaged for two of his own damaged. His pilots were Sergeant Major Kobayashi, Sergeant Ota, and Corporals Arad, Hara, and Yamaguchi.

When the raiders had gone, salvage and repair work began among the shambles on the airfields. Those who had fled returned to their units. When he arrived back from the bivouac area in the mountains, Takemori lamented the destruction of one hundred planes on the ground at Number 1 field and heavy personnel losses on Number 3. In his diary he listed the Sentai deaths: Second Lieutenant Yoshino; Sergeant Major Oshima; Sergeants Matsumura, Takeuchi, and Sawada; and Corporal Yamamoto. Second Lieutenant Aono from 33 Sentai was also killed, and 63 Sentai lost Sergeant Musubishiro.

The Japanese officially counted seventy planes destroyed by the 20-pound bombs and reported that destroyed aircraft had burned rather than been torn apart by blast and shrapnel. The Japanese described the attack as "small bombs with a dense fire net destroyed at one stroke seventy aircraft." By 2100 hours, 38 Airfield Battalion reported all runways repaired and sent messages to all subordinate companies to do their utmost to defend the airfield when the enemy returned next day.

Tadji, farther east, had also been hit by twenty-three B-25s, eighteen P-40s, and thirty-one P-47s. Twenty-nine tons of bombs hit the airstrips, put the emergency strip out of commission, and caused a two-thousand-foot-high column of smoke, which could be seen fifteen minutes after the attack. Wewak and Madang were attacked by A-20s, P-39s, and P-40s. Despite the constant air attacks of past weeks, one particular group of Japanese at Wewak seemed to have been optimists. One survivor wrote in his diary, "Thirty fighters attacked, but as we thought they were friendly, did not seek shelter and so had twenty-two killed, three wounded, and six barges sunk."

News of the devastating attack spread as far away as But, itself so recently pounded by Allied formations. One soldier was told that more than one hundred planes were destroyed on the ground by a thirty-minute B-24 bombardment. Japanese claims of damage inflicted on the raiders were quickly made known, and one diarist noted that thirty U.S. planes were claimed shot down.

While the Japanese were counting the cost of being unprepared, assessing the wreckage for salvage, carrying away the dead and wounded, and wondering how to report this disaster, to the east the next blow was gathering strength. On Allied airfields the bombers were made ready for the next mission. The fighters were refueled and rearmed, fuel consumption figures discussed, tactics rehashed, and orders and advice given. There was no doubt the mission had been a success.

Allied Air Force Intelligence Summary 196 described the mission:

A 140-ton attack during the day on Cyclops and Hollandia aerodromes, with photographs showing twenty-five airplanes destroyed and sixty-seven others damaged on the ground. Fuel dumps were hit, and one great column of smoke rose to 10,000 feet and was visible 150 miles away. About forty enemy fighters intercepted, of which ten were destroyed, and seven probably destroyed. Antiaircraft was slight, medium, and heavy—inaccurate.

The military intelligence section at General MacArthur's general headquarters compiled Intelligence Summary 739, which described the raid, repeated the figures for enemy planes destroyed and damaged, and also said that with some 41 percent of the aircraft at Hollandia out of action, the Japanese might disperse the remainder to airfields farther west, such as Sawar, Sarmi, or the Vogelkop area. It was thought air defense of Hollandia would continue, as it was from there that support to Japanese forces in eastern New Guinea had to come.

The Japanese aircraft replacement system continued to feed airplanes into the combat area. On this day another fourteen fighters were detected on radio en route to Hollandia from island transit fields to the northwest.

31 March 1944

So confident were the Allied planners and commanders that the strike force simply repeated the mission of the previous day. Approach, bombing height, and timings were the same. Four B-24s turned back, but the other sixty-seven paraded up the Markham, Ramu, and Sepik valleys and sailed over Hollandia. This time, after Japanese watchers on the coast flashed the alert to Hollandia, a warning was broadcast and seventy minutes' notice was given. The Japanese were still clearing damage from the day before when another 140 tons of 100-pound demolition bombs rained down; another carpet of destruction rolled across the airfields.

Still not recovered from the battering of their 28 March flight through the storm, the Morgan Terry crew in the Jolly Rogers Group flew this mission. Like the other crews, they were woken at 0345 hours, briefed, and took off on the eight-hour flight. They were carrying forty 100-pound demos and led an element of the 319th. In his rear turret, Dick Grills looked down at Hollandia as the bombs "really blew the hell out of it; biggest fires and most damage I have seen. A big bomb dump explosion was worst. AA not too bad; aircraft was hit. Fighters attacked after leaving the target; fired; missed." He also noted, after landing, "very tired."

For many 90th Group veterans, the bombing that day was the best they had seen. Fires sprang up among the parked airplanes. Three B-24s were damaged by antiaircraft fire, as when Lt. Paul Bundick's B-24 took a shell or material from other aircraft through a bomb bay door—an incendiary from another B-24 damaged an engine cowling.

Three hundred sixty bombs were dropped by ten 64th Squadron aircraft of the 43rd Group, and crews saw them all explode on the target. They also reported a diving P-38 with its left engine on fire and saw a Dinah fall into Humboldt Bay. This Japanese plane was shot down by Corky Smith of the 80th Headhunters. The second flight in the 65th Squadron formation was entirely RAAF, led by Squadron Leader (Major) O'Brien. The 65th dropped their frags and incendiary clusters, watched waves of explosions blossom below them, and saw three planes shot down by P-38s—one fell into the water about five miles offshore and two fell onto the land.

The bomber crewmen had grandstand seats for the spectacle, and all squadrons reported watching explosions march through the parked aircraft. They used phrases such as 100-pound demos through the dispersal areas; three aircraft received direct hits; another fifteen burning; direct hits on three twin-engine planes; twelve aircraft in revetments burning; a large oil fire north of the strip; large fires, smoke to seven thousand feet; thirty aircraft in the bomb pattern, fifteen burning; good bombing; covered the south side of the wooded area where many planes were parked.

Some of the bomb pattern roared across 68 Antiaircraft Battalion and killed thirty-two men and wounded thirty-three. Many other casualties were caused, and wounded began arriving at the hospitals. The doctor who quickly dug a bombshelter the day before watched the raid, saw the fighter interception, and then saw the airfield ablaze with gasoline fires. Of sixty fighters nearby he counted forty-two destroyed, and two of sixteen antiaircraft guns were also destroyed.

Among the parked aircraft destroyed were the Tonys of 68 and 78 Sentai. As well as airplanes, the bombs destroyed most of the mechanical and maintenance equipment. It was the end for both Sentai. The 63 Sentai had only eight Oscars serviceable after this attack. At the air depot, twenty-two Oscars of 77 Sentai awaiting repair were all destroyed.

Corporal "Fukuda," a twenty-three-year-old air-gunner in 208 Sentai, was impressed with the bombing "which destroyed everything except the campsites in the jungle. All our forty serviceable planes and another twenty under repair were smashed. I had a high regard for the B-24s, but was terrified of B-25s, and regarded highly the P-38, which was better than any Japanese fighter."

The antiaircraft fire this time was a little more accurate and damaged two bombers, leaving minor holing in Red Raiders aircraft.

More Japanese fighters were airborne, but fifty-two P-38 escorts engaged them. The U.S. pilots thought the Japanese seemed disorganized and dispirited, just as they had been the day before. About twenty-five Oscars were counted, scattered over the sky.

The 80th Headhunters attacked. Jay Robbins climbed left onto an Oscar and fired—many flashes were seen on the engine, left wing, and cockpit; the Nakajima went down and crashed. Robbins had problems with his fuel system and had to leave the combat area. Louis Schriber and his wingman, Jesse Corallo, continued the chase after an Oscar that Robbins had to leave. Schriber shot it down and was in time to see another hit by Corallo impact the ground a few hundred yards from his own victory.

Meanwhile, Ken Ladd flew through other flights ahead, brought his flight up to the fight, closed on the tail of an Oscar, and fired from such short range that Japanese oil sprayed back onto his windshield. Ladd saw the Oscar diving steeply near the water. After a few passes with another Japanese, Ladd also had to leave, conscious of the long return flight.

Capt. Corky Smith brought the fifth flight in, dived on some Oscars, which evaded the attack, and then Smith saw a Dinah overhead, and climbed after it. The Japanese saw the P-38s and decided to run for it. The P-38 was just able to close on the twin-engine airplane, but then Smith found his illuminating bulb for the gunsight was burned out. Smith fired and corrected by watching his tracers, to bring the hail of shot onto the Dinah. Hits sparked on the left engine. Some Oscars intervened, and Corky had to turn to cope with them, but when he was able to swing back to the Dinah, it was plunging seaward trailing smoke and flames from the left side and was confirmed by the bomber crews.

As the Headhunters left the target area, they could see one large column of smoke reaching to eight thousand feet and many smaller fires throughout the target area.

The 80th Headhunters claimed 7: 1 each to Captains Robbins and Smith and Lieutenants Caldwell, Corallo, Ladd, Schriber, and Stanifer. These brought squadron claims to 185 destroyed. Total claims for the mission were 5 Oscars and a Dinah destroyed, 1 Oscar probably destroyed, 2 damaged. The magic "200 Destroyed" was in sight.

The 33 Sentai was in action and claimed 9-0-0 for two Oscars damaged in the air but lost five destroyed and two damaged on the ground. However, one writer noted that "morale is high despite yesterday's losses and damage on the ground." In his diary Sergeant Major Takemori, who had so much bad fortune, related teaming up with two 77 Sentai Oscars in a fifteen-minute tangle with four P-38s. Again his drop tanks would not release, and he was furious, believing he could have shot down two U.S. fighters, but instead Inagaki and Kurahara were killed.

The 431st Squadron, Satan's Angels Group, fought twenty-five Japanese fighters thirty miles south of Sentani and claimed 7-0-0 for the loss of one Lightning. The Japanese were above the P-38s and approached from the north.

Fifteen Japanese dived on Green Flight, and the U.S. pilots could clearly see the mottled green camouflage over the natural metal of the Oscars.

Frank Monk, leading Yellow Flight, called to drop tanks and swung into the Japanese, slid in behind the third enemy fighter, and fired; bits of canopy, engine cowling, and fuselage flicked back. The Oscar flicked over and down, trailing smoke. Monk pulled up and saw the Oscar explode in its dive. Monk took the flight around to clear their tails, checked his men, and noticed that Lt. Robert Donald, the number four man, was missing.

Herman Zehring, the element leader, had seen Donald leave the flight to attack a Japanese below, and, looking down to watch Donald, had seen Monk's victory blow up. Zehring called out more Japanese coming in, and as Monk could not see them, he told Zehring to take flight lead. Zehring led the flight down onto ten or more Japanese below, over the bay. He shot one Oscar into the water and later shot down a second, which crashed on the bay shore. Zehring thought the Japanese were inexperienced, confused, and reluctant to fight. Yellow Flight was low on fuel, so it left the area.

Francis Lent, who claimed his first victory over Wewak on 18 August, led Blue Flight and shot down the last two of his eleven victories. Two other P-38s were tangling with an Oscar when Lent flew in to the combat, got in close to the tail of the Oscar, and fired twice; the Japanese dived away but exploded. Lent had lost his flight, so he joined three other P-38s as escort to the B-24s. He noticed smoke streaming from the right engine of one of those P-38s and called a warning with advice to turn for base. The P-38 turned, but the smoke thickened and darkened, the propeller did not feather, and the engine burst into flames; the P-38 started spinning.

An Oscar seized the chance and dived on the smoking P-38, but Lent shot down the Japanese. The P-38 began to fall to pieces, then exploded and crashed. The burning Oscar impacted about a mile to the west. Lent was joined by Lt. Merle Pearson, and they agreed that neither pilot escaped. Later it was deduced that Donald was flying the P-38.

The 432nd claimed 0-1-2, all Oscars. Their opponents probably had been from 77 Sentai, which had six Oscars in combat and claimed 3-2-0 for three Oscars damaged.

Below them, the combat was watched by many Japanese. Lieutenant Colonel Okada, commander 49 Anchorage Unit, saw "the engagement of one of our planes with three enemy. It was pitiful." He may have watched Francis Lent shoot down his victim, mentioned previously.

Somehow those on the ground who kept diaries or other personal records never saw the displays of martial brilliance reported to home audiences or higher headquarters in which a lone Oscar outperformed a formation of U.S. aircraft and shot down two or three enemy in one combat or destroyed several bombers with one bomb. Instead, the personal writings daily confirm defeats and losses inflicted on the Japanese formations with few mentions of Japanese successes.

The surviving Japanese fighters returned to land but realized that landing would not be possible in the wilderness of craters and burning planes on and around the fields. They flew to distant bases as far as Wakde, where Tsugio Shimada and his friends from 77 Sentai landed. A Japanese report stated that 166 planes were destroyed and 5 enemy shot down. Allied photos showed a total of 208 aircraft destroyed.

Word of the second big attack on Hollandia was flashed to Wewak, where Lieutenant Horie, 6 Flying Division headquarters, wrote: "We have been gradually pushed back by the enemy, and unhappy days follow one on another. I would like to celebrate next New Year in Sydney."

Not far from Horie, the Wewak branch of 27 Field Freight Depot held 3,569 tons of rice, 1,087 tons of various foods, and 476 tons of wheat. The airfields had been wrecked, shipping was becoming scarcer, and little more food would arrive in Wewak by air or sea.

Again the Japanese claimed the U.S. formations had been hit hard, but some officers and soldiers were beginning to question the figures. The doctor was told, "Our fighters intercepted over Aitape and shot down sixty of the enemy. A story like that is not very dependable." Another diarist noted that the bombers "appeared from the southeast at three thousand meters. Severe damage to all three airfields. Sixty-four B-24s shot down."

But it was obvious to many Japanese that despite their official claims of heavy losses to the AAF, the U.S. bomber formations were inflicting severe damage to the entire Hollandia complex. All units were ordered to send all available men to work under the command of the airfield battalions. As the raids caught many units by surprise, it was decided to improve the warning system, so a hilltop semaphore was established: red for alert and white for all-clear. In addition, all stores were ordered to be dispersed and camouflaged. Work across the bombed airfields went on without pause, and at 2230 that night, 38 Airfield Battalion reported work still in progress with assistance given by the survey unit and air depot. By mid-afternoon the next day, two of the three strips were usable.

Military organizations being what they are, normal air force business went on; after the raid 6 Flying Division had a conference and then established a four-man Air Accident Investigation Committee. The antiaircraft units realized their vulnerability to the bomb carpets and that their usual layout, with the guns in a diamond shape with commander and instruments in the center, was not best for this situation, so 3 Battery 66 AA Battalion began to redeploy into a line formation, with guns one thousand meters apart.

The AAF Intelligence Summary 196 described the mission:

The heavies returned for a second, successive 140-ton attack on dispersal areas at the Hollandia, Cyclops, and Sentani strips. Large fires were started and smoke was observed one hour after the attack, rising to 15,000 feet. Approximately thirty fighters intercepted, of which fourteen were destroyed. As a result of the two days' strikes, 219 airplanes were destroyed or damaged. One P-38, this date, was the only Allied airplane lost in the two raids.

As well as the Hollandia mission, Allied air forces aircraft attacked Timor, Tadji, Wewak, Hansa Bay, New Britain, and one B-24 went as far as the Caroline Islands. At Allied GHQ level, Intelligence Summary 740 referred to the Hollandia raids and the concurrent U.S. Navy attack on the base at Truk. In both operations, a total of 220 enemy aircraft were claimed destroyed, for a loss of 1 P-38 and 3 B-24s. The summary pointed out that the Japanese had repeatedly lost their air strength in New Guinea, had recently built it up to 300 aircraft, and were fast losing it again. The summary ended: "How quickly the enemy reacts, and the manner of his reaction, will be a good indication of his immediate defensive intention for the whole of the South West and South Pacific." Public Relations Communiqué 721 described the Hollandia raid and quoted a figure of 92 Japanese planes destroyed or damaged on the ground, and 10 more in the air, with U.S. losses as "negligible."

Lieutenant General Itabana, commanding 6 Flying Division, was removed and made a farewell address to his units. He recapitulated the events of the past sixteen months under his leadership, apologized for the enemy superiority as due to his own inefficiency, and then praised officers and men for their efforts in operating from inadequate bases with no replacements, despite which they had dealt the enemy "punishing blows."

As an example of the state of proficiency gained by the U.S. bomber units, the 90th Jolly Rogers Bomb Group had flown 730 sorties; 90 percent of airplanes dispatched had passed over their targets. Three aircraft had been lost with thirty-three men.

In the European theater, the 8th Air Force flew 11,943 sorties on twenty-three days of March 1944 and lost 349 heavy bombers. Five bomber groups' worth of airplanes and crews had gone down, but German aircraft production and war production in general actually increased.

SEVEN

Pounded to Destruction

Hollandia, April 1944

Pressure was maintained on Wewak on 2 April, when thirty-five B-24s with twenty-two A-20s escorted by sixteen P-40s attacked Wewak and Hansa Bay. Lieutenant Horie, HQ 6 Flying Division, who witnessed the March aerial assault on Wewak, flew into Hollandia on this day, saw destruction from the attacks on 30 and 31 March, and thought the airfields in "a pitiful state."

The public relations office communique from MacArthur's general head-quarters, referring to the 31 March attack on Hollandia, said:

Our escorted heavy units continuing their attack dropped 140 tons of bombs on the enemy airdrome, starting large fires, with smoke rising 15,000 feet. Fifty-seven planes were destroyed on the ground and an attempted interception cost the enemy 14 others destroyed and 8 probably. This brings the total for two days to 189 certains and 15 probable. Our own losses were extremely light. Only one-third of the enemy aircraft gathered at this base for aerial reinforcement in this sector now remain serviceable.

On 3 April Hollandia was pounded again, but now strafers added their weight of destruction and terror to the force brought against the Japanese. One B-24 of the Ken's Men Group 403rd Squadron crashed on takeoff, killing four of the crew and blocking the runway so another four bombers could not join the mission.

It was two years since the U.S. 8th Attack Squadron sent a mere five A-24s over the Owen Stanley Range to Lae, escorted by six P-40s of the RAAF 75 Fighter Squadron, itself a unit that had existed for less than one month. Long gone were the days when all the Allies could do was pinprick the victorious Japanese.

By April 1942 the Japanese had conquered a huge part of the Asia-Pacific area and enjoyed naval supremacy, air supremacy, and overwhelming superiority in land forces, with the great advantage of having done so with trained and experienced units that suffered few losses. Since that time the Japanese had failed to defend their gains. They had failed to provide development support to the fighting elements in the combat areas; had failed to provide adequate defense materials such as radar, radio, antiaircraft artillery, or modern fighters; and worst of all, had repeatedly failed to understand their enemies and consistently underestimated the capabilities of those enemies.

The rosy dawn of the new expanded Japanese Empire had faded to be replaced by a series of ever-strengthening violent storms. It was the Japanese who invaded New Guinea and instigated a military campaign there, as well as other ventures in the Pacific and Burma and their long-running campaign in China. By 1944, trying to fight everywhere, realization was slowly growing in Tokyo that nothing could be held.

Now, over a major Japanese base which they had thought to be safe, 236 U.S. bombers, including 67 four-engine B-24s, dropped 400 tons of bombs and fired 250,000 rounds of .50-caliber and 25,000 of .30-caliber machine-gun bullets into the airfields and logistics targets.

The 312th Bomb Group, based at Gusap, had rested on 2 April, and late in the afternoon the Grim Reapers 3rd Attack arrived to spend the night at the field. The distance to the target and back would be 860 miles, requiring close attention to fuel management. During briefing the CO of the 312th, Colonel Strauss, emphasized this part of the mission. Charles Lindbergh had been in the Pacific advising units how to make the most of engines and gasoline supplies. Engine revolutions per minute was to be reduced to well below what had been considered normal, despite fears that this might have a damaging effect on the engines.

The diary of the Grim Reapers 90th Squadron noted that it was "the mission the boys have been sweating out for a long time." Major Rosebush led the 90th's twelve aircraft, loaded with one-hundred-pound parachute-retarded demolition bombs—parademos. A year before Rosebush had been a second lieutenant co-pilot during the Battle of the Bismarck Sea.

John Shemelynce, 3rd Attack Group photographer, often flew with Group CO Jock Henebry. Shemelynce did not know what the target was but met Henebry at the A-20, and after the aircraft was ready, both of them lay down, resting their booted feet on one main wheel. Overhead thundered B-24s, climbing to altitude, heading west. Henebry gestured to them and told Shemelynce that after the B-24s got far enough ahead, in forty minutes, the group would also take off, with Hollandia as the target. The idea was to let the Japanese send their fighters to engage the B-24s, so that they would have landed and be refueling when the strafers arrived; it had been done several times before, with much success.

The intention was to have the strafers fly inland, pass the target, and then swing onto it from the west; each squadron would attack in line abreast: twelve squadrons of twelve aircraft machine-gunning and strewing parafrags.

The 3rd took off followed by the 312th, and the A-20s began a long two-and-a-half-hour flight to the target area. The raid passed the place on the coast where Tommy Lynch had been shot down three weeks before, and the Japanese diarist there noted "sixty or seventy enemy fighters and bombers flew toward Hollandia." This was the B-24 and P-38 formation. The strafers were flying inland.

Karl Foster, pilot of B-25 #246 in the Sunsetters Group 71st Squadron, led the third flight with a load of twenty 100-pound parademo bombs. Like the others, he was well aware of possible fuel problems due to the long distance to and from the target and noted that it was the first mission for the 38th Bomb Group out of the Australian-mandated part of New Guinea against "the last important Jap air base" on the island. There had been much speculation as to the possible success of the mission because only limited information was available from photos and maps.

Many people in the Hollandia target area had made their own decisions about personal safety. They realized the bombers arrived at about the same time and left the danger zones. A petty officer of 90 Garrison Unit described how, at about 0900, "everybody would leave for the jungle, as the bombers came at 1000. Liaison was bad and there were no air-raid warnings for us. The first we would know was when the bombs were dropping. All three of our radios were destroyed anyway."

At 0900 local Japanese time (Tokyo time) at Hollandia the alarm was given; Tonys and Oscars took off, watched by a navigator-gunner in 75 Sentai. He saw them return an hour later without combat. Then, ten minutes after the fighters landed, the B-24s were overhead.

At 1050, B-24s of the 64th Squadron, 43rd Group, bombed while crews watched six Oscars and Tonys in combat with P-38s to the west. After them came the other B-24 squadrons, some unable to observe the results of their strings of 1,000-pounders. They reported "excellent bombing"; "hits and near misses on the gun positions"; "target covered with smoke"; "saw one enemy shot down by P-38s"; "bombs fell among single-seat fighters"; and "twenty-four bombs in the target." Some Japanese fighters slipped through the escort and made about ten passes at the B-24s but did no damage. The escort fighters claimed twenty-four Japanese and the bombers two for the loss of a P-38.

Far below in Bougainville Bay, nine Japanese ships were attacked by strafers, and B-24 crews of the Jolly Rogers Group 319th Squadron watched two sink. The Group's 400th Squadron reported dropping their forty-eight bombs through clouds onto antiaircraft positions at the western end of Hollandia Strip but believed the bombs fell well south of the target. The squadron flew around barrage antiaircraft fire and saw three Japanese fighters break away from a bunch of twenty to make determined passes at the lead B-24. The nose gunner exploded one and the right waist gunner sent another down in flames. Although the Japanese were more eager to engage than on previous Hollandia missions, there were no further determined passes.

The Japanese antiaircraft artillery positions had been targeted for an avalanche of high explosives to prepare the way for the strafers. In the thirteen minutes between 1049 and 1102, 492 1,000-pounders fell onto the gun areas. The 66 AA Battalion had just redeployed from diamond-shaped battery formations into lines of guns, and a twenty-three-year-old private later wrote: "As the guns were set up in a single line we were an easy target and twenty men were killed. We had thirty or forty minutes' warning from Wewak, and the fighters took off, but we did not see them. We were told six were shot down and later that twenty were lost."

Dick Grills, rear gunner in the 320th Squadron, Jolly Rogers Group, watched their eighty 100-pound bombs fall away and thought the results were okay, but he had his attention on the Japanese fighters that were all around the B-24s over the target after they left. Two sat at high six o'clock, and one started in, but Grills fired twenty rounds and he turned away. The rest stayed back; P-38s attacked and one of those two Japanese was shot down. At the end of the seven-hour and forty-minute flight, Grills had a bad headache from glare; he did not have sunglasses.

T.Sgt. Francis Reddy, in the lead aircraft of the second element of the 321st Squadron, was credited with destruction of a fighter last seen spinning in flames down through the clouds.

An estimated thirty Tonys and Oscars attacked during the bomb runs. The Lightnings of the 80th Headhunters dived onto the Japanese and claimed ten destroyed: four to Cy Homer, two to Leland Blair, and one each to Lieutenants Jesse Corallo, Bud Fletcher, Ken Ladd, and Charles Ray. This was later revised to two each to Blair and Homer, and one each to Corallo, Fletcher, Ladd, Ray, Bill Caldwell, and Jenner. Three P-38s were damaged and one pilot landed at Gusap for medical attention for arm and hand wounds.

Ken Ladd's first confirmed victory came on 29 July 1943, and by this date he had nine destroyed plus two probables. He dived onto the Oscars, came in astern of one, held his fire, and then hammered it at two hundred yards' range. He saw several cannon strikes on the fuselage, and his wingman saw the Japanese go down burning. Ladd hit two other Oscars, one last seen diving vertically, but claimed neither.

Corky Smith and Charles Ray went after two Oscars that were going for the B-24s. Ray started firing at 300 yards and closed to 150; his hits flashed on the cockpit and wingroots. The Oscar blew up.

Cy Homer led Blue Flight and saw three Oscars above. One dived away and the other two began a gentle turn toward Homer. He fired at the second Oscar, which was carrying a bomb under the starboard wing, and followed it into a dive. As the Japanese pulled into level flight, Homer fired from directly behind. The Oscar went down and crashed into the mountainside. The bomb probably was one of the air-to-air bombs that the Japanese thought were very effective.

Homer saw two P-38s climbing gently, unaware two Tonys were closing fast from below and behind. Homer called a warning, but the Tonys were in position and fired, hitting both P-38s; each had engine damage. The Tonys saw Homer and dived for Cyclops Strip, his P-38s in chase. Homer closed on the second Tony and fired, breaking away as the Japanese fell off to the left and crashed. A large brush fire flared at the site. Homer and his wingman, Bud Fletcher, then fired on the first Tony, which rolled into the ground close below.

Fletcher attacked an Oscar, but another one slipped in behind him; Homer drove it off and then witnessed Fletcher destroy an Oscar. Ten more Oscars appeared and six more P-38s joined in. Homer shot another Oscar into the water but looked around to see a Tony behind, firing at him. Homer went forward into a 400 mph dive, doing vertical reverses, and pulled out at sea level. Gradually the Tony fell back and then turned away. Homer turned after him, but when the Tony joined five others and no other P-38s were in sight, Homer broke off and turned for base. On the way he joined with Lieutenant Dwinell, who had his right engine feathered, and stayed with him to Nadzab.

Later, as commander of the 80th, Homer contributed his combat principles at the request of higher headquarters. He said that as long as the enemy could be seen, his chance of success would be slim, and a vertical dive with jinking until 400 or 500 mph was reached would be effective. Homer added that coming out to level flight allowed the P-38 to outrun the enemy, "Or better yet," he said, "pull up into a shallow climb." Homer recommended then that a head-on attack be made unless other enemy were following. If caught at treetop height, "anything to make him overshoot" should be tried. Homer repeated some of the oldest fighter rules: clear your tail before firing, surprise, close in and use short bursts, use sun and cloud, hit the enemy in the middle of their formation, and always join friendly aircraft. To Cy Homer, the squadron leader's role was to attack aggressively into the enemy and not worry about picking off stragglers and high lone enemy to increase the leader's personal score.

Speeding along at treetop height toward the smoke from the B-24 targets were the fast A-20 strafers of the Grim Reapers and 312th Groups. The Japanese gunners had been on the receiving end of three high-level B-24 bombardments, and it was time for the A-20s and B-25s to go in. In the rear cockpit of Jock Henebry's A-20, John Shemelynce knew that yet another dangerous low-level attack was to be made and felt the now-familiar drying of his mouth. He prepared his camera, unaware that he was to record some of the most dramatic photographs of the destruction of a large number of enemy aircraft to come out of the war.

As they came streaking in, hoping to catch the fighters on the ground, Colonel Henebry called that he was watching six Japanese fighters that seemed to be circling to land. Then the strafers were firing. Henebry went over a gasoline truck and had time to glimpse two Japanese trying to hide near it. The windshield splintered, sparkling in the sun, as his .50s shattered it, and Shemelynce was able to lean over and get a photograph. He noticed the antiaircraft shell bursts behind them: the gunners had been unable to adjust quickly from high-level attacks to speeding low-level A-20s. Shemelynce flew forty-six strafer missions and recalled: "Ground fire played hell with us, but fighters did not seem to bother us low-level people."

Seven A-20s of the Grim Reapers 13th Squadron claimed a direct hit on a bomber and other aircraft also hit. They noted the many different types of Japanese aircraft scattered below them, silenced two antiaircraft positions, and counted forty to fifty wrecks along their path. Behind them came the 89th and 90th Squadrons, who claimed six enemy planes destroyed, counted about forty wrecks along their own flight paths, and noted large stores dumps; 90th crews saw three P-38s crash in the target area. Major Rosebush had his hydraulics shot out and began the long return flight with Staff Sergeant Hansford in the turret, knowing a normal landing would be impossible. They made it to Gusap, but the A-20 was destroyed in the landing.

The last squadron of the 3rd Group to attack was the 8th, led by Maj. Chuck Howe. Andrew Weigel noted that the whole first team was present: Howe, Smith, Vinson, Patten, Sounheim, Dunkel, D. W. Brown, Flanagan, Gossom, Shook, Trout, and Madden. The squadron came in from the south, passed the target, and swung back onto it, making a rather high turn to attack from west to east. Weigel, leading the second element, could not see much on the actual runway and managed to make a run on two serviceable single-engine fighters, but his bombs hung up and he later salvoed them into Sentani Lake. The 8th crews reported that a string of 100-pound parafrags fell among twenty to twenty-five twin-engine Japanese airplanes at the northwest end of Hollandia airfield, and crews reported seeing many blow up or burn fiercely. Two fighters were blown apart; two twin-engine bombers were left burning at the southern end of the field; many aircraft were in the open, unprotected by revetments; anti-aircraft burst overhead and machine guns on the ground fired too far ahead of the speeding A-20s; and antiaircraft emplacements were torn up. The P-38 cover was "beautiful to watch," as three Japanese fighters were seen shot down; a "huge mushrooming red flame" blossomed north of Hollandia Strip.

During attacks, it always seemed to John Shemelynce that "it's not so dangerous when you're strafing, you're going down and doing all the damage. Then you look back at it. . . . I'd count so many seconds then look back, and some of that machinegun fire, ground fire, had so many tracers it'd look like a hose, you'd get farther and farther away, the anti-aircraft fire would get farther and farther back. In a matter of minutes, when the engines check out OK, you know you're going to make it. Open the C rations. Your mouth is dry."

At 1145, thirty-seven A-20s of the 386th, 387th, 388th, and 389th Squadrons of Colonel Strauss's 312th Bomb Group attacked the airfields. They reported many aircraft hit and damaged, the Sentani radio station destroyed, barges sunk in Humboldt Bay, and smoke from the burning fuel dump visible forty miles away. One Oscar that tried to attack was chased off by P-38s. Twelve A-20s of the 386th passed along the southeastern side of Hollandia, straddled their bombs across a group of twenty-five to thirty twin-engine bombers, and reported all had been hit. The A-20s flew through smoke from many oil fires burning all around Hollandia.

Maj. Bill Kemble led the 388th Squadron and was impressed by the large number of 5th AF planes en route to the target. The squadron began its attack "six ships abreast. I picked a spot ahead and then jumped California Sunshine up and down like a cork in the water to avoid the AA." Kemble's gunner, Sgt. William Ernst, was suddenly hit by what he thought was a bullet, but then he found that a piece of antiaircraft shrapnel had hit the ammunition belt for his twin .50-caliber machine guns, detonated the round, and a piece of this hit him smack on the dog-tags, bending one. The feeling of relief was such that he burst into laughter, so much so he had tears in his eyes.

Last of the 312th across the target was the 389th. They swung into line abreast attack formation while pilots opened bomb doors and switched guns to "fire." Roaring across, taking evasive action at ground level, Slade in "Ravin Rachael" hit a tree, but there was no damage to the A-20. His speed across the field was 310 mph. As they reached the fighter strip, they swung into a right-hand turn, and he machine-gunned some buildings ahead. Then they were through with no losses but some damage. Ever hopeful, Lt. Ewing McKinney was waiting for a Japanese fighter to fly in front of him, so he could shoot him down with the nose guns. "My head and eyes were on the proverbial swivel" as he dipped and rose on the attack, looking for targets, avoiding ground fire. Colonel Strauss thought the target was well pounded by the heavies, who could have finished the job without the strafers. His gunner, Sgt. Leo Mandabach, was surprised to see an A-20 pass them, landing lights bright, and assumed the pilot hit the wrong switch in excitement.

The 475th Fighter Group Satan's Angels had used time off missions since 31 March to work on their P-38s, and the group launched fifty-five P-38s. As they flew toward Hollandia at Annenberg, a lone P-38 joined the 432nd Squadron's eighteen-plane formation. It was Capt. Dick Bong, leading ace in the theater with twenty-four victories, who was allowed by General Kenney to fly with any outfit he chose. The 432nd Fighter Squadron of the group covered the A-20s and attacked twenty Japanese, claiming 12-1-0 for the loss of one P-38. The squadron reported that the bombers were spread over an area of fifty miles by thirty miles, far too much for one squadron to cover.

Two 432nd pilots, already aces, added more victories. John Loisel, who began scoring on 21 August at Wewak, destroyed his ninth and tenth victories. Loisel led Blue Flight at eight thousand feet, and when the A-20s called Japanese fighters were in the area, Loisel saw two small formations of Japanese below. Loisel attacked the lower formation of Oscars and selected as targets the leader and his wingman, firing as the P-38 closed to fifty yards' range. Hits sparked on the Oscar's fuselage and wing roots, and the Japanese banked left and fell to the ground. Blue Flight then was fighting in the midst of the Japanese, and finally Loisel found himself behind another Oscar. A short burst hit, and the Oscar spun into the side of a mountain. Loisel's wingman witnessed the victory.

Perry Dahl and Joe Forster made up the other two in Blue Flight. Forster found two Oscars flying along the lakeshore where they both crashed after his gunnery pass. Dahl witnessed these victories, and saw Lt. John Temple, Green Flight, with an Oscar behind him. Temple pulled up into cloud, came out, and looked back to see his opponent going down burning, hit by Dahl. Temple shot down another into the lake, and Dahl sent down another at the end of Sentani Strip. These were Dahl's fourth and fifth victories.

Meanwhile, Forster had been making head-on passes at another Oscar, hit it, and saw the pilot climbing out onto the wing as the Oscar fell toward a mountainside just before Forster fired again to complete the destruction. These were the first three of Forster's nine victories.

Lt. Henry Condon, Green Flight, noticed a single Oscar under attack by six P-38s. The Oscar pilot was using the superior maneuverability of his fighter to turn and skid continuously at about 150 mph, unhit by the faster P-38s that overshot him time and again. Condon throttled back and slid in behind the Oscar. He fired and the Oscar turned right. Condon applied deflection and fired again; hits hammered the wings and cockpit, and the Oscar went into the trees close below.

The Group commander, Col. Charles MacDonald, led Red Flight against six Oscars flying toward the A-20s on the southeast side of the lake. All but one broke away, and that one, more determined than careful, pressed on after the A-20s. White Flight, led by Elliott Summer, went after the Oscar; Summer shot it down from behind and then pulled up to fire on another Japanese who was firing on a P-38 above them. The Oscar destroyed was Summer's seventh; he had also made his first claims on the 21 August mission to Wewak.

Jack Hannan, Red Flight, later shot down an Oscar that started to burn but turned so tightly that it almost rammed him before falling in flames.

Dick Bong fought a well-flown Oscar that managed to avoid his fire and several passes by a flight of P-38s. Finally Bong got into position behind and slightly below the Oscar, and his hits caused fire on the bottom of the engine; it went down to crash about fifty yards west of the lake. Joe Forster witnessed this victory. This was Bong's twenty-fifth and brought the squadron score for this mission to twelve. However, newcomer Flight Officer Joe Barton was last seen diving into cloud followed by two Tonys. An A-20 crew reported seeing a burning P-38 crash at about this time, at the south end of Sentani Lake.

Seventy-five B-25 strafers from the 38th Sunsetters and 345th Air Apaches Groups came hurtling in ten minutes later, restoking the fires and confusion on the airfields. Pacing them were thirty-six P-38s of the 431st and 433rd Squadrons, and the P-38s claimed three Japanese fighters. Maj. Warren Lewis of the 433rd became an ace with his fifth victory.

Col. Clinton True led the 345th Air Apaches in the lead ship of the 501st Squadron. Antiaircraft positions and dispersal areas were bombed by the 501st, who claimed three twin-engine bombers set ablaze by strafing and two antiaircraft positions destroyed, and noted the road lined with stores under tarpaulins. One strafer claimed four single-seat fighters destroyed when he caught them taxiing south of Sentani. Five planes were holed by ground fire and a gunner wounded. Behind them came Major Coltharp with the 498th, flashing by a single Oscar that made a head-on pass, but there were four 431st Squadron P-38s after him who shot him down. The 498th's nine B-25s flew across Hollandia airfield and Ifaar village, dropped 100-pound demos, noted the absence of antiaircraft fire over the target and an antiaircraft position on fire, and saw a Japanese plane crash into Sentani Lake. The 499th "Bats Outta Hell" were led by Major Baird, who had an engine hit and landed at Saidor. Four Lilys destroyed or burning were claimed by the squadron, who sighted the extensive stores dumps as they went past. The 500th Squadron carved a trail of destruction along the road to the coast and along the south and east shores of Tanamerah Bay.

The 38th Sunsetters Bomb Group came in just before midday, flying into smoke and dust of preceding attacks. Larry Tanberg led the group, and such destruction had been done by the heavies and strafers before them that he was "practically on instruments due to the fires and smoke." He had charged his nose guns and tested them, but as he hurdled the hill and saw "the first batch of airplanes, or what was left that looked like airplanes, I pushed the trigger and nothing happened." He had to pass across the target and over a ship that was directly in front as he went over the harbor without being able to fire. The 822nd Squadron, Sunsetters Group, reported it as "the most destructive the squadron has yet flown" after they hurtled across the northwest area of the runway and northern dispersal area. They praised the fighter cover as excellent and strafed a 1,500-ton freighter in Humboldt Bay. "A tremendous fire" was seen by the 823rd Squadron as they attacked the west side of the eastern revetment area and strafed two bombers into flames; they counted twenty-five burning planes and two fuel dumps on fire with large amounts of supplies stacked throughout the area. Three B-25s were damaged. Eighteen B-25s from the 71st and 405th Squadrons of the Sunsetters Group strafed their way across the target area, showering 100-pound parademos behind them. Crews saw thirty fires, at least twenty-five planes burning as well as those they machine-gunned and set ablaze, and eight fuel dumps. A truck convoy was strafed as the B-25s sped overhead. Dense smoke prevented accurate damage assessment.

Karl Foster, 71st Squadron, saw the target area "covered with fire and smoke when we entered, making the ack-ack positions hard to find. My run was directly over a line of ack-ack positions, which for some reason did not fire a shot at me, possibly due to the terrific strafing and bombing they were receiving. The run continued out to Sentani Lake and to Humboldt Bay, strafing targets all the way." The squadron re-formed over the water and had an uneventful flight home, followed by a single P-38, which was assumed to be lost.

Ed Maurer, 405th Squadron, thought it was "a well-organized mission. By the time we made this raid, we had come up to a very high level of competence, and the attack was really accurate."

Hard-pressed by the strafers roaring past were the antiaircraft gun crews who had already suffered the rain of bombs from B-24s. Some gunners abandoned their positions or took cover, and the strafers reported empty gun pits in some locations. But others fought back, either brave enough or at the stage where anger takes over from fear. Despite grass burning around gun pits, some crews fought on, loading, traversing, elevating, and clearing empty shell cases, shouting fire control orders amid smoke, explosions, hammering .50 calibers from A-20s and B-25s, and the howl of Pratt and Whitney and Wright engines a few feet overhead; all around them, as far as they could see through the chaos. Hollandia was taking a heavy pounding yet again. One private from 3rd Battery, 66 AA Battalion, was in the stage of near exhilaration that some experience after a period of intense fear. After the terror of repeated B-24 bombings and the storm of explosions from the rain of 1,000-pounders, he dared the strafers to hit him and stayed at his post; the entire gun crew operated the weapon throughout the attack.

At Hamadi, a detachment of 68 AA Battalion was attacked by what one private estimated was two hundred bombers, with eleven killed and three wounded, four guns disabled, and five hundred drums of fuel burned, plus ammunition stored nearby all destroyed. The medical officer at 113 Hospital wrote: "Low level attack by North Americans. Thought my last moment had come. The airfield in the direction of Hamadi seems to be burning endlessly. Heard only four of our thirty fighters returned." Another member of the hospital staff: "Thought my end had come. Into the shelter. Gasoline drums blew up one after the other. Air raids are fearful things." From the distance, members of 90 Garrison Unit who had left the danger zones watched the raid. Nagamitsu Tsukada noted:

"About 130 took part in today's raid and none of ours engaged them. Great columns of smoke are rising from Sentani. It appears the airdrome suffered severe damage."

Other observers wrote in their diaries and letters what had happened, describing it as: "considerable damage from today's raid"; "terrific damage, gasoline drums burned fiercely"; "watched food, fuel, and trucks burning"; "Hollandia lacks facilities and immediate action is necessary"; and "strafed for nearly an hour. It is strange to be still alive after this terrific attack. We are hoping for powerful new fighters but are determined to fight on." With diarrhea added to his problems, Lieutenant Colonel Okada, commander 49 Anchorage Unit, watched the attack destroy his personal quarters, fifteen hundred drums of precious fuel, and ammunition. By the end of the day, one report had 4 Air Army's fighter strength as twenty-one Oscars and seven Tonys.

Claims of punishment meted out to the attackers were high again. 3rd Battery, 66 AA Battalion believed it had destroyed twenty B-24s and seven P-38s, while the other two batteries claimed another twenty U.S. planes.

The 33 and 77 Sentai launched eighteen Oscars but lost five pilots killed, four of them from 33 Sentai: Lieutenant Shigeura, Corporal Nakamura, and Sergeant Majors Chikara and Takemori. After surviving combats despite balky wing tanks, faulty oxygen, and no gunsight light, Takemori finally fell to the P-38s.

The speed with which replacement aircraft reached Japanese units in New Guinea was greater than that in the Allied system. Chikara was flying a brand-new Oscar, #6740, which came out of the Nakajima factory in Japan on 8 March, delivered to Manila, and then sent to 33 Sentai on 31 March.

The 77 Sentai had seven Oscars airborne. The first flight of four was led by Major Matsumoto, with Sergeant Major Ota, Sergeant Kobayashi, and Corporal Ota, the second flight of three led by Captain Matsuo, with Corporals Hara and Yamaguchi. These two units claimed 10-1-0; 33 Sentai included four P-38s in the total.

Other figures for Japanese claims were given by 7 Flying Division headquarters: 39 Japanese fighters intercepted 240 U.S. aircraft and claimed to have shot down or damaged 13 P-38s, with 10 Japanese admitted losses in combat and 4 destroyed on the ground along with 1,600 drums of fuel. But another Japanese report gave the figure of 36 destroyed in combat, and yet other Japanese sources quote 11 lost in combat and 8 destroyed on the ground. In addition, personal diary entries refer to 20 or 30 fighters lost in air combats. U.S. fighter claims for the day were 25 destroyed and 3 damaged. With those claimed by the bombers, the figure of 30 Japanese destroyed could well be accurate.

It is hard to be unsympathetic to one of the Japanese at Hollandia at this time. On this day 6 Flying Division issued Operation Order C12 to the commander of 14 Field Air Supply Depot and made him responsible for all the dumps of fuel, ammunition, and food around the lake. The B-24s, strafers, and P-38s had just hammered the area again; all available manpower was needed at the airfields and the sky was black with smoke from burning fuel drums, ammunition, and aircraft. The defenses of Hollandia were having little or no effect on the waves of attackers. It was the sort of scene Hollywood might have ended with the officer committing hara-kiri.

Work began at once to make the airfields serviceable. At 1640, 38 Airfield Battalion reported twenty-two killed or wounded in the attack but the unit was busy with runway repairs. The defenders learned that positioning antiaircraft guns close to airfields invited destruction, and now the commanders ordered their dispersal five or ten kilometers from the fields, with only one gun at a position and with concealed approach roads.

Air raids were not the only thing to occupy the Japanese in the Hollandia area. A small party of Australians had been infiltrated into the neighborhood to observe and report but had been betrayed by natives. Japanese ground troops were led to the location; in the battle three of the team were killed, and three boatloads of arms and ammunition were captured. The hunt for survivors continued.

For the U.S. pilots and crews, the mission was not over until they had landed and been debriefed, but others began to relax a little earlier. Once John Shemelynce had "crossed the Sepik, I knew I had it made. I could probably walk back. But that river was wide and I didn't know if I could cross it. And it was patrolled by Japanese . . . and crocodiles."

Referring to the almost certain death awaiting crews who crashed into the trees or sometimes parachuted, Shemelynce recalled that when possible, photos were taken of the crash site, or area where the parachutes were seen, but "everything looked the same. The photograph was worthless."

The A-20s refueled at Gusap and went on to Nadzab. Jock Henebry recalled it as a long day, a total of twelve hours for the flight crews, who had made three takeoffs and three landings, refueled twice, and flown six hours and thirty-five minutes over enemy territory, the deepest penetration yet made for the strafers.

Jock Henebry flew a total of 219 combat missions in his time in the SWPA and rose from lieutenant to full colonel, squadron pilot to group commander, in one of the most outstanding combat careers in the U.S. Army Air Corps.

The composers of the AAF Intsum described the attack in Number 197: "In a raid lasting one hour and thirteen minutes, 400 tons were dropped from high and low levels, demolishing all remaining airplanes, leaving runways unserviceable, and heavily damaging supplies and installations. Of sixty intercepting enemy fighters, twenty-six were shot down. AA opposition dwindled to nothing. Advanced Echelon (HQ 5th AF) records 288 enemy airplanes destroyed or damaged in three strikes on 30, 31 March and this date."

At theater level, the military intelligence section of the general staff issued Intelligence Summary 743, which also quoted the destruction of 288 enemy aircraft in the recent raids. The Summary went on to state:

> The destruction of upward of 300 planes in the Hollandia area over a five-day period has been completed concurrently with heavy loss of enemy fighters over the Truk airdromes and with possibly big air losses at Palau. With Truk and Hollandia under regular attack, the enemy again has shown himself to be incapable of providing an adequate air cover at least at the latter two locations. It is doubted that he holds in reserve sufficiently large forces to make his air operations effective at so many distant points. He is committed, it would appear in his defenses, to an air war of attrition, which, coupled with his losses in other theaters, possibly requires his full monthly production to maintain.

Public Relations Communique 726 described the raid as the heaviest so far, told how the heavies first attacked the antiaircraft defenses and strafers then attacked the aircraft areas, and finished by quoting the figure of 288 aircraft destroyed since 30 March. AAF aircraft had also attacked Kai Islands, Timor, Wewak, and Bogia, and five formations had hit the Madang region. The next day, 4 April, fifty-two B-24s attacked Wewak, Timor, Hansa Bay, Tanimbar Island, and Cape Orford on New Britain.

The diarist of 90 Garrison Unit who had recorded the shooting down of Tommy Lynch and the flights past his position of the attacking forces going to

Hollandia wrote: "Yesterday, the anniversary of the birthday of the Emperor Meiji, we received from the enemy greetings, which amount to the annihilation of our Army Air Force in New Guinea."

Another indication of the high rate of destruction of Japanese aircraft in the war zones was a report from their Southwest Asia Air Arsenal, which had branches at Surabaya (Indonesia), Penang, Malaya, and Manila, the Philippines, and advised that throughout the branches on 2 April only twenty-five aircraft were available, with another twenty-nine under repair.

The U.S. flight crews were dismayed to receive a new directive. As of 4 April, the three-hundred-hour combat tour no longer applied—crews were to remain flying until they had been overseas for one year. Several crews who were near or had achieved the three-hundred-hour mark were now required to stay in theater, a blow to morale.

Hollandia, 5 April 1944

With the airfields reduced to a graveyard of Japanese army air force units, the 5th Air Force turned its attention to the mass of supplies in the area. Forty-five B-24s from the 22nd Red Raiders, 43rd Ken's Men and 90th Jolly Rogers Groups bombed Hollandia town, warehouses, and antiaircraft positions there and along the coast as well as shipping lines. Huge explosions were reported and smoke rose to twelve thousand feet. At the same time, other squadrons of the 43rd and 90th Groups attacked Wewak and Boram. Japanese on the ground were helpless witnesses to the destruction. Direct hits fell on the Hollandia Signal Station and Navy Garrison Unit, but because the personnel had left, prudently keeping away during the danger period, no one was hurt.

For those on official duty, it was a bad time to be in the area. A member of an infantry unit "went to Kotabaroe to get cement. On the way we were caught in an air raid; five killed. Heard the battalion had heavy casualties." Many of those caught in the fury of attacks were busy "camouflaging our tents and dispersing rations. Orders are to place all equipment in air raid shelters." Despite his diarrhea, Lieutenant Colonel Okada set to and dug an air raid trench amid the damage. Standing on a hill north of Sentani was Lieutenant Horie, headquarters staff, who had flown from Wewak. Enraged at continued attacks that met little effective resistance, "All I could do was grind my teeth and wave my

fist in anger." Nagamitsu Tsukada wrote, "Enemy planes bombed the AA positions along the coast for two hours. Great black columns of smoke are rising
from the positions and exploding ammunition. The explosions from gasoline
drums were terrific. Thirty wounded, twenty-five killed."

While others could seek haven in the hills and caves, the antiaircraft gun
crews had to man their posts under the hail of bombs and now were exposed to
the massed .50-caliber machine guns in the strafers. Kiichi Ishii, 68 AA
Battalion, had taken part in the earlier actions, and on this day "about 100
enemy planes attacked. They came as low as 150 meters and strafed. We could
see the pilots' faces. How provoking it all is! The section leader and men on the
right were killed. The oil drums at Hamadi were all blown away. Only 20 percent of the bombs hit, the others fell in the sea. Now wooden guns are placed
in our position. We shot down two B-25s."

The 68 AA Battalion was heavily hit in these attacks. At Imbi, a twenty-four-
year-old private in 3 Battery at his post watched oncoming B-24s shower demolition bombs. Then the B-25s howled in, right for them, hit the battery, put
three guns out of action, and killed or wounded an entire section. The survivors
fired for a while, but there were so many U.S. planes in the air, bombing, strafing, and roaring past in all directions, that fire control collapsed and the gunners
just gave up and took cover. The private saw no U.S. losses. Another 3 Battery
soldier was resigned to death because casualties were mainly among the gun
crews. A third member of the battery recalled thirteen gunners killed. Despite
the attack, the explosions, smoke, death, and wounds, when the battery fired
its guns, it claimed four B-24s destroyed and three damaged.

A man in 2 Battery said, "as the enemy formations appeared, we immediately
opened fire. The first and second shells burst forward of the enemy plane, the
third scored a direct hit, and the Boeing disintegrated. Then enemy bombs
exploded in front of the personnel shelter—blast flung me and I was unconscious. Eight killed, four wounded, but we shot down two enemy."

The paymaster of 68 AA Battalion married before departing Japan for the
South Seas. He did not want to go but thought Japan had to win or be oppressed
like Germany after 1918. As the bombers came over he ran to his trench. The
area shook to the bombardment; others in the trench were killed and wounded.
Climbing out, he looked around and saw bomb craters everywhere, some of
them ten to fifteen meters across. He did not see any U.S. losses.

The strafers flew the same route as two days before. They bombed and machine-gunned the supply dumps along the roads. The 8th Attack Squadron hit Tanahmerah with thirty-seven 500-pound bombs, but results were unknown due to the speed of the A-20s, lack of height, and the thick foliage of the trees in the target area. Eight from the 90th Squadron, led by Captain Prokopovitz, dropped thirty-one 500-pounders among stores and supplies along the south side of Jautefa Bay. They started several fires and "100 large boxes believed to contain aircraft engines were given a going over" recorded the unit diary. At 1146, seventeen B-25s of the Sunsetters Group's 71st and 405th Squadrons sped across Humboldt Bay. Other squadrons swept the roads from Jautefa to Sentani, leaving sunken barges, burning fuel, and shattered stores areas. Secondary explosions sent smoke ballooning to six thousand feet. The *Fukutoku Maru* and five army barges were sunk, and there were "great casualties on *Shunko Maru.*"

The effect of the attack on one unit was reported as "damage to air material is great; half the fuel and ammunition at both places burned. Damage to food minor. The coastal region along the Hollandia lines of communication wiped out. Sixteen killed, twenty-three wounded."

The 388th Squadron, 312th Group, had twelve A-20s barreling along the road, trailing 250-pound bombs behind them. Walter Bartlett, flying "My Akin Back" in the 388th, saw two antiaircraft guns swinging onto him, and with his eyes on them, he instinctively eased the fast bomber lower, lower, until his gunner jolted him with a call that they were on the grass. He eased up, then hurtled over a small knoll, but almost stalled the A-20. He was learning a lot quickly. On Jautefa Bay, the 389th scored a direct hit on three barges, fuel dumps, piles of supplies, and stores, and they left fires behind them.

The formations returned to Gusap over cloud. The 312th began to descend through cloud to Gusap, and Lt. Thomas Freeman of the 387th called out that he was having trouble with his right engine. Lt. Glen Benskin was on Freeman's right and noticed puffs of fuel vapor from Freeman's aircraft as the pilot juggled with fuel transfer switches. His left engine failed; the A-20 slowed to stalling speed, and Freeman tried to put the plane down in a small clearing but hit the trees and exploded. Orange flame and black smoke bubbled up, and almost at once there was no other sign that the crash had occurred. Benskin and his gunner agreed about the site, but searchers failed to locate it as Benskin expected.

Jungle closed over the wreckage and bodies; it was twenty-three years before they were discovered and recovered.

On this day, AAF Situation Report 299 stated that Japanese losses for all of March had been 300 airplanes; 149 had been destroyed on the ground by B-24 attacks. The 5th Air Force Advanced headquarters stated that 210 bombers had delivered 320 tons of bombs in attacks on antiaircraft positions, buildings, stores, shipping, and personnel. Antiaircraft positions had been hit and silenced; the fire of others slackened and became "nominal." Only two enemy aircraft were sighted airborne; there were no combat losses.

AAF Intsum 197 stated:

> AA positions near Challenger Cove appeared to be well covered by the heavy bombing from 11,000 feet. Guns in the target area were active before, but not after, the attack. The town area was partially destroyed, one warehouse was set afire, and a ship at the dock was left in flames. Stores and villages around Humboldt Bay were vigorously strafed. Two enemy planes were airborne, but there was no interception and no combat losses. Three hundred twenty tons of bombs and over a quarter of a million rounds of ammunition were expended in the strike.

Other Allied formations attacked Timor, Jefman Island, Kaimana, Talasea, Wewak, Hansa Bay–Bogia, and Marienberg. There had been no Japanese air attacks in New Guinea between 30 March and 5 April. The 275 U.S. aircraft that flew to Hollandia were not intercepted by a single Japanese airplane.

It was obvious to the Japanese that the situation in the area was not in their favor. Twenty-six female nurses were evacuated "because of the increased intensity of the war." Nagamitsu Tsukada noted that after the raid the hospital patients were evacuated to the mountains. The remaining bombers of 61 Sentai withdrew to the Halmaheras; 68 Sentai had four Tonys and sixteen pilots; 77 had five Oscars and twenty-one pilots; 78 Sentai had only five Tonys, three of which were operational, and fourteen combat-ready pilots of twenty-two on strength; 248 had three Oscars and twenty-eight pilots. The 14 Hikodan headquarters was established at Hollandia Number 3 Strip (Cyclops). On 7 April, 14 Hikodan ordered its units to train in "ambush formation." There still remained many Japanese aircraft available in rear areas, and on 6 April another thirty-six Tonys were issued to 68 and 78 Sentai.

The 4 Air Army rather plaintively signaled on 6 April for headquarters to "please give special consideration to replacing flying personnel for 33 and 77 Sentai," and added that 68 Sentai had a total of sixteen pilots, of whom only four were in the first-class category and a total of seven in the next grades.

On 7 April the flying units were reminded, "We must seize control to the east of Hollandia from the enemy. If enemy air units gain complete dominance of the situation, supply to the east of Hollandia will be cut off."

For the next two days the weather precluded missions to Hollandia, but on 8 April the bombing campaign resumed.

8 April 1944

Over Europe on this day, the 8th Air Force lost 34 heavy bombers and 247 were damaged. The Luftwaffe was being consumed in preparation for the invasion of Europe. No matter what enormous lists of victories were piled up by the heavily bemedaled German fighter *experten,* the Third Reich had lost the initiative and could try to counter Allied attacks only when they appeared. The Luftwaffe flew and fought to the last in defense of an evil regime.

Over New Guinea, 5th Air Force twin-engine bombers attacked Wewak and Hansa; B-25s of the 345th Air Apaches bombed Brandi Plantation near Wewak, the Sunsetters 38th Group targeted Moem, and the A-20s of the Grim Reapers 3rd Attack Group went after targets at Hansa Bay. Five B-24s of the 403rd Squadron pounded But field again, to keep up pressure, while squadrons of all three B-24 groups returned to Hollandia. They flew in bad weather all the way to Hollandia and almost turned back several times.

Fifty-one B-24s from the three groups paraded over Hollandia in a strike that began at 1122 and ended at 1133. It was another successful attack on the massed target area below, and some squadrons described it as "excellent bombing"; "direct hits on warehouses, smoke to 5,000 feet"; "fires and explosions"; "excellent bombing along the jetty and inland"; and "flames to 900 feet and smoke to 6,000." Dick Grills, in the rear of Morgan Terry's B-24, watched their eight 1,000-pounders hit the target with the rest of the 320th bombs but believed the other squadrons of the 90th Group missed. Three squadrons of the 90th did miss the town. Some of these aircraft retained bombs and dropped them on But airdrome and Nubia on the way back.

In the target, bombing effects were recorded by several Japanese. Lieutenant Horie wrote, "7,000 barrels of fuel destroyed." Toyotara Miyata wrote, "Naval barracks destroyed." Nagamitsu Tsukada wrote, "Hollandia suffered terrific bombardment for the second time. Losses were great. Barracks and important buildings burst into flame." In 27 Ordnance Depot, Private "Yamada" was in his trench as the Liberators passed overhead; he heard the scream of descending bombs and six 1,000-pound bombs impacted around him. Only one exploded. The infantryman who went to Kotabaroe on 5 April to get cement and was caught in that attack was unlucky again: "On the way back, caught in an air raid."

Under the rain of bombs from squadrons of attackers so confident that they came at the same time for each raid, people began to despair of any form of defense. Thirty Tonys and Oscars were reported to have taken off but failed to intercept. A weary private who had survived the Wewak bombardments and made his way to Hollandia thought that the antiaircraft was definitely ineffective, and he had never seen, during any raid, Japanese fighters attacking the formations on the bomb run. One patient in the hospital was told that by this time the number of destroyed aircraft had reached 350. The constant battering was having deep personal effects as well as destroying material targets. Kiichi Ishii, 68 AA Battalion, wrote: "Now even the noise of thunder makes me shake. I am willing to die, but I fear death."

The Hollandia radio station went off the air and was not heard for fifty-six hours.

Unable to scatter the approaching U.S. formations, or interfere with their bombing, the Japanese resorted to camouflage, dispersal, burying supplies or building revetments around them, and even a little subterfuge. On 10 April, Colonel Saito, commanding the air sector, ordered decoy fires and smoke be made in the area south of Hollandia, to draw the bombers away from what remained of the real targets. On the same day, thirty-three Japanese fighters gathered to patrol Hollandia, but the Allied air forces, despite bad weather, attacked Hansa, Wewak, and Aitape.

Pistol Pete Scores Again at Hansa

Two hundred twenty-seven tons of bombs were dropped on Hansa. In the Jolly Rogers Group, after briefing, two photographers, Bill Moran and his best friend,

Bill Handleman, went by mistake to the wrong B-24s, accidentally swapping places. Handleman climbed aboard "Hot Garters," the lead aircraft of the 321st Squadron flown by Lt. Bryant E. Poulsen. The Poulsen crew was among many who had been informed that a combat tour no longer was three hundred combat hours but was extended. This was Poulsen's first mission after reaching the three-hundred-hour mark.

Over the target, the airplane was hit by accurate antiaircraft fire from the known and respected accurate Japanese gun position "Pistol Pete." The B-24 started to burn in the number two engine, left the formation, and began to go down. The left wing collapsed, the Liberator began spinning, and the tail assembly broke off; five parachutes were seen and then the plane exploded.

Poulsen salvoed his bombs as the B-24 started down. The rest of the 321st bombed, but few results were noted as all watched Poulsen. Lt. George Anderson, to Poulsen's rear, reported that flames streamed back from the burning engine past the tail. Anderson circled until the five parachutes reached the ground. Other crews watched, confirmed five parachutes opened, and reported that two men landed in a clearing near the wrecked B-24, but the others fell into the trees; one parachute was caught on treetops. P-38s also circled the parachutes.

Like many men on other missions in all the theaters of war, Bill Moran had to watch as his friend's aircraft was destroyed, not knowing if he was among the survivors.

PBY Air Sea Rescue aircraft allocated to the mission dropped supplies to the survivors, four of whom were later identified as Lt. Donald Greenman and Staff Sergeants Donald Crotteau, William Hyler, and Bill Handleman. Local natives told them that Japanese troops were at the next village, but the Americans decided to try to reach the Ramu River valley and find friendly forces there. In the next two days, all four were captured.

The Japanese policy of not keeping flight crew prisoners alive was in force. Warrant Officer Hanada went to take charge of the men after news of their capture at Hansa was relayed to headquarters at Wewak. Two of the prisoners were later reported to have died and two were shot. Hanada is mentioned in the murder of prisoners in at least one other captured document. According to research by Wiley O. Woods for his history of the 90th Group, the four men were beaten by the Japanese when they were captured. On the thirteenth, Major Nakahara of the Kempei Tai arrived and interrogated the prisoners, and on the seventeenth they were handed over to a Corporal Morita of 20 Division Military Police Unit to move to Bogia. Because Lieutenant Greenman was not fit enough to walk, due to injuries, he was shot. Handleman apparently struck a Japanese and was beaten to death. On 24 April the Japanese shot the other two men. All four were buried by local people.

When Australian forces liberated the area, the graves of Greenman, Handleman, and Hyler were located and the remains reinterred in a U.S. cemetery. Crotteau's grave was not found. The identity of the fifth parachutist was never discovered, and it was believed he died soon after landing or in the air. All other crew members were believed to have died in the aircraft. So many Japanese died in later campaigns that no one involved in these murders could be located after the war for trial. However, on the evidence gathered by an Australian army officer, Capt. Geoff Waters, Japanese commander Gen. Hatazo Adachi was convicted of war crimes. One vital document for the prosecution was located by Captain Waters among the numerous translated captured papers—an order by Adachi that prisoners need not be kept alive. Adachi committed suicide before his death sentence could be carried out.

11 April 1944

The Empire struck back with some success. Japanese bombers with fighter escort flew east, staging through Hansa to attack Allied targets, including destroyers that had shelled Hansa. This naval action was part of the Allied deception plan to draw Japanese attention to the Hansa area, well away from Hollandia. Major Matsumoto, 77 Sentai, was in command. The decimated fighter Sentai—33, 63, 68, 77, 78, and 248—managed to put into the air between three and ten airplanes each, and eighteen bombers were escorted by thirty fighters. These made total victory claims of 15-3-0 U.S. aircraft shot down for two Japanese airplanes lost and five damaged. The most successful was 68 Sentai, with claims for 8-3-0; 77 Sentai claimed 3-3-0, and 33 Sentai claimed one P-47. The 68 Sentai recorded four aircraft damaged and one unnamed pilot had to parachute. The 78 Sentai flew Tonys, and lost Corporal Nakagawa who was killed. Lt. Edward Glascock, U.S. 8th Fighter Squadron, claimed a Tony destroyed over Wewak; almost certainly, Nakagawa was his victim. This was the only U.S. claim accredited for the day, but two Japanese airplanes were lost according to their own records.

However, 33 Sentai now was reduced to six aircraft. 33 Sentai, which had been in action in New Guinea for little more than a month, was reduced to so few aircraft; one week later, the seven remaining pilots flew to the Philippines. Forty-two victories were claimed for a loss of fourteen pilots.

Five P-47s were lost that day. Four were from the new 58th Fighter Group, who had very little combat experience and were plagued with accidents. Lieutenants Bullington, Graham, and Rothman were shot down, and later Lieutenant Theed apparently crashed while searching for the missing three. Ralph Wandrey, 9th Fighter Squadron ace, who had single-handedly attacked the Japanese fighter formation over Wewak on 19 March, described the 58th:

> That bunch was born to trouble. They flew from the opposite end of our airstrip and every day they had at least one accident. Their record was five planes wrecked in just one hour. We used to sit and watch them pile up about twenty yards from our alert shack, until one of them burned and his ammunition exploded all over the place. After that we hung around our trenches when those guys took off! They piled up sixteen planes in one week, with no combat involved, and finally the whole outfit was grounded.

The 58th Group unit history recorded six major accidents in February 1944 for no combats, fifteen more accidents in March for no combat, and another twelve accidents in April. In fairness to the 58th Group, it must be stated that its P-47s were fitted with the northern hemisphere winter-style "mud and snow" tires, which had deep diamond-shaped lugs, and these combined with the pierced steel plate runways were responsible for many landing and takeoff accidents. Later, smoother tires were fitted with better results.

12 April 1944: Yankee Doodle Dandy Dies . . .

After a four-day break, the 5th Air Force reapplied its power to Hollandia. The invasion was ten days away, but the Japanese still had to think it would be Wewak or Hansa. On 12 April another 251 tons were dropped on Hansa, while a similar but heavier attack was made on Hollandia. Fifty-one B-24s, 137 strafers, and 67 P-38s went back to Hollandia, expending 322 tons of bombs and 89,000 machine-gun rounds to create more destruction. At 1150, the much-bombed antiaircraft positions, personnel and supply areas, barracks, and shipping areas were attacked again. 1,000-pound demos showered down, with direct hits and near misses reported on the antiaircraft gun positions. Smoke and dust covered the target areas and some bomber squadrons crossing the target after the lead squadrons could not assess bombing accuracy. Squadrons commented on the lack of antiaircraft fire from parts of the target area. Depending on casualties to the gun crews, damage to the positions, and leadership and personal bravery, some antiaircraft units were not firing. In 2 Battery, 68 AA Battalion, a soldier wrote: "Big air raid. The battery personnel took shelter. Even in the large cave we could feel the earth tremor from exploding bombs. Our fear increases as one raid follows another."

The Japanese army air force was active again and attacked B-24s over the target. As the Ken's Men Group 403rd Squadron passed over Sentani Lake, an Oscar came boring in from nine o'clock. A waist gunner fired, the fighter went into a loop—the pilot probably was hit and jerked the stick back into his stomach—came over the top of the loop, and went on down to the water eleven thousand feet below.

On its 101st mission with the Jolly Rogers Group 319th Squadron was "Yankee Doodle Dandy," flown by Lt. Howard Golden. According to Wiley O. Woods in his history of the 90th Group, Golden became separated from his parent squadron and joined the formation of the 400th Squadron. As the 400th approached the target, the bombsight in the lead B-24 malfunctioned and the squadron formation changed to allow another airplane to take the lead. This maneuvering caused Golden to lag from the formation.

An antiaircraft shell hit the B-24, and it began to fall back from the formation. Below, the crews of 3 Battery, 66 AA Battalion shouted "Banzai!" when they saw the hit. Almost at once, Tonys and Oscars noticed the wounded B-24 and ignored other bombers to concentrate on Golden's ship. Watching, other crews could see flashes of 20 mm hits on the cockpit and engines; Yankee Doodle Dandy went into its death dive.

Other B-24 crews reported varying numbers of parachutes—some saw two, others six—but the victorious Japanese pilots machine-gunned them.

Yankee Doodle Dandy exploded in the kunai about a mile from the southwest end of Hollandia Strip. According to Japanese reports, six men died in the crash and four parachuted. S.Sgt. Eugene A. Ivers was found dead in his parachute by local people who buried him. Golden and 2nd Lt. Bernard Donohue were captured, taken to the 6 Flying Division headquarters, interrogated, and both beheaded, apparently by a Sergeant Major Aoyama, one on 18 April and the other a few days later. Nothing is known of what happened to the other man who parachuted. It is thought he fell into the lake and his body was not recovered. An Australian graves registration team searched the crash site and recovered the remains of four unidentified crew members. Ivers was exhumed and returned to the United States for reburial.

The B-24s had wreaked more havoc in the collections of material stored around Hollandia. In 90 Garrison Unit, Nagamitsu Tsukada wrote that enemy attacked in great numbers, the town was completely destroyed, and Sentani suffered great losses. The 27 Freight Depot reported forty-three hundred bundles of supplies destroyed at Kotabaroe and Imbi. Another diary recorded that not a single complete building remained, and the personnel of the lines of communication unit and naval development unit had gone into the hills. The doctor at 113 LofC Hospital saw the airfield at "three-fork road" afire, and he counted thirty airplanes burning.

The army air service radio at Hollandia had been off the air since 9 April, and when it did come alive again, found that it could not contact Wewak. The Hollandia station went off the air again on 13 April and was still silent on 18 April.

Major Matsumoto Lost to P-38s

The 80th Headhunters Fighter Squadron was over the target, and Capt. Burnell Adams claimed his fifth and sixth victories. Five Tonys were seen, a threesome and a pair, about four thousand feet above the P-38s some five miles northwest of Hollandia. Adams took his flight right up behind the pair of Tonys, who did not seem to know the P-38s were there until Adams fired. One split-s'ed and dived, but his target "began smoking and went into a steep dive. He broke into flames and crashed about two miles northwest of Hollandia Strip."

The other two P-38s with Adams went after the single Tony, so Adams dived, reunited with his wingman, made a pass at an Oscar, and "gave it a long burst and saw my .50s and cannon breaking on it. It turned sharply, and next thing I know he's sitting on my tail firing at me. I don't know how the hell he did it, but he did it damn fast."

Adams evaded this Oscar by diving "with everything shoved forward." He fired at five other Oscars and missed four due to insufficient deflection, but he did damage another Oscar, who escaped by using his superior maneuverability at low level, split-s'ing at low altitudes where Adams did not care to imitate him.

Dick Bong was flying with the Headhunters that day. Bong and Adams alternated firing on another Oscar, which Adams finally sent down in flames but from so close that oil spattered back onto the P-38's windshield. Bong confirmed the victory. Adams later zoomed over a hill in time to see Bong at minimum altitude shooting another Oscar down into the water.

Another Headhunter who scored was Jay Robbins, who maneuvered through the Tonys and P-38s, chased some Tonys from the tails of P-38s, and then followed another Tony down through a series of split-s'es until the Japanese began a gentle climb. Robbins was behind and lower "and drove right up behind before he saw me. He made a very sharp left turn, and I fired at close range. He burst into flames and crashed on the shore of Sentani Lake."

Robbins climbed toward a dogfight, picked a Japanese, fired, and saw hits, but the agile fighter escaped. Robbins climbed toward three other Japanese. One broke toward him, swung away, and Robbins chased him to low level over Hollandia before breaking away. He saw another Japanese and followed him through a series of dives and turns until this Japanese also turned toward the strip. Robbins flew right up on him, fired, and "knocked him down right on the strip."

Corky Smith went to assist Robbins. Two Oscars seemed determined to get Robbins, and Smith dropped some combat flap to turn more tightly and fired at 90 degrees; hits sparked on the Oscar, and Smith passed overhead. Behind him, Lt. Vernon Jenner saw the Oscar fall into the lake.

The fighter defenses gathered twenty-seven airplanes for the interception, and claimed 4-5-0 for a loss of 3-0-0. The 77 Sentai had received orders on 10 April to prepare to move to the Philippines. The unit launched six aircraft and admitted the loss of two dead: the CO, Maj. Kunio Matsumoto and Sgt. Waikichi Fukushima, both reported as shot down by P-38s. In 68 Sentai Captain Takenawa was killed. According to the Japanese report, 33, 63, and 248 Sentai did not engage.

U.S. fighter claims were for 9-2-3 for Bong, Adams, Robbins, Russell Roth, Corky Smith, Vernon Jenner, and Edward Robertson. These victories brought the 80th Squadron's total to 203 and made them the world's most successful twin-engine day-fighter squadron.

Bong claimed a probable victory, which fell into Tanamerah Bay, but there were no witnesses or camera gun confirmation. Bong closed to close range as usual, fired, and saw hits on the left wing, engine, and cockpit. After Hollandia was occupied, General Kenney had a diver go down at the spot reported by Bong. Sure enough, there was a Japanese fighter with the hits as described by Bong; the pilot had been killed. This was Bong's twenty-eighth victory and equaled the WW I score of the leading U.S. ace in that war, Capt. Eddie Rickenbacker.

Maintaining the U.S. pattern of attack, half an hour after the B-24s bombed, strafers skipped over the hills and treetops, striking airfields, storage areas, and shipping. The 89th and 90th Squadrons of the 3rd Attack went for freighters, luggers, and barges along the beaches and claimed hits on three. One A-20 had crashed five miles south of Kaiapit. Eleven A-20s of the 13th Squadron attacked three freighters in Challenger Cove and claimed two direct hits on one, destroying it. Other pilots unable to make a run on the ships dropped their bombs on Hollandia town. At 1225, the 8th Squadron charged across the bay, saw two burning freighters between Imbi and Challenger Cove, and roared past to attack storage areas at Sentani, then others along to Jautefa Bay. All around them, crews of the 8th saw other targets smoking and burning. Lieutenant Colonel Okada, CO 49 Anchorage Unit, noted that the vessel *Narita Maru* "with three direct hits, sank in the harbor." Also recorded sunk were *Tenyu Maru* and *Fukuei Maru*.

Yet another raid had been made on the major Japanese base in West New Guinea. Behind the raiders were rising columns of smoke from burning fuel and destroyed aircraft, buildings, and ships. AAF losses had been slight—one of each type aircraft. Allied Air Forces Intsum 199 described the mission: "Huge fires were observed, with smoke to 10,000 feet. One 2,000-ton freighter was fired and blown up. Two small freighters, five to seven luggers and barges, were left burning. Enemy fighters attacking the heavies lost eight of their number shot down and eleven damaged. One B-24 was lost. AA opposition was moderate, medium and heavy, inaccurate and accurate."

The Japanese had been continually searching for a way to cope with the heavy bomber formations, trying to find the weak points. Finally, 14 Hikodan headquarters said in Intelligence Report No. 7: "B-24s have no parts specially vulnerable to intense machine-gun fire. The reason for the shoot-down on 12 April is that the oxygen tank in the nose caught fire. The tail is the weakest part."

By now the bomber and fighter Sentai were in a perilous situation, certain of heavy losses regardless of whether they went onto the attack, if they flew in defense of the bases, or if they remained on the ground within range of the B-24, B-25, and P-38 team. Shimada, 77 Sentai, noted in his last diary entries that the unit was to leave its planes and withdraw from New Guinea. The weak air strength is typified in a diagram detailing a four-Sentai formation issued by 14 Hikodan in order A-30: nineteen aircraft were all that could be flown; 77 Sentai was not included.

In addition to Hollandia, Allied missions were flown against Timor, Wewak, Hansa Bay, Karkar Island, Madang area, and Alexishafen area. On following days attacks were mounted on the same targets, never releasing pressure from the air. It was to be four days before the 5th Air Force returned to Hollandia.

On a direct order by General Kenney, Dick Bong was banned from combat flying and informed of immediate promotion to major. Kenney sent Bong back to the United States for a rest. A flood of publicity followed the announcement of Bong's twenty-eighth victory because then Bong was recognized as the leading U.S. fighter ace, having broken the WW I record of twenty-seven victories by Eddie Rickenbacker. The U.S. Air Force commanders were worried at the constant stream of losses of high-scoring U.S. fighter pilots in all theaters, and there was no objection to Kenney's decision to send Bong home for a while. During this time in the United States, Bong completed a gunnery course. When he returned to the SWPA, he said that he now knew how to shoot. Jay Robbins, commander of the Headhunters, had traveled to Australia in the same batch of young fighter pilots as Bong. En route, Robbins assessed the likelihood of each man becoming a fighter ace. Robbins had put Bong last.

Despite radar and fighter patrols around the Admiralties, sometimes a Japanese reconnaissance flight was able to get close enough to see the buildup of Allied shipping there. On 15 April one such recon airplane radioed that sixty-seven Allied ships were counted near the Admiralties. This report was intercepted by one of the RAAF signals intelligence units and included in SIB 350 of 21 April. But although the Japanese did find the ships around the Admiralties and had a reasonable idea of their opponent's strength and location, the third and other important factor was his intentions, and they were wrong. The Japanese higher command had deduced that the next Allied landings would be around Madang, Hansa, or Wewak, or in the Bismarcks area to the east.

16 April 1944: "Black Sunday"

The Japanese had been unable so far to inflict serious loss on the 5th Air Force formations. On this day the hostile environment was to intervene. One hundred seventy-one U.S. fighters and bombers set out to attack targets in the Tadji-Hollandia area. Because of bad weather reports, takeoff had been delayed, but finally word came to go. Six other attacks on the area had been cancelled due to weather.

By this time the Japanese defenses could do little to hinder the onslaught. The heavies roared over at height, untouchable. From his tail turret, Dick Grills watched their eight 1,000-pounders sail down, and as the bombers departed he counted four big oil fires behind them. Squadron reports described the mission as "all in the target, eight fires"; "bombs hit in or near the AA position"; "fuel fire, smoke to 2,000 feet"; "100 percent in target"; "fires, smoke, debris in the air"; "fires with smoke to 6,000 feet"; "two direct hits on the jetty"; and "fuel dump fire."

The Grim Reapers 3rd Attack led the strafers, the 8th Squadron at the head. The formation passed south of the target and flew on for a considerable distance, level with Wakde Island, and then turned back to Hollandia and began the attacks. Maj. Chuck Howe was at the head of the mass of ten strafer squadrons with Intelligence Officer Lt. Rignal Baldwin as observer in the rear cockpit. Baldwin closely followed the map, realized they were off course, and repeatedly called Howe to correct to the north. Howe ignored him until he had passed Hollandia, and the coastline east of Wakde became visible. Only then did Howe turn back, in a wide left turn, having dragged the entire formation on an extra forty-five minutes of flying time. Andrew Weigel believes they were an hour late over the target, and the following groups tagged along, burning up valuable fuel soon to be needed. The P-38 escort could not afford the wasted fuel either.

The strafers roared across a wasteland of Japanese airpower, but it was attacked in case the enemy had flown in new aircraft since the last attack.

Morale of some Japanese gun crews had been destroyed. A soldier from 68 AA Battalion was walking from one position across country to another. Then he met "everyone fleeing down the slope away from the position. Nobody stopped to answer my questions. I found the enemy had attacked with small parachutes and leaflets." The gunners were so demoralized they abandoned the position when the strafers flew over.

Maj. Bill Kemble was leading the 388th Squadron, 312th Group, the squadron flying "almost wingtip to wingtip. A radio tower appeared ahead, which I sprayed as best I could, but I didn't dare veer off course." Then his wingman sped ahead a little and released his parafrags, which streamed out and back, one looped over Kemble's wing but fortunately slipped off. The squadron was amazed to see B-25s of the 345th Air Apaches coming across the target, head-on for the A-20s, at a closing speed of about 550 mph. Somehow, they all jinked correctly and both waves went on their ways. What impression was gained by watching Japanese can only be imagined!

The airplanes raced out of gun range, re-formed, and began the return flight, all pilots conscious of the fuel problem. Some reached for the thermos flask nearby, about which jokes had been made at the dispersals, saying the flasks should be filled with gasoline as well as all the tanks.

Once more, the Japanese catalogued their losses. The 27 Freight Depot lost twenty-seven hundred bundles of clothing and supplies. The infantryman who had been caught during an earlier attack on Kotabaroe road wrote, "Big air raid. Rations, clothing, goods, and the camp destroyed." In his diary, Lieutenant Colonel Okada noted, "2,000 drums, large amounts of clothing and goods destroyed. Thirteen buildings damaged; fourteen killed, sixteen wounded."

Allied Air Forces Intsum 200 reported the mission:

Supply and personnel areas near Imbi Bay, Challenger Cove, Hollandia Strip and town, Hamadi Island, and Jautefa Bay were well covered with 285 tons, starting numerous fires, some with black smoke to 2,000 feet. A jetty, 15 to 20 barges, and several AA positions were believed destroyed. Eight 500-lb. bombs were dropped at a 1,500 to 2,000–ton freighter, resulting in a 50' miss. The vessel was then damaged by strafing. Two villages near Tepier Bay were also strafed.

The battered and bleeding defenders of Hollandia might have gained some measure of joy had they known the situation confronting the returning U.S. squadrons. The dreaded New Guinea weather had closed in, separating the

Hollandia strike force from its bases at Nadzab, Gusap, Saidor, and other fields.

Aircraft that had turned back and others on separate missions closer to Nadzab encountered the developing cloud masses. A B-24 of the Red Raiders returned early with hydraulic problems and had to go to treetop height to follow the coast. P-39s on a barge hunt reported the worsening conditions. But the main armada attacking Hollandia was on the far side of the wall of clouds.

Larry Tanberg, CO of the Sunsetters 38th Bomb Group, later recalled: "This is one time we got caught. We went up and the front moved across and just socked in everything and it was a fiasco from then on."

Six main formations, with stragglers between them, flew back east toward the cloud mass. The B-24 squadrons led. Then came the 345th Group B-25s, followed by the 312th, and Major Howe's trailing series of A-20 and B-25 squadrons; last were six F-7 photoreconnaissance versions of the B-24s. Overhead were the P-38s.

The front came into view and was described by 475th Group pilot Carroll Anderson as "fascinating," stretching from left to right with a "black and mean-looking" base at treetop level. There were few choices for the approaching pilots, determined by each man's instrument flying experience: go through, go under, or bail out and take your chances in the jungle.

The Sunday afternoon hours were filled with incidents as the returning bomber and fighter pilots tried to find somewhere to land before running out of fuel over jungle or sea. Planes squeezed in wherever they could. There were collisions, crash landings; planes crashed into mountains, landed on beaches, in grassy clearings or in the water.

When the Grim Reapers 8th Squadron left the target, Andrew Weigel found that the leading element went too fast and, as leader of the second element, brought home the six aircraft with him, plus three of the 89th Squadron. Well aware by listening to radio talk of bad weather on the return route, he turned inland at Vanimo and went back along the valley. From Annenberg to Dumpu they flew through heavy rain and clouds with a two-hundred-foot ceiling.

Colonel Strauss led the 312th Group back, carefully conserved fuel, and listened to growing radio chatter as pilots discussed the matter or called for advice and help. He insisted on tight radio discipline in the group; there were few of his pilots cluttering up the radio channels that day. Strauss considered taking the group to Saidor, but that was only an emergency strip at the time and could not accommodate his squadrons. If the weather did not improve, or a gap appear, then within an hour the aircraft would begin to fall out of the sky. Ken Hedges, flying "Queen of Spades" in the 389th Squadron, suddenly saw what seemed to be a brighter patch of sunlight and called Strauss to say he was going to head for it. Mindful of the long formation trailing them, Strauss told him to wait for another circuit of the circle they were holding at that moment. Discipline held, they circled, and Strauss led them through and over the hills, into clearer weather, and back to Gusap. Relief flooded many of the crews as they slipped through the murk and into the valley where the Ramu River was visible. As it was, the flight had been dangerously long. "Je Reviens" was checked after the flight, and the crew chief announced that the only fuel left was in the carburetors. Bill Kemble, leading the 388th, had both engines cut as he taxied "California Sunshine" after landing; he was the last of the Group. Andrew Weigel, leading the mixed 8th/89th formation, claims the 312th followed him, then speeded up to get into Gusap first. He landed after a seven-hour mission with thirty gallons of gasoline.

Ralph Wandrey, 9th Squadron ace, spent nearly three hours airborne that afternoon, in company with fellow ace Gerry Johnson, flying out from Gusap to locate the returning formations or single aircraft and guide them in. The weather had formed a series of pockets, or large "rooms" of clouds—the floor provided by hills and jungle. Wandrey and Johnson found groups of circling aircraft of various types, called them on the radio, told them to follow, and then led them back through the treetop clouds to Gusap. Noting that the circuit at Gusap was crowded, Wandrey took one batch of followers to Saidor. One F-5A began to land as a B-25 did so at the other end of the strip; they collided head-on and exploded. Wandrey decided that the worsening weather made landing soon his personal best choice, so he returned to Gusap and did so. Johnson was already there after shepherding his own bunch of arrivals. Bill Moran, photographer with the Jolly Rogers Group, was aboard a B-24 that found its way to Saidor, a fighter strip, "But it was any port in a storm."

John Stanifer, P-38 pilot with the 80th Headhunters Fighter Squadron "lucked out. I dropped to the deck and followed the coastline, flying in heavy rain almost to Madang. However, the controller there advised all aircraft not to land due to a head-on on the runway and zero visibility. I flew back up the coast until I found a river, the Ramu, that led me into the Markham Valley where the weather was surprisingly clear."

Robert Smith, another Headhunter pilot, realized his options were few. Before this, he had always been able to avoid the weather or turn back. Now was the moment of truth. He listened to talk between Liberator pilots ahead and knew that some of those men were very scared; he turned the radio volume low. On his instrument panel was a hole where the artificial horizon had been removed for repair two days before. The faces of the pilots on either side showed the same feeling of disquiet.

The leading squadron of the Red Raiders Group plunged into the clouds at twenty-two thousand feet, and the wall towered up another fifteen thousand feet above them. To compound matters, many of the 22nd Group only recently had transitioned to the B-24, and the squadron leader, Col. Jim Sweeney, was on only his third B-24 mission. The turbulence tossed the big B-24s around and holding position became hazardous. Sweeney looked down and saw water through a gap in the clouds, called the squadron, and led them down in a spiral to 150 feet. Rain was so heavy that the pilots combined instrument flying by one while the other watched from a side window to avoid collisions. With fuel problems looming, some of the B-24s squeezed into Saidor. The 408th Squadron of the Red Raiders lost a B-24 soon after takeoff; now in the clouds another B-24 simply disappeared. The crew of a third B-24 baled out at eighteen thousand feet. Two men were never heard from again, but the rest filtered through to Saidor after surviving hardships in the jungles.

Morgan Terry led the Jolly Rogers Group 320th Squadron on this mission and put into effect his policy that the fastest way home was a straight line. He had gained the respect of his crew on several previous occasions with his flying ability and did it again this day. "He was a little bitty guy but had a whole lot of guts," was Dick Grills's opinion. Dick and the others had been listening to the chatter and arguments among pilots, but Terry kept the 320th together after other squadrons turned away. He took them in single file through the heavy rain, straight into the clouds, under the storm, down the valley, so low that the smell of the jungle came into the airplanes and crews could see birds frightened by the noise darting away and around the treetops. The big airplanes could not maneuver in the valleys, could not turn back, and had to go onward. In the rear the gunners could see how low they were and "stood there, scared to death. We could see a big outcropping sticking out once in a while, but we got home," said Grills. A break in the weather occurred as they neared Gusap, and Terry led them in line abreast at two hundred feet over the strip. The squadron got back to Nadzab.

When a B-25 of the 38th Sunsetters Group and an F-5A collided head-on and exploded at Saidor, the Saidor Strip, which was already crowded, then became unusable. Lt. Joe Price of the 475th Fighter Group appeared, out of fuel, ignored signals not to land and touched down without undercarriage, slid through the blazing mass of the B-25 and F-5, and stepped out of the ruined P-38. Then he collapsed. The runway was partially cleared and two more landings took place, but then the runway was blocked again. The circling A-20s of the 417th Sky Lancers Group turned away for Finschhafen.

The 475th Fighter Group had sent forty-eight P-38s on the mission. Enemy presence was negligible, and one formation of the 475th indulged in skylarking around the bomber formations—a happy time, but the use of fuel soon was regretted when the weather on the way home was encountered. The formations fragmented and the P-38 pilots struggled to remain calm and fly smoothly through the clouds and rain.

In the 433rd Squadron, Calvin Wire had turned back because of fuel shortage and found himself confronted with the towering wall of cloud stretching as far as the eye could see. Wire tried to go over it; no luck. He led his wingman up and down the cloud-wall looking for a break; no luck. The other 433rd airplanes, coming along behind Wire, could hear Wire and his wingman discussing the situation, and then heard B-24s talking about it, so the squadron realized all was not well. Attempts to follow bombers failed, and in desperation Wire led his wingman down to sea level to follow the coast through the tiny forty-foot gap between sea and cloud base. Rain was so intense that the two pilots had to look through the side windows of their canopy.

Wire hit a palm tree in a desperate move to avoid flying into the coastal hills and damaged his right engine and had to shut it down. His wingman called that he'd had enough and turned away to climb on instruments through the clouds. Wire knew only that he was flying along the coast toward Lae. Suddenly he saw a small strip right on the coast and tried to maneuver for a landing. But the clouds started to sag to water level; Wire saw that waves were breaking higher than his cockpit and abruptly his P-38 flew into the top of a wave. Almost instantly the P-38 was underwater and sinking.

Wire undid his seat belt and shot to the surface, and then managed to inflate and climb into his dinghy. He was about eight hundred yards from shore. Two U.S. soldiers set out in a canoe to rescue him, but Wire did not recognize them as Americans and tried to fire his .45-caliber pistol—which fortunately refused to shoot. His rescuers took Wire ashore, and he found that he was at Yamai Point, built for Piper L-4 Grasshopper liaison puddle-jumpers. Two B-24s and two B-25s also crash-landed there. Wire ended up in hospital in Sydney but returned to the 433rd in August.

Bob Tomberg of the 433rd Squadron bailed out, evaded the Japanese, met friendly natives, and was led to Saidor, where the local people were rewarded for saving Tomberg. He hitched a ride to Finschhafen on an A-20 but was refused transportation to Nadzab by officious base operations staff for the very good administrative reason that Tomberg had no orders for such a move. Tomberg was told unofficially that a C-47 was about to depart; he should speak to the pilot. He arrived back at the sprawling Nadzab base and was left at the far side, away from the 433rd. No telephone call was answered, so Tomberg had to thumb a lift and then persuade the driver to make a detour to the 433rd tent area.

The 475th battled through the weather, but six men were lost.

The B-25s of the 345th Air Apaches Group stayed together for some time after entering the clouds, but eventually the leader, Capt. Dale Speicher, had to order a descent. The squadrons spiraled down and pulled out over the trees. The 499th Squadron split into three flights of three and hugged the coast, eventually to land at Finschhafen, with the exception of "Stingeroo," which ditched after an engine fire. As the 500th Squadron came up to Saidor, they witnessed the collision and fireball and realized that they could not use that runway. They went on in the rain and gathering dark and found Lae by the lights. After seven hours fifteen minutes airborne, the B-25s touched down. One B-25 was not seen again after the spiral descent through the clouds.

General Kenney described it as the worst blow he took in the SWPA. When the final tally was done, thirty-two air crew had been killed and thirty-seven aircraft lost. Fifteen were damaged or written off at Saidor alone.

Some of the wrecks were soon found and some were discovered later, but many simply vanished. In May 2002, fifty-nine years later, U.S. military teams went to two mountain crash sites and identified the B-24 aircraft and crew remains of 2nd Lt. Ray Cooley's crew, of the 403rd Squadron, 43rd Bomb

Group, and that of Capt. Tom Paschal's, of the 408th Squadron, 22nd Bomb Group. Each had flown into mountainsides in the clouds.

There was, however, little doubt in anyone's mind that Hollandia had been well and truly battered into submission. Despite the dangerous weather, the 5th Air Force fighters, strafers, and heavies had again given a demonstration of airpower. As well as the Hollandia missions, Allied air attacks were made on Roti, Timor, Wakde Island, Hans, and the coast of New Britain.

To the Landings, 22 April

The Japanese had not sighted the Allied naval strike force since 1 April. Ultra intercepts once again kept the Allied high command informed of the Japanese situation. While the 5th Air Force had been engaged in New Guinea, the U.S. naval force had attacked Palau and Yap. Taking into account bad weather, unusable airfields from which searches could have been made, and their own radio intelligence, which reported signals traffic, the Japanese naval command believed the Allied fleet was en route to Espiritu Santo, located between the Solomons and Noumea.

From 16 April until the landings, the 5th Air Force attacked coastal targets, and the 380th Bomb Group, from Darwin, Australia, attacked airfields farther west at Noemfoor, Manokwari, and others that might be used by the Japanese to launch attacks into the Hollandia area. On 20 April the invasion fleet of eighty ships steamed northwest from the Admiralties. The next night the Tadji invasion detachment left the convoy, and the remainder went on to Hollandia. Both landings were made against little opposition, and Japanese aircraft that normally patrolled the coast did not sight the fleet until it had anchored. The success of the Allied deception plan was as great as could be wished in a military operation.

On 21 April, the day before the invasion, the Japanese estimated Allied intentions:

The signs of an enemy plan to make a new landing in the New Guinea area are clear. The probability of a landing between Madang and Hansa or on the Karkar Islands is estimated to be greatest. According to the general situation a landing in the Wewak sector is next in probability. In light of the recent bombings of Hansa, of reconnaissance and naval bombardment of Wewak, and the dropping of pamphlets by the enemy stating they would land on Wewak on 24 April, precautions must be taken in the Wewak sector.

It is also possible that the enemy will land in the Hollandia sector. However, since there was no reconnaissance carried out in this region by submarines, destroyers, or other means, and since air attacks were of a purely destructive nature, no signs of usual prelanding operations are discernible. Furthermore, the enemy has no airbase at present from which to neutralize our airdromes west of Sarmi. Therefore, probability of a landing in this sector is thought to be minor.

The estimated fourteen thousand defenders of Hollandia had been reduced to about five thousand men. Some went to Wewak and Hansa to meet the expected invasion there, and others evacuated inland or to the west.

With hardly any Japanese resistance, the Allied force landed, the airfield sites were captured, and work began at once to prepare them for Allied use. The airfield at Aitape was ready for use after forty-one hours of work, which began on the afternoon of the invasion. Brig. Gen. Paul Wurtsmith landed one of the first two P-38s on a steel-planking strip 100 feet wide and 3,900 feet long.

This work had been done mainly by RAAF engineers, two units of which had been in New Guinea for sixteen months without any leave for members of the units. The continual demand for airfield construction meant these men could not be spared. Too few tributes are paid to the work of the U.S. and Australian construction units, of all types, without whom the Allied advances would not have been possible. Work began on the Hollandia fields on 27 April, and Cyclops was usable the next day.

On 24 April Hollandia radioed Biak with a message: "All the troops would give all for the Emperor, their country, and their commander; code books would be burned and destruction already had started; the enemy was two kilometers away."

Three hundred forty wrecked or unflyable Japanese aircraft of all types littered the Hollandia airfields area. The Japanese 6 Flying Division had been destroyed. Its few remaining aircraft came under command of 7 Flying Division, which had headquarters at Ambon Island to the west and which itself was reduced to about one hundred aircraft. The fortunes of Japanese units and individuals in New Guinea varied, but most were bad. Morale fell and was not helped by the rumor that some B-24 pilots were women. This probably came from U.S. publicity given to organizations such as Jacqueline Cochran's WASPs and Nancy Love's WAFs, who ferried all types of USAAF aircraft outside the combat zones and piloted a variety of aircraft on duties in the United States.

The 208 Sentai selected thirty pilots and maintenance men to go to Manila on 19 April to collect replacement Lily bomber aircraft. From March 1943 until mid-April 1944, in just a little more than one year, this single Japanese bomber Sentai lost 230 twin-engine Lilys: about 50 on operations and the rest to air raids and nonoperational causes. One member of the unit believed 60 aircraft of the Sentai had been lost at Hollandia alone.

Of the Japanese fighter units, 13 Sentai was withdrawn to the Halmaheras, while 63 was told to walk to Sarmi, and 77 Sentai moved into the jungle. The 248 Sentai had no aircraft, and under Major Kuroda the unit began to walk to Sarmi. The 248 lost twenty-four pilots killed in air combat, but optimistically claimed ninety-seven enemy destroyed or damaged. General Inada, commanding 6 Flying Division, was removed from his post; he sent a farewell message to some units, telling them that they left a splendid record of convoy patrols, interceptions, and attacks on shipping and then urged all ranks to "work toward full recovery of your fighting power" so they could return to action.

But the trained and experienced flight and ground crews had been annihilated. Those who survived air combat, bombing, and strafing were left to fend for themselves in the jungle or to go overland to the next base; only a few irreplaceable personnel were evacuated by air or sea. On 25 July Inada's 6 Flying Division was disbanded. So was 63 Sentai: the men became ground troops, and at the surrender in August 1945, only 3 remained alive. Of 130 men of the Sentai left at Wewak, only 17 survived. The 68 Sentai personnel also became ground troops, and about 20 survived until the surrender. Led by Maj. Shigechika Tomari, 78 Sentai began the march to Sarmi. By the end of the war, not a single pilot who was at Hollandia on 22 April survived, and only some 20 men got back to Japan. The 248 Sentai went by foot and boat to Sarmi, and only 3 or 4 pilots are thought to have survived. The unit was disbanded, and only about 20 members reached Japan.

Earlier, on 17 April, the 7 remaining Oscars of 33 Sentai were flown out of Hollandia to island bases in the north, and eventually arrived in the Philippines. Lt. Tameyoshi Kuroki flew his damaged Oscar to Biak and on to Manila, with his wingman squeezed aboard. A few of the pilots and ground crew who remained escaped the invasion force and reached Japanese positions in October.

The unit flew in defense of Sumatra and the Philippines, returned to Sumatra, and was there when the war ended.

The RAAF and U.S. radio intercept units were able to keep track of the movements of the Japanese air headquarters and the air units, and were the unseen force behind many of the successful fighter interceptions of Japanese raids that were sent later against Allied bases. Not a hint of this special work could be permitted for decades after the war, but many fighter pilots with a string of victories to their credit owe a small debt to the men and women of the Ultra organization.

All that remains of some of the men who endured the Wewak and Hollandia bombing campaigns are their diary entries. Some end with the entry, "Assembling to oppose the landing," while others record the miserable existence eked out by those who fled into the mountains and refused to surrender. Sgt. Tsugio Shimada, pilot in 77 Sentai, made his last entry when going into the jungle on 15 April. No pilot of 77 Sentai is known to have survived the war, and only four or five other members of the unit returned to Japan. Toshikazi Kudo survived the attacks, went into the jungle with the rest of his unit, and dutifully kept his diary: "29 April. Even the CO is eating coconut now. 3 May. Only six of us left. 7 May. Slept in native huts; as we stole from them they got angry."

A member of 113 Hospital, who recorded the events of the past month, had gone to Hollandia and been appalled by the devastation, then went into the jungle, had several close escapes from U.S. troops, and finally was killed, his last entry being 17 May. The doctor from the hospital probably was with the same group, as his diary records similar incidents and ends on 18 May. The soldier who began to shake at the sound of thunder, Kiichi Ishii, 68 AA Battalion, also roamed the mountains. "It rains here three times a day and makes me mad. Caught some red frogs and ate them." His diary ended on 1 June. Lieutenant Colonel Okada, CO 49 Anchorage Unit, went into the battle to repulse the landing. A few entries from his diary portray the end of the Japanese at Hollandia: "23 April. I am in command of reserves in the hills to the west. 13 May. Eating leaves and grass. 17 May. 1,000 men decreased to 700. 2 June. There is no food. 5 June. No food. My body is weak."

Perspectives

The U.S. 5th Air Force blossomed from the ashes of the 1941 defeats in the Philippines and Netherlands East Indies and from the days of adversity in 1942 in Papua New Guinea to eventually span the Pacific from south to north. The 5th grew from an organization in which, in mid-1942, mechanics had to make their own tools to use on the collection of aircraft to one basing squadrons on Okinawa in July 1945. Its exploits in the South West Pacific have been over-shadowed by those in the European theater. Comparisons are invidious, but a case can be made that the U.S. 5th Air Force, from mid-August 1943 to late April 1944, conducted a campaign of aerial warfare unequaled in World War II in which, despite the severe limitations imposed by weather, terrain, and distance, it repeatedly destroyed the opposing air arm and contributed to the destruction of another at Rabaul.

The 5th Air Force's major base area, Australia, was undeveloped and unprepared for modern war. The areas of the region into which the 5th Air Force advanced were primitive and offered little hope of survival to personnel who came down there. The towns and communications facilities, such as existed in the combat zones, were either destroyed in the fighting or left in the hands of enemy to "wither on the vine"; everything needed had to be transported and constructed, and disease and illness were always a major concern. Personnel were often ruined mentally and physically by service in the SWPA, yet the theater produced some of the greatest individualists and teamworkers in the history of the war.

Airpower experience in the Pacific campaigns showed that prewar concepts of operations in the region had been incorrect. It had been thought that naval surface forces would engage in decisive battles and that Japan would have to be invaded to bring any war to a successful conclusion. Both presumptions were shown to be wrong. There were few naval forces available to the SWPA until the invasion of the Philippines was imminent, so airpower was used to a greater extent than in other theaters. By mid-April 1944, Rabaul had been effectively isolated, the Japanese air forces in New Guinea had been destroyed, and the move to the Philippines was in planning.

Instead of identifying airpower as a force in its own right, as were land and sea power, the Japanese subordinated their air component to the other two, using it as little more than longer-range artillery or torpedo launchers. They did not, as a national force, apply the principles of war to their air elements. The selection of positions for major Japanese bases and bastions was dictated by a concept of operations in two dimensions. Once the third dimension—height (or air)—became crucial, and the Allies controlled the skies, the Japanese were at a disadvantage.

In the Pacific even more markedly than other theaters, airpower dominated air, land, and sea operations; it displayed strong independent logistical capabilities, established more effective interdiction of enemy areas, and finally, delivered to the assigned targets the atomic weapons that made it unnecessary to execute an invasion of Japan. The Allied forces included people of senior and high rank who understood the use of airpower, grasped the opportunity presented by the war, and demonstrated what could be achieved with intelligent use of aircraft. But the Japanese hierarchy never really understood that potential.

The Japanese army air force performance in the SWPA was marked first by senior staff who seemed incapable of using what they did have to best effect and, in a national characteristic, who seem to have avoided honest reporting to higher headquarters about the true situation so correct policies could be devised and implemented. Second, optimistic verbal reports of battle results were accepted and passed to higher headquarters without a requirement for proof by independent sources. Third, there was a continuous high rate of destruction of units that were fed into the area with accompanying losses of pilots and crews. Fourth, there was no experimentation to get better results from the aircraft, no field modifications to improve performance, no willingness to consider new ideas. In its simplest terms, there was no evolution of the force as there was on the Allied side.

The Allied air forces in 1944 bore little resemblance to the struggling Allied formations of mid-1942, but on the Japanese side there was negligible change: the same types of aircraft, the same poorly developed airfields, and the same operations policies. Despite the problems imposed by weather and terrain, and the quality of available radios, the Allied forces worked tirelessly to perfect the coordination of air and ground forces so that close support of ground forces became an accepted part of operations in the SWPA, while the Japanese supply system came under relentless attack. The Japanese were incapable of such efforts.

The capabilities of Japanese ground attack aircraft were puny compared to those of the Allied air forces. They simply did not develop any equivalent to the powerful P-47, the P-38, or even the sturdy workhorse P-40.

A sign of their basic incompetence was evident in the Kokoda campaign July to November 1942. Even when every factor was in their favor, when they enjoyed air superiority, naval supremacy, and overwhelming numbers on the ground and were equipped with artillery, heavy infantry weapons, engineers, packhorses, and a logistics organization, the Japanese did not employ their air units for reconnaissance ahead of their troops, for air support of those units in contact, or for air resupply, and they simply ignored the operating airstrip at Kokoda itself. A few Australian infantry battalions, without heavy weapons, supported by supplies carried through the mountains on the backs of men and an imperfect but developing air supply system and air attack squadrons, fought delaying actions and made the Japanese force spend their most precious commodity—time.

The Japanese should have won the Kokoda campaign and taken Port Moresby but failed because their available airpower did not assist the land elements. Again, in the Buna-Gona campaign, when the Australian and U.S. land forces were dependent on air resupply, the Japanese failed to recognize this opportunity and exploit it with their superior naval and air forces.

Quite simply, the Japanese command in New Guinea was outperformed in every aspect of military activity, and tens of thousands of Japanese soldiers and airmen paid with their lives for that incompetence.

Rabaul and other bypassed positions were reduced to making polite vague references to the air situation and sending courteous suggestions to higher headquarters that Japanese airpower could return.

Postwar histories of the Japanese air units refer to heroic claims by individual pilots in actions that often cannot be located in Allied records. Somehow these personal techniques for success could not be adopted by the main body of Japanese pilots, crews, or units, something which one would expect to occur as the level of experience broadened. References are also made in some of these histories to combats that never took place—over the Admiralties in early 1944, for example.

What was indisputable was that flying units lost their allocation of aircraft several times over in a few months, and frequent expeditions had to be made to Manila to collect new aircraft, while at the same time a constant stream of replacement airplanes came down the chain of airfields to Wewak. The sortie rate of the entire Japanese bomber force in the SWPA for the period August 1943 to April 1944 was abysmally low and probably would be surpassed by that of any single Allied squadron.

Despite entering the SWPA with the experience of up to five years or more of war, with equipment of which the shortcomings should have been obvious, the Japanese army and navy air forces failed to change with the times and the situation and became irrelevant to military operations in the theater. It is not too much to say that by 1944 the main function of the Japanese air arms came to be that of provision of real targets for enthusiastic Allied pilots operating with superior training, superior tactics, and superior aircraft, all of which incorporated improvements found to be necessary in combat.

The Japanese air arms in the SWPA failed in every category of air operations: reconnaissance, attack, defense, maritime protection, maintenance, planning, and execution of combat missions.

The overall picture of Japanese army operations in New Guinea is of incompetence at command level accompanied by technical inferiority at frontline level, both unrelieved by any concept of evolution or improvement in overall performance. As usual, in whichever force this is present, this combination resulted in widespread slaughter in the ranks of the combat personnel. The patriotic Japanese servicemen in the ranks below major were badly served by their superiors in uniform and in the aviation industry.

Both the German and Japanese servicemen were fed a series of lies about the situation to convince them to hold out a little longer, to allow the dramatic change to take place when their enemies would be defeated once and for all. The Germans were told of the coming wonder weapons, while the Japanese were told of the huge decisive battle force gathering in the Home Islands—all that was needed was determination to endure a little longer. As time went by, only the most fanatical believed these stories.

The following few points from Allied air force operations in the SWPA to the end of April 1944 are made for their relevance at that time and relevance to the present:

Land-based aircraft alone supported operations in the SWPA—aircraft range was the major factor in destruction or neutralization of the enemy.

Sustained attack was necessary to destroy or neutralize enemy land-based airpower.

The best defense against attack demands possession of aircraft with longer range than the enemy's.

Attack aircraft that approach at low altitude for considerable distances defeat radar and achieve surprise.

The success of the Wewak-Hollandia operations was one of the brightest achievements of the 5th Air Force and effectively opened the way to the

Philippines. On 27 May U.S. forces landed at Biak. The first warning the Japanese had of this operation was the sighting of the fleet off Biak at 0500 hours that day.

Fitting concluding comments on the Wewak-Hollandia bombing campaign are perhaps best made by a Japanese who suffered the bombing and by a B-24 bombardier.

Private Ozeki related: "It seems that our units at Hansa and Wewak have recently been taking a terrific beating from enemy airplanes. They say that each time hundreds of drums, ammunitions, provisions, ships, medical supplies, and important unassembled machinery are being turned to ashes. It must be the American air force, the lords of the South Seas. They have many planes and are brave as well. They are skillful in bombing and strafing."

Tom Fetter of the Jolly Rogers 90th Bomb Group:

It was an exciting time in our lives. We did not think of ourselves as heroic. What we were doing was the way that war was fought. The issues seemed clearly drawn, the stakes were high, and we had no doubt we were doing the right thing. Perhaps we were naive, but I can still remember and recapture that mood when thinking about those long ago events. There will never again be a war in which formations of bombers will attack a target, fighting off interceptors and flying through the flak. It was a great war, and I wouldn't have missed it for anything.

Appendix A

The U.S. Army 5th Air Force
Wewak Strike Force, August 1943

Heavy Bombers

43rd Bomb Group (B-17s): 63rd, 64th, 65th, and 403rd Squadrons
The 43rd Bomb Group, Ken's Men, operated the Boeing B-17 Flying Fortress, a four-engine heavy bomber designed to operate by day at great heights, with an accurate bombsight, to destroy enemy war capacity by pinpoint bombardment. Ken's Men was about to re-equip with B-24s.

90th Bomb Group (B-24s): 319th, 320th, 321st, and 400th Squadrons
The Consolidated B-24 Liberator four-engine heavy bomber equipped the 90th Bomb Group, the Jolly Rogers—the CO was Col. Art Rogers. The B-24 became the major type used in Pacific campaigns. It has been described as the first truly modern aircraft, with features that set a new standard for aviation.

Strafers

3rd Attack Group (B-25s): 8th, 13th, 89th, and 90th Squadrons
38th Bomb Group (B-25s): 71st and 405th Squadrons
The North American B-25 Mitchell, intended as a twin-engine medium bomber, was adapted by the 5th Air Force to become a treetop strafer with eight .50-caliber machine guns in the nose. The 3rd Attack Group, the Grim Reapers, was the first attack unit in the theater, closely followed by the 38th Sunsetters.

Fighters

9th, 39th, and 80th Fighter Squadrons (equipped with the P-38)
475th Fighter Group (P-38s)
431st, 432rd, and 433rd Squadrons
The Lockheed P-38 Lightning twin-engine fighter was the star of the SWPA and was the first Allied fighter to inflict sustained heavy losses on the Japanese. Many U.S. fighter pilots became aces using the P-38's superior combination of power to climb, speed, and firepower. The 9th, 39th, and 80th Squadrons all had operated the inferior Curtiss P-40 or Bell P-39 (or P-400 export version) in the early days of the New Guinea campaign, but the 475th Fighter Group, Satan's Angels, had been formed in Australia by General Kenney on the understanding that he would find the men if Washington supplied the Lockheed fighters.

Appendix B

*Organization of Japanese 4 Air Army,
Late July 1943*

The 14 Flying Brigade: with 68 and 78 Sentai, plus 20, 72, and 81 Chutai, as well as a raider unit and a photographic unit. Note on the fighter units: 68 Sentai formed in March 1942 in Manchuria, with the Ki-61, and its only area of operations was the SWPA; disbanded 25 July 1944. 78 Sentai had a similar history.

The 12 Brigade: 21 and 22 Airfield Battalions, 23 Airfield Company; 1 Regiment, two telephone/radio companies, 5 Air Signals Unit; 4 Air Intelligence Unit; 6 Meteorology Unit, 12 Field Meteorology Unit; 14 Air Repair Depot, 209 Base Depot, 14 Air Supply Depot, and 17 Ship Aircraft Depot.

The 6 Flying Division included an Air Training Brigade, and 10, 13, 14, 24, 45, and 208 Sentai plus 83 Chutai; and 25, 47, 48, 51, and 209 Airfield Battalions; 22, 23, 24, 25, and 26 Airfield Companies; 5, 6, 10, and 11 Airfield Construction Units; 2 through 9 Mobile Repair Squads; 73 and 81 Ground Companies; and 9 Transport Unit.

Note on the fighter units: 13 Sentai formed in July 1938 in Japan and operated in Korea before moving to the SWPA, where successes were scored against 43rd Bomb Group B-17s around Rabaul. After the New Guinea campaigns, the unit operated in the East Indies, Indochina, and Formosa, where it ended the war. The 24 Sentai formed in September 1938 in Manchuria, from 11 Sentai, and flew in the Nomonhan "war," China, Formosa, and the Philippines before moving to the SWPA, after which it operated in the East Indies and Okinawa.

The 7 Flying Division comprised 3 and 9 Flying Brigades: 5, 7, 59, 61, and 75 Sentai with 70 and 74 Chutai; 20, 28, 35, 38, and 40 Airfield Battalions; 7 and 29 Airfield Companies; 4 and 9 Airfield Construction Units; three repair squads; 298 Automobile Company; 69 and 123 Ground Companies; 43 Construction Company.

Note on the fighter unit: 59 Sentai formed in July 1938 in Japan and operated in China, Manchuria, Indochina, and East Indies before going to the SWPA. After New Guinea the unit flew in defense of Okinawa and Japan.

Appendix C
Identified JAAF Losses,
August 1943 to April 1944

This list is of Japanese fighter pilots mentioned in captured documents, decoded signal messages, diaries, letters, et cetera, referring to the Wewak and Hollandia missions of August 1943 to April 1944, and in postwar Japanese histories. A few flight crews of other types of aircraft are included, but emphasis is on the losses inflicted on the JAAF fighter force in New Guinea.

This is by no means a complete record because not all documents were captured and translated and not every radio message was intercepted and decoded. This and the following appendixes give an indication, based on original documents created at the time in the field, of the severe losses suffered by the JAAF in the SWPA. For some days of intense combat, there is no captured document or intercepted message.

Ranks and given names are included where known. Detail is from RG38 and RG457 at NARA2, Maryland; Japanese unit histories translated by IR&P; post-

war works by Messers Hata, Izawa, and Shores; or ATIS translations held by the
Australian War Memorial. The detail of the loss of Lieutenant Motoyama and
Sergeant Tabata on 22 December 1944 was kindly supplied by Mr. Koji Takaki
via Henry Sakaida. Rick Dunn's deductions on the encounters also were valuable in identifying opponents in some combats.

POW = prisoner of war
KIA = killed in action
WIA = wounded in action
KIFA = killed in flying accident
dnr = did not return
s/d = shot down
b/out = bailed out
f/ld = forced landing
(?) = English spelling not certain from Japanese characters
(H/I/S) = Hata, Izawa, Shores

The name of the U.S. pilot or unit that can be linked to the loss follows the
Japanese name and unit detail.

14 Hikodan

Onda, Kenzo	Lieutenant Colonel	KIA 22 Apr 44 at the landing
Teranishi, Tamiji	Lieutenant Colonel	KIA 11 Oct 43; Neel Kearby, 348FG

10 Sentai

Hamanishi, Yoshihide	Lieutenant	dnr 20 Dec 43; observer; Capt. W. Banks, 342FS
Matsutani, Joichi	Lieutenant	dnr 20 Dec 43; pilot; Capt. W. Banks, 342FS

13 Sentai

Asahi, Rokuro	Captain	KIA 16 Oct 43
Fujii, Shigekiechi	Sergeant Major	s/d 16 Oct 43
Fujino, Hiroyuki	Lieutenant	KIA 20 Aug 43; Tommy Lynch?
Harada, Yoshihira	Lieutenant	KIA 21 Aug 43
Ikeda, Hikosaburo	Sergeant Major	KIA 16 Oct 43
Kashima, Takeo	Corporal	KIA 02 Sep 43
Kudo	Sergeant	
Nagano, Tsunao	Major	KIA 16 Oct 43 (Hata has 16/11/43)
Nakamura, Daishiro	Lieutenant	KIA 21 Aug 43
Nishide, Toranosuke	Lieutenant	KIA 16 Oct 43 (Hata has 16/11/43)
Ogata, Morishi	Corporal	KIA 27 Oct 43 (H/I/S)
Sakata, Koichi	Lieutenant	KIA 07 Nov 43 (H/I/S)
Sato	Corporal	KIA 20 Aug 43
Sato, Kazuhiro	Corporal	KIA 13 Sep 43 (H/I/S)
Sugiura, Shigeo	Sergeant Major	KIA 13 Sep 43; Capt. V. Jett, 431FS
Terada, Fumio	Sergeant Major	KIA 21 Aug 43
Wakai, Okito	Corporal	KIA 27 Oct 43 (H/I/S)
Yasuda, Yoshimitsuro	Lieutenant	KIA 29 Aug 43; Lt. R. Adams, 80FS

24 Sentai

Aoki, Tomio	Sergeant Major	KIA 29 Aug 43
Ishiguro, Takuo	Captain	KIA 20 Aug 43
Mizuno, Shoji	Sergeant	KIA 17 Aug 43
Saito, Chiyoji	Lieutenant	KIA 20 Aug 43 (Hata has 02 Sep)
Sato	Corporal	KIA 20 Aug 43 (Sahara, viz Hata?)

Shiroto, Tadao	Sergeant Major	KIA 29 Aug 43 (Shirato, viz. Hara?)
Sumida, Ryohei	Sergeant Major	KIA 02 Sep 43 (H/I/S)
Utsunomiya	Lieutenant	KIA 17 Sep 43
Yamaji	Lieutenant	KIA 01 Dec 43; reported dead plus 7 NCOs

26 Sentai

Baba	Corporal	KIA 18 Nov 43
Ishikawa, Kenzo	Sergeant	dnr 18 Dec 43; Second Lt. D. Graham, 82 Recon?
Nakamichi, Iwao	Sergeant	with Ishikawa

33 Sentai

Aono, Kiku-ichi	Lieutenant	KIA 30 Mar 44
Chikara, Nobuaki (?)	Sergeant Major	KIA 3 Apr 44 (Hata has Chigira, Nobuo)
Hara, Shoji	Corporal	KIA 3 Apr 44
Hashimoto, Soichi	Sergeant	KIA 13 Mar 44
Inagaki		KIA 31 Mar 44
Kumagai, Joshu	Master Sergeant	KIA 13 Mar 44; Ralph Wandrey, 9FS (Hata has Kumagaya, Shironushi)
Kumatani, Shirokazu,	Sergeant Major	KIA 13 Mar 44
Kurahara		KIA 31 Mar 44
Matsumoto, Koh	Sergeant	KIA 14 Mar 44 (Hata has Mitsuo)
Matsumura, Takuzo	Sergeant	KIA 30 Mar 44
Nakamura, Hisayoshi (?)	Corporal	KIA 3 Apr 44
Ohya, Seishi	Corporal	KIA 14 Mar 44 (Hata has Seiji)
Oshima	Sergeant Major	KIA 30 Mar 44
Sakaeda, Toshitaro	Sergeant Major	KIA 02 Mar 44 (H/I/S)

Sawada	Sergeant	KIA 30 Mar 44
Sugiura	Lieutenant	KIA 3 Apr 44
Takemori, Harumi	Sergeant Major	KIA 3 Apr 44 (Hata has Shigeharu)
Takeuchi	Sergeant	KIA 30 Mar 44
Tomatsu, Tatsuo	Sergeant Major	KIA 11 Mar 44 (Hata has 12 Mar)
Yamamoto	Corporal	KIA 30 Mar 44
Yoshino	Second Lieutenant	KIA 30 Mar 44

59 Sentai

Agemura	Sergeant Major	KIA 18 Aug 43
Fukuhara, Shozo	Lieutenant	KIA 09 Nov 43 (H/I/S)
Genbu	Lieutenant	KIA 18 Aug 43
Hara	Lieutenant	KIA 18 Aug 43
Kato, Akijiro	Sergeant	MIA 22 Dec 43
Kawakoshi, Yoshio	Lieutenant	MIA 01 Dec 43
Kitahara, Shigeo	Lieutenant	MIA 14 Feb 44
Kubo, Shinichi	Sergeant	KIA 21 Aug 43
Makino, Masao	Lieutenant	KIA (?) 43
Masuzawa, Masanao	Lieutenant	MIA 04 Jan 44 (Hata: KIA 17 Dec 43)
Nakamura, Hideji	Lieutenant	KIA 23 Nov 43 (H/I/S)
Nango, Shigeo	Captain	KIA 23 Jan 44
Nishino, Toichi	Sergeant	KIA 26 Nov 43 (H/I/S)
Ochi, Saburo	Sergeant	KIA 28 Sep 43 (H/I/S)
Onozaki	Captain	Evac19 Aug 43
Sato	Sergeant	MIA 14 Feb 44
Shimanto, Kikuo	Sergeant	KIA 07 Nov 43 (H/I/S)
Shinzaki	Sergeant	MIA 14 Feb 44
Sugano, Tatsuo	Sergeant Major	KIA 15 Nov 43 (H/I/S)
Takarabe, Hisao	Sergeant Major	KIA 09 Nov 43 (H/I/S)
Umeoka, Kazumi	Lieutenant	KIA 29 Aug 43; Lt. H. Round, 39FS

Umetani, Zenjiro	Sergeant	KIA Aug 43
Uno, Suezo	Warrant Officer	KIA 16 Nov 43 (H/I/S)
Yahata, Juro	Lieutenant	KIA 09 Nov 43 (H/I/S)

61 Sentai (bomber unit)

Sakai, Kazuo	Second Lieutenant	KIA 3 Mar 44; Dick Bong

63 Sentai

Hamasuna, Takeshi	Lieutenant	KIA 11 Mar 44 (Hata has 13 Mar)
Hasegawa, Kiyoshi	Lieutenant	KIA 16 Jan 44
Iwamitsu, Isao	Sergeant Major	KIA 16 Jan 44 (H/I/S)
Matsumoto, Tomio	Captain	KIA 18 Jan 44
Musubishiro, Hikimitsu	Sergeant	KIA 30 Mar 44
Ogi, Yasuji	Lieutenant	KIA 15 Mar 44
Shimoura, Shigekachi	Lieutenant	KIA 15 Mar 44
Ueki, Toshimasa	Lieutenant	s/d 3 Apr 44
Watanabe, Hajime	Sergeant	KIA 11 Mar 44
Yamada	Corporal	MIA 14 Feb 44
Yamamoto, Takaaki	Corporal	KIA 13 Mar 44 (Hata has Takamitsu)
Yoshii	Corporal	MIA 14 Feb 44

68 Sentai

Chiba, Shigeru	Sergeant	KIA 22 Oct 43 (H/I/S)
Fujimoto, Masuichi	Sergeant	KIA 10 Dec 43 (H/I/S)
Hashimoto, Kikuo	Lieutenant	KIA 21 Aug 43
Hazama, Hajimi	Warrant Officer	KIA 10 Dec 43 (H/I/S)
Hirahara, Kinji	Warrant Officer	KIA 04 Mar 44 (H/I/S)
Ideta, Takayuki	Lieutenant	KIA 27 Sep 43 (H/I/S)
Ikeda, Hideo	Sergeant	KIA 21 Dec 43 (H/I/S)
Ito, Kiyoshi	Sergeant	KIA 16 Oct 43 (H/I/S)

Izuta, Yushi	Captain	KIA 26 Sep 43 (H/I/S)
Kagaguchi, Saburo	Lieutenant	KIA 26 Jan 44
Kajita, Yoshizo	Sergeant Major	KIA 23 Jan 44 (H/I/S)
Kato, Michijiro	Lieutenant	MIA 15 Mar 44
Kawamoto, Masaru	Sergeant	KIA 16 Jan 44 (H/I/S)
Kawano, Manju (?)	Sergeant	KIA 06 Mar 44
Kimura, Kiyoshi	Major	KIA 16 Jan 44
Kirihara, Tasuku	Sergeant	KIA 02 Mar 44
Kobayashi, Sen-ichi	Sergeant	KIA 09 Jan 44 (H/I/S)
Kono, Mitsuhiro	Corporal	KIA 16 Jan 44 (H/I/S)
Koyama, Shigeru	Captain	KIA 11 Oct 43; Neel Kearby, 348FG
Kuroiwa, Tomohiko	Sergeant Major	KIFA 15 Dec 43 (H/I/S)
Motoyama, Akinori	Lieutenant	KIA 22 Dec 43
Nagae, Kiyo (?)	Sergeant Major	MIA 15 Mar 44
Nagashima, Hideshi	Sergeant Major	KIA 21 Dec 43; Merkus Cape
Nakamura, Rokusaburo	Sergeant	KIA 14 Feb 44
Nishikawa, Sadao	Sergeant	KIA 21 Aug 43
Noguchi, Takashi	Warrant Officer	POW 16 Jan 44 (H/I/S)
Shibakiyo, Tadashi	Sergeant	KIA 10 Dec 43 (H/I/S)
Tabata, Iwao	Sergeant	WIA 22 Dec 43
Takahashi, Hirasuke	Sergeant	KIA 10 Mar 44
Takahashi, Kenji	Captain	KIA? Feb 44; near Sarmi
Takenawa	Captain	KIA 12 Apr 44
Takeuchi, Shogo	Captain	KIFA 21 Dec 43
Tanaka, Satoshi	Lieutenant	MIA 15 Feb 44
Tsujii, Ryuzo	Lieutenant	KIA 22 Oct 43
Yagi	Lieutenant	MIA 15 Feb 44
Yamamoto, Kazue	Lieutenant	KIA 04 Mar 44
Yamauchi, Masahiro	Lieutenant	KIA 03 Sep 43 (accident; Hara)
Yamazaki, Tamisaku	Sergeant Major	MIA 18 Dec 43

74 Chutai

Sakamoto, Susumu	Lieutenant	MIA 2 Sep 43
Tanaka, Masaki	Lieutenant	MIA 2 Sep 43

77 Sentai

Aoyanagi		WIA 14 Mar 44
Arad	Corporal	
Fujii	Lieutenant	s/d 12 Mar 44
Fukushima, Waikichi	Sergeant	s/d 12 Mar 44 KIA 12 Apr 44
Hashimoto, Soichi	Sergeant	s/d 12 Mar 44 KIA 13 Mar 44 (Hata has KIA 18 Mar 44)
Kobayakawa, Kiyoshi	Sergeant Major	KIA 12 Mar 44 (H/I/S)
Kuwabara, Yoshiro	Major	KIA 14 Mar 44
Matsumoto, Kunio	Major	KIA 12 Apr 44
Matsuo, Yoshihide	Captain	WIA 12 Mar 44; died mid-44
Mitoma, Koichi	Warrant Officer	KIA 12 Mar 44
Miyamoto, Hakuo	Lieutenant	KIA 5 Mar 44; Tommy Lynch
Nagasaka, Shuhei	Corporal	KIA 14 Mar 44
Obakayawa, Kiyoshi	Master Sergeant	KIA 5 Mar 44
Obakayawa,	Corporal	KIA 13 Mar 44
Shimada, Tsugio	Sergeant	died mid-44
Taguchi		KIA 12 Mar 44
Tamaguchi	Corporal	s/d 14 Mar 44
Watanabe		KIA 14 Mar 44

78 Sentai

Asai, Mitsusada	Lieutenant	MIA 06 Feb 44 (Hata has 06 Mar 44)
Azuma, Yoshi-ichi	Sergeant Major	KIA 01 Jan 44 (H/I/S)

Fuj	Lieutenant	KIA 22 Oct 43
Kaneuchi, Gosaburo	Lieutenant	KIFA 11 Dec 43 (H/I/S)
Kimura	Lieutenant	KIA 17 Sep 43
Kobayashi, Komehiko	Sergeant Major	s/d 18 Aug 43 died 22 Aug; Tommy McGuire?
Matsumoto, Makoto	Sergeant	KIA 26 Dec 43 (H/I/S)
Miyagawa	Lieutenant	KIA 25 Feb 44
Mori, Ryosuke	Lieutenant	KIA 13 Sep 43
Mutaguchi, Yoshichika	Captain	KIA 15 Oct 43
Nakagawa	Sergeant	KIA 11 Apr 44; Lt. Edward Glascock, 8FS
Nakahama, Sadao	Captain	KIA 15 Nov 43
Nitta, Isoo	Warrant Officer	KIA 09 Nov 43 (H/I/S)
Nonaka, Shiro	Warrant Officer	KIA 16 Oct 43
Saito, Shogo	Lieutenant	MIA 15 Mar 44
Sakuma, Kanematsu	Sergeant Major	KIA 05 Nov 43
Shimoe, Masashi	Corporal	KIA 20 Dec 43 (H/I/S)
Tajimi, Shoichi	Sergeant Major	KIA 15 Mar 44
Takahashi, Kenji	Captain	WIA 14 Feb 44 (Hata has KIA 23 Apr)
Takatsuki, Akira	Major	KIA 22 Dec 43
Takimiya, Keiji	Lieutenant	KIFA 1 Feb 44
Tanaka, Naotoshi	Sergeant Major	MIA 15 Mar 44
Tanogami, Fujiro	Sergeant Major	KIA 16 Oct 43
Tejima, Tadatoshi	Sergeant	KIA 26 Nov 43
Ushijima, Hajime	Warrant Officer	KIA 17 Sep 43
Waku, Takeo	Sergeant Major	KIA 05 Nov 43
Yagi, Kyutaro	Lieutenant	KIA 15 Feb 44 (H/I/S)
Yamamoto, Tetsushi	Captain	KIA 14 Jan 44 (H/I/S)

248 Sentai

Aihara, Takeshi (?)	Corporal	parachuted 16 Nov 43; Maj. Meryl Smith, 475thFG

Ando, Yukiharu	Corporal	WIA 7 Nov 43; KIA 15 Feb 44
Ejiri, Hisamatsu	Lieutenant	MIA 9 Nov 43, "did not return 1 Dec 43"
Fueki, Shoji	Lieutenant	MIA 15 Nov 43; "did not return 1 Dec 43"
Furukawa, Masahaku	Sergeant	MIA 26 Nov 43
Hakuda	Corporal	forced landing 9 Nov 43
Ichikawa, Ryoichi	Lieutenant	KIA 9 Nov 43
Ikakura, Kaneji	Captain	KIA 18 Apr 44 (H/I/S)
Kato, Yoshimoto	Warrant Officer	KIA 9 Nov 43
Kitajima	Sergeant Major	s/d 15 Nov 43
Koga, Keiji	Lieutenant	MIA 3 Feb 44
Koshima, Shigeo	Captain	KIA 18 Jan 44 (Hata has Kojima)
Maekwa, Yoshihara	Lieutenant	WIA 6 Nov 43; KIA 22 Dec 43
Minamoto	Sergeant	WIA 7 Nov 43
Murakami	Lieutenant	forced landing 7 Nov 43 (with three others)
Muraoka, Shinichi	Major	KIA 2 Jan 44; Lt. Duncan C. Myers, 7 FS
Nakatsuda, Tadeo	Sergeant	forced landing 9 Nov 43; KIA 22 Dec 43
Nakayama, Ichiro	Corporal	MIA 15 Nov 43
Ogawa, Matsutaro	Sergeant Major	WIA 15 Nov 43
Oita	Corporal	MIA 15 Nov 43
Ota, Hideo	Lieutenant	KIA 6 Nov 43
Saito, Yasuo	Sergeant Major	KIA 23 Jan 44
Sakoda, Sumio	Corporal	KIA 15 Nov 43 (H/I/S)
Shimizu, Eizo	Lieutenant	KIA 15 Nov 43
Suzuki, Sosaku	Sergeant Major	KIA 7 Nov 43
Tabouchi, Shiro	Sergeant	f/ld 26 Nov 43
Toda, Shiro	Sergeant	KIA 7 Nov 43
Tozuka	Captain	MIA 23 Jan 44 (Hata: Totsuka)

| Tsutsui, Matsuo | Corporal | MIA 26 Nov 43 |
| Yoshida, Hiroshi | Sergeant Major | MIA 9 Nov 43 |

Unidentified unit losses, undated, mentioned in captured document.

Mayekawa	First Lieutenant	killed chasing a B-25
Tamura	Corporal	parachuted
Zuka	Sergeant	lost to "sudden attack"

Appendix D
Chronological Arrangement of Identified
JAAF Fighter Losses, August 1943 to April 1944

This is a chronological arrangement of Appendix C, with names in alphabetical order by date, with U.S. claims and admitted Japanese losses as available. Detail is provided by captured Japanese documents in the Allied Translator and Interpreter Section reports held at the Australian War Memorial, unit histories postwar, memoirs postwar, signals intelligence records, Hata-Izawa-Shores 2002, and Frank Olynyk's Victory List No. 3. The only dates included here are those for which Japanese documents or publications above have names or losses. There were many other missions or sweeps. The probable successful U.S. unit is listed also.

18 Aug 43

KIA	Agemura, Ekiro	Sergeant Major	59 Sentai	431FS
	Genbu	Lieutenant	59 Sentai	431FS
KIA	Hara, Takeshi (?)	Lieutenant	59 Sentai	431FS
f/ld	Shigeki, Nanba	Captain	59 Sentai	431FS
s/d	Kobayashi, Komehiko	Sergeant Major 22 Aug; died	78 Sentai	
	Tommy McGuire			431FS?

United States claims 15-3-2 near Wewak by 431 and 432FS; 59 Sentai reduced to eight operable airplanes.

19 Aug 43

Onozaki, Hiroshi	Captain	59 Sentai	evacuated (68 and 78 Sentai pilots go to Manila to re-equip)

20 Aug 43

KIA	Fujino, Hiroyuki	Lieutenant	13 Sentai Tommy Lynch?
KIA	Ishiguro, Takuo	Captain	24 Sentai ram B-24
KIA	Sahara, Toshio	Corporal	24 Sentai (H/I/S)
KIA	Saito, Chiyoji	Lieutenant	24 Sentai
KIA	Sato	Corporal	24 Sentai

United States claims 13-1-3 near Wewak by 39 and 80FS; 6-0-27 identified in Japanese records.

21 Aug 43

KIA	Harada, Yoshihira	Lieutenant	13 Sentai
KIA	Hashimoto, Kikuo	Lieutenant	68 Sentai
KIA	Kubo, Shinichi	Sergeant	59 Sentai
KIA	Nakamura, Daishiro	Lieutenant	13 Sentai
KIA	Nishikawa, Sadao	Sergeant	68 Sentai
KIA	Terada, Fumio	Sergeant Major	13 Sentai

United States claims 35-5-7 near Wewak by 39, 80, 431, and 432FS; six above named in Japanese records.

24 Aug 43

United States claims 1-0-1 at Wewak by Duncan and Denton 39FS; Japanese record admits 174 destroyed or damaged since 19 August.

29 Aug 43

KIA	Aoki, Tomio	Sergeant Major	24 Sentai
KIA	Shiroto, Tadao	Sergeant Major	24 Sentai or Shirato, Masao, by Hata-Izawa-Shores
KIA	Umeoka, Kazumi	Lieutenant	59 Sentai Lt. H. Round, 39FS
KIA	Umetani, Zenjiro	Sergeant	59 Sentai
KIA	Yasuda, Yoshimitsu	Lieutenant	13 Sentai died of wounds; Lt. R. Adams, 80FS

dnr	Hikofuji	Lieutenant	unknown unit, from Gasmata

United States claims 7-4-3 at Wewak by 39, 80, and 431FS; Japanese records show 4-0-16 lost last week of August; but above five KIAs named for this date alone and Shigeki Nanba stated that four 59 Sentai did not return on this day.

02 Sep 43

s/d	Kashima, Takeo	Corporal	13 Sentai	9FS
w/off	Momotomi, Mitsugi	Warrant Officer	13 Sentai	9FS
KIA	Saito, Chiyoji	Lieutenant	24 Sentai	(H/I/S)
KIA	Sumida, Ryohei	Sergeant Major	24 Sentai	(H/I/S)
s/d	Wakai, OKi-ndo	Corporal	13 Sentai	9FS

United States claims 14-4-1; 9-3-1 Wewak and Madang; history of Nick unit admits three Nicks off Cape Gloucester, lost to 9FS, who claimed 5-1-0. 68 Sentai pilots return with new Tonys.

09 Sep 43

KIA	Tomoi, Hisashi	Sergeant Major	68 Sentai	(H/I/S)

13 Sep 43

KIA	Sugiura, Shigeo	Sergeant Major	13 Sentai	Capt. V. Jett, 431FS
s/d	unnamed Oscar pilot		13 Sentai	2nd Lt. V. Elliott, 431FS? (Corporal Sato, Kazuhiro, by Hata-Izawa-Shores)

United States claims 11-1-0; Japanese records show 3-0-6, but as 45 Sentai loss. Eleven Oscars notified en route.

15 Sep 43

KIA	Ushijima, Hajime	Warrant Officer	78 Sentai	(H/I/S)
				Lt. D.
				McGee,
				80thFS?

United States fighter claims 9-2-1; Japanese records show 7-0-20; 90BG claim forty-four. Thirty-three fighters en route.

17 Sep 43

KIA	Kimura	Lieutenant	78 Sentai
KIA	Ushijima	Warrant Officer	78 Sentai
KIA	Utsunomiya	Lieutenant	24 Sentai

No U.S. claims for this date, but these KIAs might refer to 15 September when 80FS claimed 1 Tony and 8-2-1 Zekes, Haps, and Oscars at Wewak. 78 Sentai makes second journey to Manila to re-equip.

26 Sep 43

KIA	Izuta, Yushi	Captain	68 Sentai	(H/I/S)

United States claims 6-3-0; Japanese losses 13-0-12.

27 Sep 43

KIA	Ideta, Takayuki	Lieutenant	68 Sentai	(H/I/S)

United States claims 3-0-0; Tonys—one, thirty miles south, two near Wewak-Boram.

28 Sep 43

KIA	Ochi, Saburo	Sergeant	59 Sentai	(H-I-S)

United States claims 7-1-1; Japanese admit 23-0-38 for month. 68 Sentai reduced to two Tonys in less than a month.

02 Oct 43

24 Sentai moved from combat; twenty pilots killed since arrival in May. 59 Sentai pilots fly to Manila to re-equip. 130 aircraft notified as delivered in month.

11 Oct 43

KIA	Koyama, Shigeru	Captain	68 Sentai	Neel Kearby, 348FG
KIA	Teranishi, Tamiji	Lieutenant Col	14 Hikodan	Neel Kearby, 348FG

United States claims 9-0-0; two above admitted in Japanese records; Kearby's CMOH mission.

15 Oct 43

KIA	Mutaguchi, Yoshichika	Captain	78 Sentai

16 Oct 43

KIA	Asahi, Rokuro	Captain	13 Sentai	(Alexishafen)
s/d	Fujii, Shigekiechi	Sergeant Major	68 Sentai	(Madang Lt. G. Haniotis, 9FS)
KIA	Ikeda, Hikosaburo	Sergeant Major	13 Sentai	(Alexishafen)
KIA	Ito, Kiyoshi	Sergeant	68 Sentai	(H/I/S)

KIA	Mutaguchi, Yoshichika	Captain	78 Sentai	(H/I/S)
KIA	Nagano, Tsunao	Major, CO	13 Sentai	(Alexishafen)
KIA	Nishide, Toranosuke,	Second Lieutenant	13 Sentai	(Alexishafen)
KIA	Nonaka, Shiro	Warrant Officer	78 Sentai	(H/I/S)
KIA	Tanogani, Fujio	Sergeant Major	78 Sentai	(H/I/S)

U.S. claims 12-3-0 at Alexishafen-Madang, 80FS claim four Tonys and an Oscar at Boram; captured Japanese records admit six KIA, one WIA, with those named above. 78 Sentai pilots return with new Tonys.

22 Oct 43

KIA	Chiba, Shigeru	Sergeant	68 Sentai	(H/I/S)
KIA	Fujii,	Lieutenant	78 Sentai	
KIA	Tsujii, Ryuzo	Lieutenant	68 Sentai	(H/I/S)

U.S. claims 3-0-0; Japanese admit 5-0-3 since 19 October. 78 Sentai re-equipped but in two weeks is again using Oscars. Twenty Tonys en route.

27 Oct 43

KIA	Ogata, Morishi	Corporal	13 Sentai	(H/I/S)
KIA	Wakai, Oki-to	Corporal	13 Sentai	(H/I/S)

United States claims 13-7-3 in Finschhafen-Satelberg area, including 6-2-1 fighters; Japanese admit bomber losses for 7 and 61 Sentai as 3-0-2; 13 and 78 Sentai fighter losses as 4-0-0. 68 Sentai pilots make second return to Manila to re-equip. 78 Sentai reduced to only twelve Tonys; flew Oscars.

31 Oct 43

59 Sentai returns from Manila with twenty-three Oscars; 248 Sentai arrived with thirty Oscars; 24 Sentai delivered twenty-one Oscars.

05 Nov 43

KIA	Sakuma, Kanematsu	Sergeant Major	78 Sentai	(H/I/S)
KIA	Waku, Takeo	Sergeant Major	78 Sentai	(H/I/S)

United States claims six by 348FG.

06 Nov 43

WIA	Mayekawa	Lieutenant	248 Sentai	(Alexishafen)
KIA	Ota, Hideo	Lieutenant	248 Sentai	(Alexishafen)

Note: might refer to losses on 7 November, following.

07 Nov 43

WIA	Ando	Corporal	248 Sentai	(Alexishafen)
WIA	Minamoto	Sergeant	248 Sentai	(Alexishafen)
f/ld	Murakami	Lieutenant	248 Sentai	(Alexishafen) (with three unnamed others)
KIA	Sakata, Koichi	Lieutenant	13 Sentai	(Nadzab, Hata et al.)
KIA	Shimanto, Kikuo	Sergeant	59 Sentai	(H/I/S)
KIA	Suzuki, Sosaku	Sergeant Major	248 Sentai	(Nadzab)
KIA	Toda, Shiro	Sergeant	248 Sentai	(Nadzab)

United States claims 13-14-2 in Alexishafen-Nadzab area, including 12-3-0 fighters.

09 Nov 43

MIA	Ejiri, Hisamatsu	Lieutenant	248 Sentai	(Nadzab mission)
KIA	Fukuhara, Shozo	Lieutenant	59 Sentai	(Nadzab, Hata et al.)

f/ld	Hakuda	Corporal	248 Sentai	(Alexishafen)
KIA	Ichikawa, Ryoich	Lieutenant	248 Sentai	(Alexishafen)
KIA	Kato, Yosh imoto	Warrant Officer	248 Sentai	(near Lae)
f/ld	Nakatsuda	Sergeant	248 Sentai	(Hansa)
KIA	Nitta, Isoo	Warrant Officer	78 Sentai	(Nadzab, Hata et al.)
KIA	Takarabe, Hisao	Sergeant Major	59 Sentai	(Nadzab, Hata et al.)
KIA	Yahata, Juro	Lieutenant	59 Sentai	(Nadzab, Hata et al.)
MIA	Yoshida, Hiroshi	Sergeant Major	248 Sentai	(PW, Nadzab); 2nd Lt. Carl Weaver, 35FS

United States claims 15-11-3, all fighters, in this area.

15 Nov 43

KIA	Fueki, Shoji	Lieutenant	248 Sentai	
f/ld	Kitajima	Sergeant Major	248 Sentai	(south of Madang)
MIA	Nakayama, Ichiro	Corporal	248 Sentai	
KIA	Nakahama, Sadao	Captain	78 Sentai	
WIA	Ogawa, Matsutaro	Sergeant Major	248 Sentai	(in Alexis hospital)
MIA	Oita	Corporal	248 Sentai	
KIA	Sakoda, Sumio	Corporal	248 Sentai	(H/I/S)
KIA	Shimizu, Eizo	Lieutenant	248 Sentai	(south of Hansa)
KIA	Sugano, Tatsuo	Sergeant Major	59 Sentai	(H/I/S)

United States claims 23-8-1; Japanese records admit ten lost, at Wewak and Marawasa, plus U.S. one forced landing; 248 Sentai flew eighteen aircraft, lost six; one bomber also lost.

16 Nov 43

b/out	Aihara, Takeshi (?)	Corporal	248 Sentai	Major Smith	475th FG?
KIA	Nagano, Tsunao	Major	13 Sentai		(H-I-S)
KIA	Nishiide, Torasuke	Lieutenant	13 Sentai		(H-I-S)
KIA	Uno, Suezo	Warrant Officer	59 Sentai		(H-I-S)

United States claims 5-1-0, Japanese admit 5-0-0; 248 Sentai flew 12, lost one.

17 Nov 43

A Japanese naval report for GHQ, in ATIS Bulletin 1889, admitted aircraft losses in attacks on Allied convoys and Bougainville 31 October–2 November were fifteen; on 8 November, twenty; on 11 November, thirty; on 13 November, two; on 17 November, five; total seventy-five (*sic*).

18 Nov 43

KIA	Baba	Corporal	26 Sentai

P-38s shot Baba down into the sea ten miles west of But; no U.S. claim for this found—was it 15 November?

23 Nov 43

KIA	Nakamura, Hideji	Lieutenant	59 Sentai	(H/I/S)

United States claims 2-1-1 in Saidor area.

26 Nov 43

MIA	Furukawa, Masahaku	Sergeant	248 Sentai	
MIA	Nishino, Toichi	Sergeant	59 Sentai	
f/ld	Tabouchi, Shiro	Sergeant	248 Sentai	(at Hansa)
MIA	Tejima, Tadatoshi	Sergeant	78 Sentai	
MIA	Tsutsui, Matsuo	Corporal	248 Sentai	

United States claims 9-6-0 fighters Saidor-Finschhafen area; 248 Sentai flew fourteen airplanes to Heldsbach, lost three as above.

30 Nov 43

| MIA | Hayashi, Hachiro | Captain | 208 Sentai |

This probably refers to claim by Major F. Tompkins, 432FS, for a "Betty" probable at Finschhafen.

Note: end of November: Japanese admit 26-0-35 lost in November; 68 Sentai through November reduced to three pilots; receive twenty-six new Tonys from Manila. 248 Sentai lost thirteen of its thirty-four pilots in November.

01 Dec 43

dnr	Ejiri, Hisamatsu	Lieutenant	248 Sentai
dnr	five unnamed NCOs		248 Sentai
dnr	Fueki, Shoji	Lieutenant	248 Sentai
dnr	Kawakoshi, Yoshio	Lieutenant	59 Sentai
KIA	Yamaji	Lieutenant	24 Sentai plus seven
			NCOs KIA/MIA

United States claims 5-0-0 by 341 and 36FS at Wewak; 248 Sentai admits losing seven as above. 24 Sentai was withdrawn in October; this report is perhaps wrongly dated.

10 Dec 43

KIA	Takasugi, Isami	Sergeant	78 Sentai?
WIA?	Tanaka, Go (?)	Sergeant Major	78 Sentai?
WIA	Terada, Shinobu	Warrant Officer	78 Sentai

United States claims for six Tonys Gusap/Alexishafen area; and 1-0-1 Oscars.

16 Dec 43

United States claims 14-1-3; 248 Sentai flew nine aircraft as bomber escort to Cape Gloucester; lost three unnamed pilots.

17 Dec 43

KIA	Masuzawa, Masanao	Lieutenant	59 Sentai	(H/I/S)
				Lt. Ken
				Ladd 80FS,
				Cape Gloucester

United States claims eleven at Arawe, but only one at Cape Gloucester.

18 Dec 43

dnr	Ishikawa, Kenzo	Sergeant	26 Sentai	
	Nakamichi, Iwao	Sergeant	26 Sentai	(with above)
KIA	Yamazaki,	Sergeant	68 Sentai	Lt. Robert
	Tamisaku	Major		Tomberg,
				433FS

United States claims 1 Tony and 2-0-1 Zeke and Val; claims check.

20 Dec 43

dnr	Hamanishi, Yoshihide	Lieutenant	10 Sentai	
dnr	Matsutani, Joichi	Lieutenant	10 Sentai	
KIA	Shimoe, Masashi	Corporal	78 Sentai	(H/I/S)

Only one 5AF fighter claim: Capt. Bill Banks, 342FS, Dinah 70m NW Arawe.

21 Dec 43

KIA	Ikeda, Hideo	Sergeant	68 Sentai	(H/I/S)
KIA	Nagashima,	Sergeant	68 Sentai	C. Merkus
	Hideshi	Major		

| KIA | Takeuchi, Shogo | Captain | 68 Sentai | after battle damage |

United States claims 20-3-1; Japanese admit loss of six fighters and six bombers in attack on Allied ships. Ten JNAF losses apply here, with three JAAF as above.

22 Dec 43

MIA	Kato, Akijiro	Sergeant	59 Sentai	
KIA	Maekawa, Yoshihara	Lieutenant	248 Sentai	(convoy escort)
s/d	Motoyama, Akinori	Lieutenant	68 Sentai	died 25 Dec; 80FS
KIA	Nakatzuka, Takeo	Sergeant	248 Sentai	(convoy escort)
s/d	Tabata, Iwao	Sergeant	68 Sentai	wounded; Capt. P. Murphey, 80FS
KIA	Takatsuki, Akira	Major, CO	78 Sentai	80FS?

United States claims 19-1-2; Japanese memoirs and documents name those above. Thirty-six more fighters en route.

26 Dec 43

| KIA | Matsumoto, Makoto | Sergeant | 78 Sentai | (H/I/S) |

United States claims 61-4-3, JNAF-JAAF; JAAF records show five bombers and two fighters lost; fighters from 78 Sentai.

29 Dec 43

Fifteen more Oscars en route.

30 Dec 43

Ten more Tonys en route.

01 Jan 44

KIA   Azuma, Yoshi-ichi   Sergeant Major   78 Sentai   (H/I/S)
No U.S. fighter claims this date.

02 Jan 44

KIA	Muraoka, Shinichi	Major, CO	248 Sentai	(Saidor); Lt. Duncan C. Myers, 7FS
KIA	Tatsuo	(untranslated but loss notified)	78 Sentai	Lt. Robert Dehaven, 7FS

U.S. claims 5-0-1, including 3-0-1 fighters, by 7FS, Saidor area.

03 Jan 44

MIA	Masuzawa, Masanao	Lieutenant	59 Sentai	Neel Kearby
s/dn	Onota, Akimasu	Lieutenant	75 Sentai	Neel Kearby
s/dn	Takanu, Shinji	Warrant Officer	75 Sentai	Neel Kearby

Twelve more fighters en route.

06 Jan 44

Fifteen more Tonys en route.

09 Jan 44

KIA   Kobayashi, Sen-ichi   Sergeant   68 Sentai   (H/I/S)
Neel Kearby claimed two Tonys at 1215 and 1220, at Wewak.

12 Jan 44

Nine more fighters en route; twenty-four already sent.

13 Jan 44

63 Sentai arrived at Wewak.

14 Jan 44

| KIA | Yamamoto, Tetsushi | Captain | 78 Sentai | (H-I-S) |

No U.S. fighter claims this date.

15 Jan 44

Six more Tonys en route.

16 Jan 44

KIA	Hasegawa, Kiyoshi	Lieutenant	63 Sentai	Saidor
KIA	Iwamitsu, Isao	Sergeant Major	63 Sentai	(H/I/S)
KIA	Kawamoto, Masaru	Sergeant	68 Sentai	(H/I/S)
KIA	Kimura, Kiyoshi	Major, CO	68 Sentai	Saidor
KIA	Kono, Mitsuhiro	Corporal	63 Sentai	(H/I/S)
POW	Noguchi, Takashi	Warrant Officer	68 Sentai	Saidor
KIA	Oishi, Tadashi	Sergeant Major	63 Sentai	(H/I/S)

U.S. claims 19-1-2; Japanese records show ten, including five from 63 Sentai.

18 Jan 44

KIA	Koshima	Captain	248 Sentai	(Hata: Kojima, Shigeo)
KIA	Matsumoto, Tomio	Captain	63 Sentai	
KIA	Suko (?)	Sergeant	78 Sentai	
b/o	unnamed		59 Sentai	

United States claims 14-3-1 at Wewak; Japanese admit 8-0-0 lost for January to date.

22 Jan 44

Sixteen more fighters en route.

23 Jan 44

KIA	Kajita, Yoshizo	Sergeant Major	68 Sentai	(H/I/S)
KIA	Nango, Shigeo	Captain	59 Sentai	
KIA	Saito, Akeji	Sergeant Major	248 Sentai	
MIA	Tozuka, Nobuyoshi	Captain	248 Sentai	

United States claims 19-2-4 at Wewak; Japanese admit six; 248 Sentai flew eight, lost two.

27 Jan 44

KIA   Kagaguchi, Saburo   Lieutenant   68 Sentai   on convoy escort
No 5AF fighter claims near this date; engine trouble?

31 Jan 44

248 Sentai had no officer pilots left.

01 Feb 44

KIA   Takimiya, Keiji   Lieutenant   78 Sentai   (accident)

03 Feb 44

MIA   Koga   Lieutenant   248 Sentai
United States claims 15-0-0; 57 admitted destroyed on ground at But.

04 Feb 44

Fourteen Oscars received.

06 Feb 44

MIA	Asai	Lieutenant	78 Sentai

U.S. claims 4-0-0 at Wewak, 7 and 8FS.

14 Feb 44

MIA	Kitahara, Shigeo	Lieutenant	59 Sentai
KIA	Nakamura, Rokusaburo	Sergeant	68 Sentai
MIA	Sato	Sergeant	59 Sentai
MIA	Shinzaki	Sergeant	59 Sentai
WIA	Takahashi	Captain	78 Sentai
MIA	Yamada, Akio (?)	Corporal	63 Sentai
MIA	Yoshii	Corporal	63 Sentai

U.S. claims 7-0-0 at Wewak-Dagua, by 7 and 8FS; Japanese records agree.

15 Feb 44

KIA	Ando, Yukiharu (?)	Corporal	248 Sentai
MIA	Tanaka, Satoshi	Lieutenant	68 Sentai
MIA	Yagi, Kyutaro	Lieutenant	68 Sentai

U.S. claims 9-1-2 Wewak area, 8FS and 35FG.

Note: U.S. fighter claims 1–15 Feb 44 are 36-1-2; 36-0-40 admitted in Japanese documents as lost 1–15 Feb 44; also see ATIS Bulletin 1165, a report from 14 Air Repair Depot: losses at Wewak 1–15 Feb 44 were seventy-six.

17 Feb 44

Surviving ten pilots of 59 Sentai depart the area for Japan.

19 Feb 44

Eighteen more fighters en route.

25 Feb 44

KIA	Miyagawa	Lieutenant	78 Sentai

Note: Japanese records admit New Guinea losses August 43 to February 44 totaled 710: 225 air combat, 373 on ground, 112 in accidents.

26 Feb 44

Fifty-seven fighters notified as sent.

02 Mar 44

KIA	Kirihara, Tasuku	Sergeant	68 Sentai	(H/I/S)
KIA	Nagae, Seiichi	Sergeant Major	68 Sentai	(H/I/S)
KIA	Sakaeda, Toshitaro	Sergeant Major	33 Sentai	(H/I/S)

All three lost at Admiralty Islands; United States claims 7-1-0.

03 Mar 44

KIA	Sakai, Kazuo	Lieutenant	61 Sentai
KIA?	Ushijima, Shigeyoshi	Lieutenant	60 Sentai

Dick Bong claimed two bombers at Tadji. U.S. claims four in Tadji area by Dick

Bong and Tom Lynch; Sakai the only name found in captured documents and Ushijima in decoded message.

04 Mar 44

KIA	Hirahara, Kinji	Warrant Officer	68 Sentai	(H/I/S)
KIA	Yamamoto, Kazue	Lieutenant	68 Sentai	(H/I/S)

Hata et al have these lost at Nadzab; Lts. P. Lorick and E. Park, 41FS, claim Tonys over Bogadjim Road, south of Nadzab. Other U.S. claims for 2-2-2 at Wewak and Gusap.

05 Mar 44

KIA	Miyamoto, Hakuo	Lieutenant	77 Sentai	Tommy Lynch
KIA	Obakayawa, Kiyoshi	MSergeant	77 Sentai	

United States claims 5-1-2; 1-1-2 to Bong and Lynch at 1325, confirmed in 77 Sentai records; and other documents confirm three bombers and one Oscar lost at 1740 to Kearby, Blair, and Dunham; Neel Kearby was KIA. Hata et al. have Miyamoto as lost on 7 Mar, in "New Guinea" but captured 77 Sentai documents state the loss as 5 Mar.

06 Mar 44

KIA	Asai, Mitsusada	Lieutenant	78 Sentai
KIA	Kawano, Manju	Sergeant	68 Sentai

No U.S. claims for 6 Mar; could be for previous day.

08 Mar 44

United States claims 1-0-0 by Capt. Arland Stanton, 7FS; Japanese admit 1-0-0; seven more Tonys en route.

10 Mar 44

KIA   Takahashi, Hirasuke   Sergeant   68 Sentai

No U.S. fighter claims this date, but Hata et al. have the loss at Wewak. Six more Oscars en route.

11 Mar 44

KIA	Hamasuna, Takeshi	Lieutenant	63 Sentai
KIA	Tomatsu, Tatsuo	Sergeant Major	33 Sentai
KIA	Watabe, Hajime	Sergeant	63 Sentai

United States claims 23-0-1 at Wewak; Japanese admit 9-0-0 lost.

12 Mar 44

s/d	Fujii	Lieutenant	77 Sentai	
s/d	Fukushima, Waikichi	Sergeant	77 Sentai	KIA 12 Apr 44
s/d	Hashimoto, Soichi	Sergeant	77 Sentai	KIA 13 Mar 44
KIA	Kobayakawa, Kiyoshi	Sergeant Major	77 Sentai	(H/I/S)
WIA	Matsuo, Yoshihide	Captain	77 Sentai	died mid-44
KIA	Mitoma, Koichi	Warrant Officer	77 Sentai	
KIA	Taguchi	unknown	77 Sentai	
KIA	Tomatsu, Tatsuo	Sergeant Major	33 Sentai	(H/I/S)

United States claims 18-1-0 at Wewak; Japanese admit 12-0-0.

13 Mar 44

| KIA | Hamasuna, Takeshi | Lieutenant | 63 Sentai | (H/I/S) |
| KIA | Hashimoto, Soichi | Sergeant | 77 Sentai | |

KIA	Kumagai, Joshu	Sergeant	33 Sentai	Ralph Wandrey, 9FS
KIA	Kumatani, Shirokazu	Sergeant Major	33 Sentai	
WIA	Takemura, Koji	Captain	63 Sentai	7FS victory
KIA	Yamamoto, Takaaki	Corporal	63 Sentai	7FS victory
s/d	unnamed, parachuted		63 Sentai	7FS victory

United States claims 5-1-2 by 7 and 9FS, 49FG, and 41 FS; Japanese admit 6-0-0 destroyed; checks with U.S. claims.

14 Mar 44

WIA	Aoyanagi	unknown	77 Sentai	41FS victory
KIA	Kuwabara, Yoshiro	Major	77 Sentai	41FS victory
KIA	Matsumoto, Koh	Sergeant	33 Sentai	9FS victory
KIA	Nagasaka, Shuhei	Corporal	77 Sentai	41FS victory
KIA	Ohya, Seishi	Corporal	33 Sentai	9FS victory
s/d	Tamaguchi	Corporal	77 Sentai	41FS victory
KIA	Watanabe	unknown	77 Sentai	41FS victory

United States claims 7-1-0 by 9 and 41FS at Wewak; Japanese admit eight destroyed. One 77 Sentai fighter shot down by 320BS.

15 Mar 44

MIA	Kato, Michichiro	Lieutenant	68 Sentai	
MIA	Nagae, Kiyo (?)	Sergeant Major	68 Sentai	
KIA	Ogi, Yasuji	Lieutenant	63 Sentai	(H/I/S)
MIA	Saito, Shogo	Lieutenant	78 Sentai	
KIA	Shimoura, Shigekatsu	Lieutenant	63 Sentai	(H/I/S)

KIA	Tajimi, Shoichi	Sergeant Major	78 Sentai
MIA	Tanaka, Naotoshi	Sergeant Major	78 Sentai
MIA	Tsuneo	Sergeant Major	79 Chutai, plus three others
MIA	Watanabe, Hajimi	Corporal	63 Sentai

United States claims 9-0-0 in Wewak area; Japanese admit 10-0-0, in radio message.

8 Mar 44

| KIA | Hashimoto, Shoichi | Sergeant | 77 Sentai | (H/I/S) |

No U.S. claims for Wewak this date, but could be next day.

19 Mar 44

United States claims 1-0-0, Lt. R. Sutcliffe 342FS at Wewak; Japanese admit 1-0-0.

22 Mar 44

Fifteen Tonys en route.

25 Mar 44

Twenty-one Oscars issued.

30 Mar 44

KIA	Aono, Kikuichi	Second Lieutenant	33 Sentai (on ground)
KIA	Matsumura, Takuzo	Sergeant	33 Sentai
KIA	Musubishiro	Sergeant	63 Sentai
KIA	Oshima	Sergeant Major	33 Sentai

KIA	Sawada	Sergeant	33 Sentai
KIA	Takeuchi	Sergeant	33 Sentai
KIA	Yamamoto	Corporal	33 Sentai
KIA	Yoshino	Second Lieutenant	33 Sentai

United States claims 8-2-7 near Hollandia by 80FS and 431FS; Japanese records confirm these losses.

31 Mar 44

KIA	Inagaki	unknown	33 Sentai
KIA	Kurahara	unknown	33 Sentai

United States claims 14-1-1 near Hollandia by 80, 431, and 432FS; Japanese admit the above 2-0-0.

Note: Japanese records show sixty-five Oscars supplied February–March to two unidentified fighter units; forty are recorded separately as issued in March.

03 Apr 44

KIA	Chikara, Nobuaki	Sergeant Major	33 Sentai
KIA	Hara, Shoji	Corporal	33 Sentai
KIA	Nakamura, Hisayoshi	Corporal	33 Sentai
KIA	Sugiura	Lieutenant	33 Sentai
KIA	Takemori, Harumi	Sergeant Major	33 Sentai
s/d	Ueki, Toshimasa	Lieutenant	63 Sentai

United States claims 25-0-3 near Hollandia by 80 and 432FS; Japanese admit ten, eleven, or thirty-six (different sources).

06 Apr 44

Thirty-six Tonys issued to 68 and 78 Sentai.

11 Apr 44

KIA	Nakagawa	Sergeant	78 Sentai	Lt. Ed Glascock, 8FS
s/d	unnamed pilot		68 Sentai	
	parachuted			

U.S. claim 1-0-0 at Wewak; Japanese admit 2-0-0.

12 Apr 44

KIA	Fukushima, Waikichi	Sergeant	77 Sentai
KIA	Matsumoto, Kunio	Major	77 Sentai
KIA	Takenawa, Toshio(?)	Captain	68 Sentai

U.S. claims 9-2-3 near Hollandia by 80FS and Dick Bong; Japanese records admit these three by name.

17 Apr 44

Last seven pilots 33 Sentai escape from Hollandia; unit arrived in March.

18 Apr 44

| KIA | Ikakura, Kaneji | Captain | 248 Sentai | (H/I/S) |

No 5AF fighter claims this date.

23 Apr 44

63, 68, 248 Sentai ceased to exist.

mid-1944

| died | Matsuo, Yoshihide | Captain | 77 Sentai |
| died | Shimada, Tsugio | Sergeant | 77 Sentai |

Appendix E
JAAF Aircraft Numbers,
Late 1943 to March 1944

This appendix lists Japanese Army Air Force aircraft numbers notified as held at or passing through Manila, or supplied direct to a unit, and reported unit strengths of aircraft available and flight crews available, in the forward areas, from late 1943 to end of March 1944.

A glance at these figures will indicate the continuous loss of aircraft in New Guinea at this time. Though combat reports exist only for some dates, the true situation within Japanese air units is indicated by the figures in this appendix. Manila air depot did not supply aircraft only to New Guinea, but to Japanese units in Indochina, Indonesia, Burma, and Thailand. Where aircraft were reported as specifically for New Guinea, that detail has been recorded in this appendix.

Source for this detail is the RG457 collection of decoded Japanese air force messages at U.S. Archives, College Park, Maryland, captured documents in the

ATIS SWPA G2 collection, research by Sam Tagaya, and postwar writings. Aircraft numbers are in **bold** to assist in discerning them among the numbers representing units and aircraft types.

The Aircraft Replacement Flow to New Guinea

Aircraft reported as en route to, at Manila, or passed through to New Guinea

5 Sep 43	**33** Ki-21 and Ki-49 bombers arrive Hollandia; fly east next day.
	4 aircraft 9 Flying Brigade arrive Wewak from Hollandia.
6 Sep 43	**16** more aircraft flying east from Namlea.
7 Sep 43	**9** aircraft arrive Wewak from the west; others arrive Hollandia.
9 Sep 43	**70** aircraft move through Hollandia; **20** more Ki-21 and Ki-49 arrive Hollandia.
10 Sep 43	**3** aircraft 61 Sentai arrive Hollandia; **7** other aircraft arrive Babo.
11 Sep 43	**4** aircraft arrive Hollandia from Ambon.
12 Sep 43	**11** Ki-43 in transit, escorted from Babo.
	7 aircraft 61 Sentai arrive Hollandia.
14 Sep 43	**6** bombers 14 Sentai arrive Namlea from Davao.
16 Sep 43	**32** aircraft en route Hollandia from Manila.
18 Sep 43	**33** aircraft en route Hollandia from Manila.
19 Sep 43	**18** aircraft arrive Wewak from east; **14** arrive Hollandia from Wewak.
20 Sep 43	**9** aircraft arrive Hollandia from west; **6** more following.
21 Sep 43	**1** escorted flight arrives Hollandia from Davao.
24 Sep 43	**5** fighters and escort arrive Namlea from Menado.
27 Sep 43	**42** aircraft moving east across West New Guinea.
2 Oct 43	**13** Ki-43 delivered to New Guinea by 24 Sentai.
4 Oct 43	**12** aircraft moving east from Hollandia.
5 Oct 43	**7** aircraft arrived Wewak from Rabaul.
17 Oct 43	**65** aircraft en route from Manila, including **43** Ki-21.
18 Oct 43	**43** Type 97 bombers depart Ambon for Hollandia.

	Aircraft of 7 Flying Brigade en route Palau-Wewak.
19 Oct 43	24 aircraft en route Davao-Hollandia.
22 Oct 43	20 fighter aircraft en route Hollandia from Manila (see following).
24 Oct 43	20 Ki-61 arrive Hollandia with 78 Sentai.
25 Oct 43	5 aircraft depart Menado for Hollandia.
26 Oct 43	4 aircraft flights depart Menado for Hollandia.
28 Oct 43	4 medium bombers depart Davao; 3 others land Ceram en route.
30 Oct 43	48 flights en route to Manila and Hollandia; types not stated.
	23 Ki-43 ferried "late October" by 59 Sentai.
	21 Ki-43 "end of October" ferried by 24 Sentai.
	30 Ki-43 arrive New Guinea with 248 Sentai.
2 Nov 43	4 Type 100 recon aircraft arrive Wewak from west; 14 Sentai aircraft arrive Rabaul from west. Six escorted flights arrive Hollandia and But.
3 Nov 43	Radio traffic Manila to Wewak concerning air movements reached an all-time high.
5 Nov 43	4 escorted Ki-43 arrive Ambon from Davao.
6 Nov 43	5 aircraft en route to Namlea.
10 Nov 43	4 aircraft en route from Davao.
13 Nov 43	7 aircraft arrive Hollandia from Davao.
18 Nov 43	10 Type 100 bombers arrive Namlea.
20 Nov 43	4 aircraft depart Davao; others depart Menado; all for Hollandia.
23 Nov 43	Three flights arrive Ambon from Menado and Davao.
25 Nov 43	8 aircraft depart Wakde.
26 Nov 43	6 aircraft of 61 Sentai arrive But from the west.
27 Nov 43	7 aircraft of 61 Sentai active along coast of New Guinea.
28 Nov 43	Several Type 97 bombers en route to Hollandia.
29 Nov 43	4 Type 97 bombers from Babo en route Hollandia.
30 Nov 43	26 Ki-61 ferried to New Guinea by 68 Sentai.
19 Dec 43	Reported at Manila: total 105 aircraft, including 4 Ki-46; 4 Ki-48; 17 Ki-49; 23 Ki-51.

20 Dec 43	Reported at Manila: **31** Ki-43; **21** Ki-61; **4** Ki-46; **4** Ki-48; **15** Ki-49; **23** Ki-51; plus **8** others needing repair work; total **106**.
22 Dec 43	At Manila: **33** aircraft. At Manila: **59** aircraft in a total "being supplied" (separate message).
23 Dec 43	Reported as arrived at 6 Flying Division: **6** Ki-43; **1** Ki-21; en route Wewak: **28** Ki-43 for 63 Sentai; **8** Ki-61 for 68 Sentai; **9** Ki-21 carrying ground crews for 63 Sentai plus **2** other aircraft.
24 Dec 43	Due at Manila: **6** Ki-49; **11** Ki-61.
25 Dec 43	Reported at Manila: **139** aircraft, including **65** Ki-43; **4** Ki-46; **4** Ki-48; **18** Ki-49; **23** Ki-51; **25** Ki-61.
26 Dec 43	Reported at Manila: **32** aircraft.
28 Dec 43	Reported at Manila: **60** aircraft, including **14** Ki-43 for 63 Sentai. A separate report states **118** aircraft were at Manila, some undergoing repairs: **47** Ki-43; **4** Ki-46; **12** Ki-48; **18** Ki-49; **21** Ki-51; **16** Ki-61.
29 Dec 43	Reported at Manila: **24** Ki-43; **11** Ki-48; **31** Ki-61; reported en route from Manila to Hollandia: **15** Ki-43 for 63 Sentai, and **3** Ki-49; **14** Ki-61.
30 Dec 43	Reported at Manila en route Hollandia: **14** Ki-43 for 63 Sentai: **10** Ki-61.
January 1944	Aircraft allocation for New Guinea for the month: fighters **117**; bombers **92**; transport **8**.
1 Jan 44	Reported arrived Hollandia: **2** Ki-43 for 248 Sentai, and **4** Ki-48; **4** Ki-61.
2 Jan 4	Reported at Manila: **45** Ki-43; **2** Ki-48; **17** Ki-49; **25** Ki-61.
3 Jan 44	At Babo, en route from Manila: **6** Ki-43 for 63 Sentai, **6** Ki-61 for 68 Sentai, and **1** Ki-51.
4 Jan 44	At Manila, a total of **125** aircraft, including **26** twin-engine bombers, and **35** Ki-43; **20** Ki-51; **29** Ki-61.
5 Jan 44	At Manila: **35** Ki-43; **3** Ki-46; **12** Ki-48; **26** Ki-49; **19** Ki-51; **24** Ki-61.

6 Jan 44	Reported left Manila, en route to Hollandia: **11** for **68** Sentai, **4** for **78** Sentai, plus **8** aircraft in separate formations.
7 Jan 44	At Manila: **49** aircraft.
9 Jan 44	At Manila: **15** Ki-45; **3** Ki-46; **4** Ki-48.
10 Jan 44	At Manila: **41** Ki-43; **2** Ki-46; **7** Ki-48; **26** Ki-49; **17** Ki-51; **23** Ki-61.
11 Jan 44	At Manila: **47** Ki-43, plus **1** under repair; **7** Ki-48; **23** Ki-61, plus **6** under repair. Reported arrived at Hollandia: **3** Ki-49.
12 Jan 44	Reported at Manila, for New Guinea: **29** aircraft; and already notified as sent were **31**: **1** Ki-21; **16** Ki-43; **1** Ki-46; **5** Ki-49; **3** Ki-51; **14** Ki-61; total: **40** [*sic*].
15 Jan 44	En route to Hollandia: **6** Ki-61.
17 Jan 44	At Manila: **12** Ki-43; **10** Ki-61; delivered to New Guinea: **2** Ki-49; **2** Ki-61; ready for delivery: **1** Ki-21; **10** Ki-45; **2** Ki-46, and **8** others; being prepared: **9** Ki-43; **6** Ki-48; **6** Ki-49; **8** Ki-51; **6** Ki-61; **66** others.
18 Jan 44	At Manila: 5 Sentai **2** Ki-45 in the "Matsumoto formation"; 75 Sentai **4**, equipped with 20 mm guns.
19 Jan 44	At Manila: **53** Ki-43; **7** Ki-48; **27** Ki-61.
22 Jan 44	At Manila: a total of **33** aircraft, plus **6** Ki-48; **12** Ki-51 for 73 Independent Chutai, and **16** fighters en route for Hollandia. 7 Flying Division reported receipt of **9** Ki-21, and **3** other aircraft.
25 Jan 44	At Manila: **25** Ki-43; **11** Ki-48; **2** Ki-49; **22** Ki-61.
26 Jan 44	At Manila: **71** Ki-43; **22** Ki-61; **3** Ki-48; **25** Ki-49. In a separate report, at Manila: **30** Ki-43; **22** Ki-61; en route to Hollandia: **14** Ki-43; **3** Ki-49.
27 Jan 44	At Manila: **43** Ki-43, some under repair; **31** Ki-61, some under repair, plus **27** twin-engine aircraft. En route to Wewak: **4** Ki-46; **5** Ki-61.
28 Jan 44	At Manila: **32** Ki-43; **6** Ki-46; **11** Ki-48; **26** Ki-49; **15** Ki-51; **31** Ki-61.

31 Jan 44	At Manila: **11** Ki-43; **11** Ki-48; **23** Ki-49; **26** Ki-61.
4 Feb 44	7 Flying Division received: **5** Ki-21; **14** Ki-43; **5** Ki-48.
6 Feb 44	En route Wewak: **32** Ki-43; **5** Ki-45; notification sent that five more Sentai to go to New Guinea.
14 Feb 44	Advice to 7 Flying Division: **95** aircraft scheduled to move to Hollandia; fuel arrangements required for these at Babo; arrangements at Ambon for 33 Sentai and arrangements at Halmaheras for 60 Sentai and 77 Sentai.
19 Feb 44	7 Flying Division received: **6** Ki-43; **7** Ki-46; **6** Ki-48; 45 Sentai reports **16** aircraft arrived Menado, en route Babo.
20 Feb 44	En route to Hollandia:
	45 Sentai **16** aircraft at Babo
	60 Sentai **19** aircraft at Galela
	77 Sentai **12** depart for Halmaheras
26 Feb 44	4 Air Army advised these aircraft already sent to New Guinea for:
	33 Sentai **20** Ki-43; 63: **9** Ki-43; 77: **10** Ki-43; 248: **3** Ki-
43	
	68 Sentai **6** Ki-61; 78: **9** Ki-61
	45 Sentai **10** Ki-45
	75 Sentai **12** Ki-48; 208: **13** Ki-48
	60 Sentai **6** Ki-49
	61Sentai **15** Ki-21
	70 Chutai **3** Ki-46 en route
	Hollandia informed it was to receive **130** aircraft in March.
5 Mar 44	At Manila: **81** aircraft; including: **20** Ki-43, plus **2** under repair.
	2 Ki-46, plus **2** under repair **21** Ki-49; from Japan; **20** other aircraft arrived Manila.
6 Mar 44	At Manila:
	15 Ki-43, plus **2** under repair; **5** others depart for Hollandia
	4 Ki-46; **6** Ki-48; **21** Ki-49
	1 Ki-51, to depart for Hollandia
	20 Ki-61, plus **1** under repair; **3** others to depart for Hollandia.

7 Mar 44	At Manila: **9** Ki-43; **6** Ki-48; **9** Ki-49; **16** Ki-61.
8 Mar 44	En route to Hollandia: **7** Ki-61; **3** Ki-46.
10 Mar 44	At Wasile, Halmaheras, en route Hollandia **6** Ki-43, with engine trouble; **1** Ki-49.
13 Mar 44	At Manila: **18** aircraft.
14 Mar 44	**14** unspecified aircraft arrive Hollandia.
22 Mar 44	En route to Wewak: **15** Ki-61.
23 Mar 44	Tokyo informed Manila that **6** Ki-43 are in storage; no others available. Manila advised there were **8** aircraft for New Guinea; **15** damaged aircraft at the depot; **27** others under repair; **20** other aircraft at the depot.
25 Mar 44	Hollandia advised that **21** Ki-43 were issued to units.
31 Mar 44	In March, **40** fighters issued from Hollandia air depot.
2 Apr 44	At Manila: **25** aircraft available; **29** others under repair.
6 Apr 44	**36** Ki-61 issued to 68 and 78 Sentai.

Reported Sentai Strengths, August 1943 to March 1944

Though no figures exist for some dates in the period, these indicate the steady fluctuation in unit aircraft strengths during the time.

Sentai	Aircraft	Date	Quantity
5	Ki-45	18 Jan 44	(2 at Manila)
		24 Jan	16
		8 Feb	15
		26 Feb	16
		9 Mar	15
		12 Mar	33
		16 Mar	14
7	Ki-49	18 Aug 43	6
		23 Sep	3
		1 Oct	4 (to 3 Oct)
		4 Oct	5 (to 7 Oct)
		8 Oct	7 (to 13 Oct)
		14 Oct	9 (to 20 Oct)
		21 Oct	8 (8, 7, 7, to 24 Oct)
		25 Oct	6 (to 27 Oct)

Sentai	Aircraft	Date	Quantity
		28 Oct	4 (2, 1, 1 to end Oct)
		1 Nov	3
		5 Nov	5 (maximum 8 on 14 Nov)
		27 Nov	4 (to end of month)
		7 Dec	6
		25 Dec	2
		29 Dec	1
		31 Dec	25
		9 Jan 44	25
		15 Jan	1
		21 Jan	2
		28 Jan	0
		10 Feb	8
		26 Mar	2
10	Ki-46	23 Sep 43	6
		1 Nov	5 (for Nov, between 1 and 5)
		30 Nov	2
		1 Dec	0
		30 Jan 44	3
		15 Feb	3
		24 Feb	5
		7 Mar	6
		15 Mar	4
		26 Mar	3
13	Ki-45/Ki-43	9 Jul 43	20 Ki-45 at Boram
		17 Aug	2 Ki-45
		18 Aug	2 Ki-45
		23 Sep	2, 6 (Ki-45, Ki-43)
		1 Oct	8 Ki-43
		3 Oct	17 Ki-43 (also 4 Oct)
		5 Oct	16
		6 Oct	15

Sentai	Aircraft	Date	Quantity
		7 Oct	10
		8 Oct	12 (also 9 Oct)
		10 Oct	2, 15 (Ki-45, Ki-43)
		11 Oct	1, 15
		12 Oct	0, 15
		13 Oct	1, 15
		14 Oct	1, 16 (also 15 Oct)
		16 Oct	16 (Ki-43 for rest of Oct)
		17 Oct	10
		18 Oct	11 (also 19 Oct)
		20 Oct	10 (11, 11 to 22 Oct)
		23 Oct	13 (also for 24 Oct)
		25 Oct	15
		26 Oct	17
		27 Oct	10 (11,12 for 28, 29 Oct)
		30 Oct	17 (also for 31 Oct)
		1 Nov	16 (to 5 Nov)
		6 Nov	15
		7 Nov	17 (and 8 Nov)
		9 Nov	14 (and 10 Nov)
		11 Nov	4
		12 Nov	14
		13 Nov	4
		14 Nov	16
		15 Nov	15
		16 Nov	13
		17 Nov	10 (to 20 Nov)
		21 Nov	8
		22 Nov	7
		23 Nov	9
		24 Nov	10
		25 Nov	8 (to 28 Nov)

Sentai	Aircraft	Date	Quantity
		29 Nov	7 (also 30 Nov)
		17 Jan 44	to use Ki-43
		18 Jan	17
		31 Jan	11
		8 Feb	40
		26 Feb	10
		12 Mar	29
14	Ki-45-2	18 Aug 43	1
		23 Sep	10
		1 Oct	9 (to 5 Oct)
		6 Oct	6 (to 14 Oct)
		15 Oct	5 (4, 4, 3 to 18 Oct)
		19 Oct	4 (to 27 Oct)
		28 Oct	7 (to end of Oct)
		1 Nov	7 (to 5 Nov)
		5 Nov	9
		6 Nov	11
		7 Nov	9
		8 Nov	0
		9 Nov	7
		10 Nov	3 (to 16 Nov)
		17 Nov	2 (to 18 Nov)
		(no figures available to end of year)	
		9 Jan 44	13
		31 Jan	13; and 26 (separate report)
		8 Feb	15
		26 Feb	16
		9 Mar	14
		12 Mar	25
		16 Mar	4
26	Ki-51	31 Oct 43	13
		1 Nov	27 (also for 2 Nov)

Sentai	Aircraft	Date	Quantity
		3 Nov	18 (to 10 Nov)
		9 Nov	19 (17, 18, 19 to 13 Nov)
		14 Nov	12 (15, 17, 14 to 17 Nov)
		18 Nov	9
		19 Nov	15
		20 Nov	13
		21 Nov	15 (15, 16 to 24 Nov)
		25 Nov	13 (to 26 Nov)
		27 Nov	16 (to 29 Nov)
		30 Nov	19
		7 Dec	12
		14 Dec	12
		26 Dec	9
		29 Dec	11
		30 Dec	3
		1 Jan 44	7
		2 Jan	10
		3 Jan	14
		5 Jan	11
		10 Jan	12
		15 Jan	5
		21 Jan	12
		28 Jan	10
		30 Jan	10
		6 Feb	6
		8 Feb	6
		10 Feb	12
		14 Feb	5
24	Ki-43	18 Aug 43	7
		23 Sep	9
		1 Oct	11
		2 Oct	removed from operations; lost 20 KIA since May 43

Sentai	Aircraft	Date	Quantity
28	Ki-46	15 Jan 44	comes under command
	(training unit)		4 Air Army
		20 Feb	4
		28 Feb	4 (in 3rd Chutai)
		5 Mar	10
		7 Mar	4
		15 Mar	5
33	Ki-43	8 Feb 44	30 aircraft on strength
		18 Feb	arrive Ambon
		21 Feb	arrive Hollandia
		26 Feb	20 aircraft supplied in February; total 50
		29 Feb	24
		3 Mar	20
		5 Mar	12
		7 Mar	12
		8 Mar	9
		10 Mar	18
		14 Mar	16
		15 Mar	13
		17 Mar	15
		18 Mar	14
		19 Mar	13
		22 Mar	18
		25 Mar	13
		26 Mar	16
		31 Mar	(20 aircraft issued in March)
		8 Apr	6
		12 Apr	6
		17 Apr	7
34	Ki-48	20 Feb 44	11
	(training unit)	26 Feb	10
		28 Feb	17

Sentai	Aircraft	Date	Quantity
		2 Mar	12
		3 Mar	13
		5 Mar	9
		5 Mar	22 (separate report)
		6 Mar	12 (to 14 March)
		15 Mar	10
		18 Mar	11
		22 Mar	10 (to 26 March)
45	Ki-45	19 Aug 43	4
		23 Sep	15
		1 Oct	11
		2 Oct	14
		3 Oct	19 (to 6 Oct)
		7 Oct	16
		8 Oct	15 (no figures for 2 days)
		11 Oct	14
		12 Oct	13
		13 Oct	6 (also for 14 Oct)
		15 Oct	14
		16 Oct	6
		17 Oct	7
		18 Oct	3 (also for 19 Oct)
		20 Oct	9
		21 Oct	5 (to 25 Oct; no figures for rest of year)
		8 Feb 44	30
		19 Feb	16
		20 Feb	16 aircraft to Babo
		26 Feb	(10 supplied in Feb [*sic*])
		28 Feb	9
		2 Mar	15
		3 Mar	13

Sentai	Aircraft	Date	Quantity
		5 Mar	8
		5 Mar	11 (separate report)
		7 Mar	8
		10 Mar	12
		14 Mar	1
		15 Mar	12 (to 26 March)
59	Ki-43	18 Aug 43	8
		23 Sep	16
		30 Sep	15
		1 Oct	15 (nil for rest of month)
		31 Oct	23
		1 Nov	22
		5 Nov	24
		8 Nov	17
		9 Nov	16
		10 Nov	9
		11 Nov	16
		16 Nov	11
		18 Nov	13
		19 Nov	16
		20 Nov	14
		23 Nov	8
		24 Nov	13
		27 Nov	12 (11, 12, 13 to end of month)
		14 Dec	12
		26 Dec	11
		29 Dec	12
		30 Dec	13 (to 2 January)
		3 Jan 44	12
		5 Jan	10
		10 Jan	15
		23 Jan	25

Sentai	Aircraft	Date	Quantity
		28 Jan	8
		30 Jan	9
		3 Feb	3
		6 Feb	3
		7 Feb	7
		8 Feb	6
		9 Feb	23
		10 Feb	1
		13 Feb	7 (also for 14 Feb)
		15 Feb	4
60	Ki-21	14 Feb 44	22
		18 Feb	arrive Galela, Halmaheras
		20 Feb	19 aircraft at Galela
		26 Feb	5; 6 others supplied in February
		2 Mar	18
		3 Mar	25
		5 Mar	15 (for next week)
		12 Mar	15
		14 Mar	12
		15 Mar	2
		18 Mar	12 (to end of month)
61	Ki-49	23 Sep 43	4
		1 Oct	5 (4, then 5 to 10 Oct)
		11 Oct	6 (6 or 7 to 27 Oct)
		28 Oct	4 (also for 29 Oct)
		30 Oct	2 (also for 31 Oct)
		1 Nov	3 (same number until 6 Nov)
		6 Nov	2 (until 9 Nov)
		9 Nov	5 (until 11 Nov)
		12 Nov	3
		13 Nov	4 (until 17 Nov)

Sentai	Aircraft	Date	Quantity
		17 Nov	5
		18 Nov	4 (until 26 Nov)
		27 Nov	5 (to end of Nov 43)
		7 Dec	7
		14 Dec	4
		25 Dec	5 to Wakde
		29 Dec	2 to end of month
		1 Jan 44	2
		15 Jan	1
		18 Jan	15
		21 Jan	1
		28 Jan	0 to end of month
		6 Feb	1
		10 Feb	7
		14 Feb	1
		20 Feb	6 or 5 to end of month
		26 Feb	(15 supplied in Feb)
		2 Mar	4
		5 Mar	3 (for next few days)
		10 Mar	5 (no change for one week)
		18 Mar	5 (no change for next week)
		25 Mar	5
		26 Mar	4
63	Ki-43	23 Dec 43	28 Ki-43 en route from Manila
		28 Dec	14 Ki-43 en route from Manila
		3 Jan 44	6 en route land at Babo
		7 Jan	28
		28 Jan	6
		30 Jan	8
		3 Feb	10

Sentai	Aircraft	Date	Quantity
		6 Feb	8 and for next day
		8 Feb	10 (to 10 February)
		13 Feb	4
		14 Feb	8
		15 Feb	6
		20 Feb	5 (to 24 February)
		25 Feb	9
		26 Feb	(9 supplied in Feb)
		29 Feb	18
		3 Mar	8
		5 Mar	27
		7 Mar	8
		8 Mar	7
		10 Mar	10
		11 Mar	9
		14 Mar	6
		15 Mar	7
		17 Mar	6 (for next week)
		25 Mar	7
		26 Mar	8 (to end of month)
		20 Apr	8
68	Ki-61	17 Aug 43	6
		18 Aug	6
		28 Sep	2
		1 Oct	0, 6 (Ki-43, Ki-61)
		2 Oct	10, 7
		3 Oct	8, 7
		4 Oct	7, 7 (also for 5 Oct)
		6 Oct	9, 8
		7 Oct	10, 6
		8 Oct	7, 4 (also for 9 Oct)
		11 Oct	10, 4 (also for 12 Oct)
		13 Oct	11, 5
		14 Oct	9, 5

Sentai	Aircraft	Date	Quantity
		15 Oct	11, 5
		16 Oct	12, ? No figure given
		17 Oct	6, 3
		18 Oct	6, 2
		19 Oct	5, 3 (to 22 Oct)
		23 Oct	6, 5
		24 Oct	7, 3
		25 Oct	6, 4
		26 Oct	5, 4
		27 Oct	0, ? No figure given; to end Oct
		1 Nov	0 (to 29 Nov)
		30 Nov	8
		12 Dec	9
		14 Dec	12
		23 Dec	8 depart Manila
		26 Dec	6
		29 Dec	5
		30 Dec	5
		1 Jan 44	8
		2 Jan	8 (and 3 Jan)
		3 Jan	6 en route at Babo
		5 Jan	11 at Manila (and same on 6 Jan)
		10 Jan	10
		28 Jan	8
		30 Jan	10
		3 Feb	11
		6 Feb	4
		7 Feb	1
		8 Feb	3; then 10 (separate report)
		10 Feb	4; then 14 (separate report)

Sentai	Aircraft	Date	Quantity
		14 Feb	4
		15 Feb	3
		20 Feb	2 (to 23 Feb)
		24 Feb	1
		25 Feb	6
		26 Feb	(6 supplied in Feb)
		29 Feb	8
		2 Mar	8
		3 Mar	10
		5 Mar	8; then 12 (separate report)
		7 Mar	3
		8 Mar	10
		10 Mar	9
		11 Mar	10
		12 Mar	7 for next three days
		17 Mar	8
		18 Mar	7 for next week
		26 Mar	11
		5 Apr	4
		20 Apr	3
75	Ki-48	25 Dec 43	to Amahai, Ceram
		18 Jan 44	45
		31 Jan	40
		18 Jan	29
		18 Jan	4 at Manila
		24 Jan	28
		5 Feb	21 (to 8 February)
		21 Feb	to Hollandia
		2 Mar	15
		3 Mar	5
		5 Mar	9; then 15 (separate report)
		6 Mar	15

Sentai	Aircraft	Date	Quantity
		7 Mar	15
		10 Mar	17
		12 Mar	25; then 20 (separate report)
		14 Mar	20
		15 Mar	19
		18 Mar	18
		22 Mar	11 for next three days
		26 Mar	16
77	Ki-43	8 Feb 44	6
		14 Feb	26 in transit
		19 Feb	due Miti, Halmaheras
		20 Feb	12 aircraft at Halmaheras
		26 Feb	(10 others supplied in Feb)
		28 Feb	12 (day), 6 (night ops)
		29 Feb	20
		3 Mar	13
		5 Mar	11
		7 Mar	8
		8 Mar	9
		10 Mar	12
		12 Mar	6; then 11 (separate report)
		14 Mar	5
		15 Mar	6
		18 Mar	4
		22 Mar	4
		25 Mar	5
		26 Mar	4
		31 Mar	(27 aircraft issued in March)
		5 Apr	5

Sentai	Aircraft	Date	Quantity
78	Ki-61	18 Aug 43	0
		1 Oct	nil (to 15 Oct)
		15 Oct	7 (Ki-61 unless identified as Ki-43)
		16 Oct	11
		17 Oct	4
		18 Oct	6 (also for 19 Oct)
		20 Oct	8 (also for 21 Oct)
		22 Oct	7
		23 Oct	5
		24 Oct	5, but 20 replacement aircraft arrived
		25 Oct	7
		26 Oct	5
		27 Oct	6, 12 (Ki-43, Ki-61)
		28 Oct	4, 8 (also for 29 Oct)
		30 Oct	0, 11
		31 Oct	3, 10
		1 Nov	4, 11 (Ki-43, Ki-61)
		2 Nov	4, 10
		3 Nov	4, 12
		4 Nov	5, 12 (also for 5 Nov)
		6 Nov	5, 10
		7 Nov	5, 9 (also for 8 Nov)
		9 Nov	0, 9
		10 Nov	0, 8
		11 Nov	0, 6
		12 Nov	4, 7
		13 Nov	0, 6
		14 Nov	4, 12
		15 Nov	0, 10
		16 Nov	0, 8 (nil Ki-43 and 8, 9, 10 Ki-61 to 19 Nov)

Sentai	Aircraft	Date	Quantity
		20 Nov	0, 8 (0, 8 or 0, 7 to end of month)
		12 Dec	7 (Ki-61 unless otherwise noted)
		14 Dec	10
		26 Dec	10
		29 Dec	9
		30 Dec	9
		1 Jan 44	8 (and 2 Jan)
		3 Jan	6
		5 Jan	11
		6 Jan	4 at Manila
		10 Jan	8
		28 Jan	10
		30 Jan	8
		3 Feb	5
		7 Feb	3
		8 Feb	4; then 10 (separate report)
		10 Feb	4; then 11 (separate report)
		14 Feb	3
		15 Feb	5
		20 Feb	4 for five consecutive days
		25 Feb	9
		26 Feb	(9 supplied in Feb)
		29 Feb	10
		2 Mar	7
		3 Mar	6
		5 Mar	10
		7 Mar	16
		8 Mar	10
		10 Mar	6

Sentai	Aircraft	Date	Quantity
		11 Mar	7
		12 Mar	8
		14 Mar	7
		15 Mar	8
		17 Mar	7
		18 Mar	7
		19 Mar	10
		22 Mar	9
		25 Mar	10
		26 Mar	11
		5 Apr	5
		20 Apr	6
208	Ki-48	18 Aug 43	1
		1 Oct	training until 10 Oct
		11 Oct	19
		12 Oct	17
		13 Oct	18
		14 Oct	8 (also for 15 Oct)
		16 Oct	11 (also for 17 Oct)
		18 Oct	7 (to 21 Oct)
		22 Oct	8 (9, 7, to 24 Oct)
		26 Oct	6 (to 29 Oct)
		30 Oct	7
		31 Oct	15
		1 Nov	15 (until 9 Nov)
		10 Nov	18 (between 15 and 18 to 16 Nov)
		16 Nov	6
		17 Nov	9
		18 Nov	14
		20 Nov	15
		21 Nov	9
		23 Nov	12
		26 Nov	10

Sentai	Aircraft	Date	Quantity
		27 Nov	12 (12 or 13 to end of month)
		7 Dec	11
		25 Dec	11
		29 Dec	10 (also for 30 Dec)
		1 Jan 44	12
		7 Jan	10
		9 Jan	8
		10 Jan	11
		15 Jan	7
		20 Jan	2
		28 Jan	13
		30 Jan	13
		6 Feb	12
		8 Feb	37
		10 Feb	15; then 12 (different report)
		13 Feb	15
		14 Feb	8
		21 Feb	11
		22 Feb	11
		25 Feb	9; then 11 (second report)
		26 Feb	(13 supplied in Feb)
		28 Feb	15 (for day), 8 (for night ops)
		2 Mar	9
		3 Mar	6
		5 Mar	10; then 28 (separate report)
		6 Mar	5
		7 Mar	10
		10 Mar	9
		12 Mar	6

Sentai	Aircraft	Date	Quantity
		14 Mar	7 for next 4 days
		22 Mar	6 for next four days
248	Ki-43	31 Oct 43	30 on arrival
		2 Nov	32 (30, 32, 31 to 6 Nov)
		7 Nov	21
		9 Nov	24
		10 Nov	14
		11 Nov	17 (to 13 Nov)
		14 Nov	21
		15 Nov	18
		16 Nov	13
		17 Nov	10 (10 or 11 to 20 Nov)
		21 Nov	12 (to 24 Nov)
		25 Nov	11
		26 Nov	14
		27 Nov	8 (to 29 Nov)
		30 Nov	7; (lost 13 KIA in Nov)
		14 Dec	11
		26 Dec	9
		29 Dec	9
		30 Dec	10
		1 Jan 44	12
		1 Jan	2 at Hollandia
		2 Jan	10
		3 Jan	6
		5 Jan	6
		10 Jan	11
		20 Jan	8
		21 Jan	10
		23 Jan	18
		28 Jan	6
		3 Feb	7

Sentai	Aircraft	Date	Quantity
		6 Feb	5
		7 Feb	7
		8 Feb	5; then 13 (separate report)
		10 Feb	5
		13 Feb	4 to 15 February
		20 Feb	3; then 11 (separate report)
		21 Feb	3 to 29 February
		3 Mar	5
		5 Mar	3; then 14 (separate report)
		6 Mar	1
		7 Mar	0
		11 Mar	2
		17 Mar	0
		18 Mar	2
		22 Mar	5
		25 Mar	5
		26 Mar	4
		5 Apr	3
		20 Apr	6

Chutai	Aircraft	Date	Quantity
20		1 Mar 44	3
		5 Mar	6
		26 Mar	4
70	Ki-46	18 Aug 43	0
		31 Dec	11
		1 Jan 44	12
		31 Jan	15
		2 Feb	10
		11 Feb	5
		26 Feb	6

Chutai	Aircraft	Date	Quantity
		9 Mar	2
73	Ki-51	31 Dec 43	14
		1 Jan 44	12
		2 Feb	12
		11 Feb	4
		26 Feb	8
		12 Mar	17
74	Ki-46	17 Aug 43	0
		23 Sep	3
		1 Oct	0 (for Oct 43, between 1 and 3 aircraft)
		1 Nov	2 (for Nov 43, between 1 and 3 aircraft)
		18 Jan 44	4
		30 Jan	2
		31 Jan	6
		9 Feb	5
		15 Feb	1
		24 Feb	1
81	Ki-46	23 Sep 43	0
		1 Oct	nil until 30 Oct
		30 Oct	1 (also for 31 Oct)
		1 Nov	1 (for Nov 43, between 1 and 4 aircraft)
		30 Jan 44	1
		15 Feb	1
		21 Feb	6
		24 Feb	1
83	Ki-51	18 Aug 43	5
		23 Sep	3
		1 Oct	0
		2 Oct	3 (remained at 3 for October)
		1 Nov	3 (remained at 3 for November)

Chutai	Aircraft	Date	Quantity
		26 Dec	3
		20 Jan 44	1
		28 Jan	6
		8 Feb	6 (remained at 6 for Feb)
		15 Mar	1
		25 Mar	20
		26 Mar	3

Reported Flight Personnel Available

Date	Unit	TOE Pilots/ Flight Crews	Available
30 Nov 43	68 Sentai	(no figure stated)	2
9 Jan 44	7 Sentai	20 officer pilots	10
		48 enlisted pilots	18
	14 Sentai	20 officer pilots	18
	75 Sentai	17 officer pilots	11
		65 enlisted crewmen	28
31 Jan 44	248 Sentai	0 officer pilots	
8 Feb 44	6 Flying Division strength return		
	63 Sentai		10
	68 Sentai		10
	78 Sentai		10
	208 Sentai		56
	248 Sentai		5
10 Feb 44	7 Flying Division strength return		
	13 Sentai		11 pilots
	59 Sentai		10 pilots
	75 Sentai		13 pilots

Date	Unit	TOE Pilots/ Flight Crews	Available
19 Feb 44	59 Sentai		10 pilots
5 Mar 44	4 Air Army	strength return	
	28 Sentai		5 offr, 9 EM
	34 Sentai		16 offr, 36 EM
	45 Sentai		11 offr, 12 EM
	63 Sentai		11 offr, 19 EM
	68 Sentai		8 offr, 9 EM
	75 Sentai		12 offr, 21 EM
	208 Sentai		15 offr, 36 EM
	248 Sentai		9 offr, 7 EM
5 Apr 44	68 Sentai		16 pilots
	77 Sentai		21
	78 Sentai		22
	248 Sentai		28
6 Apr 44	68 Sentai		16
7 Apr 44	4 Air Army	strength return	
	33 Sentai		27 pilots
	78 Sentai		22 pilots
8 Apr 44	33 Sentai		7 pilots

4 Air Army Reports of Totals Available for Operations

10 Sep 43	97
1 Oct 43	75
5 Oct 43	80
7 Oct 43	68
11 Oct 43	72
12 Oct 43	75
13 Oct 43	68
15 Oct 43	86
18 Oct 43	57
21 Oct 43	62 (61, 63, 62 next three days)

22 Oct 43	56 (in separate report)
30 Oct 43	49
31 Oct 43	62
1 Nov 43	134
8 Nov 43	106
10 Nov 43	86
14 Nov 43	124
16 Nov 43	88
23 Nov 43	85
24 Nov 43	94
29 Nov 43	77
30 Nov 43	92
25 Dec 43	71
9 Jan 44	82
23 Feb 44	43
29 Feb 44	176
1 Mar 44	120
3 Mar 44	133
11 Mar 44	28
13 Mar 44	(46 fighters)
21 Mar 44	114 (48 fighters)
25 Mar 44	120 (48 fighters)

Reported Aircraft Types on Hand and Requested

18 Aug 43	6 Flying Division: 28 all types.
	7 Flying Division: 12 all types.
10 Sep 43	6 Flying Division: 63 all types.
	7 Flying Division: 34 all types.
22 Oct 43	At Wewak in p.m.: 24 fighters, 13 light bombers, 19 heavy bombers.
9 Dec 43	4 Air Army request for January allotment: Ki-43 70; Ki-46 20; Ki-48 10; Ki-51 20; Ki-61 50—Total: 170.
27 Dec 43	7 Flying Division: request five reconnaissance aircraft by mid-January.

3 Jan 44	4 Air Army report; does not identify units or if in reserve: 2 Ki-48 lost; aircraft available: Ki-48 10; Ki-43 18; Ki-61 14—Total: 42.
10 Jan 44	7 Flying Division February allotment request: Ki-21 12; Ki-46 2; Ki-48 7; Ki-51 3—Total: 24.
15 Jan 44	4 Air Army report; does not clarify if with units or in reserve: Ki-46 4; Ki-51 17; Ki-49 2; Ki-48 11.
18 Jan 44	75 Sentai: Ki-48 29 operational, 14 for maintenance, 2 damaged.
24 Jan 44	7 Flying Division report: 5 Sentai Ki-45 34; 13 Sentai Ki-45 17; 75 Sentai Ki-48 41.
28 Jan 44	At Manila: Ki-43 33; Ki-46 6; Ki-48 11; Ki-49 24; Ki-61 31; Ki-51; 15—Total 120.
2 Feb 44	4 Air Army report, aircraft held at Hollandia: Ki-43 22; Ki-61 1; Ki-45 1; Ki-46 13; Ki-48 15; Ki-49 28; Ki-51 2—Total 82.
6 Feb 44	4 Air Army report: Ki-46 6; Ki-51 12 59 Sentai Ki-43 3 63 Sentai Ki-43 8 248 Sentai Ki-43 5 208 Sentai Ki-48 12 61 Sentai Ki-4 1
8 Feb 44	4 Air Army report to Davao, 2 Area Army and Tokyo: 10 Sentai Ki-46 5 26 Sentai Ki-51 6 33 Sentai Ki-43 31 59 Sentai Ki-43 6 77 Sentai Ki-43 6 248 Sentai Ki-43 5 68 Sentai Ki-61 3 78 Sentai Ki-61 4 45 Sentai Ki-45 30 60 Sentai Ki-27 18 75 Sentai Ki-48 21

10 Feb 44	4 Air Army report:
	(unit unknown) Ki-46 4
	59 Sentai Ki-43 6
	63 Sentai Ki-43 10
	248 Sentai Ki-43 5
	68 Sentai Ki-61 4
	78 Sentai Ki-61 4
	26 Sentai Ki-51 5
	61 Sentai Ki-49 1
	208 Sentai Ki-48 15
12 Feb 44	7 Flying Division request for supply in March:
	Ki-45 30; Ki-46 12; Ki-51 5.
13 Feb 44	4 Air Army report:
	(unit unknown) Ki-46 5
	59 Sentai Ki-43 7
	63 Sentai Ki-43 4
	248 Sentai Ki-43 4
	61 Sentai Ki-49 1
	208 Sentai Ki-48 15
16 Feb 44	4 Air Army report:
	Ki-43 11; Ki-46 6; Ki-48 10; Ki-49 1; Ki-51 8; Ki-61 4—
	Total 40.
19 Feb 44	4 Air Army report:
	Ki-43 8; Ki-46 5; Ki-48 12; Ki-51 6; Ki-61 6—Total: 37.
21 Feb 44	4 Air Army report:
	Ki-43 8; Ki-46 6; Ki-48 11; Ki-49 5; Ki-51 6; Ki-61 6—
	Total 42.
22 Feb 44	7 Flying Division refers to "shortfall to our request for
	February 1944" and asks for the Ki-43s to go to
	Hollandia and the Ki-21s to go to Galela in the
	Halmaheras, plus the following:
	33 Sentai Ki-43 30
	60 Sentai Ki-21 15
25 Feb 44	4 Air Army report:
	Ki-43 13; Ki-46 7; Ki-48 11; Ki-49 6; Ki-51 6; Ki-61 15—
	Total 58.

26 Feb 44	4 Air Army is advised the following aircraft already sent to New Guinea:
	33 Sentai Ki-43 20; 63 Ki-43 9; 77 Ki-43 10; 248 Ki-43 3
	68 Sentai Ki-61 6; 78 Ki-61 9
	45 Sentai Ki-45 10
	75 Sentai Ki-48 12; 208 Ki-48 13
	60 Sentai Ki-49 6
	61 Sentai Ki-21 15
	70 Chutai Ki-46 3 en route
	Total: 116.
28 Feb 44	4 Air Army report:
	328 Sentai 4; 34 17; 45 9
	75 Sentai 18; 208 23; 15 Ki-43; 20 Ki-61
	Total: 106.
29 Feb 44	4 Air Army report:
	68 Sentai 8; 78 10
	33 Sentai 24; 63 18; 77 20; 248 3
	Total fighters: 83.
1 Mar 44	4 Air Army request for March 1944:
	50 fighters, 15 two-seat fighters, 15 heavy bombers.
4 Mar 44	4 Air Army:
	7 Flying Division message; to Tokyo; requests 32 Ki-61.
5 Mar 44	4 Air Army report:
	60 Sentai Ki-21 27 "three have over 250 hours and three have over 300 hours."
11 Mar 44	4 Air Army, morning (partial report):
	63 and 248 Sentai, Ki-43 11;
	68 and 78 Sentai Ki-61 17.
13 Mar 44	4 Air Army to 2 Area Army: please supply in April:
	Ki-43 26; Ki-46 5; Ki-51 3.
3 Apr 44	4 Air Army:
	Ki-43 21; Ki-61 7.
12 Apr 44	14 Flying Brigade:
	19 fighters available.
20 Apr 44	6 Flying Division reports available are:

	63 Sentai 8; 248 6; 68 3; 78 6
	Ki-46 4; Ki-48 3; Ki-51 2
	Total: 32.
1 May 44	4 Air Army request for May:
	Ki-21 10; Ki-49 30.

Works Consulted

Every documentary source consulted is included in this list. Much information came from material in the Australian War Memorial, particularly the large collection of reports created by the WWII G2 office of GHQ SWPA Allied Translator and Interpreter Section (ATIS). In Australia, these are in AWM archival collection AWM 55, while other WWII written documents are in AWM 54. ATIS information is contained in ATIS Interrogation Reports (ATIS Intg), ATIS Bulletins (ATIS Bull), Current Translations (CT), or Enemy Publication (EP). The Special Intelligence Bulletins, the signals intelligence Ultra reports, are from the MacArthur Memorial archives, Norfolk, Virginia. Much detail of JAAF unit strengths in the appendices was gleaned from the RG457 collection in the U.S. Archives at College Park, Maryland. Other sources were U.S. Strategic Bombing Surveys and Group histories written in September 1945 and information from interviews and translated material held by Larry Hickey's International Research & Publishing (IR&P), as well as some detail from volumes in the Bibliography.

Chapter 1: The Preliminaries: New Guinea 1942–43

Australian War Memorial records used in this chapter were:

AWM 54 423/11/199 Part 6 Index U1, AWM 54 14/1/4, AWM 54 14/1/1, AWM 54 AAF Int Memo 31, AWM 54 AAF Int Memo 32, AWM 54 Japanese Monograph 34

AWM 55 ATIS Interrogation Report (Intg) 388

AWM 66 18/2/1

ATIS Bulletin 297, 373, 52, 615, 618, 1034, 1149

ATIS Intg 298, 393, 449, 475, 494

Other sources:

Volumes in the bibliography, Craven and Cate Vol. VII P.420, SIB 100–109, John Brogan—author, 1983, and International Research & Publishing, Colorado

Chapter 2: A Sea of Fire: Wewak, August 1943

Australian War Memorial records used in this chapter were:

AWM 54 423/11/199 Pt 2 Index C39, AWM 54 1010/9/80 and 779/4/11, AWM 54 423/11/199 Pt 2 Index C39, AWM 54 423/11/199 Pt 2 Index E16 ATIS Bulletins 857, 1344, 1146, 1157, 2020; ATIS EP 270; ATIS Intg 427, 485, 704

Allied Air Forces (AAF) Intsum 132, 133 SIBs 110–22

U.S. Strategic Bombing Survey (USSBS) Intg 338, 483

Other sources:

Australian Archives file 614/1/25 Pt 6; volumes in bibliography

International Research & Publishing supplied the following:

Maurer-IR&P, Middlebrook-IR&P, Radnik-IR&P 1989—author, Webster-IR&P—author, IR&P Japanese language translations, Lynch combat report via IR&P

Veterans:

Hallett diary to author 1988, Swanson—author 1988, Wandrey—author 1987.

63 BS diary, 80 Squadron history

Steve Birdsall *Flying Buccaneers* Doubleday, 1977

John Stanaway supplied the Lent combat report Frank Olynyk *Victory List No.3,* 1985

Chapter 3: Locked Horns: September 1943–March 1944

Australian War Memorial records used in this chapter were:

AWM 54 423/11/199 Pt 3 Index H13, AWM 54 423/4/61AWM 55 Japanese Monograph 34

AAF Intsum 197, AAF Sitrep 270

ATIS Bulletins 745, 995, 999, 1011, 1017, 1045, 1048, 1066, 1071, 1075, 1087,
    1090, 1091, 1099, 1100, 1108, 1109, 1110, 1124, 1125, 1154, 1159, 1161,
    1165, 1171, 1248, 1281, 1282, 1285, 1299,1302, 1324, 1393, 1471, 1560, 2068
    ATIS CT 109, 110, 127, 130, 133 ATIS EP 268, 270, 282 ATIS Intg 330, 415,
    470, 485, 515, 531, 540, 569, 599, 600

Other sources:

IR&P

Chapter 4: The Mincing Machine: Wewak, March 1944

Australian War Memorial records used in this chapter were:

AWM 54 423/11/199 Pt 5 Index 528, AWM 54 423/11/199 Pt 6 Index W16

AWM 54 Japanese Monograph 34

AAF Intsum 192, 193, 194, 195; AAF Sitrep 277 ATIS Bulletins 977, 999, 1034,
    1040, 1066, 1069, 1071, 1090, 1109, 1110, 1125, 1126, 1157, 1159, 1194,
    1227, 1237, 1269, 1277, 1283, 1285, 1286, 1299, 1327, 1333, 1372, 1456,
    1560 ATIS CT 102, 129; ATIS EP 218, 268, 305 ATIS Intg 402, 454, 485, 515,
    529, 557, 600, 707.

USSBS #72 "Interrogation of Japanese Officials"

Other sources:

SIB 309, 311, 313, 314, 316, 317, 319, 327, 322

Veterans:

Grills—author 1988, Hampshire—author 1985, Parker—author 1988, Stafford—
    author 1983, Wandrey—author 1985–87

International Research & Publishing: Claringbould-IR&P, Foster-IR&P, Stanaway-
    IR&P, 90th Squadron diary-IR&P 3 BG history, September 1945

Chapter 5: In the South West Pacific Area

All anecdotal items from the person concerned to the author, 1982–90

Chapter 6: Hammer-Blow

Australian War Memorial records used in this chapter were:

AWM 54 423/11/199 Pt 3 Index H14, Index C63

ATIS Bulletins 1014, 1066, 1072, 1090, 1157, 1171, 1195, 1196, 1199, 1208, 1213,
    1222, 1227, 1238, 1239, 1269, 1286, 1299, 1304, 1309, 1361, 1425

ATIS Intg 362, 373, 441, 467, 495, 529, 567, 600

Other sources:

Grills—author 1988, SIB 330, 331; Frank Olynyk *Victory List No.3*, 1985

Chapter 7: Pounded to Destruction

AWM 54 423/11/199 Pt 2 Index C63, AWM 54 423/11/199 Pt 2 Index H13

AWM Japanese Monograph "Operations of 18th Army"

AAF Intsum 201—Addams/Robbins

ATIS Bulletins 745, 1066, 1071, 1080, 1090, 1091, 1108, 1110, 1134, 1137, 1146,
1149, 1153, 1157, 1166, 1195, 1196, 1199, 1204, 1213, 1222, 1227, 1247,
1264, 1269, 1284, 1299, 1310, 1358, 1372, 1449, 1451, 1463, 1586

ATIS Enemy Publication 305

ATIS Interrogations 345, 372, 400, 407, 435, 437, 438, 447, 467, 529, 567, 585,
600, 672

USSBS #72 "Japanese Air Operations—Interrogations of Japanese Officials"

International Research & Publishing: Claringbould-IR&P, Foster-IR&P, Maurer-
IR&P, Tanberg-IR&P, 90 BS diary-IR&P

Veterans:

Fetter, Grills, Moran, Shemelynce, Stanifer, Wandrey and Weigel—author 1983–89

Squadron report, 80th Squadron history

Frank Olynyk *Victory List No.3*, 1985

COMAFADVON 5 Report

Bibliography

General

USSBS. *The Allied Campaign Against Rabaul.* U.S. government, 1 September 1946.
———. *The Campaigns of the Pacific War.* U.S. government, 1946.
———. *Japan's Struggle to End the War.* U.S. government, 1 July 1946.

South West Pacific Area

Abraham, Walter V. *AIRIND in Retrospect.* Self-published, Australia, 1996.
Drea, Edward J. *MacArthur's Ultra.* University Press of Kansas, USA, 1992.
Henebry, John P. *The Grim Reapers at Work in the Pacific Theater.* Pictorial Histories, Montana, 2002.
Odgers, George. *Air War Against Japan 1943–45.* Australian Official history, 1957.
Rothgeb, Wayne P. *New Guinea Skies.* Iowa State University Press, 1992.
Sakaida, Henry. *JAAF Aces 1937–45.* Osprey UK, 1997.

5th Air Force

Birdsall, Steve. *Flying Buccaneers.* Doubleday & Co, USA, 1977.

Bong, Carl, and Mike O'Connor. *Ace of Aces.* Champlin Fighter Museum, USA, 1985.

Claringbould, Michael. *Black Sunday.* Aeroasian Publications, Australia, 1995.

———. *Lost Liberators in the Mist.* Flightpath Vol. 14, No. 3, 2003.

Hata, I., Y. Izawa, and C. Shores, *Japanese Army Air Force Fighter Units and Their Aces 1931–1945.* Grub St, UK, 2002.

Hess, William N. *Pacific Sweep.* Doubleday, USA, 1974.

Kenney, George C. *Dick Bong, Ace of Aces.* Duell, Sloan & Pearce, USA, 1960.

———. *General Kenney Reports.* Duell, Sloan & Pearce, USA, 1949.

Maloney, Edward T., ed. *Fighter Tactics of the Aces' S.W.P.A.* Aviation Book Co., USA, 1978.

Martin, Charles A. *The Last Great Ace.* Fruit Cove Publishing, USA, 1998.

Rust, Kenn C. *Fifth Air Force Story.* Historical Aviation Album Pub, USA, 1973.

Stafford, Gene B. *Aces of the Southwest Pacific.* Squadron/Signal, USA, 1977

Stanaway, John. *Peter Three Eight.* Pictorial Histories Publishing Co, USA, 1986

Unit Histories

8th Fighter Group

Stanaway, John, and Lawrence Hickey. *Attack & Conquer.* Schiffer, USA, 1995.

8th Photo Squadron

Stanaway, John, and Bob Rocker. *The Eightballers.* Schiffer, USA, 1999.

49th Fighter Group

Ferguson, S. W., and W. K. Pascalis. *Protect & Avenge.* Schiffer, USA, 1996.

McDowell, Ernest R. *49th Fighter Group.* Squadron/Signal Pubs, USA, 1989.

90th Bomb Group

Alcorn, John S. *The Jolly Rogers.* Historical Aviation Album, USA, 1981.

Lord, Andrew M. *Tales of the Jolly Rogers.* Auburn Letter House, USA, 1985.

McDowell, Ernest R. *The Jolly Rogers.* John Sands P/L, Australia, 1944.

Woods, Wiley O. *Legacy of the 90th Bombardment Group.* Turner Publishing, USA, 1994.

312th Bomb Group
Sturzebecker, Russell L. *The Roarin' 20s.* KNA Press, USA, 1973.

345th Bomb Group
Hickey, Lawrence J. *Warpath Across the Pacific.* IR&P Corp, USA, 1984.

348th Fighter Group
Stanaway, John. *Kearby's Thunderbolts.* Phalanx, USA, 1992.

475th Fighter Group
Stanaway, John. *Possum, Clover & Hades.* Schiffer, USA, 1993.

Index

About the Author

Lex McAulay was born in Australia in 1939. He served three tours of duty in South Vietnam and has since written more than a dozen books on Australian involvement in World War II and Vietnam. *MacArthur's Eagles* completes a trilogy on the U.S. airwar in the South West Pacific Area, the other two parts being *The Battle of the Bismarck Sea,* the destruction of the March 1943 convoy to Lae, New Guinea, and *Into the Dragon's Jaws,* the 5th Air Force bombing of Rabaul in October–November 1943.

Lex McAulay lives in Maryborough, eastern Australia, with his wife and is involved in local and international community service organizations. His other interests include history and the big band music of the 1930s and '40s.

The Naval Institute Press is the book-publishing arm of the U.S. Naval Institute, a private, nonprofit, membership society for sea service professionals and others who share an interest in naval and maritime affairs. Established in 1873 at the U.S. Naval Academy in Annapolis, Maryland, where its offices remain today, the Naval Institute has members worldwide.

Members of the Naval Institute support the education programs of the society and receive the influential monthly magazine *Proceedings* and discounts on fine nautical prints and on ship and aircraft photos. They also have access to the transcripts of the Institute's Oral History Program and get discounted admission to any of the Institute-sponsored seminars offered around the country. Discounts are also available to the colorful bimonthly magazine *Naval History*.

The Naval Institute's book-publishing program, begun in 1898 with basic guides to naval practices, has broadened its scope to include books of more general interest. Now the Naval Institute Press publishes about one hundred titles each year, ranging from how-to books on boating and navigation to battle histories, biographies, ship and aircraft guides, and novels. Institute members receive significant discounts on the Press's more than eight hundred books in print.

Full-time students are eligible for special half-price membership rates. Life memberships are also available.

For a free catalog describing Naval Institute Press books currently available, and for further information about joining the U.S. Naval Institute, please write to:

Membership Department
U.S. Naval Institute
291 Wood Road
Annapolis, MD 21402-5034
Telephone: (800) 233-8764
Fax: (410) 269-7940
Web address: www.navalinstitute.org